Pro Java™ EE 5 Performance Management and Optimization

■ ■ ■

Steven Haines

Apress®

Pro Java™ EE 5 Performance Management and Optimization

Copyright © 2006 by Steven Haines

ISBN-13: 1-59059-610-2

ISBN-10: 978-1-59059-610-4

Printed and bound in the United States of America 9 8 7 6 5 4 3 2

Lead Editor: Steve Anglin
Technical Reviewers: Mark Gowdy, Dilip Thomas
Editorial Board: Steve Anglin, Ewan Buckingham, Gary Cornell, Jason Gilmore, Jonathan Gennick,
    Jonathan Hassell, James Huddleston, Chris Mills, Matthew Moodie, Dominic Shakeshaft, Jim Sumser,
    Keir Thomas, Matt Wade
Project Manager: Beth Christmas
Copy Edit Manager: Nicole LeClerc
Copy Editors: Heather Lang, Nicole LeClerc
Assistant Production Director: Kari Brooks-Copony
Production Editor: Laura Cheu
Compositor: Susan Glinert
Proofreader: Liz Welch
Indexer: Broccoli Information Management
Artist: Kinetic Publishing Services, LLC
Cover Designer: Kurt Krames
Manufacturing Director: Tom Debolski
Distributed to the book trade worldwide by Springer-Verlag New York, Inc., 233 Spring Street, 6th Floor, New York, NY 10013. Phone 1-800-SPRINGER, fax 201-348-4505, e-mail orders-ny@springer-sbm.com, or visit http://www.springeronline.com.

For information on translations, please contact Apress directly at 2560 Ninth Street, Suite 219, Berkeley, CA 94710. Phone 510-549-5930, fax 510-549-5939, e-mail info@apress.com, or visit http://www.apress.com.

The source code for this book is available to readers at http://www.apress.com in the Source Code section.

This book is dedicated to my wife, Linda, and my son, Michael.
Your love has been my inspiration and the purpose of life.
Thank you for loving me the way that you do!

Contents at a Glance

PART 1 ▪▪▪ Fundamentals

PART 2 ▪▪▪ Application Life Cycle Performance Management

PART 3 ▪▪▪ Performance Management in Production

PART 4 ▪▪▪ Tips and Tricks

Contents

PART 1 ■■■ Fundamentals

PART 2 ■■■■ Application Life Cycle Performance Management

PART 3 ■■■ Performance Management in Production

PART 4 ■■■ Tips and Tricks

About the Author

STEVEN HAINES is the author of three Java books: *The Java Reference Guide* (InformIT / Pearson, 2005), *Java 2 Primer Plus* (SAMS, 2002), and *Java 2 From Scratch* (QUE, 1999). In addition to coauthoring and contributing chapters to other books, as well as providing technical editing for countless software publications, he is also the Java Host on InformIT.com. As an educator, Haines has taught all aspects of Java at Learning Tree University and at the University of California, Irvine. By day, he works as a Java EE 5 performance architect at Quest Software, defining performance tuning and monitoring software, as well as managing and executing Java EE 5 performance tuning engagements for large-scale Java EE 5 deployments, including those of several Fortune 500 companies.

About the Technical Reviewer

MARK GOWDY is the manager of the systems consultants for Java Solutions at Quest Software. He has been consulting and working in Java performance for four years and has been active in the Java industry for over eight years. As a consultant, he has assisted Fortune 500 organizations in finding and resolving performance issues in their Java applications.

Acknowledgments

First off, I would like to thank my personal Lord and Savior, Jesus Christ, through whom all of this has been possible. I would like to thank my mother for her support and for helping me stay focused on writing this book. I would like to thank my technical reviewer, Mark Gowdy, for going the extra mile to ensure the quality of this book on an accelerated schedule. I would like to thank John Newsom and Rini Gahir for their internal book reviews and great ideas, and I would like to especially thank Emerald Pinkerton for her hard work and dedication in promoting this book within Quest Software.

I want to thank the top-quality staff at Apress who have helped make all of this possible: Steve Anglin, Beth Christmas, Stephanie Parker, Heather Lang, Nicole LeClerc, and Laura Cheu.

Many thanks to Dr. Bradstreet and the staff at ICDRC for taking care of my son and giving us hope. God's hands are upon all of you and the great work you are performing.

Finally, I would like to thank you, the reader, for giving this book your serious consideration. Performance management is a new and much needed practice in Java EE, and I hope that this book equips you to take control of the performance of your complex enterprise environments.

Introduction

This book is divided into four parts:

- Part 1: Fundamentals

- Part 2: Application Life Cycle Performance Management

- Part 3: Performance Management in Production

- Part 4: Tips and Tricks

In the first part, we explore the nature of application performance and define what is meant by "performance management." Specifically, Chapter 1 sets the stage by reflecting on the state of the Java EE market, provides insight into why performance management is so difficult in a Java EE application, and defines the role of the Java EE administrator. Chapter 2 defines how we quantify and measure performance and explores the costs of measuring application performance. Chapter 3 is dedicated to the details you need to gather to assess the health of your applications' performance and the mechanisms used to gather them. Chapter 4 concludes the part by diving deep into the underlying technologies used in gathering performance information.

The second part, Application Life Cycle Performance Management, addresses every performance-related task that you perform prior to deploying your application into a production environment. Specifically, Chapter 5 addresses how to ensure the performance of your applications during the architecture phase and the performance testing steps required in application development, QA, and production staging to manage performance as applications are developed. Chapter 6 provides an overview of the wait-based tuning approach for applications and application servers. Chapter 7 looks deep under the hood of an application server, at the important metrics to consider when tuning your application server, showing you how to realize 80 percent of your tuning impact with 20 percent of your tuning efforts. Chapter 8 discusses high-performance deployments and deployment strategies that can be employed to maximize performance while considering high-availability and failover requirements. Chapter 9 concludes this section by discussing performance and scalability testing, specifically how to assess the capacity of your environment.

Once your applications are running in a production environment, you have a new set of challenges to address. Part 3, Performance Management in Production, discusses performance from a production standpoint. Chapter 10 proposes using a performance assessment periodically performed against your production environment to assess its health and identify tuning points in both your applications and environment to improve performance. Chapter 11 presents the theory behind a formal production support workflow to help you efficiently resolve production issues when they occur. Chapter 12 looks to the future of your application by providing strategies to trend analysis, forecasting, and capacity planning. Chapter 13 concludes this part by helping you assemble a full life cycle performance management plan.

The book concludes with Part 4, Tips and Tricks, which includes a chapter on common performance problems and next steps. Chapter 14 presents common performance issues that I have encountered in Java EE environments over the past two years troubleshooting production performance issues for companies ranging from government organizations to Fortune 500 companies, as well as strategies to resolve these issues. Chapter 15 closes the book by providing references to additional resources, an action plan, and a guide to your next steps in implementing performance management in your organization.

Although this book builds on itself, chapter by chapter, you can read any chapter individually to address your needs. Where appropriate, the chapters cross-reference other areas in the book for additional information. For example, if your role is production support, then you might start directly in Part 3 and refer back to Parts 1 and 2 as needed for additional information.

Performance management is a serious practice that has been greatly neglected in the Java EE space, and we are counting the costs in lost revenue, credibility, and productivity. My hope is that this book will empower you to take control of the performance of your applications and enable you to focus on more important things than troubleshooting performance issues—namely, providing your customers with the high-quality applications that they deserve.

PART 1

■ ■ ■

Fundamentals

CHAPTER 1

■■■

An Introduction to Application Performance Management

John was driving home from work on Saturday night; it was late by most people's reckoning, but not by his these days. He's the director of development at Acme Financial Services, and his team has been laboring for two years to migrate the company's legacy mainframe business-to-business transaction processor to a Java EE environment. Acme facilitates the transfer of funds from one bank to another. One bank stops earning interest the second the funds are transferred, while the other starts earning interest as soon as it receives them. Working in business banking, Acme's transferring millions of dollars from point to point: they have no room for failure, because missing funds can add up to hundreds of thousands of dollars in only a couple hours.

Over the past four months, John and his team have worked nights and weekends revalidating the architecture, testing the thousands of use cases that it must support, and ensuring that not one cent is lost in a transaction.

"Honey, you're home!" his wife exclaimed at seeing him arrive bleary-eyed at the early hour of 11:00 PM.

"It's been a hard few months, but it's finally over. I'll have more time for you and the kids, I promise. The guys really put in extra effort to make our deadline. Everything is installed and tested, so when the Eastern European market opens in a few hours, we'll be ready for them." He spoke with the confidence derived from months of building architecture, careful design, detailed implementation, and testing. "We did everything right and have nothing to worry about. Let's just get some sleep; we can celebrate in the morning."

At 4:18 AM, his wife was shaking him awake.

"John, it's Paul on the phone for you, and it sounds important!"

"Hi Paul, what's up?" he said with as much clarity as he could.

"John, you have to come in. We're having problems, and I mean big problems! Japan, uh, you've got to come in!"

"Slow down. Tell me what's going on, one thing at a time." Whenever Paul got excited John could make neither heads nor tails of what he was saying.

"John, the servers are crashing. The market opened about fifteen minutes ago, and ten minutes ago the first server crashed. We brought it back up, and then the next two went down. We're bringing servers up just to watch them fall down. What's going to happen when Western Europe opens in a couple hours and our load triples?"

"Okay, hold on, I'm on my way. I'll be there in twenty minutes. . . ."

What happened at Acme Financial? Are they facing a unique issue? Did they simply fail to test their application well enough, or is the problem larger?

Unfortunately Acme's case is more the rule than the exception. In my line of work, I troubleshoot and diagnose production problems in the enterprise environments of companies like Acme all over the world, ranging from small shops with a handful of developers to Fortune 500 companies employing hundreds, even thousands, of developers. The same situation comes up at each company: developers built and tested an application that is either under duress and not meeting its service level agreements or crashing on a weekly, daily, or even hourly basis.

This chapter will consider the definition and implications of quantifiable performance in a Java Platform, Enterprise Edition 5 (Java EE) environment, some hazards to and pitfalls in ensuring quality, and the role of the Java EE systems administrator in this process. The chapter will also briefly outline numerous details within these topics, to be explored in further detail later in the book, such as particular functions of a skilled Java EE systems administrator.

Forrester reported that among companies with revenue of more than $1 billion, nearly 85 percent reported experiencing incidents of significant application performance degradation.[1] Furthermore, in the Network World and Packeteer survey that Forrester references, respondents identified the application architecture and deployment as being of primary importance to the root cause of application performance problems.[2] This means that nearly 85 percent of applications are failing to meet and sustain their performance requirements over time and under increasing load. Formal performance requirements are detailed in service level agreements. A *service level agreement*, or SLA, is a contract that explicitly defines the terms of service that a vendor will provide to an end user. For an application provider, an SLA prescribes the amount of time in which a unit of work must be completed. For example, logging in on a Web site must be completed in less than five seconds.

SLAs can be defined internally by a business to ensure the satisfaction of its end-user experience, such as the speed of at which a Web search engine retrieves results, or it can be a legally binding contract, such as a business-to-business e-commerce application. In the former case, users have been occasionally tolerant of a sluggish application in the past, but increasingly, users now demand better performance, and daily raise the bar on acceptable speeds. A few years ago, a Web request serviced within seven seconds was considered acceptable, and a user would continue to utilize that service. Today however, when a simple request does not respond within three seconds, the user frequently reinitiates the request (thinking there is a problem) or leaves the site for a quicker responding competitor. Even seven seconds is not an option anymore.

In the case of an SLA serving as a legally binding contract, a company uses a provider's services under the promise that those services will, in fact, satisfy the SLA as defined in the contract. The penalty for violating that can be severe, including financial restitution for damages incurred because of the violation or the dissolving of the contract altogether.

Impact of Poor Performance

The impact of poor performance can be quantified in three areas:

---

1. Jean-Pierre Garbani, "Best Practices in Problem Management," Forrester, June 23, 2004.
2. Denise Dubie, "New apps can be a real pain in the net," Network World, July 21, 2003, http://www.networkworld.com/news/2003/0721appmgmt.html.

- Lost productivity

- Lost customer confidence and credibility

- Lost revenue

Poorly performing applications can impact productivity in two ways. First, when internal applications (for example, an intranet application) perform poorly, companies are paying their employees to wait for applications to respond. I once worked for a computer hardware manufacturer deciding on the hardware components that would go into the machines and building software bundles to install on them. We used a manufacturing plant to assemble and verify their quality. When a problem was discovered, the line lead would shout, "Stop the line!" All assembly workers would cease building the computers, and we were then called in to troubleshoot and fix problems. Meanwhile the assembly workers sat idle, being paid an hourly wage to watch us troubleshoot problems, and at the end of the day, the number of computers produced was reduced. The loss of productivity for idle workers had to be applied to the manufacturing cost of our computers (our overhead), which cut into our profitability. Similarly, when your employees accomplish less work in the day because of poorly performing applications, it directly impacts your financial overhead and profitability.

Second, when an issue arises in an internal application, those responsible for troubleshooting the problem, who in many cases are developers, must divert their attention from other tasks. This diversion may mean that new features targeted for the next release of a product may be dropped or the delivery schedule may be impacted. Either way, the internal performance issue affects your competitiveness.

Also, poorly performing applications that service other corporate entities directly impact the confidence that they have in both your corporate and personal reputations. When you claim that you can perform a service in a specified amount of time and fail to do so, then losing your credibility is only natural. Consider an employee who commits to delivering a report to you every Friday, but he consistently delivers it Monday afternoon. You grow accustomed to his tardiness, but you know that if you have a task that must be completed by a specific time that he is not the one to give it to. Similarly, a corporation that relies on your services will undoubtedly seek out your competition if your services are not reliable. And as the individual who guarantees and promises these services to your customer, you lose their respect.

Finally, applications that perform poorly can directly affect your revenue by causing you to lose customers. Take one of my own recent purchases for example. Because I travel extensively for my company, I am writing this book, and airplane seats are shrinking on a daily basis, I researched personal digital assistants (PDAs) to which I can connect an external keyboard. Being a technical geek, I did all of my research online, found a couple of models that I was interested in, and then started comparing vendors. My success criteria for selecting a PDA vendor were customer feedback, reputation, availability, and finally price. My search returned 14 vendors, and I connected to their sites to gather information. Two of these vendors did not respond within an acceptable period of time. (My tolerance for something like this is about ten seconds.) I simply skipped those vendors and moved on to the next one on my list. Regardless of how you define performance criteria, your users' perception of your application is really all that matters—and there are ways to mitigate the poor perception of performance, such as a progress bar or a running countdown. I may very well have missed the vendor with the best reputation, price, and delivery schedule, because its application did not perform acceptably or appropriately use mitigating features. This needlessly lost sale is a reality facing businesses at present.

Regardless of whether you are developing business-to-business, business-to-consumer, or internal applications, you need to address the performance and reliability of these applications. The impact of a poorly performing application can vary from mild to severe, but it can always be measured if you take the time to analyze it. Only a proactive approach of implementing a formal, performance-based methodology will maximize your chances of success.

Complications in Achieving Application Performance

If 80 percent of all production Java EE applications are failing to meet their performance requirements, then achieving Java EE application performance must be complicated, but why? This section explores some of the reasons Java EE application performance considerations can be overwhelming.

Evolution of Java Applications

As technology evolves so does the way that we use that technology. Consider the evolution of computer hardware. Today's desktop computers are exceedingly faster and have more memory and storage capacities than they did a decade ago, but how much faster is Microsoft Windows XP than Windows 3.1? The speed difference is minimal, but its capabilities and appearance are far superior. Instead of allowing faster hardware to run existing operating systems faster, the extra processing capabilities have been used to develop more robust operating systems and, as a result, have greatly improved productivity.

The evolution of Web applications has followed a similar progression. The first Web sites served static content: when a vendor added new products to his catalog, he was required to update the physical HTML files that rendered it. This requirement quickly became a management nightmare, so databases were incorporated with scripts built to generate HTML pages from database content. Tools and frameworks evolved to accomplish dynamic Web content generation more efficiently and soon standards emerged.

In 1997, Sun released the servlet specification which enabled developers to build Java programs that used existing code and a robust set of classes to generate HTML pages. But difficulties arose in implementing presentation details inside a Java servlet (for example, changing a font size meant changing Java code, recompiling it, and redeploying it to a servlet container), so Sun released the JavaServer Pages (JSP) specification in 1999. JavaServer Pages enable us to build HTML-looking documents that contain embedded Java code to generate dynamic content. At run time, JSPs are translated into servlet source code, compiled, and loaded into memory. Therefore simple changes to presentation details could be accomplished on the fly without requiring a real person to recompile and redeploy the servlet.

Shortly after, it became apparent that complicated business logic hindered the readability and maintainability of JSPs. Understanding that servlets were very good at implementing application business logic and JavaServer Pages were equally good at generating HTML pages, we, as an industry, began implementing a variation of the *Model-View-Controller (MVC)* design pattern. In MVC architecture, JavaBeans represent data (Model), JSPs performed the presentation (View), and servlets represent application business logic (Controller). This delegation of programmatic responsibility resulted in more vigorous and maintainable applications.

As business requirements utilized new technological capabilities, Sun introduced the concept of Enterprise JavaBeans (EJB) to provide transactional integrity and a strong delegation of responsibilities within the business tier. Servlets are now only responsible for application flow and logic, while Enterprise JavaBeans are responsible for business logic and object persistence. Using Java to build enterprise applications presented both positive and negative effects, and by analyzing those effects we discovered best practices that led to a collection of design patterns. These patterns are equipped to solve more complicated problems, which allowed business requirements to evolve.

Web applications evolved into portals with user-customizable content subscription, a single sign-on, and an advanced user-security model. The next wave of evolution came with the advent of Service-Oriented Architecture (SOA) built on top of Web services. SOA facilitated the integration of disparate systems, including interoperability between applications written in different programming languages and running on different operating systems.

The more that Java EE developers increase what we can do, the more users require of us. This brief historical overview of Java's dynamic Web-content generation evolution demonstrates that as our technology improves, our business requirements evolve to use that technology. Java Web-based applications written in 1997 were infinitely simpler than today's. As the complexity of the code increases, our capability to easily identify performance problems decreases.

Layered Execution Model

The first complication in Java EE application performance is the inherent architecture of the Java EE platform, which necessitates a layered execution model. The benefit gained by embracing Java EE as a deployment platform is hardware and operating system independence. To utilize these benefits, we write our applications to adhere to formal specifications and deploy them to an application server running in a Java Virtual Machine (JVM) on an operating system on a physical computer (hardware). In its simplest form, a Java EE application requires all of these components running on a single machine, shown in Figure 1-1. We refer to this complexity of a single application server instance as *vertical complexity*.

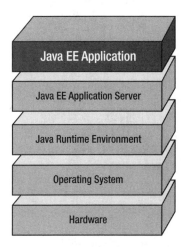

Figure 1-1. *A Java EE application requires a layered execution model.*

Because of this layered model, the location of a performance problem can be in the application code, in the application server configuration, in the JVM configuration, in the operating system configuration, or in the hardware itself. To ensure proper performance of your application and diagnose performance problems, you need to master of each of these layers and understand how to attain their ideal configurations. To further complicate matters, most significant Java EE applications do not run inside of a single application server instance but, rather, run in a distributed environment. In a *distributed environment*, the same layered execution model is spread across multiple machines. Then too, for your application to accomplish anything beyond simple dynamic-content Web page generation, it will need to interact with other systems such as databases and legacy systems. Figure 1-2 puts all of these components together.

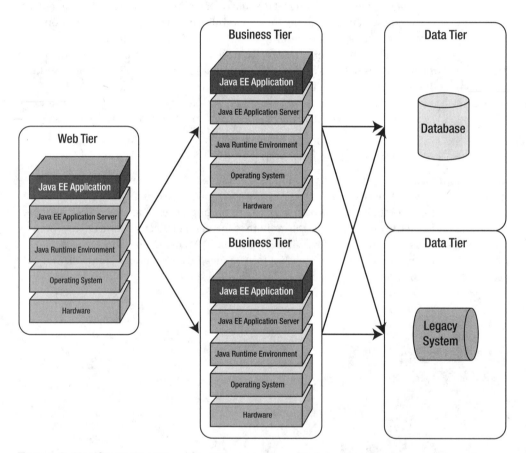

Figure 1-2. *Significant Java EE applications require multiple application server nodes and interactions with other external systems such as databases and legacy systems.*

When your users complain that your application is running slow, identifying the root cause is a daunting task, because the problem can be in any layer in any tier on any application server instance or in an external dependency. We refer to this distributed complexity as *horizontal complexity*. Horizontal complexity issues can manifest themselves when your application is subjected to a significant load: the nature of certain performance problems is to arise only outside the context of a single JVM. Large loads cause seemingly small issues to become large issues.

The combination of horizontal and vertical complexities equates to more moving parts in your application environment than a typical Java EE developer can be expected to handle. Because the proper deployment of a Java EE application requires mastery not only of an application server environment, but of the application server topology as well as detailed skills in the configuration of each external dependency, the best operational model is not a single individual, but a team of skilled individuals specializing in each respective arena.

Prebuilt Frameworks

As you may surmise from the previous discussion, the generation of a robust MVC enterprise application is not a trivial task. As a result, several organizations built application frameworks that simplify the demands on the application: the application integrates its business logic into the framework, and the framework manages the application flow and logic. Most of these frameworks have open source licenses, with the more popular ones being Apache Software Foundation's Jakarta Struts and Velocity, and the Spring Framework.

Prebuilt frameworks offer a number of benefits:

- Productivity increases because most of the mundane work of building infrastructure is removed.

- Large open source development communities offer rapid development.

- Wide adoption means that many developers have tested the framework before you, and those who wrote the code have already handled initial troubleshooting.

- Implementation of application enhancement requests is quick. Because prebuilt frameworks are targeted at solving generic problems, changes to your application requirements will most likely already be supported.

While these benefits should persuade you to adopt an existing application framework, incorporating someone else's code into your application has dangers. Unless you spend the time to become an expert on the internal workings of the prebuilt framework, troubleshooting subsequent problems is difficult because using that framework introduces a black box into your application. A *black box* is a component or piece of functionality that you understand how to use but not necessarily how it works: you provide the inputs to the black box, it performs its functions, and it returns its results to you. Therefore when a problem arises you have another layer in your layered execution model to analyze to discover the root of your problem.

Furthermore, if the framework does, in fact, have a performance issue that impacts your business, then you either must fix it yourself or request that the framework provider fix it. In the former case, if your changes are not committed back to the formal framework repository, then you could have problems upgrading to future releases of the framework. In the latter case, your issue might take weeks or months to reach an acceptable resolution.

I fully support implementing prebuilt frameworks in new development efforts, but I also recommend that you spend the time up front to understand the architecture of the framework that you choose. This way, if a performance problem does occur, you will be better equipped to troubleshoot it. Furthermore, I suggest you research the existing frameworks and choose a popular one that best fits your business requirements. The popularity of the framework will help you when it comes time for acquiring bug fixes and obtaining troubleshooting guidance.

Java EE Expertise

Understanding how to use a technology is a far cry from being an expert at using it. In this respect, Java EE is especially dangerous as its specifications define recommended approaches to application design, but they do not force any particular implementation. This was done by design, because although a full MVC Web architecture is more scalable and robust than a stand-alone servlet, it may not be the best tool to solve a problem. The flexibility of Java EE empowers you with all of the capabilities to develop a small, lightweight application or a large enterprise-scale application; the choice is yours.

However, a Java EE developer can develop a functional application that performs adequately in unit tests, but falls apart under heavy loads. Having the knowledge to build the application does not necessarily mean having the experience to build it to meet your business require-ments. Because Java EE has been gaining in popularity over the years, particularly as a platform for enterprise applications, more and more developers are moving over to Java EE and becoming acclimated as quickly as possible. Many of these developers may bring bad habits from other programming languages, and some learn enough to build an application, but not enough to comprehend the impact of their implementation decisions.

Java EE is a relatively new technology, so it is not as easy to find a seasoned Java EE architect as it is to find a seasoned C or C++ architect. This shortage in Java EE experts can directly impact the performance of your applications if you do not take precautions to ensure that someone with rock-solid experience leads your team. A competent developer can become competent in any language and environment given proper time to acclimate; just be sure that your architects and team leads are already well acclimated before your project begins.

Development Tools

Development tools are evolving in two ways that *may* negatively impact the performance of Java EE applications. I emphasize the word "may," because, while a good tool can work miracles, a good tool in the hands of an unknowledgeable person can wreak havoc on your environment.

First, tools are being developed to relieve many of the mundane activities performed by Java EE developers. This will undoubtedly improve productivity as long as the developer understands the impact of decisions made inside the tool. During the days of early Windows programming there was a debate between Visual Basic and C. C and C++ programmers argued that Visual Basic programmers did not know how to program, while Visual Basic programmers flaunted their productivity; they could build a robust application in a quarter of the time that a seasoned C++ expert could. The underlying problem was that Visual Basic covered up many details about how the resultant application worked, so that someone who was not familiar with the fundamental structure of a Windows application (for example, the message pump, window messages, or threading models) could develop an application that satisfied the functionality of the business requirements, but performed atrociously. On the other hand, empowering a knowledgeable person with such a tool would increase his productivity. Likewise, many of the underlying details involved in building a Java EE application can be automated and as long as the developer understands the implications of his inputs into that automation process, then he will be more productive and still retain high-performance.

A second evolution to consider is the new breed of Java EE tools coming to the market to facilitate application assembly. The idea is that an application architect will be able to assemble an application from existing components using a graphical tool without writing a single line of Java code. The concept is fascinating, and if these vendors deliver on their promises, then productivity will certainly improve. One of the biggest tools in this market is BEA AquaLogic, a relatively new tool with unknown industry acceptance that could revolutionize enterprise application development if it delivers on its promises. But again, this technology heightens the risk of allowing tools to do our work for us without requiring us to understand what they are doing.

Service-Oriented Architecture and Web Services

Every time new technology enters the software industry, it is met with a combination of skepticism, in wondering if the technology will deliver on its promises, and enthusiasm for its potential impact on the way we develop software. In my experience, no technology has ever met all promises and only time can tell how much impact it has on our lives. One thing is for sure: CIOs like buzzwords and eagerly adopt best-of-breed technologies, even if they are not ready for prime time.

Service-Oriented Architecture (SOA) is an example of a technology that has crossed over from fad into widespread adoption, and is only now beginning to deliver on its promises. SOA promotes the concept that software components should be written as services and expose their functionality openly: any component needing the functionality provided by a service simply calls the service rather than reimplementing the functionality itself. The current practical application of SOA is in the integration of disparate systems. SOA and its implementation on top of Web services make connecting the functionality of a .NET server with a Java EE server and a legacy application incredibly simple. Simply drop a service in front of your functionality and voilà—instant integration.

Please note that SOA and Web services are not the same thing. SOA is a design methodology or architectural concept, while Web services are a collection of technologies that enables SOA. Web services itself is a platform- and technology-agnostic collection of specifications by which services can be published, be discovered, and communicate with one another. SOA is the software engineering concept through which you build applications.

From a technology standpoint, Web services are incredible. But from a management and performance standpoint, they can be tricky if you are not prepared. You now have server platforms with different operating systems running multiple applications and application servers to comprise a single application. Figure 1-3 shows this graphically.

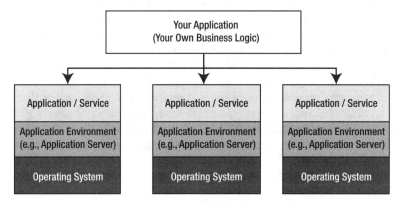

Figure 1-3. *Developing an application from a collection of Web services integrates different application environments, operating systems, and hardware.*

In order to effectively manage this type of environment, you need visibility at all technology points, including

- Each operating system upon which each service is running

- Each technology component in each layer of the distributed layered execution model that supports the service in Java EE environments

- The performance of the enabling technologies as well as the application components that are supporting the service in non-Java EE environments

- Other external dependencies such as database and external servers that may be hosted offsite

- The network communication behavior between your application and its services

The benefits of using Web services outweigh many of these concerns, but the inherent complexity and verboseness of a Web services implementation are prohibitive to optimal performance. Consider the steps that must be performed for a single Web service call:

1. The caller creates a complex XML file.

2. The caller then transmits that XML file to the service.

3. The service infrastructure translates the XML file into an instruction set that the service understands.

4. The service implements its business logic.

5. The service infrastructure constructs a complex XML document containing the results of the business logic implementation.

6. That resultant XML file is then transmitted back to the caller.

7. Then the results of the service call must be translated back to application-specific values.

If these are the steps involved in using a single Web service, consider the steps for an application built by an application assembler that may access half a dozen Web services to service a single Web request. If one Web service call translates to the construction, transmission, and disassembly of two complex XML documents, then doing this six times requires the construction, transmission, and disassembly of twelve complex XML documents. Regardless of how well-written the code and fast the network, performance is going to be abysmal. So while the technology enables many sought-after capabilities, the inherent complexity of implementing that technology necessitates careful planning and analysis in order to benefit your organization.

With all of these pitfalls, should we simply avoid using Web services? Can we count on their adoption being minimal? Or should we take a proactive yet cautious approach to embracing the technology?

The industry analysts have voiced their approval of the technology:

IDC Researcher Sandra Rogers in a 2005 study predicted that the worldwide Web services market will hit $15 billion by 2009, driven by major vendors such as IBM, Microsoft, BEA Systems, and Sun Microsystems.[3]

"Gartner's Positions on the Five Hottest IT Topics and Trends in 2005" includes a review of Service-Oriented Architecture and predicts that by 2006 more than 60 percent of the $527 billion market for IT professional services will be based on Web services standards and technology.[4] By 2008, 80 percent of software development projects will be based on SOA.

SOA is not a fad but, rather, a technology that has the potential to greatly increase productivity and save companies millions of dollars if implemented intelligently.

Application Performance

When someone asks you about the performance of your enterprise applications, what do you think they mean? What does performance means to you?

Performance means different things to different people, usually based on their role in measuring and ensuring the performance of their area of responsibility. When we break down the development organization into groups, we call each group a *stakeholder*. And each stakeholder has an area of responsibility that dictates what that person considers to be the definition of performance.

From the perspective of an application support engineer, whose panicked life is framed by user complaints, the primary criterion for performance measurement is application response time. If the application responds in a reasonable amount of time, then users do not complain, and the engineer's efforts can be spent on more interesting tasks.

A Java EE administrator is more concerned with the supporting environment and hence measures performance through resource utilization and availability. The Java EE administrator determines when to add application server instances, when to change configurations, when to add hardware, and so on. The worst time to make major architectural changes to an environment is when users are complaining; when users complain, then it is already too late. Rather it is best to perform a capacity assessment of the environment and correlate current usage patterns with resource utilizations to determine if the application is approaching its saturation point. Recognizing the environment's saturation point and being able to discern how soon it will reach it empowers the Java EE administrator to plan application server architectural changes. Another significant consideration in his job role is the availability of the application servers. If the application servers are not available, then the code execution, database, and network traffic performance levels are meaningless. For the Java EE administrator, then, good performance implies effective resources that are readily available.

A database application programmer's perspective is primarily concerned with the response time of the Structured Query Language (SQL) and how quickly it services database requests as well as different query execution plans. Creating or removing indices, and optimizing SQL queries to meet the demand of the application against the volume of data in the database are also of concern, particularly considering that the most optimal query for small database is not

---

3. IDC, "Worldwide Web Services Software 2005-2009 Forecast: Let the Races Begin," May 2005, `http://www.idc.com/getdoc.jsp?containerId=33418`.
4. Gartner, Inc., "Gartner's Positions on the Five Hottest IT Topics and Trends in 2005," May 12, 2005, `http://gartner.com/DisplayDocument?id=480912`.

necessarily the most optimal for a large one. If the database is servicing application requests according to the required service level agreement, then it is performing well.

A database administrator is primarily concerned with the utilization of the database resources. The relationship between the database administrator and database application programmer is analogous to the relationship between the Java EE administrator and the application developer: the database application programmer is concerned about the code (SQL) while the database administrator is concerned about the environment (utilization of database resources). The database administrator can create indices, move physical storage around, and configure caches to enhance the performance of the underlying database code.

A network administrator's perspective focuses on how much network traffic passes between the physical machines and how much bandwidth is available. He needs to know when to change the network topology to optimize communications to maximize performance.

Finally, the CIO is concerned with the results of all the aforementioned. This company officer wants to know the bottom line, including how long the environment will run given the current configuration, how long before changes must be made, and what changes offer the best benefits. CIOs apply analyzed trends to a budget to ensure the stability of the company itself, so for them, performance is a much more global concept.

Because application performance means different things to different people, what you consider of vital importance, someone in another role may discount. Application performance encompasses the perspectives of many different stakeholders with the goal of ensuring the long-term stability and responsiveness of all applications running in the environment.

Java EE Performance Problems

Enterprise Java environments are complex and difficult to implement and configure properly, if for no other reason than the sheer number of moving parts. Throughout this book we will look at specific problems that can impede performance, but to provide you with a general introduction to the symptoms of these problems, consider the following:

- Slow-running applications

- Applications that degrade over time

- Slow memory leaks that gradually degrade performance

- Huge memory leaks that crash the application server

- Periodic CPU spikes and application freezes

- Applications that behave significantly differently under a heavy load than under normal usage patterns

- Problems or anomalies that occur in production but cannot be reproduced in a test environment

Unfortunately, no simple one-to-one solution exists for each of these symptoms, but once equipped with the tools and methodologies presented in this book, you will be prepared to build a plan of attack when one of these problems occurs.

Application Performance Management

When you see the phrase "Application Performance Management," you probably think of "Application Performance Tuning." While Application Performance Management includes performance tuning, it is far broader in scope. *Application Performance Management* (APM) is a systematic methodology for ensuring performance throughout the application development and deployment life cycles. APM is sometimes called a full life cycle approach, because it begins during the architecture of an application, is applied during development, is practiced during the quality assurance (QA) and testing processes, and remains a lifestyle in production.

Application Performance Management should start early in the development life cycle, because we have learned that *earlier is cheaper*. The earlier in the development life cycle you find a performance problem, the less the cost to fix it (in terms of both dollars and time spent).

As Figure 1-4 shows, the rate in which the cost to fix a problem grows is exponentially proportionate to the stage in the development life cycle it is discovered. For example, an incorrect choice to use entity beans to represent data can be changed in architecture documents in a couple hours, but if the problem goes undiscovered into development, then code has to be changed. If it is found in QA, then the solution has to be designed again, redeveloped, and retested. But in production, not only does the cost affect architecture, development, and QA, but also it affects end users. And we have already established that poorly performing applications accessible to end users cost you in terms of productivity, reputation, and revenue.

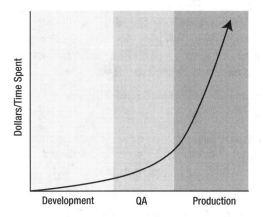

Figure 1-4. *The cost to fix a performance problem, measured in dollars and in time spent, increases exponentially the later in the development life cycle that it is discovered.*

APM in Architecture

The architecture of any application must at least include (if not be based upon) performance considerations. The architecture of an enterprise application must consider object life cycles as well as how objects will be used. In the entity bean example, the best choice for data persistence management must be heavily based on how the objects will be used, how long they will exist, and what operations can be performed on them. For instance, a read-only object is not a good candidate for an entity bean, because entity beans force transactional participation that is not required if the data is truly read-only. However, if an object will be accessed frequently, then caching it in memory is a good idea, and if the data requires transactional integrity then an entity bean is a good choice. As with all performance considerations, the final decision depends on the specific circumstances.

Too often architects neglect to address performance concerns in their artifacts. To remedy this, I promote the practice of integrating SLAs into use cases. This integration requires additional effort by the architect to initiate communications with the application business owner, but by working together to define these SLAs they provide realistic success criteria to evaluate the use case. Note here that SLAs must be decided upon by both the application business owner, to ensure that the business case is satisfied, and the application technical owner to ensure that the SLA is reasonably attainable. For example, the application business owner may want a particular request to respond in less than one second, while the technical application owner understands that the complexity of the functionality cannot complete in less than three seconds.

Performance success criteria can be measured throughout the development of the application and quantified during QA cycles. Furthermore, mutually-decided-on SLAs add the awareness of acceptable performance as a success criterion to QA testing in addition to functional testing.

APM in Development

The development of large-scale applications involves the subdivision of an application into components, which are then developed by different teams. For example, one team might be responsible for the application and framework logic, another team manages the persistence and business logic, and a third team develops the presentation logic. Each team is composed of one or more developers who build their respective subcomponents.

When applying APM to development teams the emphasis is on educating individual developers to properly unit test their subcomponents. Typical unit tests focus on functionality but neglect two key problematic performance areas: memory usage and algorithm efficiency. To mitigate these potential performance obstacles, developers need to test the following:

- *Memory*: Perform deep analysis into heap usage, looking specifically for lingering objects as well as object cycling.

- *Code profiling*: To assess the efficiency of algorithms, breaking down processing time in a line-by-line analysis to allow the developer to better identify potential bottlenecks in the code.

- *Coverage*: Use a coverage tool to display each area of code that was, and was not, executed during a performance test, because, as unit tests are running, it is important to understand which portions of code are being executed.

Integrating these performance measures into the development life cycle creates confidence in integrating code from disparate development teams. For example, consider building a car. If you gather parts from the junkyard, assemble the car, turn the key, and it does not start, then where is the problem? Because you did not test the individual components, you do not know whether you have a bad part (for example, alternator or carburetor) or have integrated the parts incorrectly. On the other hand, if you thoroughly test each component independently, then when the components are integrated, you have the foreknowledge that each part works properly in isolation. In the second scenario, if your car does not start then you can look to the integration of the parts (for example, did you connect all of the wires and hoses properly?).

Understanding that we would not want to build a car from untested parts seems obvious, but all too often we do not apply the same principle to software. By implementing performance-focused unit tests, integration phases will be quicker and more successful.

APM in QA

After application components have been tested and successfully integrated, then the QA team ensures that the application functions properly. In the context of APM, QA testing extends beyond simple functional testing to include testing to verify satisfaction of performance criteria. As previously mentioned, architects must define SLAs in their use cases to give QA personnel the performance success criteria for each use case. As a result, if a use case functions properly but does not meet its SLA, then it will fail the QA test and be returned to the development team for revision. Failure to meet an SLA should be viewed in the same light as an application bug: it either needs to be addressed in development through refactoring code or through rearchitecting the solution. By holding fast to such strict guidelines, you can feel more confident that the final version of your software will meet SLAs and be delivered on time.

I learned the lesson of delaying performance testing until the last iteration of a software project painfully. My company only employed QA to test a large-scale application project for functionality. After working through all of the bugs found during one iteration, we pressed on, adding features to the next iteration. Only when the application was complete did we turn our attention to performance testing. As you might guess, the performance was horrible. In the end, the proper resolution to the performance problems was to refactor the data model, which meant refactoring the entire persistence layer, as well as many of the components that interacted with it. This failure demonstrates a case in which spending additional time in performance testing early in the development life cycle would have reduced our cost to fix the problem substantially, because, as you recall from Figure 1-4 the cost to fix a performance problem, measured in dollars and in time, increases exponentially the later in the development life cycle that it is discovered.

Depending on the organization, performance load testing might be performed by QA or by a performance team; in this case we will group the task into the QA role. After each use case has been verified for adequate performance against its SLA, the next step is to implement *performance load testing*, which measures the performance of the application under the projected usage. In order to successfully pass this stage of QA, the application's use cases need to maintain their SLAs under that projected usage load. Performance load testing reveals many things about an application, including algorithm inefficiencies and memory usage. The development team tests algorithm efficiencies and memory usage in isolation, but seemingly insignificant problems can become large-scale problems when subjected to the usage load. For example, consider an application that stores 1MB of information in each user's session. During both unit testing and integration testing, this 1MB would most likely be ignored, but with 1,000 users in the application, 1GB of memory is lost, and the problem becomes painfully apparent. By implementing performance load testing during each appropriate iteration (recognizing that some early iterations may not lend themselves to load testing), performance problems such as the one just mentioned can be tamed before they become insurmountable.

APM in Preproduction

Prior to moving an application into production, a capacity assessment must be performed. The QA team would already have verified that the application meets its SLAs under the projected load, but a capacity assessment answers the following additional questions:

- How well does each use case perform at the expected usage?

- At what usage point does each use case fail to meet its SLA?

- As usage increases to the point where use cases miss their SLAs, what is the pattern of degradation?

- What is the application's saturation point?

Even if QA confirms that your use cases perform within their service level agreements for the projected 1,000 users, how can you know how to expect the application to behave as usage patterns increase? If the application continues to successfully meet its service level agreements at 2,000 users, then you can feel confident that performance will be acceptable when the application meets the real world. On the other hand, if the use cases are barely meeting their SLAs at 1,000 users and 10 additional users forces the environment into its saturation point, then you should be afraid; you should be very afraid! Without the information that a capacity assessment provides, you could not foresee an inevitable crash.

Figure 1-5 shows the interrelationships between resource utilization, application server throughput, and end user response time as the user load increases. As the user load increases, resource utilization and throughput increase similarly until the resource utilization becomes saturated. At this point throughput decreases, and the response time increase becomes noticeable to the end user. The application then enters the *buckle zone*, a state where application performance "buckles" and response time increases exponentially, and all hope is lost for your users.

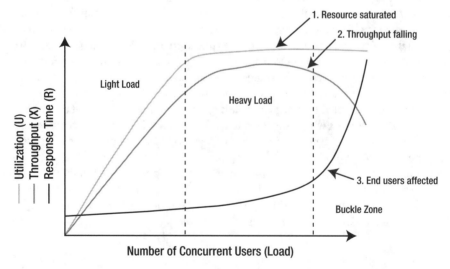

Figure 1-5. *Resource utilization, application server throughput, and end-user response time as user load increases*

You need to use a capacity assessment to understand how the application will react to changing usage patterns in the current deployment topology, how much buffer you have before you miss SLAs, and when your application will completely fail. With this information you can make decisions about the application server topology, and if need be, add additional hardware to put yourself into a comfort zone.

APM in Production

After an application is deployed to production, the real fun begins. You need to monitor your environment to ensure that end users are following projected usage patterns: performance tuning is only valuable if it was performed against load that reflects real-world usage patterns. If users are not using your application as expected, then you need to mimic their behavior in a preproduction environment, perform a new performance tuning exercise, and execute a new capacity assessment. Predicting exactly what your users will do and how they will use your application before you present it to them is impossible, but detailed analysis of use cases can increase your predictions' accuracy.

For example, a large automotive company once experienced memory leaks in production that could not be reproduced in preproduction. They thought that the load tests accurately reflected user behavior, but mistakenly expected their users to log out of their application when they were finished. In actuality, most users closed their Web browsers, which left the application in a waiting state. The application was forced to maintain user session information for several hours before discarding it, whereas if the users had logged out appropriately, then sessions would have been discarded and memory would have been immediately reclaimed. The company's presuppositions were reasonable, but end user behavior caused the company to reboot their servers every two days. Knowing your users is vital to the success of all projects.

In addition to monitoring user behavior, you need keep an eye on all aspects of application resource utilization, as well as capture accurate end-user response times. You need to determine whether users are in fact receiving the end-user experience that you projected in preproduction or not. Application server resource utilization assessments help warn of impending performance issues and can offer time to take proactive steps to avoid them.

Finally, historical data recorded from application usage and user behavior can aid in trend analysis and forecasting application server topology and configuration changes. Trend analysis and forecasting with identified trends is an art in and of itself, therefore Chapter 12 is dedicated to guidelines you can apply to such efforts.

The Role of the Java EE System Administrator

Because databases are complex pieces of software the role of the database administrator (DBA) emerged to manage them. Java EE environments are similarly complex, and the Java EE system administrator role is slowly evolving to manage them. In large corporations, we already see specific jobs serving this responsibility, with titles such as WebLogic administrator and WebSphere administrator, and in small corporations we see people serving this role in addition to other responsibilities (usually either application architecture and development or system administration). In the coming years, though, expect to see this role become more and more prevalent as applications become more complex and less manageable.

DBAs have a distinct set of job responsibilities, and so should Java EE system administrators, but few have taken the opportunity to formally list those responsibilities. The following section describes the basic set of job responsibilities that should be expected of a formal Java EE system administrator.

Application Server Topology Configuration

Before installing and configuring an application server instance, the Java EE system administrator needs to work with various stakeholders to plan the application server topology. The topology considerations include the decision to implement clustering, the number of physical servers to configure, and the number of logical servers to install per physical server.

Application servers can be clustered together to enable multiple servers to behave as one large server. The user load is distributed across the servers within a cluster, so the application can service more users. Clustering can come in one of two forms: horizontal clustering and vertical clustering. *Horizontal clustering* refers to using multiple physical machines in a cluster to service user requests, while *vertical clustering* refers to using multiple application server instances on a single machine to service user requests. Most clusters can benefit from both types of clustering, because horizontal clustering ensures hardware failover, and vertical clustering enables JVMs to better use operating system resources.

Then too, multiple application server instances can function as a group outside the context of a cluster. The choice to implement a cluster must follow a logical argument, because although clusters offer benefits such as failover, they incur additional overhead above using individual application server instances. Specific business requirements help you make the determination of whether or not to implement clustering. Chapter 8 looks deeply into the issues surrounding clustering and presents guidelines to help you implement the optimal configuration.

Application Server Tuning

In order to service high volumes of user requests in disparate applications, application servers maintain a large number of moving parts to configure their behavior. For example, user requests are sent to an application server through a listening socket and placed in a queue awaiting processing. Each queue is assigned a thread pool that removes the request from the queue and assigns it to a thread for processing. During its processing it may access a stateless session bean (that is maintained in a pool) that references an entity bean (that is maintained in a cache) that reads a database (through a JDBC connection pool). Each of the aforementioned infrastructure components is configurable: the size of the thread pool, the size of the bean pool, the size of the cache, and the number of connections in the JDBC connection pool.

The optimal configuration for an application server is dependent on its applications and associated usage patterns. Only by tuning an application server with a load tester generating balanced and representative user requests can you have any confidence that the application will perform adequately. *Tuning to representative user requests* means that the simulated user requests must reflect actual user behavior and *tuning to balanced user requests* means that the simulated user requests are executed in the appropriate percentages in relation to one another.

Application server tuning is not limited to application server resource configuration, but also includes the JVM. The dynamic nature of the JVM and its memory management support, which utilizes different garbage collection algorithms, means that the JVM must be tuned specifically to the applications running in the application server. Chapter 7 extensively discusses tuning memory, one of the biggest causes of performance problems in Java EE applications. Many times performance problems caused by application architectural deficiencies can be masked by tuning the JVM; the architectural issues continue to exist, but the JVM heap configuration can hide them long enough for the application architecture to be refactored.

Application server tuning is difficult in a single application server instance and the introduction of additional vertical instances (clustered or not) further complicates the issue. The Java EE system administrator needs expert knowledge of the internal behavior of the application server and JVM in order to be successful; a superficial knowledge will inevitably lead to problems. Chapter 7 provides a conceptual overview of the various moving parts in a Java EE 5–compliant application server that you need to apply to your specific application server.

Application Deployment

Application deployment can be as simple as deploying a Web archive (WAR) file or Enterprise archive (EAR) file to an application server, but in large-scale environments it usually involves configuring application resources and potentially altering the application server environment to support the new components. From a resource perspective, new application components may require any of the following:

- A database connection pool and associated data source

- A Java Message Service (JMS) server and associated topics and/or queues

- An external Java Connector Architecture (JCA) connection pool

And to support increased load and application footprint, the Java EE system administrator may need to modify the application server configuration settings. For example, the heap may need additional memory capacity or repartitioning and thread pools sizes may need to be increased to manage the additional application overhead.

Most people view application deployment as simply walking through a set of wizard pages to deploy an application, but the formal responsibilities of the Java EE system administrator are to configure the environment to support the components and to assess and mitigate the impact of deploying the new component to the environment. In some cases these responsibilities may require the creation of new application server instances, additional hardware, or a combination of the two.

Application Production Integration

In addition to configuring an application to run in your environment and ensuring that it is given the required resources, you must assess the impact of integrating that application into the environment. I have seen successful customer environments where the integration of a new component followed a formal procedure that required automated performance testing to measure this impact, and I have seen unfortunate customer environments where essentially untested code was pushed out to a live production environment. In one case, a multi-billion-dollar company's complete business-to-consumer Web site was brought to its knees by a faulty outsourced Flash game.

As you embrace a full APM methodology in your organization by integrating SLAs into use cases, requiring developers to implement performance-based unit tests, and requiring QA to uphold performance success criteria and execute performance load tests, why would you choose to deploy a piece of code that has not been held to similar standards? As the Java EE system administrator, you own this environment and you make the rules (within reason, of course). Would a DBA let you add unauthorized tables, indexes, and stored procedures to the databases without evaluating them? Not a chance, so why should your standards be any lower?

The cost in adopting this firm stance is a longer release time for new code, but it is balanced against a greater assurance of success. Earlier in this chapter when we identified the cost of failure for a poorly performing application, we saw very clearly that whether the application is internal, business-to-consumer, or business-to-business, the cost can be quantified and in some cases can cost a company its livelihood. As a professional in your position, you do not want to be responsible for this loss and must take every precaution to avoid it.

Capacity and Scalability Assessment

Recall our brief discussion of capacity assessment, and its representation in Figure 1-5 earlier in the chapter. The Java EE system administrator must understand and interpret the results of the capacity assessment. QA assurance teams may facilitate the load test, but the Java EE system administrator assigns the results business values.

Performance is not the same as scalability, and this distinction will be explored in great depth in Chapter 9. In brief, consider the key differentiator between performance and scalability to be that while performance describes the speed with which a single request can be executed, scalability describes the ability of a request to be executed quickly under an increasing load. More specifically, performance is a measure of the capabilities of your system; scalability is of the capacity of your application. In the development life cycle, we work hard to ensure performance and build our solution so that we can then enable and test for scalability. In a scalability test, we execute performance-based load tests against a sample deployment environment using balanced and user-representative use cases. The goal is to assess the capacity of a single application server instance and then measure the capacity of the environment to tell us how that application scales as new application server instances are added into the environment. We will use this information later when we delve into trend analysis, forecasting, and capacity planning.

If for any reason an application cannot be deployed to multiple application server instances or to a cluster, then the application has serious architectural issues that need to be resolved or the application cannot ensure high availability, nor can it service significant load. A developer once asked me if he should use stateless session beans to implement his business logic or standard Java classes. He questioned the need for stateless session beans, which offer transactional support and an EJB container-managed pooling mechanism to help ensure reliability and scalability. He did not require the transactional support, and he could easily attain the pooling mechanism from a third party (such as the Apache Jakarta Commons Pool). Although he did not need the transactional support, I advised him to implement his solution using stateless session beans and configure them to ignore transactions because it would make his solution more scalable. At some point in the future, he may need to support transactions and ensure transactional integrity across a multitude of Java EE objects and services running on multiple application server instances, and his standard Java objects would be no help.

Trending, Forecasting, and Capacity Planning

Trending, forecasting, and capacity planning are often confused. *Trending*, or *trend analysis*, involves analyzing historical data looking for predictive patterns. *Forecasting* takes these trends and projects futures with them. Finally, *capacity planning* reads forecasts and builds an infra-structure that can support what they report. Chapter 12 delves deeply into these topics, but this section provides a 10,000-foot overview of the roles.

Trend analysis can be applied to a wide variety of enterprise application facets, but it is applied most commonly to usage patterns, end-user response times, and various resources to be utilized, such as CPU, memory, thread pools, JDBC connection pools, caches, and pools. Regardless of the metric being analyzed, we are interested in the following:

- A change in usage, either increasing or decreasing

- The rate of that change, such as the slope of linear change or the degree of an exponential one

- Trend correlation—that is, whether different trends are changing in a similar pattern

Once trends have been identified, the next step is to interpret them, in light of current user and resource behavior, using capacity assessments to establish forecasts projecting when resources will become saturated and cause end-user response times to exceed SLAs. The presupposition is that trends will continue to follow their identified patterns, so care must be taken to ensure that forecasts are valid.

Another core component to creating accurate forecasts is routinely interviewing the appli-cation's business owners to uncover any auxiliary factors that may disrupt current trends. For example, the marketing team may run a promotion that puts a link to your application on America Online's (AOL) login screen. They are thinking about increased corporate awareness and might neglect to think about the impact it could have on the application itself. If you have not had the pleasure of watching usage patterns when receiving AOL login page traffic, let me assure you that it is not for the squeamish. Previously I experienced this while watching at ten-second samples as the user load increased at literally a near-exponential rate: 10 users, 20 users, 50 users, 200 users, 500 users, and so on. Without being aware of this change in usage pattern and preparing for it, your entire Java EE environment may be compromised.

Finally, these forecasts directly feed into capacity planning, because forecasts reveal when resources will become saturated and SLAs will be missed, and your job is to plan your environ-ment to maintain your SLAs. Capacity planning utilizes capacity and scalability assessments to estimate the hardware and application server deployment and configuration requirements necessary to meet your SLAs. To satisfy the AOL scenario, we might increase both the vertical and horizontal scaling of the application to ensure we are maximizing hardware use and have enough hardware to support the load.

Application Production Troubleshooting and Triaging

Chapter 11 explores a formal production support methodology, but, at this point, simply know that the role of the Java EE system administrator is vital to troubleshooting production issues. When a production issue occurs, the first step is to triage the problem to identify the subgroups within an organization that own the problem. *Triaging* is the process of identifying the compo-nent within an enterprise application (such as the application code, application server, database, Web server, or legacy system) responsible for the issue. Competent triaging is essential to efficiently resolving production issues.

In your organization today, how do you resolve production issues? For example, if your application were suddenly not meeting its SLAs, what would you do? For many corporations, the problem diagnosis phase involves all parties sitting in a room pointing fingers at one another. This company's process would be to bring together the application technical owners, the DBAs, the lead QA representative, the customer support team members who received notification of the problem, the development managers, and sometimes the CTO or CIO to brainstorm theories about the problem's location. This meeting recurs until the issue is resolved.

The proper way to diagnose the problem is to have a set of robust tools monitoring your entire application stack (Web server, application server, application code, database, legacy system) that identifies the offending component(s) for you. This way, if the problem is in the application server, the DBAs do not need to be involved, or if the problem is in the database, then the development team does not need to be involved. Implementing such as solution results in a faster resolution cycle and increased productivity throughout your organization, because only necessary parties are required to troubleshoot the problem.

If the problem lies inside the application server or the application itself, the Java EE system administrator becomes engaged to troubleshoot the problem. With a command of the Java EE environment and tools that lend insight into the environment, the Java EE system administrator can quickly identify whether the issue is an application server resource issue, a load issue, or an application performance issue. In other words, the Java EE system administrator is responsible for triaging issues within the Java EE tier.

Summary

Most Java EE applications fail to meet their performance requirements. Regardless of the type of application (internal, business-to-consumer, or business-to-business), the impact of poor performance is quantifiable in the areas of corporate productivity, credibility, and revenue. Java EE environments are difficult to tune because of both inherent architectural complexity, such as the distributed layered execution model of application servers, and a lack of true Java EE expertise.

In order to mitigate production performance issues, you need to first understand the meaning of performance and how to measure it and then adopt an Application Performance Management (APM) methodology that spans the entire development life cycle. Only through extensive planning and forethought do you have any chance of being part of the 20 percent of Java EE applications that meet their performance requirements.

Looking back to our friend John at Acme Financial Services, we can see that he and his team performed diligent functional testing but neglected performance testing until it was too late. Furthermore, the performance testing that they did perform did not represent real-world usage patterns and thus was performed in vain. Had John embraced APM, he would be enjoying the weekend with his family but, rather, he needed to call in someone skilled in Java EE performance tuning and troubleshooting to analyze and refactor his architecture. John and Acme Financial Services are fictional, but unfortunately the problems they experienced are real and representative of what happens in development organizations across the country.

CHAPTER 2

Quantifying Performance

John got out of his car in the Acme Financial Services parking lot and rubbed his forehead.

"I just don't know how this could have happened," he said to himself in disgust. At 5:05 on a Sunday morning he was at work. The morning fog hadn't cleared yet, and he could still see his breath. What a start to the day!

Paul met John at the door and took him back to the war room, where he found every DBA, architect, network operations specialist, and QA person who could be mustered out of bed at this early hour.

"Okay, we need to get to the bottom of this problem fast. Take a look at each of your components, and let's meet back here in fifteen minutes. I want to know what's happening in the database, in the application server, and on the network. I want answers, and I want them now!" John walked out of the room with Paul at his heels and headed straight for his office.

"The best place to start looking is the application server," Paul said uncomfortably as he saw John's forehead wrinkle. "We can turn on monitoring and see what it tells us."

"Do it," John said, his mind preoccupied with the call he was going to have to make to the CEO. The CEO was going to have to do some damage control while the team brought the systems back up; he would not be happy about this.

When John hung up the phone, his ears still ringing from one of the most unpleasant conversations of his career, he saw Paul standing at the door, sweat starting to run down his forehead.

"John, I turned on the monitoring and now the servers are crashing before I can get to the monitoring screens to see anything! What should I do? I can't even turn it off!"

Defining Performance

In Chapter 1, we discovered that performance means different things to different stakeholders. However, to cultivate a discussion about the subject, we need to narrow our focus and outline definitive metrics that we will collectively refer to as *performance*. Focusing specifically on Java EE, including applications and application servers, the most common and relevant performance metrics are end-user response time, request throughput, resource utilization, and application availability. This section explores the rationale behind why we include each metric into our overall picture of application performance.

End-User Response Time

End-user response time defines the core of the end-user experience, so although other performance metrics are important, this one is the most evident. A slow response time can cause losses to your customer base in a business-to-consumer application, losses to productivity in an internal application, and losses to your credibility and potentially your entire relationship in a business-to-business application. Even a relatively small number of long response times makes a bigger impression on your users than many shorter ones. According to Arnold Allen, "The perceived value of the average response time is not the average, but the ninetieth percentile value: the value that is greater than 90 percent of all observed response times."[1] The other performance criteria that we will discuss are measured and balanced to ensure that our end-user response times remain acceptable under changing conditions.

We can measure end-user response time in a two ways: active monitoring through synthetic transactions and passive monitoring.

A *synthetic transaction* consists of a series of service requests representing a unit of business functionality that is executed against your environment over a regular time interval. The response times of synthetic transactions are recorded for two purposes: trending and alerting.

Synthetic transaction trend analysis provides insight into the impact on end users as a result of other performance trends, hopefully before those users are impacted. You may see thread pool usage and memory usage trending upward, and while those trends need to be addressed, the paramount concern is whether your end users are being affected by the upward trend. Synthetic transactions also act as the perfect catalyst for triggering alerts. Monitoring systems analyze the response time of a synthetic transaction against a predefined service level agreement (SLA) and alert the system administrator if it is exceeded. Alerts can be simple notifications, such as an e-mail or a page, or they can trigger a deeper diagnostic component to gather additional and more expensive diagnostic information.

In large-scale applications, synthetic transactions are played from multiple geographical locations throughout the world. The purpose is to gain an understanding of the end-user response time along various Internet pathways. In some cases, when a corporation has applications hosted at multiple physical sites, traffic can be redirected as a result of a slow pathway.

Synthetic transactions are referred to as *active monitoring*, because they actively engage the application; another valuable mechanism to measure end-user response time is *passive monitoring*. Passive monitoring watches or samples real-time requests as they occur in the enterprise environment. As a result, they provide a much better overall picture of the end-user response time, and we can compute metrics to give us even better data. For example, from a pool of 20 requests that occur within a minute we can compute the mean, minimum, maximum, standard deviation, and variance. While small changes that may pass by unnoticed may not necessarily affect the mean, they can drastically affect the standard deviation—this could result in awful end-user response time for a percentage of users that we would otherwise never know about.

Request Throughput

Throughput defines the number of things we can accomplish in a time period. In Java EE terms, we typically define *request throughput* as the number of requests we can service in a

---

1. Arnold O. Allen, *Introduction to Computer Performance Analysis with Mathematica* (San Diego, CA: Academic Press, 1994).

second. Our goal is to maximize our request throughput and measure it against the number of simultaneous requests we receive. A high request throughput means that we are quickly and efficiently servicing requests, and it reflects a quick response time. A high request throughput also highlights the overall efficiency of the application itself.

Resource Utilization

In addition to the health of our application response times and the measure of work our application can accomplish, another important aspect of our application server performance is the utilization of its resources. *Resources* are services that support or facilitate applications and include the following:

- The heap

- Thread pools

- JDBC connection pools

- Caches

- Pools

- JMS servers

- JCA connection pools

This list is ordered by relative importance, according to my observations in my tuning efforts, considering both impact and problematic frequency.

The first resource to analyze is the heap. We are interested in the heap usage as well as the rate, duration, and pause time of garbage collections. Considering that your entire application runs inside the heap, a misconfigured heap can result in degraded performance regardless of how well the application code is written and the application server is configured. One of the most compelling features that draws developers to Java is its automatic memory management. Java memory management is facilitated by a garbage collection process that tracks down dereferenced objects and frees them on your behalf. This feature is both a blessing and a curse—a blessing because C++-style memory leaks are eliminated, and a curse because manual memory management is not an option. The garbage collector is the only mechanism through which memory is reclaimed. As a result, a considerable amount of time has been spent by JVM vendors optimizing garbage collection algorithms, and at present, a host of differing implementations are available. Each different implementation, vendor, and algorithm requires its own set of fine-tuning configuration parameters that you need to be familiar with. Unfortunately, when the heap manages long-lived objects, the only way to clean up their memory is through a *stop-the-world* garbage collection. During a stop-the-world garbage collection, all execution threads in the JVM are frozen until the garbage collection completes. Chapter 7 takes an in-depth look at heap tuning, but it suffices to say that anytime the JVM is frozen, the impact is severe and all other tuning options are not effective at that point.

When an application server receives a user request, it places it into a request queue. That request queue is serviced by a thread pool, which removes the request from the queue and processes it. The utilization and performance of that thread pool can have a significant impact on the performance of the application. If the utilization is consistently low, then the thread pool is taking system resources away from the application server that could be better used elsewhere.

On the other hand, if the thread pool is overused, meaning that its utilization is above 85 percent with pending requests possibly waiting in the queue, the application throughput is compromised. In order for your application to accomplish a unit of work, it needs a thread, so effective thread pool utilization is very important to your application. No available threads equates to no work.

Another key resource to consider is the JDBC connection pool. Most applications are backed by a database, or at some point interact with one. All database interactions are funneled through a database connection pool. A request that resolves in a database query must first obtain a connection from the connection pool before it can execute its query. If the connection pool does not have any available connections, then the request must wait for a connection to be returned to the pool before proceeding. This wait time can have a significant impact on the overall response time of the service request.

A strategy to reduce the number of calls, and hence network trips, to a database is to serve requested data from a memory-resident cache. Serving content from memory will always be faster than a network call to a database, but the infrastructure required to manage the cache must be carefully configured. Consider that caches, by nature, must be of a finite size; an unrestricted cache could quickly deplete the heap of memory and crash the application server. Because the number of entries is finite, a request for a noncached entry made against a full cache requires the removal of an existing object from the cache to make room for the newly requested object. In Java EE terms, objects are removed from a cache and persisted to a database through a process called *passivation*. New objects are loaded from the database and placed into a cache through a process called *activation*. Excess occurrences of activations and passivations result in a condition called *thrashing*. When a cache is thrashing, it spends more time managing cached data than serving data and hence loses all of its benefit. Therefore, cache utilization, activation, and passivation rates greatly impact performance.

Stateless resources are stored in pools. When a process needs a pooled resource, it obtains a resource instance from the pool, uses it, and then returns it back to the pool. Subsequent utilization of a pooled resource does not necessitate the same instance but, rather, any instance from the pool. Stateless resources naturally lend themselves to pooling and high-performance utilization. Stateless resources become application bottlenecks only when the pool is sized too small. Pooling resources well involves balancing the amount of memory required to maintain the resource instances against maintaining enough resource instances to satisfy application requests. Therefore, pool overutilizations can introduce wait points into request processing and dramatically affect the performance of your applications.

Applications that make use of messaging, either to support communication with legacy systems such as mainframes or to provide asynchronous processing, typically interact with JMS servers. JMS servers define various destinations in the form of topics and queues that applications interact through, and depending on the implementation, they can define constraints about the maximum number of messages and/or bytes allowed in the server at any given time. If the JMS server is full, then attempts to add new messages to the server will fail. This failure results in either a total service request failure or a performance bottleneck, as the application retries until it is successful or finds another JMS server. Regardless, the utilization of JMS servers is an important performance metric to monitor for applications that use these servers.

Java Connection Architecture (JCA) connection pools are similar to database connection pools, with the difference being the destination that the connection interacts with: database connections interact with a database, while JCA connections interact with any system that supports the JCA specification. Most practical applications of JCA connections are to communicate with legacy systems that have exposed their functionality using the Java Connection Architecture. For applications that use JCA connections, the utilization of JCA connection pools becomes another potential application bottleneck.

Application Availability

The final measure of application performance that I'll discuss is application availability. *Availability* refers to the running and accessible states of an application in the wake of component failures in the system. *High availability* refers to an application that is available when it is supposed to be available a high percentage of the time. Obviously if an application is not available, then its performance is compromised. In order to satisfy performance requirements, an SLA usually states the percentage of time that an application must be available. And depending on the nature of your business, violating this SLA may have financial repercussions.

Before Quantifying Performance Requirements

Performance requirements are quantified through service level agreements. SLAs are not defined arbitrarily but, rather, systematically after a deep problem analysis by key stakeholders.

SLA Stakeholders

The stakeholders required to define an SLA are the application business owner and the application technical owner. The application business owner, who is sometimes the application product manager, analyzes the business cases and brings customer requirements to the SLA. The application business owner therefore ensures that, as long as the SLA is satisfied, customer needs will also be satisfied. The application technical owner, who is sometimes the application architect, analyzes the technical requirements necessary to solve the use case and ensures the feasibility of the SLA. The technical business owner therefore ensures that the service level is attainable.

   Not involving both parties when defining an SLA is dangerous. If the SLA is left solely in the hands of the application technical owner, then the end users' needs may not be satisfied. On the other hand, if the SLA is left in the hands of only the application business owner, the SLA might not be attainable. Consider the SLA for a database search against a projected 100 million rows. The application business owner may try to define a subsecond SLA to satisfy his end users, but the application technical owner realizes the complexity of the query and may propose a seven-second response time to give his team some breathing room. In the end, they will likely compromise on a five-second SLA. End users who want this functionality as defined must accept a five-second response time, and the development team must spend additional time optimizing the query, all in the spirit of enhancing the end-user experience.

SLA Properties

An effective SLA exhibits three key properties:

- Specificity
- Flexibility

- Realism

An effective SLA must include specific values. Stating that a use case must complete in about 5 seconds is not definitive and hence is difficult to verify; 5.25 seconds is *about* 5 seconds. The use case analyses performed by the application business owner and the application technical owner yield a specific value for a reason—the application business owner preserves the requirements of the end user, while the application technical owner ensures that the SLA is attainable. When these two application representatives arrive at a specific value, it should be used, because it is a definitive value that QA teams can test before moving the application to production. Then, when the application is in production, a definitive SLA value provides alert criteria for both active and passive monitoring. Furthermore, the use case documents the environmental profiles for which the SLA should be valid, including expected user load, the nature of data that changes hands during the use case, the number of objects and their sizes, and acceptable degradation for extreme deviations from the expected profile.

An effective SLA must also be flexible in the context of its distributed variance. The use case must adhere to the specific SLA value for a predefined percentage of time, allowing for a measurable degree of flexibility in anticipation of unexpected conditions. For example, consider the popular search engine that you use on a daily basis. When you execute a search, would you consider it acceptable if your results were presented in less than two seconds 95 percent of the time? Are you willing to accept a seven-second response time on 1 out of every 20 searches you perform? Most users find this level of variance acceptable. Now, if 10 out of 20 searches returned your results in seven seconds, then there is a good chance that you would change search engines. But the level of flexibility must be restrained, because no matter how much you love your search engine, after ten seconds of unresponsiveness you will leave.

Not only must an SLA be specific, yet flexible, but it must also be realistic. Requiring the SLA to be defined by both the application business owner and the application technical owner ensures that it will be realistic. I mention realism specifically as a key property of an effective use case, because frequently SLAs are defined solely by the application business owner without the opinion of the application technical owner. When the technical team receives the performance requirements, they simply ignore them. Having an unrealistic SLA is probably worse than not having one in the first place.

Measuring Performance

Performance is measured by first acquiring performance data and then interpreting the data. Acquiring data is the technical aspect that can be learned by reading through application server documentation. Interpreting data is more of an art than a science that can be learned only through detailed instruction, experience, or a combination of both.

But before we dive into how to acquire data, you first need to know what data you want to acquire. In order to form a complete picture of the application's health, you need to capture the following metrics:

- Application performance

- Application server performance

- Platform

- External dependency

You need to gather information not only about the application itself, but also about the infrastructure that supports it, the platform that it runs on, and any external dependencies that it interacts with. This is a result of Java EE applications running inside a layered execution model, as discussed in Chapter 1.

Acquiring Data

Performance data can be acquired in several ways:

- Public APIs

- Proprietary APIs

- Code instrumentation

- System APIs and tools

In the past, obtaining performance data was considered something of a black art, but the monitoring and management industry has evolved to the point where the task is primarily mechanical today. Most application server vendors have embraced the Java Management Extensions (JMX) interface to expose programmatic monitoring and management functionality. Chapter 3 delves into the specifics of interacting with an application server using JMX, but for the purposes of this discussion, the benefit to using this standard is that monitoring applications are able to extract performance information using the same code across application servers.

You may be using an older version of an application server or one that is late to adopt JMX. In that case, a proprietary interface most likely obtains performance data. For example, IBM WebSphere has always built its monitoring and management capabilities on top of its Performance Monitoring Infrastructure (PMI). In version 4.x, IBM provided a set of tools and APIs that allowed access to this data, but in version 5.x and later, a JMX interface into the PMI data is provided.

To discover information that is not available through a public or proprietary API, such as method-level response times or detailed SQL tracing, the solution is to use code instrumentation. Code instrumentation comes in two forms: custom and automatic.

Custom code instrumentation is performance monitoring code inserted by the developer. The benefit to using custom code instrumentation is that you can extract the exact data that you are interested in and present it in the format of your choice.

Automatic instrumentation is performance monitoring code inserted by a tool. The benefits to using a tool to instrument your applications are as follows:

- Source code files are not convoluted by monitoring code.

- The tool can instrument the entire application; doing so by hand is a tedious task (and computers are good for performing tedious tasks).

- The code is scalable up and down. You can change the amount of the data you are gathering at run time.

- Bytecode instrumentation is better optimized than Java code. Java code compares to bytecode somewhat analogously to the way high-level languages like C/C++ compare to assembly language code: if the assembly code is written in assembly and not as C code compiled to assembly, then the code is better optimized.

- Information is maintained and collated in a central repository.

- Most tools provide an intuitive user interface to present performance data and allow for deeper analysis than homegrown solutions.

- Advanced tools can rebuild an entire request that spans multiple JVMs and provide method-level call stacklike information.

My know-how derives from both backgrounds: prior to designing performance monitoring software, I implemented my own custom instrumentation. At that time, my custom instrumentation solution, which may be similar to something that you have done in the past, was self-limiting in scope—I recorded the response times and invocation counts of major business events. If something slowed down, then diagnosing the problem was my responsibility, but at least I could isolate a call path. Though I could have used a more robust solution, creating monitoring tools was not my job responsibility; developing code was. When I moved into the monitoring industry, I was elated, because then I was able to spend all of my time analyzing performance metrics and designing performance monitoring software. And to make the dream job complete, I was not responsible for implementing the solution but, rather, analyzing the problem domain while very skilled teams of software developers reaped the fruit of my analysis for me.

The final domain from which we acquire data is the set of metrics outside the context of the Java EE application and application server. This includes operating system metrics such as CPU usage, physical memory usage, network traffic, and disk I/O, and external dependencies such as databases and legacy systems. The distributed layered execution model buys us significant scalability, but as our environment scales, the complexity increases exponentially. Operating systems provide their own set of tools and system APIs that can be tapped to gather this performance information. Providing information about databases and legacy systems is beyond the scope of this book, but be aware that most databases and legacy systems provide a mechanism or API from which to obtain this data.

Interpreting Data

Data is not knowledge; rather, data applied to a model yields knowledge. Consider what a meteorologist must understand to interpret weather conditions. Taken independently, current temperature, barometric pressure, and humidity data reveal very little about weather conditions, but understanding that a temperature of 82°F, a barometric pressure of 101.5 kPa, and 100 percent humidity mean that we can expect a thunderstorm is knowledge. The meteorologist applies each of these metrics to a model that has been developed to represent weather conditions. When the metrics fall into specific ranges at the same time, they can be interpreted to provide knowledge.

■**Note** Data is not knowledge, and knowledge is not wisdom. Specific temperature, barometric pressure, and humidity values give you the knowledge that a thunderstorm is coming, but wisdom tells you not to go out and play golf. Interpreting data against a model will give you knowledge, but only experience of how to apply that knowledge to benefit your environment will give you wisdom.

In order to properly interpret the data that we have acquired, in the context of a Java EE application, we need to define a model that represents our Java EE environment. We measure three basic metric categories at various stages in Java EE request processing:

- Response time

- Throughput

- Resource utilization

Figure 2-1 displays the interrelationships between resource utilization, request throughput, and request response time as user load increases.

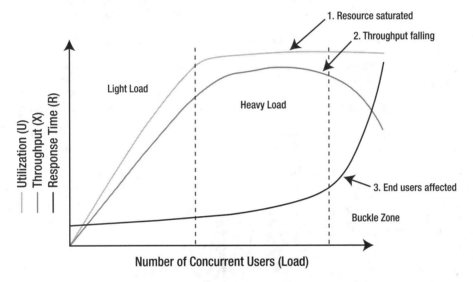

Figure 2-1. *The relationships between response time, throughput, and resource utilization*

The behavior of each of the relationships depicted in Figure 2-1 can be characterized as follows:

- The resource utilization increases with user load, because the system is being asked to do more. More users require more memory and more CPU power. This increase follows a natural and healthy progression, but the system eventually reaches a point where resources become saturated. For example, if the system is trying to process more requests than it is capable of handling, then the CPU will spend more time switching between thread contexts than actually processing the request.

- Throughput also increases as user load increases, because more users are asking the system to do more, and as a natural result it does more. But when the load causes resources to become saturated, then the system spends more time managing itself (such as in the CPU context switching example) than processing requests. When this saturation point is reached, the throughput beings to decline.

- Response time gradually increases with user load, too, because of the additional resource strain that the increased user load adds to the system. As resources become saturated, the throughput decreases (the system actually accomplishes less than it did with a lesser load). When that system is subjected to an even greater load, then the additional load backs up, and response time starts increasing at an exponential rate.

The model displayed in Figure 2-2 traces a request from the external request handling services through each application and application server component. When a request is received, it is added to a request queue. Each request queue has an associated thread pool from which a thread is assigned to process the request. The request passes through the application components, including servlets, JSPs, and EJBs, and interacts with application server resources. All of these components are running inside a JVM that runs in an operating system on hardware. At each point in this call path, we want to measure and record specific information:

- *Request handling*: The external user response time and the request throughput

- *Execution management*: The utilization of thread pools and number of requests that back up in request queues

- *Applications*: The response times of each component and, when necessary, of each method

- *Services*: The response times and utilization of services to know both how well the JDBC connection pool is being used and how long database requests take to execute

- *Operating system/hardware*: The utilizations of operating system resources

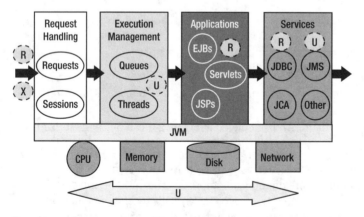

Figure 2-2. *This Java EE model groups functionality into logical categories. At each point in the model we record the measurement criteria as Response Time (R), Throughput (X), or Resource Utilization (U).*

We employ various mechanisms to gather data and each piece of data that we then interpret in light of our Java EE application model. Finally, we correlate related metrics and define rules that expose knowledge. Chapter 3 devotes an entire section to analyzing metrics.

Costs of Measuring Performance

Performance monitoring is rarely free. The more you want to know, the more expensive the knowledge is to obtain. Spending time identifying the exact data that we are interested in can minimize the cost impact of our monitoring. Most application servers can report more or less data, depending on your requirements; this is typically configured through the application server's administration console. Many of your decisions about how to configure the reporting level of your application server should be based on the volatility of your application. For example, if your application is relatively new and prone to change, then you want to capture more information, so you have enough data to diagnose problems. More mature and stable applications can be less prone to problems and require less monitoring.

But before you make any decisions about how to configure the monitoring level of your production applications, you need to quantify the cost in your preproduction environment. Monitoring overhead is variable, because each application is different, with different application server resources, and a different number of classes and methods. Therefore, a blanket statement that a particular level of monitoring incurs too much overhead is unfounded until a formal measurement has been made. I have seen environments where enabling all possible monitoring options has had virtually no observable effect on the application and others where enabling even minimal monitoring options has pushed the application over the top.

Luckily, you can quantify the impact of monitoring your environment using the aforementioned measurements of response time, throughput, and resource utilization. Most monitoring vendors take a very unscientific approach to calculating the impact of their monitoring solutions and do not account for real-world applications in their estimations. I hold to the statistics dictum: if you torture the data long enough, it will confess to anything. I like numbers that I can verify.

■**Note** Observing a system without affecting it is impossible, because the very act of observing the system introduces some level of overhead. The best solution is to observe the system at the least expensive level that offers enough data from which to assess a baseline. Then adjust monitoring parameters and calculate the difference between the baseline and the new settings—this is your measurable impact. This need to monitor the system before you can assess the impact of your monitoring is something of a paradox—it's not quite as dramatic a paradox as Schrödinger's cat, but it's worthy of mention nonetheless.

The biggest mistake individuals make when computing overhead is not accounting for changes in application server usage. For example, consider assessing the CPU overhead for enabling high-level monitoring across the entire application server. If no users are running through the application, then there is no overhead; with 10 users, the overhead is minimal; but with 1,000 users, the overhead may be substantial. The point is that we need a mechanism to normalize the utilization for changes in user patterns. The best metric to compute this normalized utilization is the *service demand*. The service demand (D) is defined in relationship to resource utilization (U) and throughput (X) as follows:

$$D = U / X$$

The service demand measures the utilization of various resources and then divides that utilization by the application throughput. As the number of users increases and the application becomes more efficient (higher throughput), the service remains relatively stable. You want to compute the service demand for at least CPU and memory usage, and potentially other application server resources such as threads and connection pools.

In addition to measuring the service demand of memory usage, observing the memory allocation rate, memory level, garbage collection frequency, and garbage collection size is also important. Figure 2-3 demonstrates that performance monitoring can increase the rate at which memory is allocated and freed, which results in more frequent garbage collection; this increase is a distinct possibility if the monitoring overhead creates a multitude of temporary objects during each service request.

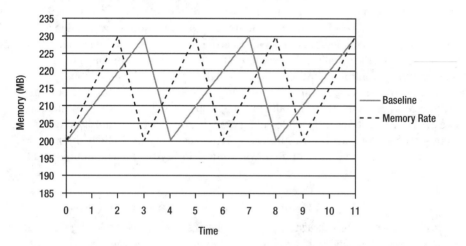

Figure 2-3. *Performance monitoring can increase the rate at which memory is allocated and the frequency of garbage collection.*

Figure 2-4 demonstrates that performance monitoring can increase the base level of memory usage as well, by introducing its own objects into the heap. As the memory level increases, the frequency of garbage collections increases, simply because less memory is available to work with. The memory level problem can be mitigated by adjusting the size of the heap to account for performance monitoring overhead, but adjustments to the heap require a lot of careful analysis and trials.

Also note that any impact that increases the duration of a garbage collection also negatively affects the response time of all service requests running during that garbage collection.

A simpler measurement of performance monitoring impact that still yields good information is the response time of your key service requests with one standard deviation. Most monitoring options have minimal impact on the mean response time, but the standard deviation (the distribution of requests) can be affected greatly, which can dramatically affect a subset of your users.

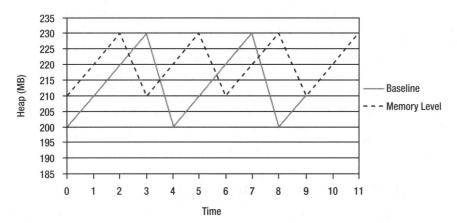

Figure 2-4. *When performance monitoring raises the base level of memory usage, available application memory decreases and the frequency of garbage collection increases.*

Mitigating the Cost of Performance Monitoring

The most effective way to address and mitigate the overhead associated with performance monitoring is to implement performance monitoring in a scaled approach. Advanced monitoring solutions refer to this scaled approach as *smart monitoring.* The process is to gather a minimal amount of statistics from which to evaluate rules that trigger deeper monitoring on a subset of the environment. The best example of this process is gathering method-level invocation and response time information in a production environment—very valuable information that is also very expensive to gather. The solution therefore is to passively observe key service requests, which is a relatively inexpensive operation, and evaluate their response times against specific SLAs. When the service request exceeds the SLA, it triggers method-level monitoring for that specific service request.

In such a capacity, a performance monitoring tool throttles its overhead to minimize its impact on your environment. It requires time and effort to determine the base set of performance statistics to monitor as well as to configure intelligent and composite rules to trigger deeper diagnostics, but the benefit to your environment offsets the effort.

Improving Performance

Acquiring and analyzing performance data is an interesting exercise, but the real question that we derive from this is, "How do we improve performance?" We take a two-phased approach:

1. Implement proven performance methodologies into our application life cycle.

2. Perform systematic tuning of our application, application server, and external dependencies.

Responding to performance issues is important to maintaining SLAs, but the goal is to address performance proactively rather than reactively. Reactive tuning is stressful and largely ineffectual, because its purpose is to extinguish fires rather than adopt best practice coding and configuration techniques to prevent those fires in the first place. Chapter 5 presents a detailed discussion about integrating performance throughout the application life cycle, and Chapter 6 offers a formalized performance tuning methodology.

Performance issues can arise anywhere in the Java EE layered execution model (including the application, application server, and external dependencies), so a smart approach to monitoring is required to minimize the monitoring overhead. The best approach to guaranteeing the performance of your applications in production is to implement proactive steps throughout the development and QA life cycles to avoid problems before they occur.

Building a Performance Test Plan

Just as you need to build a business plan to run a successful business and formalize a budget to manage your finances, developing a performance test plan is essential to the success of your application. A performance test plan satisfies two purposes:

- It formalizes your understanding of your user behavior.

- It documents each phase of performance testing that must be performed and tracked for each iteration of your application development cycle.

User behavior serves as the input to performance tests, and by consistently testing at the specific milestones we discuss later in this chapter, you can track the performance of your application as it develops and ensure that it never gets out of your control.

Know Your Users

The most important thing you can do to ensure the success of your tuning efforts is to take time to get to know your users. I do not mean calling them on the phone or going out for a round of golf with them (but feel free to do so, especially if you can expense the green fees). I mean that you need to understand their behavior inside your applications. You will seldom tune application servers in a production environment; rather, you will generate test scripts representing virtual users and execute load tests against a preproduction environment and tune it. After your preproduction environment is properly tuned, then you can safely move the configuration information to production.

If you are part of the majority of corporations that cannot adequately reproduce production load on a preproduction environment, do not lose hope. Most of the larger companies I visit do not have a firm understanding of their users' behavior and cannot generate representative load on their test environments. I commonly hear two excuses: "Production load is too large for preproduction" and "I do not have any way of knowing what my end users are really doing." To address the first point, you can build a scaled-down version of production in preproduction and scale up the configuration of your production deployment. This method is not as effective as mirroring production in preproduction, but sometimes mirroring production is not affordable. To address the second point, I will show how you can gather end user behavior in this section.

Because we try to tune our environment in preproduction to validate settings before moving them to production, it naturally follows that we are tuning our environment to support the load test scripts that are executed against the environment. To tune an enterprise application, first implement some best practice settings, and then load test the application, observe its behavior, and adjust the configuration parameters appropriately. Tuning is an iterative process, where we try to hone in on the optimal configuration settings—some changes will yield improvements, and some will actually degrade performance. Because performance tuning is an iterative process, it should not be left until the end of a development life cycle; it takes a long time to do properly.

Given that we tune our application servers to our load scripts, what does that tell you about the load scripts? They need to represent real-world user behavior. Consider tuning a Web search engine. I can write test scripts that search for apples and bananas all day, but is that what end users do? I can tune my environment to be the best "apples and bananas" search engine in the world, but what happens when someone searches for BEA or IBM? In my application, I could have grouped technical companies in a separate database from fruits and vegetables; if so, that piece of code would never be executed in preproduction, and my tuning efforts would be in vain. The better solution is to discover the top 1,000 or 10,000 search phrases and their frequencies. Then compute the percentage of time that each is requested and build test scripts that request those phrases in that percentage. For the remaining percentage balance, you might connect the load test generator to a dictionary that queries for a random word.

The difficult part of writing user-representative load scripts is the process of discovering how users are using your applications. Though discovering user patterns is not an exact science, for reasonably reliable results, look at your access logs first. I would not recommend doing this by hand, because the task is insurmountable even for a Web application of medium size. Plenty of commercial and free tools will analyze your access logs for you. They will perform the following analysis on your service requests:

- Sort service requests by percentage of time requested and display that percentage

- Zoom in and out of your analysis time period to present finer or less granular results

- Identify peak usage times of the day, week, month, and year

- Track bytes transferred and the mean time for requests

- Identify and categorize the originators of requests against your application (internal, external, geographic location)

- Summarize the percentage of successful requests

- Summarize HTTP errors that occurred

- Summarize customer loyalty, such as return visitors and average session lengths

- Track page referrals from other sites

Regardless of the software that you choose to analyze your access logs, the important thing is that you do perform the analysis and use this information as a starting point for building your test scripts. Access logs are somewhat limited in what they report, and they may not suffice in certain instances, such as if you use a single URL as the front controller for your application and differentiate between business functions by embedded request parameters. In this case, you need a more advanced tool that can monitor your usage and partition business functions by request parameters.

Access logs give you part of your solution; the next step requires a deeper understanding of the application itself. For example, when a particular service request is made, you need to know the various options that control the behavior of that service request. The best sources of that information are application use cases and the architect responsible for that functionality. Remember that the goal is to identify real-world user behavior, so your research needs to be thorough and complete. Errors at this stage will lead to the aforementioned "apples and bananas" search engine anomaly.

Before leaving this subject, you should know about the biggest mistake that I have seen in defining load test scripts: users do not log out of the system. No matter how big you make your logout button, at most 20 percent of your users are going to use it. Mostly I believe that this behavior is a result of the late adoption of the Web as a business deployment platform. Commercial Web sites dominated the Internet throughout its emergence and mass growth, and as such, users became accustomed to exiting a Web site in one of two ways: by leaving the current site and traversing to another, or by closing the browser window. Because these exit patterns are ingrained in users' Web usage patterns, you cannot depend on them to properly log out of your Web site. Therefore when you develop test scripts, you need to determine the percentage of users that log out properly, and the percentage that do not, to develop your test scripts accordingly.

One large-scale automotive manufacturer that I worked with struggled with this problem for over a year. Its application servers crashed every few days, so the staff became accustomed to simply rebooting their application servers nightly to reset the memory. After interviewing them and looking at their HTTP session usage patterns, we discovered an inordinate number of lingering sessions. We reviewed their load test scripts and, sure enough, each test scenario included the user properly logging off. They tuned their environment with this supposition and when it proved incorrect, their tuning efforts could not account for the amount of lingering session memory. They adjusted their test scripts, retuned their environment, and have not been forced to restart their application servers because of lack of memory since.

Performance Testing Phases

Performance testing must be performed at several specific points in the development life cycle. Specifically, performance testing must be integrated at the following points:

- Unit test

- Application integration test

- Application integration load test

- Production staging test

- Production staging load test

- Capacity assessment

Current software engineering methodologies break the development effort into iterations. Each iteration specifies the set of use cases that must be implemented. According to the typical pattern, the first iteration implements the framework of the application and ensures that the communication pathways between components are functional. Subsequent iterations add functionality to the application and build upon the framework established during the first iteration. Because iterations are defined by the use cases (or sections of use cases) that they implement, each iteration offers specific criteria for performance testing. The use cases define the test steps and test variations, in addition to the SLAs that quality assurance should test against. Therefore, all of the following performance test phase discussions should be applied to each iteration; the controlling factor that differentiates the work performed during the iteration is the set of use cases.

Unit Tests

Performance unit testing must be performed by each developer against his components prior to submitting the components for integration. Traditional unit tests only exercise functionality but neglect performance, even though the cost of resolving performance issues in development is drastically less than resolving them in production. Performance unit testing means that the component needs to be analyzed during its unit test by the following tools: memory profiler, code profiler, and coverage profiler.

The memory profiler runs a garbage collection and records a snapshot of the heap before the use case begins and after it completes, and from this you can see the memory impact of the use case and the list of specific objects that it leaves in memory. The developer needs to review those objects to ensure that they are intended to stay in memory after the use case terminates. Objects inadvertently left in the heap after the use case completes are referred to as *lingering objects*, and their presence represents a Java memory leak.

The next memory issue to look for is referred to as *object cycling*. *Object cycling* is caused by the rapid creation and destruction of objects, typically occurring in request-based applications (such as Web applications) when creating temporary objects to satisfy a request. Fine-grained heap samples recorded during the use case combined with creation and deletion counts show you the number of times an object was created and deleted. An object being created and deleted rapidly could be placing too much demand on the JVM. Each object that is created and deleted can only be reclaimed by a garbage collection; object cycling dramatically increases the frequency of garbage collection. Typically object cycling happens with the creation of an object inside of a loop or nested loop. Consider the following:

```
for( int i=0; i<object.size(); i++ ) {
   for( int j=0; j<object2.size(); j++ ) {
      Integer threshold = system.getThreshold();
      if( object.getThing() - object2.getOtherThing() > threshold.intValue() ) {
         // Do something
      }
   }
}
```

In this case, the outer loop iterates over all of the items in object, and for each item it iterates over the collection of object2's items. If object contains 1,000 items and object2 contains 1,000 items, then the code defined in the inner loop will be executed 1,000 × 1,000 (1 million) times. The way that the code is written, the threshold variable is allocated and destroyed every time the inner loop runs. (It is destroyed as its reference goes out of scope.) Looking at this code inside a memory profiler, you will see 1 million threshold instances created and destroyed. The code could be refactored to remove this condition by writing it as follows:

```
int threshold = system.getThreshold().intValue();
for( int i=0; i<object.size(); i++ ) {
   for( int j=0; j<object2.size(); j++ ) {
      if( object.getThing() - object2.getOtherThing() > threshold ) {
         // Do something
      }
   }
}
```

Now the threshold variable is allocated once for all 1 million iterations. The impact of the threshold variable went from being significant to being negligible.

One other common scenario where we see object cycling in Web-based applications is in the creation of objects inside the context of a request. On an individual basis, creating these objects is not problematic, but as soon as the user load increases substantially, the problem becomes quickly apparent. You must decide whether the object needs to be created on a per-request basis or if it can be created once and cached for reuse in subsequent requests. If the object can be cached, then you can stop it from cycling. Figure 2-5 shows an image of a heap when object cycling occurs.

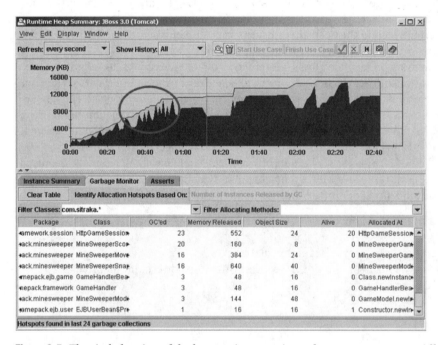

Figure 2-5. *The circled region of the heap points to a time when memory was rapidly created and freed, indicating potential object cycling.*

Application Integration Test

After components have been through unit tests and found acceptable to be added to the application, the next step is to integrate them into a single application. The integration phase occurs at the conclusion of each iteration, and its primary focus is determining if disparate components can function together to satisfy the iteration use cases. After functional integration testing is complete, and the application satisfies the functional aspects of the use cases, then you can run performance tests against the integrated whole.

The application integration test is not a load test, but one of a small-scale set of virtual users. The virtual users should perform the functionality defined earlier: attempting to simulate end users through balanced and representative service requests. The user load for the test is defined and documented in the *performance test plan* by a joint decision between the application technical owner and the application business owner. The purpose of this test is not to break the application, but to identify application issues such as contention, excessive lingering objects, object cycling, and poor algorithms, which can occur in any application when it is first exposed to multiple users. In addition to identifying application functional issues resulting from load and obvious performance issues, this test is the first one that holds the use case to its SLAs. If the application cannot satisfy its use case under light load, then subjecting it to a full load test would be pointless.

Application Integration Load Test

Now that the application is properly integrated, has passed all of its functional requirements, and has been able to satisfy its SLAs under a small load, the time has come to execute a performance load test against it. This test is a full load test replicating the number of projected users that the application is expected to eventually support in production. This test should be executed in two stages:

1. With minimal monitoring

2. With detailed monitoring

In the first test, the goal is to see if the code upholds its SLAs while under real levels of load. An application deployed to production will have a minimal amount of monitoring enabled, so in this first test you give the application every chance to succeed.

In the second test, you enable detailed monitoring, either for the entire application or in a staged approach (with filters to capture only a subset of service requests), so that you can identify performance bottlenecks. Even applications that meet their SLAs can have bottlenecks. If we identify and fix them at this stage, then they do not have the opportunity to grow larger in subsequent iterations.

This phase of the performance test plan represents your first chance at performance tuning the application, which is quite a change from the traditional approach of waiting to perform performance tuning until after the application is finished. You are already trying to tune your application when its functionality is simplistic. If you build your application from a good foundation, you ensure its success.

Production Staging Test

Your performance tuning and management tasks would be greatly simplified if your applications could always run in isolation, where you had full use of application server, operating system, and hardware resources. Unfortunately, adding hardware and software licenses for each new application that you develop is expensive, so you are forced to deploy your applications to a shared environment. Utilizing a shared environment means that while your integration load tests helped you tune your applications, you need a real-world testing environment that will mimic a production deployment.

This need imposes quite a task on QA teams, because they need to manage test scripts not only for our applications, but also for all applications running in the shared environment. QA must implement an automated solution that produces repeatable and measurable results.

Just as with the application integration test, this is not a full load test, but one to identify resources that applications may be competing for. The load is minimal and defined in the performance test plan. If contention issues arise, then deep analysis is required to identify the problem. But this requirement is the very reason that the test is automated and performed by adding one component at a time. When your new application arrives into this test bed, the test bed has already successfully performed this test in the past, so the problem can be isolated to something in your application or something in your application in conjunction with another application. Either way, your application is the only change between a working test bed and a failing test bed, which presents a good starting point for problem diagnosis.

Production Staging Load Test

When it finally appears that your application has successfully integrated into the shared environment, turn up the user load to reflect production traffic. If your application holds up through this test and meets its SLAs, then you can have confidence that you are headed in the right direction. If it fails to meet its SLAs in this test, then you need to enable deeper monitoring, filtered on your application's service requests, and identify more bottlenecks.

■**Note** Simply dropping your new application into an existing tuned environment is not sufficient. Rather, you need to retune the environment with the new application to continue supporting the existing applications and load and to support your new application load. This may mean resizing shared resources such as the heap, thread pools, JDBC connection pools, and so forth.

Capacity Assessment

When you've finally made it to the capacity assessment stage, you have a very competent application iteration in your hands. This final stage of performance testing captures the capacity of your application. In this assessment, you generate a load test on the entire environment, combining the expected usage of your application with the observed production behavior of the existing environment. In other words, you start with the production staging load test for existing applications and then add the additional load for your new application. All the while, you are testing for compliance with all SLAs.

You continue to increase the load slowly until the system resources saturate, throughput begins to degrade, and response time increases dramatically. During this test, you record the load at which each use case exceeds its SLA and then pay close attention to the response time of each use case. Knowing the rate at which performance degrades for each use case is important; it will feed back later into capacity planning.

The capacity assessment gives you the total picture of your application (and environment) so that you can assess new architectural considerations. Furthermore, recording capacity assessments on a per-iteration basis and correlating them provides insight into application code added at any specific iteration and measures the capabilities and growth of your development team.

Summary

This chapter was all about performance. We considered the definition of performance, ways to quantify it, and the costs of doing so. We also looked at improving performance and managing performance throughout the development life cycle.

We determined that performance means different things to different stakeholders, but we can generalize our performance measurements into three categories: response time, throughput, and resource utilization. We can measure each of these at various points in the Java EE application model to draw conclusions about our environment.

We saw that, in order to obtain a complete picture of our application, we need to obtain information from a breadth of components, including the application code, application server, platform, and external dependencies. Unfortunately, obtaining this information can be expensive, but that expense can be mitigated through intelligent monitoring—gathering perimeter data and gathering deeper data for only the troubled component when we observe a problem.

Finally, we saw that formal management of performance throughout the development life cycle requires a significant investment in performance testing time. But remember that 80 percent of all Java EE applications fail to meet their performance requirements and that we can measure the cost of failure in terms of loss of productivity, credibility, and revenue, so the cost of allocating time to performance testing up front can only help us on the back end.

Performance management can be burdensome and tedious, so some might consider throwing it out, because they do not want to absorb that upfront cost, but the heroes in the IT industry are not the ones who can solve production problems quickly but, rather, those who build the systems that do not have the production problems to begin with.

Had John and the Acme Financial Services folks built and followed a performance test plan, they could have avoided their problems altogether. But to add insult to injury, they did not understand the impact of enabling full monitoring on an application server that already could not handle the load. Trying to solve production problems quickly made things a lot worse for them.

At this point, their best option is to roll back to the previous version of their code. The new code needs weeks of performance testing and refactoring before it is ready to re-emerge into production. John's CEO is upset, but luckily John had proven himself in the past, so he gets one more chance. Let's see what he does with it.

CHAPTER 3

■ ■ ■

Performance Measurements

John was able to roll back his environment to the previous working version and calm his CEO. Then he called me.

"Steve, I need your help, man. We were able to pull our application out of production and roll back to the previous version. I bought myself a few weeks with the CEO, but right now my name is still mud. If I can turn this into a success, then my team will get the credit they deserve, but if not, I don't think anyone is safe from the chopping block!"

"I'm glad you called; it's time to do things right. Before we dive in and start troubleshooting your problems, let me give you a little background about enterprise Java applications and how they work inside an application server. As a foundation, you need to understand specifically what information you want to gather, where you need to gather it from, and how to interpret it. With this information, we'll find out where your application was crashing and that will show us how to fix it. Following a strict methodical approach to analyzing your environment takes time, but it is not nearly as complicated as you might imagine."

"Thanks. You're a lifesaver." John put his phone down and sighed with hesitant relief. He and his team were supposed to be basking in glory right now, enjoying well-deserved bonuses, but if they can pull this off, then there's still hope.

Performance Measurement Prerequisites

The distributed layered execution model that hosts enterprise Java applications greatly complicates our performance measurement task. Figure 3-1, which you may recall from Chapter 1, reproduces this visually. Enterprise Java applications run inside a layered execution model. The application runs in an application server that runs inside a Java Runtime Environment that runs in an operating system on a hardware platform. When applications grow, then they require multiple application server nodes and interactions with other external systems such as databases and legacy systems.

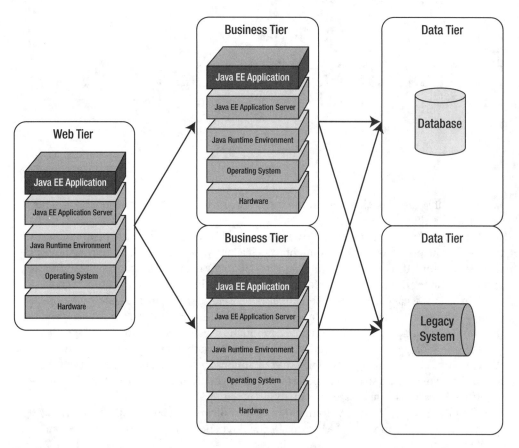

Figure 3-1. *Enterprise Java applications run inside a layered execution model.*

Because we want a representative picture of an enterprise Java application, we need visibility into the different layers in the model. Specifically looking at a Java EE node, we need to obtain the following information for the following components:

- *Application*: Service request response times (cross-JVM), service request call counts, class-level and method-level response times, class and method call counts, object allocations and deallocations, and so on

- *Application server*: Thread pool metrics, database connection pool metrics, JCA connection pool metrics, entity bean and stateful session bean cache metrics, stateless session bean and message-driven bean pool metrics, JMS server metrics, and transaction metrics

- *JVM*: Memory usage and garbage collection metrics

- *Operating system/platform*: CPU usage, physical memory usage, disk input/output metrics, and network connectivity metrics

Application metrics present the application's specific performance characteristics, which can be used to identify performance bottlenecks in both the application as well as in external resources. By recording the response times of method invocations that leave the JVM, such as calls to JDBC that execute SQL queries against a database, we can triage and isolate performance problems between application code and external dependencies. Furthermore, application metrics provide us with a strong passive monitoring mechanism. By monitoring the response times and call counts of service requests, we can better understand users' behavior and response times. Looking deeper, we can take this raw data and derive other metrics that provide additional insight; for example, instead of looking at only the mean value for the response time of a 60-second summary point, we can compute the minimum, maximum, mean, standard deviation, and variance. The response time distribution model reveals the true behavior experienced by the end user, so after reviewing the mean value, your next step is to understand the response time distribution model, as it can reveal performance problems that tracking only the mean may mask.

The application server provides the general infrastructure to support distributed applications as well as the infrastructure to support a specific application and its components. In a general sense, the application server provides a socket listener that accepts incoming requests and a request queue that prepares those requests for processing. It defines one or more thread pools that provide threads that can extract a request from the request queue and process it. On the back end, the application server provides connection pools that hold connections, which can be used to access external resources as well as messaging services. In the middle tier, it provides a transaction service that allows you to ensure the reliability of your applications, and it provides the infrastructure to manage and replicate session information across application server instances. We are interested in the behavior of each of these moving parts.

From an application-specific perspective, the application server provides all of the caches and pools for application components. For example, it provides caches for entity beans and stateful sessions beans, and pools for servlets, stateless session beans, and message-driven beans. A monitoring and measurement perspective typically separates this caching and pooling functionality from general application server functionality, because general application server infrastructure is relatively constant while application infrastructure is present for each application deployed to the application server. In the end, you need both categories of information in order to paint a valid picture of the performance of your application.

Obtaining information on the operations of the JVM is essential as well, because while enterprise Java applications run inside an application server, the application runs on top of a JVM. This layering means that any performance problems that the JVM experiences impact the performance of the application server and hence the application itself. Fortunately, developers have been working out JVM issues even longer than enterprise Java issues, so with a little education, tuning a JVM is not an insurmountable task. The principal issues with JVMs are memory management and garbage collection. When a major garbage collection runs, all processes running in the JVM pause until the collection completes. During this time, nothing can be processed; the application server freezes, which in turn freezes the application. So clearly, monitoring the JVM is of paramount importance.

Finally, you need to gather information from the operating system, specifically about the CPU utilization (sorted by process), physical memory utilization (sorted by process), disk input/output rates, and network traffic. CPU utilization is important because it is reflective of the amount of work your application server is performing. Physical memory usage can reveal information about nonheap JVM memory that can indicate a number of potential configuration issues that can adversely affect the performance of your application server. Measuring network traffic can shed light on the effectiveness of both your load-balancing and replication implementations. For example, in some instances utilizing clustering is inefficient because of the overhead of replicating session information across application server instances, but you can follow proactive steps when designing your application architecture to minimize that overhead. Each component of the layered execution model provides insight that can improve the way you configure your application servers.

Performance Monitoring and Management Using Java Management Extensions (JMX)

In the early days of enterprise Java performance monitoring, each application server vendor provided its own mechanism for exposing performance information. Some early adopters integrated performance information into the Java Management Extensions (JMX), including BEA and JBoss, while other industry leaders such as IBM and Oracle continued to maintain proprietary interfaces. Monitoring and management vendors went through considerable effort to extract and present all relevant performance information about an application server and worked together with application server vendors to compose standards. The largest vendor-neutral undertaking in performance management is known as the J2EE Management Specification, or Java Specification Request (JSR) 77.

JSR 77 proposes a standard management model for exposing and accessing management information, operations, and parameters of J2EE or Java EE components. The purpose of this management model is to

- Allow rapid development of management solutions for J2EE

- Provide J2EE integration with existing management systems

- Enable a single management tool to manage multiple-vendor implementations of the platform

- Enable a specific implementation of a platform to use any compliant management tool

Although not explicitly required, the most robust and standard technology upon which JSR 77 information can be exposed is JMX. JMX is not new; it was defined as JSR 3 in 1998 through the Java Community Process (JCP), an online community primarily charged with developing and approving the JSRs. JMX can be likened to a platform or API upon which JSR 77 is built; JMX is the enabler of the JSR 77 management model.

■**Note** Internet standards such as HTTP, FTP, and SMTP are defined through Request for Comment documents (RFCs), and similarly, Java specifications such as JMX and the J2EE Management Specification are defined as Java Specification Requests (JSRs). JSRs are hosted by the Java Community Process (JCP) and are available for browsing at `www.jcp.org`. Whenever you encounter a standard and want to understand it better, the JCP Web site is the best source for further information.

Fast forward to today and you'll find all major application server vendors support JSR 77 exposed through JMX: BEA, IBM, Oracle, Sun, JBoss, and Apache. In some cases the road was long, but we finally arrived. Because each application server vendor has embraced these technologies, it is in your best interest to understand them as well. In this section, we will explore the architectures of both JMX and JSR 77 to equip you to work with live data that will be collected in the next chapter.

JMX Architecture

The JMX specification can be found at `www.jcp.org/en/jsr/detail?id=3`. It defines itself as follows:

> *The Java Management extensions (also called the JMX specification) define an architecture, the design patterns, the APIs, and the services for application and network management and monitoring in the Java programming language . . . The JMX specification provides Java developers across all industries with the means to instrument Java code, create smart Java agents, implement distributed management middleware and managers, and smoothly integrate these solutions into existing management and monitoring systems.[1]*

JMX architecture is divided into four major areas: the instrumentation level, agent level, distributed services level, and additional management protocol APIs. Figure 3-2 presents the architecture of JMX graphically and was taken from the JMX 1.2 specification.

---

1. Sun Microsystems, Inc., *Java Management Extentions Instrumentation and Agent Specification, v1.2* (October 2002), p. 17. Also available online at `http://jcp.org/aboutJava/communityprocess/final/jsr003/index3.html`.

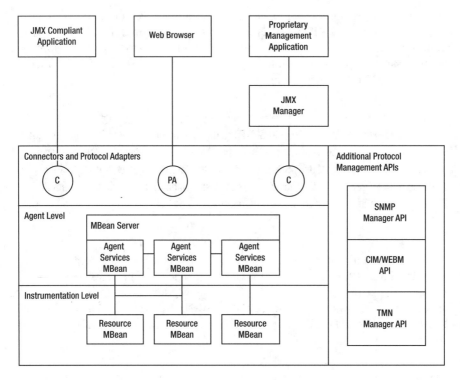

Figure 3-2. *JMX management architecture*

The JMX instrumentation level, at the lowest level, defines a specification for implementing manageable resources; a *manageable resource* can be an application, a service, or any user-defined type such as an application component or service. Manageable resource instrumentation is accomplished through the creation of one or more managed beans, called *MBeans*. An MBean can be standard or dynamic. Standard MBeans are Java objects that adhere to specified criteria, while dynamic MBeans implement a specific interface that allows for more flexible behavior at run time.

MBeans are designed to be flexible, simple, and easy to implement, and they can be developed by application server vendors as well as by application developers to make their products manageable in a standardized way, without developing a complex management system. Furthermore, MBeans can be developed in front of existing resources to make them manageable according to those same standards. For example, you can develop an MBean that exposes the management of a proprietary resource and, inside the bean, translate MBean calls to proprietary calls.

The agent level, the next in the JMX architecture, provides a specification for developing agents that directly interact with and control managed resources; the MBeans that are registered with an MBean server constitute the agent level. The JMX agent consists of an MBean server and a set of services for handling MBeans. When a managed resource is deployed to an application server, the application server registers each MBean with its MBean server. Then the MBean server facilitates MBean queries and interactions. From a monitoring perspective, the MBean server is of utmost importance acting as the gateway to the rich information you so desperately seek. JMX does not specify the distributed services level, or how the managing clients access an MBean, so you also need a connector or protocol adapter that exposes MBeans.

The distributed services level, the third tier, provides interfaces for implementing JMX managers. JMX managers can present a connector layer on top of JMX agents; expose management information through standard mechanisms such as HTTP, RMI, and SNMP; consolidate information from disparate JMX agents; and implement security measures on top of JMX agents. The distributed services level exists to complete the architecture by empowering monitoring and management vendors to develop complete management applications.

For more information about the Java Management Extensions, I strongly encourage you to read through the JMX specification. Although it is nearly 200 pages long, if one of your job responsibilities is to ensure the performance of your enterprise applications, I would consider it required reading.

JSR 77 Architecture

In order for an application server to be JSR 77 compliant, it must supply a specific set of managed objects, an event notification model, a state management model, and a statistics provider model that exposes performance monitoring information, as illustrated in Figure 3-3.

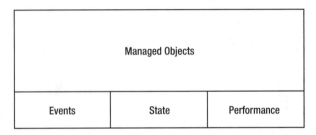

Figure 3-3. *The Java EE management model*

The set of managed objects includes the following application components as well as application server resources:

- Servlets

- EJBs, especially entity beans, session beans, and message-driven beans

- Deployed modules, such as application, EJB, and Web modules

- Java EE resources, like JCA, JTA, JDBC, JMS, JNDI, RMI, JavaMail, and URLs

- JDBC drivers and data sources

- Connection factories

- Resource adapters

- The JVM

JSR 77 describes specifically what you can expect to extract from each of these components, and later in this chapter we will look at sample data taken from a running application server. The Java EE ManagedObject class defines the base of the managed object inheritance hierarchy; managed objects extend from this base and touch all management and performance monitoring aspects of the application server and application. Figure 3-4 shows the complete managed object hierarchy graphically.

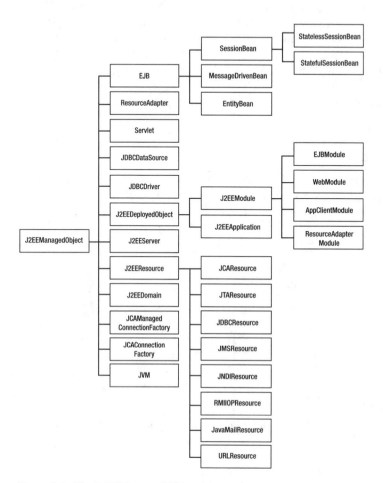

Figure 3-4. *The J2EEManagedObject hierarchy*

Not only does JSR 77 define the types of objects that each application server is required to support, but it also defines the specific format used to present each object's data metrics. Each managed object is required to provide a Stats attribute of the type

```
javax.management.j2ee.statistics.Stats
```

This Stats attribute contains a collection of Statistic elements and a mechanism to obtain their values. The Statistic interface is fully qualified as

```
javax.management.j2ee.statistics.Statistic
```

Each metric is defined by a class that implements a subinterface of the Statistic interface. These Statistic derivative interfaces, TimeStatistic, RangeStatistic, BoundaryStatistic, BoundedRangeStatistic, and CountStatistic, are shown in Figure 3-5 along with their methods.

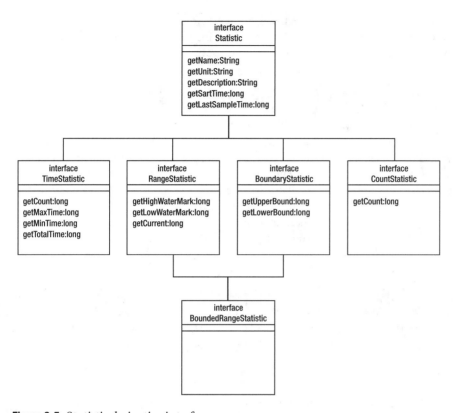

Figure 3-5. *Statistic derivative interfaces*

These statistics are defined as follows:

- CountStatistic provides a count of the number of occurrences of something, such as the total number of transactions committed or rolled back.

- RangeStatistic provides a current value, as well as high and low watermarks, such as the number of execute threads waiting for a database connection or the number of beans in a pool.

- BoundaryStatistic provides an upper and lower boundary for a statistic. This type of statistic works well for configuration information, but not so well for runtime information.

- BoundedRangeStatistic provides the current value, high and low watermarks, and range of possible values for a statistic, such as the size of a JVM heap. The heap may have a minimum size of 256MB and a maximum size of 1024MB, but currently be at 512MB, never having dropped below 384MB or risen above 768MB.

- TimeStatistic provides the execute count, execution time, minimum execution time, maximum execution time, and total execution time for an operation such as the response time of a servlet's service method.

Knowing the type of information application servers provide, and the specific format of that information, you should feel empowered to start using it. The rest of this chapter focuses on obtaining, aggregating, correlating, and presenting performance information.

Obtaining Application Server Metrics

The first step in obtaining performance information from an application server is accessing the MBean server in the JMX agent. You can access the MBean server through application server proprietary mechanisms as well as through standard ones; your eventual decision will be based on your application server and your particular intentions. You might opt to use the application server's proprietary mechanism to ease security restrictions. The application server may provide a mechanism to simply provide a username and password in a method call and return the MBean server, whereas following standard mechanisms may require additional policy modifications to permit the operation. Regardless, first get an MBean server.

■**Note** A couple of decades ago on the U.S. television show *Saturday Night Live*, Steve Martin performed a skit that taught us how to obtain a million dollars without paying taxes on it. His advice went something like this: First, get a million dollars. And then don't pay taxes on it. When the government asks, "Why didn't you pay taxes on it?" tell them, "I forgot." So in this spirit I tell you, "First get an MBean server."

MBean servers are classes that implement the `javax.management.MBeanServer` interface. This interface defines methods to create managed beans, query for managed beans, obtain managed bean attributes, obtain additional information about a managed bean, invoke a managed bean's methods, and modify a managed bean's attributes. The following code snippet shows the standard enterprise Java mechanism for obtaining all `MBeanServer` instances and returning the first one, which should be the only one, most of the time:

```
public MBeanServer getMBeanServer()
{
    try
    {
        ArrayList mbeanServers = MBeanServerFactory.findMBeanServer( null );
        for( Iterator itr=mbeanServers.iterator(); itr.hasNext(); )
        {
            MBeanServer mbs = ( MBeanServer )itr.next();
            System.out.println( "Default Domain: " + mbs.getDefaultDomain() +
                                        ", mbeans: " + mbs.getMBeanCount() );
        }
```

```
        // Return the first MBeanServer
        return ( MBeanServer )mbeanServers.get( 0 );
    }
    catch( Exception e )
    {
        e.printStackTrace();
        return null;
    }
}
```

The current specification supports more than one MBeanServer per JVM instance, but in practice most application servers provide only a single MBeanServer instance. The MBeanServer interface provides several interesting methods, shown in Table 3-1.

Table 3-1. *MBeanServer Methods*

Method	Description
void addNotificationListener(. . .)	Adds a listener to a register MBean for MBean specific notification messages
Object getAttribute(ObjectName name, String attribute)	Gets the value of a specific attribute of a named MBean
AttributeList getAttributes(ObjectName name, String[] attributes)	Gets the values of several attributes of a named MBean
String getDefaultDomain()	Returns the default domain used for naming the MBean
String[] getDomains()	Returns the list of domains in which any MBean is currently registered
Integer getMBeanCount()	Returns the number of MBeans registered in the MBean server
MBeanInfo getMBeanInfo(ObjectName name)	Discovers the attributes and operations that an MBean exposes for management
Object invoke(. . .)	Invokes an operation on an MBean
Set queryMBeans(ObjectName name, QueryExp query)	Gets MBeans controlled by the MBean server
Set queryNames(ObjectName name, QueryExp query)	Gets the names of MBeans controlled by the MBean server

For the purposes of this discussion, the most interesting method is queryNames(). This method allows you to search for specific managed beans or to pass null arguments to return all managed beans. Whenever I am analyzing the performance of a new application server, I first find all managed beans, group them by domain and type, and review their attributes. From these attributes you can not only discover the type of information available, but also infer quite a bit about the internal architecture of the application server. The first step therefore is to interrogate the `MBeanServer` class for its managed beans:

```
Set mbeans = server.queryNames( null, null );
```

This query returns a `java.util.Set` of `ObjectName` instances. An `ObjectName` uniquely identifies a managed bean and follows a loose naming convention; I say "loose" because while application servers are mostly consistent with the naming of their own managed beans, when you cross application server vendor boundaries subtle differences emerge. The format of an `ObjectName` is defined as follows:

```
Domain:Name=<bean-name>,param1=value1,param2=value2,…,paramN=valueN
```

The following is an example of an `ObjectName` extracted from BEA WebLogic's `examples` domain:

```
examples:Location=examplesServer,Name=weblogic.kernel.Default,
ServerRuntime=examplesServer,Type=ExecuteQueueRuntime
```

In this case, the name of the domain is `examples` and it exposes the following parameters:

- `Location`: The server hosting the MBean.

- `Name`: The name of the resource.

- `ServerRuntime`: The WebLogic proprietary value representing the server instance in which this managed bean runs.

- `Type`: The type of this bean. Most application servers have a type, although variations include "type" (lowercase "t") and "j2eeType".

The bean can be interpreted as a runtime managed bean exposing information about WebLogic's `Default` execute queue (denoted by the name `weblogic.kernel.Default`) running on the `examplesServer`. I chose this managed bean for this example because it is a key metric that will be analyzed later.

The following are some common facets of an object in the class `ObjectName`:

- `Domain`: A broad categorization of managed beans. Each application server organizes its managed bean differently, but as we look at more examples the organizational schemes will make more sense.

- `Name`: The name of the managed bean that uniquely identifies it within a domain.

- `Type`: The type of the managed bean that describes, for example, its behavior and function.

Most of the additional information regarding `ObjectName` objects is application server–vendor dependent.

Obtaining Application Metrics

Obtaining application metrics is another beast altogether. Some application servers expose more information about method and request call counts and response times than others, but the most useful information comes through code instrumentation. *Code instrumentation* is the process of inserting code snippets into the application methods to record information such as

- Method invocation counts.

- Method response times (the differences between method start and stop times). This can include both exclusive time (the time spent only in that method) and cumulative time (the time spent in the method and all methods that it calls).

- Object creations and deletions.

More advanced instrumentation implementations not only capture this information for individual methods, but also tag requests as they arrive at the application server and trace request method calls. Because of this tagging, they are able to reassemble the call path that a specific request followed during its execution. The response time and call count information can be used to identify the hot path(s) through the service request as well as the hot point(s) in the request that are most affecting response time. When presented with a claim that a specific request is not performing acceptably, this information empowers you with the means to discover why.

Smart instrumentation dives deeper to include arguments passed to key methods. For example, methods arguments passed to JDBC calls such as preparation and execution methods can provide valuable insight to database administrators troubleshooting a performance issue identified by such instrumentation. Telling a database administrator that a service request is not performing acceptably because of the database is almost useless; telling the database administrator that the database is not responding acceptably for a specific SQL call executed at a specific time, however, empowers that administrator to isolate the problem.

Code instrumentation comes in two flavors: custom and automatic. *Custom instrumentation* is implemented manually by programmers as they write code, whereas *automatic instrumentation* is implemented by an automated process either before an application is deployed or, more optimally, as classes are loaded into the JVM.

Custom Instrumentation

Custom instrumentation is performed by application developers. The mechanism to implement code instrumentation is tedious, but it is also easily understood. Once you understand how to instrument an application manually, writing code to instrument it for you is much easier.

At the simplest level, code instrumentation records the response time of a method. For example, consider recording the response time of a servlet's service() method, shown in Listing 3-1.

Listing 3-1. *Simple Servlet Instrumentation*

```
package com.javasrc.web;

import javax.servlet.*;
import javax.servlet.http.*;

public class MyServlet extends HttpServlet {
```

```java
    private long servletTotalTime;
    private long callCount;
    private long minTime = -1;
    private long maxTime = -1;

    public void service( HttpServletRequest req, HttpServletResponse res )
              throws ServletException {
      long startTime = System.currentTimeMillis();
      // Insert application logic here
      ...
      long endTime = System.currentTimeMillis();
      long totalTime = endTime - startTime;

      // Compute response time metrics
      this.servletTotalTime += totalTime;
      this.callCount++;
      if( totalTime < this.minTime || this.minTime == -1 ) {
        this.minTime = totalTime;
      }
      if( totalTime > this.maxTime || this.maxTime == -1 ) {
        this.maxTime = totalTime;
      }
    }

    public long getAveResponseTime() {
      return this.servletTotalTime / this.callCount;
    }

    public long getCallCount() {
      return this.callCount;
    }

    public long getMinTime() {
      return this.minTime;
    }

    public long getMaxTime() {
      return this.maxTime;
    }
}
```

Listing 3-1 demonstrates how to instrument a single service() method. The service() method calculates the response time of its application logic by calling the method System. currentTimeMillis(). System.currentTimeMillis() returns the current time in milliseconds from the operating system; the returned value is the number of milliseconds that have occurred since the *epoch*, specifically January 1, 1970. With this information, we can define a performance monitoring interface to the servlet to report this information and present it in a format that we can analyze (either graphically or in a format from which it can be imported into a graphical environment such as Microsoft Excel). By computing the derived values for the average response time, minimum and maximum response times, and call count, we keep the memory overhead low and still provide rich information. We can add additional computations to reveal the standard deviation and variance for a time period (or to date).

■**Note** With the advent of Java 5, the `System` class has added another method with a finer granularity than `currentTimeMillis()`. `nanoTime()`, the new class, returns the most precise available system timer in nanoseconds, but it can only be used for measuring elapsed time (by capturing two values and comparing them), not for recording an absolute time.

Another common metric in code instrumentation is the partitioning of method invocation information into two categories: successful method invocations and exceptional invocations. This categorization is accomplished by wrapping the method call with your own exception handling code and maintaining two categories of response time and execution count information. This basic idea is shown in Listing 3-2.

Listing 3-2. *Servlet Custom Instrumentation with Exception Counts*

```java
package com.javasrc.web;

import javax.servlet.*;
import javax.servlet.http.*;

public class MyServlet extends HttpServlet {

  public void service( HttpServletRequest req, HttpServletResponse res )
          throws ServletException {
    long startTime = System.currentTimeMillis();
    try {
      // Application code

      long endTime = System.currentTimeMillis();
      long totalTime = endTime - startTime;

      // Compute response time metrics
      this.servletTotalTime += totalTime;
      this.callCount++;
      if( totalTime < this.minTime || this.minTime == -1 ) {
        this.minTime = totalTime;
      }
      if( totalTime > this.maxTime || this.maxTime == -1 ) {
        this.maxTime = totalTime;
      }
    }
```

```
    catch( Exception e ) {
      // Calculate monitoring values
      long endTime = System.currentTimeMillis();
      long totalTime = endTime - startTime;
      this.exceptionTotalTime += totalTime;
      this.exceptionCount++;

      // Rethrow the exception
      throw e;
    }
  }
  ...
}
```

Recall that we have done all of this work for a single method; if we want to partition additional methods into successful and exceptional categories, then we have to implement similar
logic. When we do this for all of our application methods, we can derive a complete view of our
application performance. In order to obtain real value from that view, we need to assemble
these disparate method calls into a logical call tree. To assemble the call tree, we need to create
a unique key at the start of the request and pass it to each method involved in the request. We
also need a central server or process that correlates this information and builds a model of the
behavior of a single request. Each method, as it is executed, registers itself with the correlation
server, passing the unique key along with context information. The correlation engine then
keeps track of the order of method calls and the parent/child relationships (who called whom).

In Chapter 4, we build a fully functional custom code instrumentation engine that you can
use to manually instrument your own applications.

Automatic Instrumentation

Automatic instrumentation is the most technically complex subject when discussing code
instrumentation. Automatic instrumentation allows you to perform all that we did in the last
section without requiring you to incorporate instrumentation code into your application.
You can implement it either prior to application deployment or at run time in the following
two ways:

- Source code instrumentation

- Bytecode instrumentation

Source code instrumentation is simpler for an individual developer to implement than
bytecode instrumentation, because it only requires source code parsing and not bytecode
processing. Source code instrumentation can be run as an Apache Ant task or as a stand-alone
process on your source code files prior to compilation and deployment.

Bytecode instrumentation, which is sometimes called bytecode insertion, follows the
same logic, but rather than parsing your source code files, a bytecode instrumentor opens the
class Byte code file and inserts the instrumentation into your code at the bytecode level. This
can be thought of loosely as the difference between C/C++ and assembly: the Java source code
is similar to the C/C++ code while the bytecode is similar to the assembly code. The benefit in

performing bytecode instrumentation is that the overhead of the instrumentation can be less than that of source code instrumentation if it is written efficiently, because rather than requiring the Java compiler to generate the bytecode, smart programmers can write the bytecode themselves to perform the functionality optimally. This requires in-depth knowledge of the JVM and its internal machine code. For simple instrumentation implementations, bytecode instrumentation requires far too much work, but for production applications it is often the best solution.

Bytecode instrumentation can be performed at the following two points:

- Prior to application deployment

- During class instantiation

In the first case, your compiled class files can be instrumented through an Ant task or by a separate process before your application is deployed to your application server to create an instrumented Java Archive (JAR), Web Application Archive (WAR), or Enterprise Application Archive (EAR) file. In the second case, a custom classloader can be interjected into the JVM and instrument classes on the fly. Most commercial offerings provide classloader-based bytecode instrumentation.

Classloading works as follows. When a Java process creates an instance of a class, that creation call is delegated to the classloader to open the class file (bytecode). The classloader opens the class and creates what you might think of as a template (not like a C++ template, but more like a rubber stamp from which to create class instances) and stores that in the heap's permanent space. The object instance is then created, stored in the heap, and a reference is returned to the process that created the class instance.

When employing classloader-based bytecode instrumentation, a custom classloader is responsible for loading the class into memory, but as it loads the class, it interjects instrumentation code directly into the bytecode. Figure 3-6 shows this process graphically.

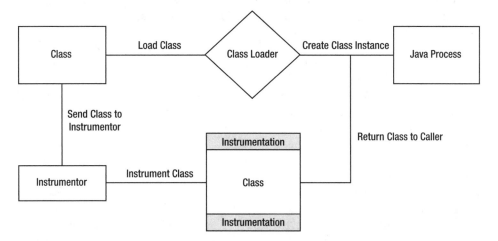

Figure 3-6. *Classloader-based bytecode instrumentation*

Most application servers, or rather most JREs, permit the user to define the classloader to use at runtime. By telling the JRE to use a specific classloader, you can control the creation and instantiation of each class. And as such you can easily facilitate automatic code instrumentation.

Obtaining JVM Metrics

Each JVM presents performance information differently and offers different Application Programming Interfaces (APIs) into their performance metrics; for example, IBM, BEA, and JBoss provide information through JMX. Although the specific implementations vary between JVM vendors, to appease the specifications common things exist across them.

But before gathering data, you need to understand what information is of interest to the performance of your application. The following list summarizes the metrics we are interested in gathering from the JVM:

- *Heap usage*: What is its current size and maximum size, and what generational information is available?

- *Garbage collection rate*: How often does garbage collection run?

- *Garbage collection duration*: When garbage collection runs, how long does it take to complete?

- *Garbage collection effectiveness*: When it runs, is garbage collection able to reclaim significant amounts of memory or is all of the work in vain?

- *Loitering objects*: As business processes run, what are they leaving in memory, and should it be there?

- *Object cycling*: Are objects being created and destroyed frequently incurring extra effort on the garbage collection process?

Some information is very inexpensive to capture, such as the heap size and heap usage, and other information is extremely expensive, such as identifying loitering objects and object cycling. Garbage collection information comes at a medium expense; Sun states that recording verbose garbage collection information at its lightest form incurs about 5 percent overhead. You can enable verbose garbage collection logging to allow you to analyze garbage collection types, rates, durations, and, after considerable computation, the collection's effectiveness.

A *lingering object* is an object that your application creates during a service request and does not dereference before the service request completes; this behavior may or may not be expected. For example, a user login request may validate a user and then store the user's identity as an HTTPSession object. Creating this object is expected and satisfies a business requirement. However, a request may query the database and retrieve 1,000 rows of data and cache it as an HTTPSession object for the user to peruse at a later date. If the user never looks at the data, but the application continues to maintain it, that data occupies memory and drains the system of resources. This condition is referred to as *maintaining lingering objects*. Java garbage collection eliminates C++-style memory leaks, but it cannot eliminate memory mismanagement that derives from poor object life cycle definition.

Object cycling, on the other hand, takes the reverse approach: rather than cache a value, re-create it on every request. Objects are thus created at the beginning of a request and then cleaned up at the end of the request. On subsequent requests, the process repeats even for the same objects. Object cycling causes the JVM to run out of memory quickly and hence increases

the frequency of garbage collection. In extreme cases, object cycling can occur inside programmatic loops. For example, the following causes object cycling inside the `for` loop:

```
public double computeSD( Set values, int callCount, long totalTime )
{
  double diffs = 0.0d;
  for( Iterator i=values.iterator(); i.hasNext(); )
  {
    double value = ( ( Double )i.next() ).doubleValue();
    Double average = new Double( totalTime / callCount );
    diffs += ( value - average.doubleValue() ) * ( value - average.doubleValue() );
  }
  double variance = diffs / callCount;
  return Math.sqrt( variance );
}
```

This method computes the standard deviation for a set of `Double` values, given the number
of executions and the total execution time. It may appear clean, but consider a set of 2,000 values
from which we want to compute the standard deviation; the average is computed 2,000 times.
Not only is this inefficient, but it wreaks havoc on garbage collection. The average is a double
that occupies 8 bytes, and we are creating 2,000 instances, each occupying 8 bytes, so that's
16 kilobytes. Not a huge problem, but if this is done 20 times a second in a Web application,
then we are inadvertently creating thousands of objects that we do not need. The method
could be rewritten as follows to eliminate this problem:

```
public double computeSD( Set values, int callCount, long totalTime )
{
  double diffs = 0.0d;
  Double average = new Double( totalTime / callCount );
  for( Iterator i=values.iterator(); i.hasNext(); )
  {
    double value = ( ( Double )i.next() ).doubleValue();
    diffs += ( value - average.doubleValue() ) * ( value - average.doubleValue() );
  }
  double variance = diffs / callCount;
  return Math.sqrt( variance );
}
```

Moving the computation of the average outside of the `for` loop improves performance by
performing the computation once, but it also means that, when computing the standard deviation for a set of 2,000 objects, we only need one instance of the average in memory rather than
2,000 instances.

Lingering objects drain memory and reduce the effectiveness of garbage collections, while
object cycling increases the frequency of garbage collection. More frequent garbage collections
mean that short-lived objects may not have time to be created and destroyed between garbage
collections causing two problems:

- Short-lived objects need to be analyzed to see if they are still alive even though they will be cleaned up in milliseconds; this increases the duration of garbage collection.

- If garbage collection runs too frequently, depending on the garbage collection algorithm, objects may move into a condition where they require a major garbage collection to free them rather than a minor garbage collection. Major garbage collections are significantly more expensive than minor collections and can hurt the performance of your application.

Figure 3-7 shows excessive object creation and destruction within a 30-second to 50-second time period, visually representing a pattern that signifies object cycling. With this background in obtaining JVM metrics, in the next chapter we will explore techniques for acquiring some of this information.

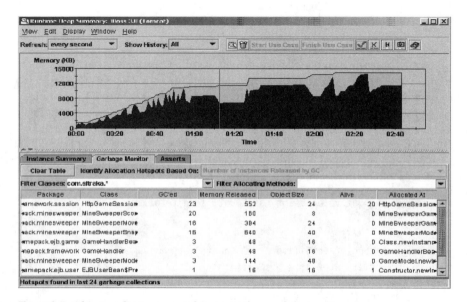

Figure 3-7. *Object cycling—excess object creation and destruction*

Aggregating Data

Raw data is powerful in many circumstances, but usually aggregate values provide deeper insight into the behavior of a metric. For example, consider the response time of a service request over a 30-minute interval. If it was executed close to 2,000 times in that 30-minute session, then observing its behavior for each individual request is unreasonable; requests may be concurrent or within a few milliseconds of each other. Instead we divide the 30-minute sample into intervals and then aggregate the data for that interval. For example, we might want the granularity of 10-second sample intervals. For a 30-minute sample, that means there will be 30 minutes multiplied by 6 samples per minute, equating to 500 data points. For each sample interval, we compute the following aggregate values: the execution count; the minimum, maximum, total, and average response times; the variance; and the standard deviation of response times. In this scenario, we would have a table with 500 rows that resembled the following:

Request	Call Count	Ave	Min	Max	Total	V	SD
/dosomething	15	1.2	0.5	7.2	18.0	0.25	0.5

From this table we can see that the service request /dosomething was executed 15 times at an average of 1.2 seconds per request, with a minimum response time of 0.5 seconds, a maximum response time of 7.2 seconds, and a total time of 18.0 seconds. This presentation is far more interesting that 15 individual rows that only report the response time for a single invocation. Now further aggregate all of this information for all 500 rows:

Request	Call Count	Ave	Min	Max	Total	V	SD
/dosomething	1526	1.25	0.07	17.2	1907.5	9.0	3.0

You cannot possibly read anything meaningful from over 1,500 values, but you can identify suspect service requests with values such as the average, maximum, and total times and the standard deviation. If I see a request that accounts for 1,907 seconds of a 30-minute sample, then I know that it is a significant method. I am probably not too worried about the average response time, but the maximum response time does concern me. Furthermore, this method has a large standard deviation relative to the average (a 3-second standard deviation rather than the 1.25-second average), so I know that, although the average is low, it is not conclusive enough to be representative of the end-user experience. If, however, the standard deviation were small, like 0.2 seconds, then I could trust the average. So, one line that aggregates 500 samples accounting for over 1,500 calls tells me far more than looking at the 1,500 requests individually.

Finally, with samples having a granularity of 10 seconds, we can zoom in on a small portion of the observed session to find troublesome time periods. In my experience, troublesome service requests tend to fall into one of two categories: overall poor performers (high average) or sporadic performers (good on average but with periodic spikes in the response time). In the former category, code instrumentation can reveal the cause of general slowdowns. In the latter, the analyzed segment needs to be narrowed to the specific time period when the response time was poor before code instrumentation can identify the cause of the discrepancy; analysis of the entire session can mask periodic problems, which is why the maximum response time is so important.

Correlating Data

As previously mentioned, knowledge differs from data: data applied to a model equates to knowledge. With that said, individual metrics do not represent business values outside the context of a model, and most metrics need to be analyzed in conjunction with other metrics. As an example, consider thread pool usage. Given an 80 percent thread pool usage, here are questions that you need to consider:

- What is the size of the pool? If we have 5 total threads and 4 of them are in use, then we need to increase the thread pool, but if we have 200 threads with 160 in use, then we have some breathing room.

- Why are the threads in use? Is it user load, or is a surplus of threads waiting for a database connection? Is there contention?

- Are users being affected by the high usage of threads? Are their response times meeting SLAs?

For true understanding, we need to evaluate a metric against the environment model and correlate it to its business impact. In the end, we need to have a complete collection of valuable metrics from which to derive meaningful values. The obviously difficult part is identifying which metrics are important. Two things can help you make this determination:

- A strong understanding of the Java EE model

- A visualization of all metrics

Knowledge of the enterprise Java model provides a core set of observations to aid in metric interpretation; specifically these observations are as follows:

- The layered execution model dictates that enterprise Java applications run inside a JVM, so we are very interested in memory-related metrics such as memory usage, garbage collection behavior (rate, duration, and effectiveness), lingering objects, and object cycling.

- Looking deeper into the layered execution model, we are also interested in hardware performance such as CPU usage, disk I/O rates, physical memory usage, network traffic, and operating system threads and processes.

- All requests are placed in an execution queue that is serviced by a thread pool; therefore, we are interested in the performance of the thread pools, specifically their usage, their throughput, and the number of pending requests in the queue.

- If an application has a back-end database, then it must do so through a JDBC connection pool, so we are interested in metrics such as pool usage, peak usage, and pending requests waiting for a connection.

- If an application uses any caching structure, such as entity beans, then we are interested in the performance of that cache; specifically we want to observe cache usage, activation rate, passivation rate, hit percentage, miss percentage, and the amount of thrashing.

- If an application makes use of messaging, then its messaging will be facilitated through the JMS. Therefore, we are interested in the performance of the JMS destinations (queues and topics). For example, for any upper limit in bytes or messages, we want to observe the usage percentage, queue depth, rate of queue growth, rate of message consumption, and assigned thread pool utilization.

- Most enterprise applications are transactional by nature, so we are interested in the performance of the `TransactionManager`, including the commit rate and percentage, rollback rate and percentage, and ratio of application to nonapplication rollbacks.

- From an application-level perspective, we are interested in overall response times of service requests, hot spots in requests, the impact of external dependencies, the top ten methods being executed (slowest as well as most popular), and the top ten SQL statements being executed.

This outline of considerations loosely fits each application server vendor's implementation, because each of the aforementioned categories of metrics is required to support the enterprise Java specifications. On top of these core services, application server vendors build their own optimizations and services to enhance the performance of enterprise applications. For example, BEA provides customizable thread pools and allows you to reserve threads for specific subsets of application functionality, and IBM provides an additional caching mechanism that holds dynamically generated content from servlets and JSPs. After observing the core enterprise Java services, you need to learn the intricacies of your vendor-specific offerings.

Finally, you need to ask the question, "What do these metrics mean to my business process?" Most of the time, you need to correlate the performance of your application server behavior with the performance of your enterprise applications. For example, consider a JDBC connection pool that always ranges between 90 and 100 percent usage, with occasional pending threads waiting for a connection. Should the size of this pool be increased? Yes, most likely, but first consider what business process is waiting on this connection pool. If it is a user request, then most definitely increase the pool size. On the other hand, if it is a background batch process that you want to allow to run, but you do not want to permit it to consume too many resources, then restricting its runtime threads and database connections can minimize its impact on the overall environment. Without an understanding of the underlying business process and requirements, you cannot assume that general recommendations are always applicable.

■**Note** I have shared the following story with all of my customers and students, and in most of my Webinars, so forgive me if you have heard this before. Whenever I talk about performance, I cannot help reflecting back to the sorting lectures of the Data Structures and Algorithm Analysis class that I taught. Sorting algorithms vary in performance from horrible to great (or in terms of algorithm orders from $O(n^2)$ to $O(nlogn)$). On the final exam, I asked my students which algorithm is better to use: Bubblesort ($O(n^2)$) or Quicksort ($O(nlogn)$)? Most of my students knew it was a trick question; I did not want an absolute answer, but rather I wanted the students to turn the question back around at me and ask, "For what size N?" The point is that Quicksort is faster than Bubblesort, but only for large numbers of objects. When sorting fewer than 100 objects, the overhead for using Quicksort is prohibitive to its viability. But with 1,000 objects, Quicksort will return results over 50 times faster than Bubblesort. The point is that you need to understand general principles, but you need to be flexible enough to adapt your thinking to serve the business processes.

After applying general principles derived from the enterprise Java model to the metrics that I am analyzing and then reflecting on the business values of those metrics, I next extract performance metrics into a visualization tool to try to identify trends between metrics that can lead to new correlations. For example, under load I might observe that the response time of a service request increases as the thread pool usage reaches capacity and then the rate of time-out rollbacks increases. Those three metrics—the response time of a specific service request, the usage of a specific thread pool, and the rate of time-out rollbacks for a handful of specific classes—empower me to write powerful rules specific to my environment. Furthermore, observing the behavior of the environment just prior to this condition may provide information that can be used to detect this problem before it greatly impacts the end-user experience. And the purpose of our tuning efforts is to satisfy our customers.

Chapter 7 provides guidance in interpreting performance metrics and how they interrelate.

Visualizing Data

While writing code to detect and provide alerts based on metric thresholds is reasonable, writing code to analyze and correlate data is a difficult task. It's not difficult programmatically, but rather the difficulty lies in identifying related metrics and interpreting their interrelationships. To identify trends in metric behaviors and correlate them, present metric data sets in a visualization tool. A visualization tool should allow you to overlay the metrics' historical performance (even if the history is only 30 minutes) to allow you to visually identify relationships. Good tools present you with performance metrics and allow you to drag and drop metrics on top of one another and then display your metrics on a single graph or on a set of them. With these graphs you should be able to interpret metric meanings specific to the context of your application.

Using a spreadsheet provides another very effective and less expensive approach, though it is just a little slower. A spreadsheet allows you to generate graphs from various table rows and columns, and thus it can be configured to plot multiple data sets. The manual component to this process is that you are required to choose the data sets either by highlighting the columns and walking through a wizard or manually choosing the data set row and column IDs (for example, A7 to C14). In the early days, before I had access to more advanced tools, I used a spreadsheet to architect both the threshold and advanced rules for our monitoring products. Many times a metric looks interesting on paper, but the observed behavior is far from spectacular. Believe it or not, many metrics that application server vendors provide do not behave as advertised or are simply of little value. The only way to be sure of the utility of a metric is to plot the metric over some time period and see if any valuable information can be gleaned from the graph.

Summary

In order to effectively measure performance, we need to first understand what to measure. The enterprise Java application model provides the framework from which we derive the type of information to measure and the components from which to measure the information. Looking specifically at the enterprise Java stack, we gather metrics from the following sources:

- *Application server*: We gather metrics through the JMX API.

- *JVM*: We gather information through exposed APIs and log files.

- *Application*: We gather metrics through code instrumentation.

Once we have these metrics, we aggregate them to transform raw values into meaningful values that help in our interpretation. We correlate these aggregate values to derive business values specific to our applications, and we visualize these business values to assess their impact on our end users. In the next chapter, we will implement performance measurement on a sample enterprise Java environment and extract meaningful values from what, at first, may appear to be a disparate set of 15s and 32s.

CHAPTER 4

■■■

Implementing Performance Measurements

"**O**kay, I understand the whole JMX thing and the depth of monitoring that we need to identify problems in our environment, but do we really need to go out and purchase a tool to do it for us, or can we build it ourselves?" John asked. "I have some very smart people in my organization that should be able to do it."

I could tell that John was looking for a quick and inexpensive solution that would solve all of his problems. This was a good opportunity to explain the technology to him at the level of detail he was looking for.

"Smart people can build anything," I replied. "But the real question is this: are you in the performance monitoring business or are you in the financial business?"

"Well, obviously, I'm in the financial business, but I could spare a couple people to work on this for a couple months if I needed to." John's confidence in his team was admirable.

"How about this? Let me show you the details of the technology and you can decide for yourself," I responded. "I have code that can read application server metrics and implement basic code instrumentation that I would love to explain to you. In my opinion, this problem is complex enough that you are better finding a prebuilt solution, but the technology is interesting and this exercise can get you through some of your initial troubleshooting."

"Great, let me get my architect on the line!"

This chapter presents an overview of the technologies that gather performance measurement metrics. Specifically, it presents code to obtain application server–specific metrics from a JMX registry and a basic implementation of a custom instrumentation engine. Because all of my previous books have been about Java programming, I had to add a "geek"-oriented chapter. If you skip this chapter, it will not hurt your understanding of the material later in the book, but reading this chapter will give you an appreciation for the technologies and a starting point if you do not currently have a commercial product that you can use to start tuning your Java EE environments today.

Reading Application Server Metrics

In Chapter 3, you learned that application server vendors publish much of their internal configuration and run-time behavior through a managed bean (MBean) registry that is accessible
through the Java Management Extensions (JMX) API. In this section, we implement a statistics
servlet that accesses an application server's MBean registry, iterates over all of its MBeans, and
returns MBean information as XML. The servlet itself displays MBean information in a raw
format; I use this servlet when determining the metrics to analyze when developing performance monitoring software. It has the capability to present *derived metrics*, or metrics with
associated business value, and it is also capable of running in *debug* mode, where it returns a
large XML file displaying all MBeans, all MBean attributes, and all attribute values that can be
easily converted to a `String`.

One of the challenges that we face when obtaining MBean information is gaining access to
an MBean server, so to address this, we implement an extension to the servlet that delegates
obtaining the MBean server to a subclass of the servlet. Furthermore, the delegate is the entry
point to building application server–specific derived metrics.

Figure 4-1 illustrates the workflow of the statistics servlet as well as the relationship
between the statistics servlet and its application server–specific delegate. As shown in Figure 4-1,
when the statistics servlet `AbstractStatsServlet` receives a request from a Web browser or other
HTTP client, it first queries the delegate servlet for its `MBeanServer` and then asks it to build its
derived metrics. Afterward, if the servlet is running in debug mode (passed a `debug=true` servlet
parameter), it then iterates over the MBeans in the MBean registry and optionally captures
MBean attributes.

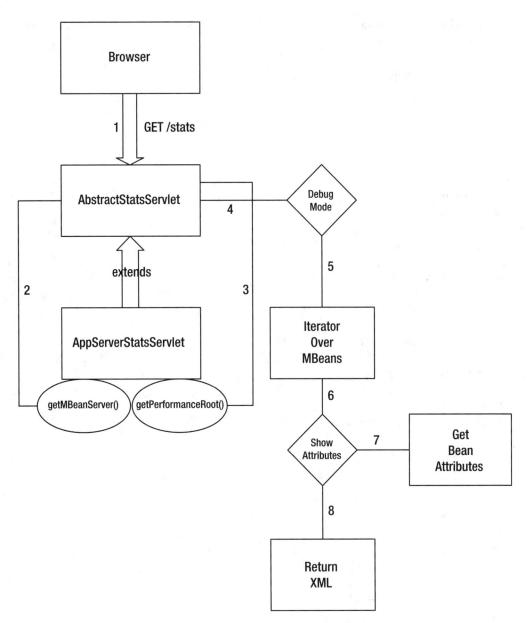

Figure 4-1. *Workflow of the statistics servlet and the relationship between the statistics servlet and its application server–specific delegate*

Listing 4-1 shows the source code for the AbstractStatsServlet class, which implements the majority of the MBean interactions.

Listing 4-1. *AbstractStatsServlet.java*

```
package com.javasrc.tuning.web;

// Import servlet classes
import javax.servlet.*;
import javax.servlet.http.*;

// Import JNDI classes
import javax.naming.*;

// Import JDOM classes
import org.jdom.*;
import org.jdom.output.*;

// Import Java classes
import java.util.*;
import javax.management.*;

import javax.management.j2ee.statistics.*;

/**
 * Abstract base class for building statistic servlets.
 *
 * Provides the following base functionality:
 *      - Queries MBean names, sorts, and caches
 *      - Debug mode to display all MBeans (with or without attributes)
 *      - Ability to refresh object names
 *      - XML output to the caller
 */
public abstract class AbstractStatsServlet extends HttpServlet
{
    protected InitialContext ic;
    protected ServletContext ctx = null;

    // Computation parameters
    protected long now = 0l;
    protected long lastSampleTime = 0l;
    protected Element lastRequest = null;
```

```java
/**
 * Obtains an MBeanServer to communicate with and uses it to build an initial
 * map of object names.
 *
 * The map of object names is stored in the ServletContext with the name
 * "object-names" The MBeanServer is stored in the ServletContext with the
 * name "mbean-server"
 */
public void init()
{
    try
    {
        // Load our contexts
        this.ctx = getServletContext();
        this.ic = new InitialContext();

        // See if we already have the ObjectName Map defined in the
        // application object
        Map objectNames = ( Map )ctx.getAttribute( "object-names" );
        if( objectNames == null )
        {
            // Get the MBeanServer from the servlet instance
            MBeanServer server = getMBeanServer();

            // Save our MBeanServer and preload and save our object names
            objectNames = this.preloadObjectNames( server );
            ctx.setAttribute( "object-names", objectNames );
            ctx.setAttribute( "mbean-server", server );
        }
    }
    catch( Exception ex )
    {
        ex.printStackTrace();
    }
}

/**
 * Converts a String to a boolean
 */
private boolean getBoolean( String str )
{
    if( str != null && str.equalsIgnoreCase( "true" ) )
    {
        return true;
    }
    return false;
}
```

```
/**
 * Converts a boolean to a String
 */
private String getBooleanString( boolean b )
{
    if( b )
    {
        return "true";
    }
    return "false";
}

/**
 * Returns an XML document to the caller containing MBean information.
 * The following are request options:
 *
 *   refresh            Refresh the object-names map to pick up any newly
 *                      added MBeans
 *   debug              Dump the object-names map of MBeans inside the
 *                      returned XML document
 *   showAttributes     When dumping the object-names map of MBeans,
 *                      include as many attribute values as we can extract
 *   showAttributeInfo  When showing attributes, display extended
 *                      information about the attribute
 */
public void service( HttpServletRequest req, HttpServletResponse res )
          throws ServletException  {
    try {
        // Load our MBeanServer from the ServletContext
        MBeanServer server =
            ( MBeanServer )this.ctx.getAttribute( "mbean-server" );

        // Get our request objects
        boolean refresh = getBoolean( req.getParameter( "refresh" ) );
        boolean debug = getBoolean( req.getParameter( "debug" ) );
        boolean showAttributes = getBoolean(
            req.getParameter( "showAttributes" ) );
        boolean showAttributeInfo = getBoolean(
            req.getParameter( "showAttributeInfo" ) );

        Map objectNames = null;
        if( refresh )
        {
            objectNames = this.preloadObjectNames( server );
            System.out.println( "Refresh object map..." );
        }
```

```
else
{
    objectNames = ( Map )this.ctx.getAttribute( "object-names" );
}
this.now = System.currentTimeMillis();

// Ask the servlet instance for the root of the document
Element root = this.getPerformanceRoot( server, objectNames );

// Dump the MBean info
if( debug )
{
    Element mbeans = new Element( "mbeans" );
    for( Iterator i=objectNames.keySet().iterator(); i.hasNext(); )
    {
        String key = ( String )i.next();
        Element domain = new Element( "domain" );
        domain.setAttribute( "name", key );
        Map typeNames = ( Map )objectNames.get( key );
        for( Iterator j=typeNames.keySet().iterator(); j.hasNext(); )
        {
            String typeName = ( String )j.next();
            Element typeElement = new Element( "type" );
            typeElement.setAttribute( "name", typeName );
            List beans = ( List )typeNames.get( typeName );
            for( Iterator k=beans.iterator(); k.hasNext(); )
            {
                ObjectName on = ( ObjectName )k.next();
                Element bean = new Element( "mbean" );
                bean.setAttribute( "name", on.getCanonicalName() );

                // List the attributes
                if( showAttributes )
                {
                    try
                    {
                        MBeanInfo info = server.getMBeanInfo( on );
                        Element attributesElement =
                            new Element( "attributes" );
                        MBeanAttributeInfo[] attributeArray =
                            info.getAttributes();
                        for( int x=0; x<attributeArray.length; x++ )
                        {
                            String attributeName =
                                attributeArray[ x ].getName();
                            Element attributeElement =
                                new Element( "attribute" );
```

```
                                attributeElement.setAttribute(
                                   "name", attributeName );
                                if( showAttributeInfo )
                                {
                                   String attributeClass =
                                      attributeArray[ x ].getType();
                                   attributeElement.setAttribute(
                                      "class", attributeClass );
                                   attributeElement.setAttribute(
                                      "description",
                                   attributeArray[ x ].getDescription() );
                                   attributeElement.setAttribute(
                                      "is-getter",
                                      getBooleanString(
                                        attributeArray[ x ].isIs() ) );
                                   attributeElement.setAttribute(
                                      "readable",
                                      getBooleanString(
                                        attributeArray[x].isReadable()));
                                   attributeElement.setAttribute(
                                      "writable",
                                      getBooleanString(
                                        attributeArray[x].isWritable()));

                                   // Handle special cases
                                   if( attributeClass.equalsIgnoreCase(
                                "javax.management.j2ee.statistics.Stats"))
                                   {
                                       Element statsElement =
                                        getStatsElement(
                                        ( Stats )( server.getAttribute( on,
                                                  attributeName ) ) );
                                       attributeElement.addContent(
                                       statsElement );
                                   }
                                }
                                try
                                {
                                   Object objectValue = server.getAttribute(
                                      on, attributeName );
                                   if( objectValue != null )
                                   {
                                       attributeElement.addContent(
                                         objectValue.toString() );
                                   }
                                }
```

```
                            catch( Exception exx )
                            {
                                attributeElement.addContent(
                                  "Error obtaining value" );
                            }
                            attributesElement.addContent(
                                attributeElement );
                        }
                        bean.addContent( attributesElement );
                    }
                    catch( Exception noAttributesException )
                    {
                    }
                }

                typeElement.addContent( bean );
            }
            domain.addContent( typeElement );
        }
        mbeans.addContent( domain );
    }
    root.addContent( mbeans );
}

// Save our last sample time
this.lastSampleTime = this.now;

// Save the last request
this.lastRequest = root;

// Output the XML document to the caller
XMLOutputter out = new XMLOutputter( "   ", true );
out.output( root, res.getOutputStream() );
}
catch( Exception e )
{
    e.printStackTrace();
    throw new ServletException( e );
}
}
```

```java
/**
 * This method extracts a JSR-77 stats metric from the specified ObjectName
 * with the specified attribute name
 *
 * @param stats          The JSR 77 Stats object
 *
 * @return               A JDOM XML node containing the statistics
 */
protected Element getStatsElement( Stats stats )
{
    Element statsElement = new Element( "stats" );
    try
    {
        Statistic[] statistics = stats.getStatistics();
        for( int i=0; i<statistics.length; i++ )
        {
            Element statElement = getStatElement( statistics[ i ] );
            statsElement.addContent( statElement );
        }
    }
    catch( Exception e )
    {
        Element exceptionElement = new Element( "exception" );
        exceptionElement.addContent( e.toString() );
        statsElement.addContent( exceptionElement );
    }
    return statsElement;

}

protected Element getStatElement( Statistic statistic )
{
    Element statElement = new Element( "stat" );
    try
    {
        statElement.setAttribute( "name", statistic.getName() );
        statElement.setAttribute( "description", statistic.getDescription() );
        statElement.setAttribute( "unit", statistic.getUnit() );
        statElement.setAttribute( "start-time", Long.toString(
            statistic.getStartTime() ) );
        statElement.setAttribute( "last-sample-time",
            Long.toString( statistic.getLastSampleTime() ) );
```

```java
// Get the specific statistic type information
if( statistic instanceof BoundedRangeStatistic )
{
    statElement.setAttribute( "type", "bounded-range-statistic" );

    BoundedRangeStatistic brs = ( BoundedRangeStatistic )statistic;
    statElement.setAttribute( "current",
        Long.toString( brs.getCurrent() ) );
    statElement.setAttribute( "low-water-mark",
        Long.toString( brs.getLowWaterMark() ) );
    statElement.setAttribute( "high-water-mark",
        Long.toString( brs.getHighWaterMark() ) );
    statElement.setAttribute( "lower-bound",
        Long.toString( brs.getLowerBound() ) );
    statElement.setAttribute( "upper-bound",
        Long.toString( brs.getUpperBound() ) );
}
else if( statistic instanceof BoundaryStatistic )
{
    statElement.setAttribute( "type", "boundary-statistic" );

    BoundaryStatistic bs = ( BoundaryStatistic )statistic;
    statElement.setAttribute( "lower-bound",
        Long.toString( bs.getLowerBound() ) );
    statElement.setAttribute( "upper-bound",
        Long.toString( bs.getUpperBound() ) );
}
else if( statistic instanceof RangeStatistic )
{
    statElement.setAttribute( "type", "range-statistic" );

    RangeStatistic rs = ( RangeStatistic )statistic;
    statElement.setAttribute( "current",
        Long.toString( rs.getCurrent() ) );
    statElement.setAttribute( "low-water-mark",
        Long.toString( rs.getLowWaterMark() ) );
    statElement.setAttribute( "high-water-mark",
        Long.toString( rs.getHighWaterMark() ) );
}
else if( statistic instanceof CountStatistic )
{
    statElement.setAttribute( "type", "count-statistic" );

    CountStatistic cs = ( CountStatistic )statistic;
    statElement.setAttribute( "count", Long.toString( cs.getCount() ) );
}
/*
```

```
            else if( statistic instanceof StringStatistic )
            {
                statElement.setAttribute( "type", "string-statistic" );

                StringStatistic ss = ( CountStatistic )statistic;
                statElement.setAttribute( "current", ss.getCurrent() );
            }
            */
            else if( statistic instanceof TimeStatistic )
            {
                statElement.setAttribute( "type", "time-statistic" );

                TimeStatistic ts = ( TimeStatistic )statistic;
                statElement.setAttribute( "count", Long.toString( ts.getCount() ) );
                statElement.setAttribute( "max-time",
                        Long.toString( ts.getMaxTime() ) );
                statElement.setAttribute( "min-time",
                        Long.toString( ts.getMinTime() ) );
                statElement.setAttribute( "total-time",
                        Long.toString( ts.getTotalTime() ) );
            }
            /*
            else if( statistic instanceof MapStatistic )
            {
                statElement.setAttribute( "type", "map-statistic" );

                MapStatistic ms = ( MapStatistic )statistic;
                Map m = ms.asMap();
                for( Iterator i=m.keySet().iterator(); i.hasNext(); )
                {
                    String name = ( String )i.next();
                    Statistic s = ( Statistic )m.get( name );
                    Element subElement = getStatElement( s );
                    statElement.addContent( subElement );
                }
            }
            */
        }
        catch( Exception e )
        {
            Element exceptionElement = new Element( "exception" );
            exceptionElement.addContent( e.toString() );
            statElement.addContent( exceptionElement );
        }
        return statElement;
    }
```

```java
/**
 * Classes extending this servlet are responsible for locating and returning
 * an MBeanServer instance. This instance is used to preload object names and
 * for managing state access.
 */
public abstract MBeanServer getMBeanServer();

/**
 * This is the main focus point of the application server-specific servlet
 * classes; through the getPerformanceRoot() method you will build an XML
 * document that you want to return to the caller
 */
public abstract Element getPerformanceRoot(MBeanServer server, Map objectNames);


/**
 * Returns a specific ObjectName with the MBean name for the specified MBean
 * type in the specified domain
 */
protected ObjectName getObjectName( Map objectNames, String domain,
            String type, String name )
{
    // Get the List of domain names
    List ons = getObjectNames(objectNames,domain,type);

    // Find the requested bean
    for( Iterator i=ons.iterator(); i.hasNext(); )
    {
        ObjectName on = ( ObjectName )i.next();
        String objectName = on.getKeyProperty( "name" );
        if( objectName != null && objectName.equalsIgnoreCase( name ) )
        {
            // Found it
            return on;
        }
    }

    // Didn't find it
    return null;
}

/**
 * Returns a List of ObjectNames in the specified domain for the specified
 * type of MBeans
 */
protected List getObjectNames( Map objectNames, String domain, String type )
{
```

```
        // Get the domain map
        Map domainMap = getDomainMap(objectNames,domain);
        if( domainMap == null )
        {
            return null;
        }

        // Get the List of ObjectNames
        List l = ( List )domainMap.get( type );
        return l;
    }

    /**
     * Returns the domain map for the specified doamin name from the map of
     * object names; map of object names must be passed instead of stored as a
     * member variable to support multithreading
     */
    protected Map getDomainMap( Map objectNames, String domain )
    {
        // Get the domain Map
        Map domainMap = ( Map )objectNames.get( domain );
        return domainMap;
    }


    /**
     * Returns all of the domain names found in the MBeanServer
     */
    protected Set getDomainNames( Map objectNames )
    {
        return objectNames.keySet();
    }

    /**
     * Preloads the ObjectName instances and sorts them into a Map indexed by
     * domain; e.g., jboss.web is a domain and Jetty=0,SocketListener=0 is the
     * ObjectName.
     *
     * For WebSphere, further categorizes by "type":
     *  Map of domain names to a vector of maps of type names to object names
     */
    protected Map preloadObjectNames( MBeanServer server )
    {
        Map objectNames = new TreeMap();
        try
        {
            Set ons = server.queryNames( null, null );
```

```java
        for( Iterator i=ons.iterator(); i.hasNext(); )
        {
            ObjectName name = ( ObjectName )i.next();
            String domain = name.getDomain();
            Map typeNames = null;
            if( objectNames.containsKey( domain ) )
            {
                // Load this domain's List from our map and
                // add this ObjectName to it
                typeNames = ( Map )objectNames.get( domain );
            }
            else
            {
                // This is a domain that we don't have yet, add it
                // to our map
                typeNames = new TreeMap();
                objectNames.put( domain, typeNames );
            }

            // Search the typeNames map to match the type of this object
            String typeName = name.getKeyProperty( "type" );
            if( typeName == null ) typeName = name.getKeyProperty( "Type" );
            if( typeName == null ) typeName = "none";

            if( typeNames.containsKey( typeName ) )
            {
                List l = ( List )typeNames.get( typeName );
                l.add( name );
            }
            else
            {
                List l = new ArrayList();
                l.add( name );
                typeNames.put( typeName, l );
            }
        }
    }
    catch( Exception e )
    {
        e.printStackTrace();
    }
    return objectNames;
}
```

The AbstractStatsServlet class delegates to its subclass to obtain an MBeanServer and then it stores that MBeanServer in the ServletContext. The ServletContext is referred to in Java Web technologies as the *application scope*, meaning that any servlet or JSP file in the Web application can access it through its attribute name, which in this case is `mbean-server`. We do this to obtain the `MBeanServer` the first time the servlet is invoked and then cache it for later use. The `AbstractStatsServlet` iterates over all of the MBeans in the MBean registry and captures each MBean's `ObjectName`. The MBean server uses each MBean's `ObjectName` to discover its attributes and attribute values.

When the servlet is invoked, it first calls the subclass's `getPerformanceRoot()` method, passing it the `MBeanServer` and the collection of `ObjectNames` so that it can build its derived metrics. If the servlet is run in debug mode, when we pass it the servlet request parameter `debug` with a value of `true`, it iterates over all MBeans and reports each MBean name. If it is configured to show attributes, when we pass the request attribute `showAttributes` with a value of `true`, it extracts and displays each MBean's attributes. Finally, if the servlet is configured to show attribute values, when we pass the request attribute `showAttributeValues` with a value of `true`, it attempts to obtain attribute values. A special type of attribute value that reports JSR-77 statistics is signified by the class name `javax.management.j2ee.statistics.Stats`. In this case, the servlet extracts those values.

You can read through the rest of the code details yourself. The majority of the code is structured around working with the MBean attribute interfaces, which can be verbose, but straightforward.

The `AbstractStatsServlet` class does not have much value without an application server–specific subclass, so Listing 4-2 presents a sample subclass that communicates with BEA WebLogic. You can download sample code for communicating with IBM WebSphere and JBoss from the Source Code area of the Apress Web site at www.apress.com and from www.javasrc.com.

Listing 4-2. *WeblogicStatsServlet.java*

```
package com.javasrc.tuning.weblogic.web;

// Import JNDI classes
import javax.naming.*;

// Import JDOM classes
import org.jdom.*;
import org.jdom.input.*;
import org.jdom.output.*;

// Import Java classes
import java.util.*;
import javax.management.*;

// Import WebLogic JMX classes
import weblogic.jndi.Environment;
import weblogic.management.*;
import weblogic.management.runtime.*;
import weblogic.management.configuration.*;
import weblogic.management.descriptors.*;
import weblogic.management.descriptors.toplevel.*;
import weblogic.management.descriptors.weblogic.*;
```

```java
// Import our base class
import com.javasrc.tuning.web.*;

public class WebLogicStatsServlet extends AbstractStatsServlet
{
    /**
     * Classes extending this servlet are responsible for locating and returning
     * an MBeanServer instance. This instance is used to preload object names and
     * for managing state access.
     */
    public MBeanServer getMBeanServer()
    {
        // Load our initialization information
        String url = null;
        String username = null;
        String password = null;
        try
        {
            String config = getServletContext().getResource(
                        "/WEB-INF/xml/stats.xml").toString();
            SAXBuilder builder = new SAXBuilder();
            Document doc = builder.build( config );
            Element root = doc.getRootElement();
            Element adminServer = root.getChild( "admin-server" );
            String port = adminServer.getAttributeValue( "port" );
            url = "t3://localhost:" + port;
            username = adminServer.getAttributeValue( "username" );
            password = adminServer.getAttributeValue( "password" );
        }
        catch( Exception e )
        {
            e.printStackTrace();
        }

        // Retrieve a reference to the MBeanServer
        MBeanHome localHome = ( MBeanHome )Helper.getAdminMBeanHome(
                                            username, password, url );
        return localHome.getMBeanServer();
    }

    /**
     * This is the main focus point of the application server-specific servlet
     * classes; through the getPerformanceRoot() method you will build an XML
     * document that you want to return to the caller
     */
```

```
public Element getPerformanceRoot(MBeanServer server, Map objectNames)
{
    Element root = new Element( "weblogic-tuning-stats" );

    // Build the document: construct derived metrics

    // Return the document
    return root;
}
}
```

The `WebLogicStatsServlet` is driven by the XML file located in the Web Archive's (WAR) `/WEB-INF/xml/stats.xml`, as shown in Listing 4-3.

Listing 4-3. *stats.xml*

```
<weblogic-stats>
  <admin-server port="7001" username="weblogic" password="weblogic" />
</weblogic-stats>
```

This XML file tells the `WebLogicStatsServlet` what port WebLogic is listing on and provides an administrator's username and password. The `WebLogicStatsServlet` returns an `MBeanServer` by using WebLogic's `Helper` class:

```
MBeanHome localHome = ( MBeanHome )Helper.getAdminMBeanHome(
                                        username, password, url );
return localHome.getMBeanServer();
```

The `getPerformanceRoot()` method is not currently configured to build derived metrics, but it provides a mechanism for you to build these metrics.

To compile these classes, you are going to need a few dependencies:

- *JDOM*: This XML parsing API is built on top of a Simple API for XML (SAX) engine. It constructs a very Java-centric representation of an XML document, built around Collections classes. You can download JDOM from `www.jdom.org`. You need to add the `jdom.jar` and `xerces.jar` files to your `CLASSPATH`.

- *JSR-77*: This API exposes a standardized representation of performance metrics. You can download it from Sun's Web site: `http://java.sun.com`. You need to add the `java77.jar` file to your `CLASSPATH`.

- *WebLogic classes*: To use the WebLogic interfaces to gain access to its `MBeanServer`, you need to include the `weblogic.jar` file in your `CLASSPATH`. This file is packaged with your WebLogic installation—for example, WebLogic 8.1 ships this file in the `{weblogic home directory}/server/lib` folder.

Finally, in order to package these classes into a WAR file, you need to add two deployment descriptors, `weblogic.xml` and `web.xml`, shown in Listing 4-4 and Listing 4-5, respectively.

Listing 4-4. *weblogic.xml*

```
<?xml version="1.0" encoding="UTF-8"?>
<!DOCTYPE weblogic-web-app PUBLIC
  "-//BEA Systems, Inc.//DTD Web Application 6.0//EN"
  "http://www.bea.com/servers/wls610/dtd/weblogic-web-jar.dtd">

<weblogic-web-app>
    <description>Statistics Web Application</description>
</weblogic-web-app>
```

Listing 4-5. *web.xml*

```
<?xml version="1.0" encoding="UTF-8"?>
<!DOCTYPE web-app PUBLIC '-//Sun Microsystems, Inc.//DTD Web Application 2.2//EN'
  'http://java.sun.com/j2ee/dtds/web-app_2_2.dtd'>
<web-app>
    <servlet>
        <servlet-name>StatsServlet</servlet-name>
        <servlet-class>com.javasrc.tuning.weblogic.web.WeblogicStatsServlet.➥
            </servlet-class>
    </servlet>

    <servlet-mapping>
        <servlet-name>StatsServlet</servlet-name>
        <url-pattern>/*</url-pattern>
    </servlet-mapping>

    <servlet-mapping>
        <servlet-name>StatsServlet</servlet-name>
        <url-pattern>/stats</url-pattern>
    </servlet-mapping>
</web-app>
```

When you build your WAR file, you need to include the following files in the following folders:

```
WEB-INF/classes/com/javasrc/tuning/web/AbstractStatsServlet.class
WEB-INF/classes/com/javasrc/tuning/weblogic/web/WeblogicStatsServlet.class
WEB-INF/lib/jdom.jar
WEB-INF/lib/xerces.jar
WEB-INF/web.xml
WEB-INF/weblogic.xml
WEB-INF/xml/stats.xml
```

Then follow the standard WebLogic mechanism to deploy this WAR file to your environment. In production mode, you need to use the administration console, and in development, you need to copy this file to your live application directory.

This servlet can be accessed through the following URL:

```
http://localhost:7001/stats/stats?debug=true&showAttributes=true& _
showAttributeValues=true
```

To give you a flavor for the type of output (my XML file running against WebLogic 8.1 is over 2MB, so I will save you from reading through 40 pages of uninteresting information), the following is an excerpt that displays the WebLogic Default execute queue for the examples server:

```
<weblogic-tuning-stats>
  <mbeans>
    <domain name="examples">
      <type name="ExecuteQueue">
        <mbean name="examples:Name=weblogic.kernel.Default,
                          Server=examplesServer,Type=ExecuteQueue">
          <attributes>
            <attribute name="MBeanInfo">weblogic.management.tools.Info@1ddcb
            </attribute>
            <attribute name="QueueLength">65536</attribute>
            <attribute name="ObjectName">
                          examples:Name=weblogic.kernel.Default,
                          Server=examplesServer,
                          Type=ExecuteQueue</attribute>
            <attribute name="Notes" />
            <attribute name="Name">weblogic.kernel.Default</attribute>
            <attribute name="Parent">examples:Name=examplesServer,
                                              Type=Server</attribute>
            <attribute name="ThreadPriority">5</attribute>
            <attribute name="PersistenceEnabled">true</attribute>
            <attribute name="ThreadCount">15</attribute>
            <attribute name="SetFields">[Name]</attribute>
            <attribute name="CachingDisabled">true</attribute>
            <attribute name="Registered">false</attribute>
            <attribute name="Type">ExecuteQueue</attribute>
            <attribute name="QueueLengthThresholdPercent">90</attribute>
            <attribute name="ThreadsIncrease">0</attribute>
            <attribute name="ThreadsMaximum">400</attribute>
            <attribute name="ThreadsMinimum">5</attribute>
            <attribute name="Comments" />
            <attribute name="DefaultedMBean">true</attribute>
          </attributes>
        </mbean>
      </type>
      <type name="ExecuteQueueConfig">
        <mbean name="examples:Location=examplesServer, _
                        Name=weblogic.kernel.Default, _
                        ServerConfig=examplesServer,Type=ExecuteQueueConfig">
```

```xml
    <attributes>
        <attribute name="MBeanInfo">weblogic.management.tools.Info@1ddcb
        </attribute>
        <attribute name="QueueLength">65536</attribute>
        <attribute name="ObjectName">examples:Location=examplesServer,
                    Name=weblogic.kernel.Default,
                    ServerConfig=examplesServer,
                    Type=ExecuteQueueConfig</attribute>
        <attribute name="Notes" />
        <attribute name="Name">weblogic.kernel.Default</attribute>
        <attribute name="Parent">examples:Location=examplesServer,
                    Name=examplesServer,
                    Type=ServerConfig</attribute>
        <attribute name="ThreadPriority">5</attribute>
        <attribute name="PersistenceEnabled">true</attribute>
        <attribute name="ThreadCount">15</attribute>
        <attribute name="SetFields">[Name]</attribute>
        <attribute name="CachingDisabled">true</attribute>
        <attribute name="Registered">false</attribute>
        <attribute name="Type">ExecuteQueueConfig</attribute>
        <attribute name="QueueLengthThresholdPercent">90</attribute>
        <attribute name="ThreadsIncrease">0</attribute>
        <attribute name="ThreadsMaximum">400</attribute>
        <attribute name="ThreadsMinimum">5</attribute>
        <attribute name="Comments" />
        <attribute name="DefaultedMBean">true</attribute>
    </attributes>
  </mbean>
</type>
<type name="ExecuteQueueRuntime">
  <mbean name="examples:Location=examplesServer,
                Name=weblogic.kernel.Default,
                ServerRuntime=examplesServer,
                Type=ExecuteQueueRuntime">
    <attributes>
        <attribute name="Name">weblogic.kernel.Default</attribute>
        <attribute name="Parent">examples:Location=examplesServer,
                    Name=examplesServer,
                    Type=ServerRuntime
        </attribute>
        <attribute name="PendingRequestCurrentCount">0</attribute>
        <attribute name="ServicedRequestTotalCount">56</attribute>
        <attribute name="MBeanInfo">weblogic.management.tools.Info@b846c6
        </attribute>
        <attribute name="CachingDisabled">true</attribute>
        <attribute name="Registered">false</attribute>
        <attribute name="ExecuteThreads">…</attribute>
```

```
                    <attribute name="ExecuteThreadCurrentIdleCount">14</attribute>
                    <attribute name="PendingRequestOldestTime">
                                1116563936093</attribute>
                    <attribute name="ObjectName">examples:Location=examplesServer,
                                Name=weblogic.kernel.Default,
                                ServerRuntime=examplesServer,
                                Type=ExecuteQueueRuntime</attribute>
                    <attribute name="Type">ExecuteQueueRuntime</attribute>
                    <attribute name="ExecuteThreadTotalCount">15</attribute>
                    <attribute name="StuckExecuteThreads" />
                </attributes>
            </mbean>
        </domain>
    </mbeans>
</weblogic-tuning-stats>
```

We look at how to analyze this data in Chapter 7, but for now, please note the following about these metrics:

- The thread pool length is 15 (Name=ExecuteQueueConfig, Attribute=ThreadCount).

- Fourteen threads are idle (Name=ExecuteQueueRuntime, Attribute=ExecuteThreadCurrentIdleCount).

- No requests are waiting in the queue for a thread (Name=ExecuteQueueRuntime, Attribute=PendingRequestCurrentCount).

- The thread pool cannot increase its size if it needs more threads (Name=ExecuteQueueConfig, Attribute=ThreadsIncrease = 0).

Therefore, if we were building a derived metric to represent this data, we would obtain the ExecuteQueueConfig and ExecuteQueueRuntime MBeans from the "examples" domain and build a friendly representation of the aforementioned metrics.

As I warned at the beginning of this chapter, this information I present here is very geeky, but it offers a relatively straightforward way of programmatically accessing performance information. The tough part—the interpretation of these metrics against business processes—is covered in Chapter 7.

Implementing Code Instrumentation

Code instrumentation comes in two flavors:

- Bytecode instrumentation

- Custom instrumentation

Bytecode instrumentation involves building a custom class loader, prepending it to the list of class loaders, and then inserting bytecode that tracks method response times, exceptions, and method time-outs into classes as they are loaded. It requires a command of bytecode operations, which is analogous in the C++ world to writing assembly code rather than C++ code. Bytecode instrumentation does not require you to make any modifications to your code and results in highly optimized instrumentation. As illustrated in Figure 4-2, when a Java process creates a class, it loads it through a class loader. That class loader loads the class, passes it to an instrumentor that instruments all of its methods by adding bytecode operations, and then returns it to the calling process.

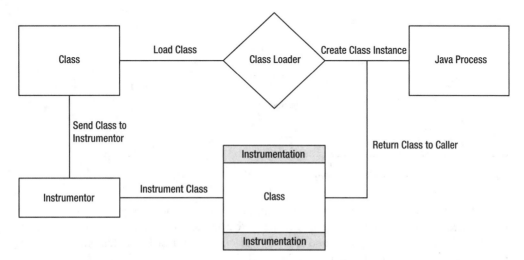

Figure 4-2. *Bytecode instrumentation process*

Custom instrumentation, on the other hand, requires you to hand-code the instrumentation code into your Java classes. It is not as efficient as bytecode instrumentation, and it's burdensome for the programmer, but conceptually it is much easier to understand and implement. Commercial offerings provide bytecode instrumentation, but it takes many months of dedicated programming effort to realize an effective implementation.

In this section, we will build a custom instrumentation engine and a simple Web interface that you can use to control the instrumentation engine. The core requirement for classes that you want to instrument is that all instrumented methods must register themselves with the instrumentor, as illustrated in Figure 4-3, and inform it when methods start and stop.

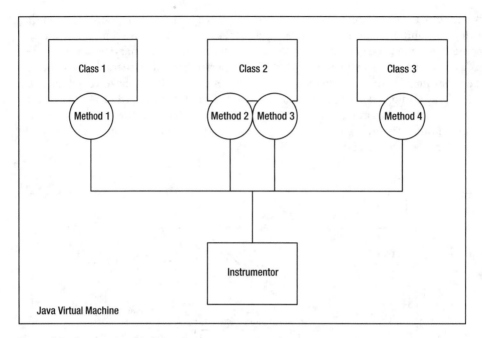

Figure 4-3. *Custom instrumentation process*

Internally, the instrumentor generates a unique identifier when a request starts. That unique identifier is then passed to each instrumented method. In this way, the instrumentor can track the order of method calls and later reconstruct the request, by implementing method tracking using a programmatic stack as illustrated in Figure 4-4.

Figure 4-4 shows the state of the internal stack as method calls are made. Because method 1 is the parent of the tree, it stays on the stack the entire time. Method 2 is pushed on the stack and then popped off when it completes. Method 3 is then pushed on the stack, and because it calls method 4, method 4 is pushed on top of method 3. When method 4 completes, then the call tree unwinds and all methods are popped off in the reverse order that they were pushed on.

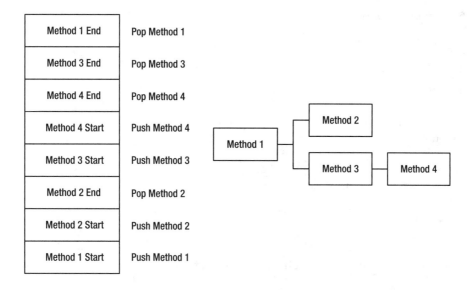

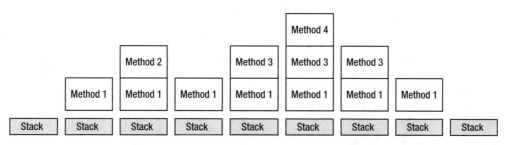

Figure 4-4. *In this scenario, method 1 calls method 2 and method 3, and method 3 makes a call to method 4. Internally, the instrumentor pushes each method onto its stack when it starts and then pops off the method when it ends.*

Instrumentation Engine

The instrumentation engine is implemented through three classes:

- `Instrumentor`
- `RequestInfo`
- `MethodInfo`

The code for the `Instrumentor` class is shown in Listing 4-6.

Listing 4-6. *Instrumentor.java*

```java
package com.javasrc.instrument;

// Import Java classes
import java.util.*;

// Import JDOM classes
import org.jdom.*;

/**
 * Singleton class that records transactions
 */
public class Instrumentor
{
    /**
     * Maps request IDs to a stack (LinkedList) of method calls
     */
    private static Map requestStacks = new HashMap( 100 );

    /**
     * Maps request IDs to request names
     */
    private static Map requestToIdMap = new HashMap( 100 );

    /**
     * Maps request names to RequestInfos
     */
    private static Map requests = new TreeMap();

    private static long startTime;
    private static long endTime;
    private static boolean instrumenting = false;

    public static void start()
    {
        startTime = System.currentTimeMillis();
        requestStacks.clear();
        requestToIdMap.clear();
        requests.clear();
        instrumenting = true;
    }

    public static void stop()
    {
        endTime = System.currentTimeMillis();
        instrumenting = false;
    }
```

```java
public static boolean isInstrumenting()
{
    return instrumenting;
}



/**
 * Returns an ID for the specified request name
 */
public static String getId( String req )
{
    return req + "-" + System.currentTimeMillis();
}

/**
 * Marks the start of a request
 */
public static void startRequest( String id, String requestName )
{
    // Only work if we are instrumenting
    if( !instrumenting )
    {
        return;
    }
    System.out.println( "Starting request: " + id + ", " + requestName );
    if( !requests.containsKey( requestName ) )
    {
        RequestInfo request = new RequestInfo( requestName );
        requests.put( requestName, request );
    }
    requestToIdMap.put( id, requestName );
}

/**
 * Marks the end of a request
 */
public static void endRequest( String id )
{
    // Only work if we are instrumenting
    if( !instrumenting )
    {
        return;
    }
    System.out.println( "Ending request: " + id );
    // Get the root element for this request
    LinkedList requestStack = ( LinkedList )requestStacks.get( id );
    MethodInfo root = ( MethodInfo )requestStack.removeLast();
```

```java
    System.out.println( "ROOT:" + root );

    // See if we already have the request
    String requestName = ( String )requestToIdMap.get( id );
    System.out.println( "\tRequest Name: " + requestName );
    RequestInfo request = null;
    if( requests.containsKey( requestName ) )
    {
        // Found the request
        System.out.println( "Found the request..." );
        request = ( RequestInfo )requests.get( requestName );
        request.addRequest( root );
    }
    else
    {
        System.out.println( "Could not find request: " + requestName );
    }
}

/**
 * Marks the start of a method
 */
public static void startMethod( String id, String qualifiedName )
{
    // Only work if we are instrumenting
    if( !instrumenting )
    {
        return;
    }

    System.out.println( "Starting method: " + id + ", " + qualifiedName );
    // Get the Stack for this ID
    LinkedList stack = null;
    if( requestStacks.containsKey( id ) )
    {
        stack = ( LinkedList )requestStacks.get( id );
    }
    else
    {
        stack = new LinkedList();
        requestStacks.put( id, stack );
    }

    // Build the method info and add it to our stack
    MethodInfo method = new MethodInfo( qualifiedName );
    method.start();
    stack.add( method );
}
```

```java
/**
 * Marks the end of a method
 */
public static void endMethod( String id )
{
    // Only work if we are instrumenting
    if( !instrumenting )
    {
        return;
    }

    System.out.println( "Ending method: " + id );
    // Get the stack for this method
    LinkedList stack = ( LinkedList )requestStacks.get( id );

    // Get the last method executed
    MethodInfo method = ( MethodInfo )stack.removeLast();

    // Tell the method that it has completed
    method.end();

    // Add this method's info to its parent method
    if( stack.size() == 0 )
    {
        // Top of the stack; push it back on for endRequest to handle
        stack.addLast( method );
    }
    else
    {
        MethodInfo parent = ( MethodInfo )stack.getLast();
        parent.addSubMethod( method );
    }
}

public static Element toXML()
{
    Element report = new Element( "instrumentation-report" );
    report.setAttribute( "request-count", Integer.toString( requests.size() ) );
    if( requests.size() == 0 )
    {
        return report;
    }

    report.setAttribute( "start-time", Long.toString( startTime ) );
    report.setAttribute( "end-time", Long.toString( endTime ) );
    report.setAttribute( "session-length",
            Long.toString( endTime - startTime ) );
```

```
        Element requestsElement = new Element( "requests" );
        for( Iterator i = requests.keySet().iterator(); i.hasNext(); )
        {
            String requestName = ( String )i.next();
            RequestInfo requestInfo = ( RequestInfo )requests.get( requestName );
            requestsElement.addContent( requestInfo.toXML() );
        }
        report.addContent( requestsElement );
        return report;
    }
}
```

The `Instrumentor` class operates by exposing the following commands:

- `start()`: This method tells the instrumentor to start recording call traces.

- `stop()`: This method tells the instrumentor to stop recording call traces.

- `getId()`: This method returns a unique identifier for a request. In this case, it takes the request name and appends the current time in milliseconds to the end of it.

- `startRequest()`: This method starts tracing a request.

- `endRequest()`: This method stops tracing a request.

- `startMethod()`: This method starts a method inside a request.

- `endMethod()`: This method ends a method inside a request.

Requests are maintained in a `RequestInfo` object, which serves to maintain a collection of `MethodInfo` objects and provide request-level aggregate data. A `MethodInfo` object represents a method and maintains a record of all of the submethods that it calls. It calculates the method timings and relevant metrics, such as call counts, minimum time, maximum time, cumulative time, and exclusive time. This relationship is illustrated in Figure 4-5.

When a request starts, `startRequest()` creates a `RequestInfo` for the request and stores it in the request map. As methods are invoked, `startMethod()` creates `MethodInfo` instances and pushes them onto the method stack, and `endMethod()` pops them off, rolling their performance metrics into the next node on the stack (the parent method). When the request completes, `endRequest()` pops the root method off the method stack and adds it to the `RequestInfo` in the request map.

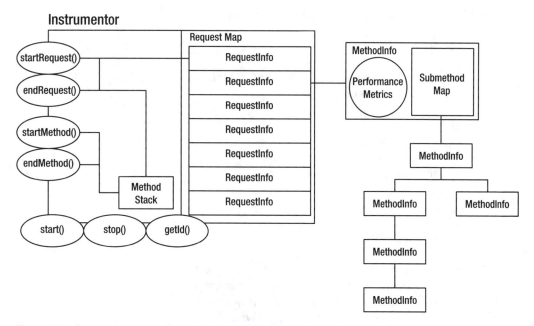

Figure 4-5. *The Instrumentor class exposes an interface to manage requests and track the methods it calls.*

The source code for the RequestInfo and MethodInfo classes is shown in Listing 4-7 and Listing 4-8, respectively.

Listing 4-7. *RequestInfo.java*

```java
package com.javasrc.instrument;

import java.util.*;

// Import JDOM classes
import org.jdom.*;

public class RequestInfo
{
    private String request;
    private MethodInfo root;

    public RequestInfo( String request )
    {
        this.request = request;
    }
```

```java
    public void addRequest( MethodInfo newRequest )
    {
        if( this.root == null )
        {
            // This is the first instance of this request; save it
            this.root = newRequest;
        }
        else
        {
            // Add this call to the request
            this.root.addCall( newRequest );
        }
    }

    public Element toXML()
    {
        Element requestElement = new Element( "request" );
        requestElement.setAttribute( "name", request );
        requestElement.setAttribute( "ave-time",
                    Long.toString( root.getAverage() ) );
        requestElement.setAttribute( "min-time", Long.toString( root.getMin() ) );
        requestElement.setAttribute( "max-time", Long.toString( root.getMax() ) );
        requestElement.setAttribute( "call-count",
                    Integer.toString( root.getCallCount() ) );
        requestElement.addContent( root.toXML() );
        return requestElement;
    }
}
```

Listing 4-8. *MethodInfo.java*

```java
package com.javasrc.instrument;

import org.jdom.*;
import java.util.*;

/**
 * Stores information about a method and its submethods
 */
public class MethodInfo
{
    /**
     * This method's class name
     */
    private String className;
```

```java
/**
 * This method's name
 */
private String methodName;

/**
 * The total time spent in this method
 */
private long totalTime;

/**
 * The number of times this method was called
 */
private int callCount;

/**
 * The minimum amount of time that this method was executed
 */
private long minTime = -1;

/**
 * The maximum amount of time that the method was executed
 */
private long maxTime = -1;

/**
 * Contains a list of all submethods that this method calls
 */
private Map submethods = new TreeMap();

/**
 * The start time of this method, used to compute method response time
 */
private transient long startTime;

/**
 * Creates a new MethodInfo
 *
 * @param qualifiedName    The fully qualified name of the method
 */
public MethodInfo( String qualifiedName )
{
    int lastPeriod = qualifiedName.lastIndexOf( '.' );
    this.className = qualifiedName.substring( 0, lastPeriod );
    this.methodName = qualifiedName.substring( lastPeriod + 1 );
}
```

```java
/**
 * The start of the method
 */
public void start()
{
    this.startTime = System.currentTimeMillis();
}

/**
 * The end of the method
 */
public void end()
{
    long endTime = System.currentTimeMillis();
    long methodTime = endTime - this.startTime;
    System.out.println( "Start time: " + startTime + ", end time: " +
                            endTime + ", method time: " + methodTime );
    this.totalTime += methodTime;
    this.callCount++;

    if( this.minTime == -1 || methodTime < this.minTime )
    {
        this.minTime = methodTime;
    }

    if( this.maxTime == -1 || methodTime > this.maxTime )
    {
        this.maxTime = methodTime;
    }
}

/**
 * Returns the fully qualified method name
 */
public String getMethodName()
{
    return this.className + "." + this.methodName;
}

/**
 * Returns the call count of this method
 */
public int getCallCount()
{
    return this.callCount;
}
```

```java
/**
 * Returns the average time that this method took to execute (in ms)
 */
public long getAverage()
{
    return ( long )( ( double )this.totalTime / ( double )this.callCount );
}

/**
 * Returns the minimum amount of time that this method took to execute (in ms)
 */
public long getMin()
{
    return ( long )this.minTime;
}

/**
 * Returns the maximum amount of time that this method took to execute (in ms)
 */
public long getMax()
{
    return ( long )this.maxTime;
}

/**
 * Returns the total time spent in this method
 */
public long getTotalTime()
{
    return this.totalTime;
}

/**
 * Returns all submethods
 */
public Collection getSubMethods()
{
    return this.submethods.values();
}

/**
 * Adds a submethod to this method
 */
public void addSubMethod( MethodInfo method )
{
    this.submethods.put( method.getMethodName(), method );
    //this.submethods.add( method );
}
```

```java
/**
 * This method was called again, so add its information
 */
public void addCall( MethodInfo newMethodCall )
{
    // Add this method's info
    this.totalTime += newMethodCall.getTotalTime();
    this.callCount++;

    // Add the new method's submethods
    Collection newMethodCalls = newMethodCall.getSubMethods();
    for( Iterator i=newMethodCalls.iterator(); i.hasNext(); )
    {
        MethodInfo newMethod = ( MethodInfo )i.next();

        // Find this submethod
        if( this.submethods.containsKey( newMethod.getMethodName() ) )
        {
            // Add a new call to an existing method
            MethodInfo methodInfo = ( MethodInfo )this.submethods.get(
                                            newMethod.getMethodName() );
            methodInfo.addCall( newMethod );
        }
        else
        {
            // Add this method to our call tree
            this.addSubMethod( newMethod );
        }
    }
}

/**
 * Returns this method info as an XML node
 */
public Element toXML()
{
    // Build a method node
    long aveTime = this.getAverage();
    Element methodElement = new Element( "method" );
    methodElement.setAttribute( "name", this.methodName );
    methodElement.setAttribute( "class", this.className );
    methodElement.setAttribute( "ave-cumulative-time",
                            Long.toString( aveTime ) );
    methodElement.setAttribute( "min-time", Long.toString( this.minTime ) );
    methodElement.setAttribute( "max-time", Long.toString( this.maxTime ) );
```

```
        methodElement.setAttribute( "total-time",
                            Long.toString( this.totalTime ) );
        methodElement.setAttribute( "call-count",
                            Integer.toString( this.callCount ) );

        // Add the submethods
        long submethodTotalTime = 0;
        for( Iterator i=this.submethods.keySet().iterator(); i.hasNext(); )
        {
            String methodName = ( String )i.next();
            MethodInfo submethod = ( MethodInfo )this.submethods.get( methodName );
            methodElement.addContent( submethod.toXML() );
            submethodTotalTime += submethod.getTotalTime();
        }
        long totalExclusiveTime = this.totalTime - submethodTotalTime;
        long aveExclusiveTime = totalExclusiveTime / this.callCount;

        methodElement.setAttribute( "exclusive-ave-time",
                    Long.toString( aveExclusiveTime ) );

        // Return the fully constructed method node
        return methodElement;
    }
}
```

Test Application

In order to use the custom instrumentation, you need to invoke the aforementioned Instrumentor's methods in the following order:

1. Obtain a unique identifier for your request by calling getId(). This involves obtaining the name of the request, which can be accomplished in a servlet by calling the HttpServletRequest's getRequestURL() method.

2. Start the request by calling startRequest().

3. Start the method by calling startMethod().

4. Call submethods, passing the unique key, and iterate over steps 3 to 5 for each submethod.

5. End the method by calling endMethod().

6. End the request by calling endRequest().

Listings 4-9, 4-10, 4-11, and 4-12 show a test application that demonstrates how to use the instrumentor. I apologize for the number of classes, but in order to see anything of consequence we need more than a single class—four classes illustrates the mechanics of the instrumentor architecture.

Listing 4-9. *TestServlet.java*

```java
package com.javasrc.instrument.test;

// Import servlet classes
import javax.servlet.*;
import javax.servlet.http.*;

// Import Java classes
import java.io.*;

// Import instrument class
import com.javasrc.instrument.Instrumentor;

public class TestServlet extends HttpServlet
{
    private boolean bool = false;
    public void service( HttpServletRequest req, HttpServletResponse res )
    {
        // Start the request
        String requestName = req.getRequestURL().toString();
        String iid = Instrumentor.getId( requestName );
        Instrumentor.startRequest( iid, requestName );
        Instrumentor.startMethod( iid,
            "com.javasrc.instrument.test.TestServlet.service( _
            HttpServletRequest, HttpServletResponse )" );

        // Business logic
        try
        {
            Thread.sleep( 100 );
            if( bool )
            {
                doNothing( iid );
            }
            else
            {
                doLessThanNothing( iid );
            }
            Controller c = new Controller();
            c.handle( iid, "something" );

            bool = !bool;
            PrintWriter out = res.getWriter();
            out.println( "<html><head><title>Test Servlet</head>
                            <body>test, test, test...</body></html>" );

            out.flush();
        }
```

```java
            catch( Exception e )
            {
                e.printStackTrace();
            }

            // End the request
            Instrumentor.endMethod( iid );
            Instrumentor.endRequest( iid );
    }

    private void doNothing( String iid )
    {
        Instrumentor.startMethod( iid,
                "com.javasrc.instrument.test.TestServlet.doNothing()" );

        // Business logic
        try
        {
            Thread.sleep( 1000 );
        }
        catch( Exception e )
        {
            e.printStackTrace();
        }

        Instrumentor.endMethod( iid );
    }

    private void doLessThanNothing( String iid )
    {
        Instrumentor.startMethod( iid,
            "com.javasrc.instrument.test. _
            TestServlet.doLessThanNothing()" );

        // Business logic
        try
        {
            Thread.sleep( 1000 );
        }
        catch( Exception e )
        {
            e.printStackTrace();
        }

        Instrumentor.endMethod( iid );
    }
}
```

Listing 4-10. *Controller.java*

```java
package com.javasrc.instrument.test;

import com.javasrc.instrument.Instrumentor;
import com.javasrc.instrument.test.handlers.*;
import com.javasrc.instrument.test.authentication.*;

public class Controller
{
    private BusinessProcess bp = new BusinessProcess();
    private Authentication auth = new Authentication();

    public void handle( String iid, String command )
    {
        Instrumentor.startMethod( iid,
            "com.javasrc.instrument.test.Controller.handle( String )" );
        try
        {
            // Business logic
            try
            {
                Thread.sleep( 100 );
            }
            catch( Exception e )
            {
            }

            if( auth.isValidUser( iid, "me" ) )
            {
                bp.execute(iid);
            }
        }
        finally
        {
            Instrumentor.endMethod( iid );
        }
    }
}
```

Listing 4-11. *Authentication.java*

```java
package com.javasrc.instrument.test.authentication;

import com.javasrc.instrument.Instrumentor;

public class Authentication
{
```

```java
    public boolean isValidUser( String iid, String username )
    {
        Instrumentor.startMethod( iid, "com.javasrc.instrument.test.
                            authentication.Authentication.isValidUser()" );
        try
        {
            // Business logic
            try
            {
                Thread.sleep( 200 );
            }
            catch( Exception e )
            {
            }
            return true;
        }
        finally
        {
            Instrumentor.endMethod( iid );
        }
    }
}
```

Listing 4-12. *BusinessProcess.java*

```java
package com.javasrc.instrument.test.handlers;

import com.javasrc.instrument.Instrumentor;

public class BusinessProcess
{
    public void execute( String iid )
    {
        Instrumentor.startMethod( iid, "com.javasrc.instrument.test.➥
                                    handlers.BusinessProcess.execute()" );

        // Business logic
        try
        {
            Thread.sleep( 300 );
        }
        catch( Exception e )
        {
        }

        Instrumentor.endMethod( iid );
    }
}
```

Figure 4-6 illustrates the architecture of this simple Web application.

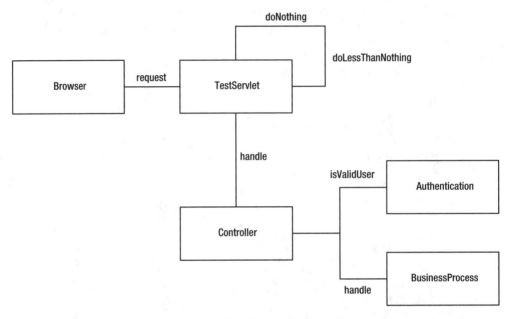

Figure 4-6. *The browser sends a request to the TestServlet that calls internal methods and forwards them to the Controller for processing.*

This test application is simple, but it demonstrates how the instrumentation engine works. Observe the sequence of events in the TestServlet: it generates a unique identifier, starts the request, and starts the service() method. And note how each instrumented method must provide an additional attribute to support the unique identifier and invoke startMethod() and endMethod() at the beginning and end of the method, respectively. It is intrusive to the development process, but it is capable of tracing requests within a single JVM. As soon as you leave a single JVM, you need to define a central repository for the instrumentor and re-create the request across the network, which presents an additional level of complexity to the instrumentation task.

Instrumentation Command Interface

The final task we need to perform to complete this example is build a command interface to start and stop instrumentation and generate a report. In this implementation, we build an instrumentation servlet and a JSP to present the command interface. The code for the InstrumentorServlet is shown in Listing 4-13.

Listing 4-13. *InstrumentorServlet.java*

```java
package com.javasrc.instrument.web;

// Import servlet classes
import javax.servlet.*;
import javax.servlet.http.*;

// Import Java classes
import java.util.*;
import java.io.*;

// Import JDOM classes
import org.jdom.*;
import org.jdom.output.*;

// Import instrument class
import com.javasrc.instrument.Instrumentor;

public class InstrumentorServlet extends HttpServlet
{
    public void service( HttpServletRequest req, HttpServletResponse res )
            throws ServletException
    {
        try
        {
            // The command controls the action of this servlet
            String command = req.getParameter( "cmd" );
            if( command == null ) command = "none";

            // The format controls the return format: HTML or XML
            String format = req.getParameter( "format" );
            if( format == null ) format = "html";
            boolean xml = format.equalsIgnoreCase( "xml" );

            String status = "Please make a selection";

            if( command.equalsIgnoreCase( "report" ) )
            {
                if( Instrumentor.isInstrumenting() )
                {
                    status = "Instrumentation is running, cannot generate a report➡
                                until you stop instrumentation";
                }
```

```
        else
        {
            // Convert the output of the report to an XML string
            XMLOutputter outputter = new XMLOutputter( "\t", true );
            status = outputter.outputString( Instrumentor.toXML() );

            if( !xml )
            {
                status = xmlToHtml( status );
            }
        }
    }
    else if( command.equalsIgnoreCase( "start" ) )
    {
        Instrumentor.start();
        status = "Instrumentor started";
        if( xml )
        {
            status = "<status>" + status + "</status>";
        }
    }
    else if( command.equalsIgnoreCase( "stop" ) )
    {
        Instrumentor.stop();
        status = "Instrumentor stopped";
        if( xml )
        {
            status = "<status>" + status + "</status>";
        }
    }

    // Update the instrumentation status
    String instrumentationStatus = "Not Running";
    if( Instrumentor.isInstrumenting() )
    {
        instrumentationStatus = "Running";
    }

    if( xml )
    {
        PrintWriter out = res.getWriter();
        out.println( status );
        out.flush();
    }
```

```
        else
        {
            req.setAttribute( "instrumentation-status", instrumentationStatus );
            req.setAttribute( "status", status );
            RequestDispatcher rd = req.getRequestDispatcher( "instrument.jsp" );
            rd.forward( req, res );
        }

    }
    catch( Exception e )
    {
        e.printStackTrace();
        throw new ServletException( e );
    }
}

private String xmlToHtml( String xml )
{
    StringBuffer sb = new StringBuffer( xml );
    int index = sb.indexOf( "<" );
    while( index != -1 )
    {
        sb.replace( index, index+1, "&lt;" );
        index = sb.indexOf( "<", index + 3 );
    }
    index = sb.indexOf( ">" );
    while( index != -1 )
    {
        sb.replace( index, index+1, "&gt;" );
        index = sb.indexOf( ">", index + 3 );
    }
    return sb.toString();
}
}
```

The code for the instrument.jsp file is shown in Listing 4-14.

Listing 4-14. *instrument.jsp*

```
<%@page import="java.io.*" %>
<html>
<head>
<title>Instrumentation Management Interface</title>
</head>
<body>

<h2>Instrumentation Management Interface</h2>
```

```
<table width="90%" align="center">
<tr><td><i>This interface allows you to control the embedded instrumentation engine
          </i></td></tr>
<tr><td>Options:

<table width="90%" align="center">
<tr><td><a href="instrument?cmd=start">Start Instrumentation</a></td></tr>
<tr><td><a href="instrument?cmd=stop">Stop Instrumentation</a></td></tr>
<tr><td><a href="instrument?cmd=report">Get Report</a></td></tr>
</table>

</td></tr>

</table>

<br>
<%String instrumentationStatus =
    ( String )request.getAttribute( "instrumentation-status" );%>
<h3>Instrumentation: <%=instrumentationStatus%>
<br>

<h3>Status</h3>
<pre>
<%String status = ( String )request.getAttribute( "status" );%>
<%=status%>
</pre>

</body>
```

The InstrumentorServlet presents three commands:

- start: Start instrumentation.

- stop: Stop instrumentation.

- report: Generate a report in XML that shows all requests, response times, and call traces.

The start command calls the Instrumentor's start() method, the stop command calls the Instrumentor's stop() method, and the report command calls the Instrumentor's toXML() method. The Instrumentor's toXML() method extracts all RequestInfo instances from its request map and asks them to generate an XML report containing all method traces.

To enable these servlets, you need to build a Web deployment descriptor, as shown in Listing 4-15.

Listing 4-15. *web.xml*

```xml
<?xml version="1.0" encoding="UTF-8"?>
<!DOCTYPE web-app PUBLIC '-//Sun Microsystems, Inc.//DTD Web Application 2.2//EN'
    'http://java.sun.com/j2ee/dtds/web-app_2_2.dtd'>

<web-app>
    <servlet>
      <servlet-name>InstrumentorServlet</servlet-name>
      <servlet-class>com.javasrc.instrument.web.InstrumentorServlet</servlet-class>
    </servlet>

    <servlet>
        <servlet-name>TestServlet</servlet-name>
        <servlet-class>com.javasrc.instrument.test.TestServlet</servlet-class>
    </servlet>

    <servlet-mapping>
        <servlet-name>InstrumentorServlet</servlet-name>
        <url-pattern>/instrument/*</url-pattern>
    </servlet-mapping>

    <servlet-mapping>
        <servlet-name>TestServlet</servlet-name>
        <url-pattern>/test/*</url-pattern>
    </servlet-mapping>

</web-app>
```

And finally, to deploy the instrumentor application to your application server, you need to construct a WAR file with the following files:

```
instrument.jsp
WEB-INF/classes/com/javasrc/instrument/Instrumentor.class
WEB-INF/classes/com/javasrc/instrument/MethodInfo.class
WEB-INF/classes/com/javasrc/instrument/RequestInfo.class
WEB-INF/classes/com/javasrc/instrument/test/Controller.class
WEB-INF/classes/com/javasrc/instrument/test/authentication/Authentication.class
WEB-INF/classes/com/javasrc/instrument/test/handlers/
WEB-INF/classes/com/javasrc/instrument/test/handlers/BusinessProcess.class
WEB-INF/classes/com/javasrc/instrument/test/TestServlet.class
WEB-INF/classes/com/javasrc/instrument/web/InstrumentorServlet.class
WEB-INF/lib/jdom.jar
WEB-INF/lib/xerces.jar
WEB-INF/web.xml
```

Recall from the previous example that the XML library employed to build XML documents is JDOM, which is available at www.jdom.org. The jdom.jar and xerces.jar files need to be packaged in the WAR file in the WEB-INF/lib folder.

You can access the instrumentation command interface through the following URL:

```
http://localhost:8080/instrument/instrument
```

■**Note** The URL http://localhost:8080/instrument/instrument is valid for Apache Tomcat and JBoss. If you are using another application server or if you changed the listening ports, then you will need to adjust that accordingly. WebLogic listens by default on port 7001, and WebSphere listens by default on port 9080.

Start the instrumentation by clicking the "Start Instrumentation" link. Then you can exercise the test application through the following URL:

```
http://localhost:8080/instrument/test
```

When you are finished, click the "Stop Instrumentation" link and then select Get Report. In my example, doing so yielded the following output:

```
<instrumentation-report request-count="1" start-time="1141940605562"
                          end-time="1141940633640" session-length="28078">
  <requests>
    <request name="http://localhost:8080/instrument/test" ave-time="1841"
          min-time="1765" max-time="1841" call-count="12">
      <method name="service( HttpServletRequest, HttpServletResponse )"
          class="com.javasrc.instrument.test.TestServlet"
          ave-cumulative-time="1841" min-time="1765" max-time="1765"
          total-time="22092" call-count="12" exclusive-ave-time="110">
        <method name="handle( String )"
            class="com.javasrc.instrument.test.Controller"
            ave-cumulative-time="692" min-time="609" max-time="609"
            total-time="8313" call-count="12" exclusive-ave-time="131">
          <method name="isValidUser()"
              class="com.javasrc.instrument.test.authentication.Authentication"
              ave-cumulative-time="225" min-time="204" max-time="204"
              total-time="2704" call-count="12" exclusive-ave-time="225" />
          <method name="execute()"
              class="com.javasrc.instrument.test.handlers.BusinessProcess"
              ave-cumulative-time="335" min-time="296" max-time="296"
              total-time="4030" call-count="12" exclusive-ave-time="335" />
        </method>
        <method name="doLessThanNothing()"
            class="com.javasrc.instrument.test.TestServlet"
            ave-cumulative-time="1000" min-time="1000" max-time="1000"
            total-time="1000" call-count="1" exclusive-ave-time="1000" />
```

```
      <method name="doNothing()" class="com.javasrc.instrument.test.TestServlet"
            ave-cumulative-time="1041" min-time="1047" max-time="1047"
            total-time="11453" call-count="11" exclusive-ave-time="1041" />
    </method>
    </request>
  </requests>
</instrumentation-report>
```

In this example, I invoked the test request 12 times in rapid succession, which was fast enough to skew the balance between the doNothing() and doLessThanNothing() calls. The XML output presents a hierarchical representation of the call traces, with each node aggregating its subnodes. The next step would be to take this XML file to a visualization tool and present it in some logical fashion.

Summary

This chapter presented an overview of the technologies required to implement performance measurements in two core areas:

- Application server metrics

- Code instrumentation

Application server metrics provide insight into the performance of the application's container, including its thread pools and connection pools. Most modern application servers present this information through JMX, so it is a simple matter of obtaining this information and locating the metrics you are interested in.

Code instrumentation provides insight into the performance of your application. Through code instrumentation, you can identify slow-running methods as well as the path that a request followed to arrive at slow-running methods. It identifies tuning opportunities.

This chapter is by far the "geekiest" chapter in the book, but I hope it gave you an appreciation for the amount of work that goes into the tools that you purchase to monitor the health of your enterprise Java environment. In closing, realize that this chapter presented only two layers of Java's layered execution model. For a complete picture, you also need information about the JVM, the operating system, the hardware, the network that facilitates communications between servers, and all external dependencies such as databases, legacy systems, and the technology stacks underlying any services that you access.

In the next chapter, we'll turn our attention to the proactive steps that you can employ at every stage of your application development life cycle to manage performance. Specifically, we'll look at performance-related activities that you should perform while architecting your application, the additional performance testing that you should perform in development, the performance criteria that QA should gauge your application by and, finally, the steps that you should perform in production staging before deploying your application to a production environment.

PART 2

Application Life Cycle Performance Management

■ ■ ■

CHAPTER 5

Performance Through the Application Development Life Cycle

"**O**kay, I understand how to gather metrics, but now what do I do with them?" John asked, looking confounded. "If I have application response time, instrumentation, and application server metrics, what should I have my developers do to ensure that the next deployment will be successful?"

"That is a very good question. At its core, it involves a change of mind-set by your entire development organization, geared toward performance. You'll most likely feel resistance from your developers, but if they follow these steps and embrace performance testing from the outset, then you'll better your chances of success more than a hundredfold," I said.

"I can deal with upset developers," John responded. "The important thing is that the application meets performance criteria when it goes live. I'll make sure that they follow the proper testing procedures; they have to understand the importance of application performance. I just can't face the idea of calling the CEO and telling him that we failed again!"

"Don't worry, I've helped several customers implement this methodology into their development life cycle, and each one has been successful. It is a discipline that, once adopted, becomes second nature. The key is to get started now!"

"Tell me more," John stated calmly, in contrast with his stressed demeanor. I knew that John had seen the light and was destined for success in the future.

Performance Overview

All too often in application development, performance is an afterthought. I once worked for a company that fully embraced the Rational Unified Process (RUP) but took it to an extreme. The application the company built spent years in architecture, and the first of ten iterations took nearly nine months to complete. The company learned much through its efforts and became increasingly efficient in subsequent iterations, but one thing that the organization did not learn until very late in the game was the importance of application performance. In the last couple of iterations, it started implementing performance testing and learned that part of the core architecture was flawed—specifically, the data model needed to be rearchitected. Because object models are built on top of data models, the object model also had to change. In addition, all components that interact with the object model had to change, and so on. Finally, the application had to go through another lengthy QA cycle that uncovered new bugs as well as the reemergence of former bugs.

That company learned the hard way that the later in the development life cycle performance issues are identified, the more expensive they are to fix. Figure 5-1, which you may recall from Chapter 1, illustrates this idea graphically. You can see that a performance issue identified during the application's development is inexpensive to fix, but one found later can cause the cost to balloon. Thus, you must ensure the performance of your application from the early stages of its architecture and test it at each milestone to preserve your efforts.

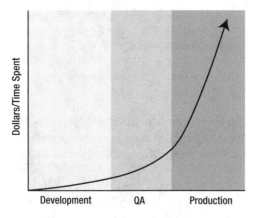

Figure 5-1. *The relationship between the time taken to identify performance issues and the repair costs*

A common theme has emerged from those customer sites I visit in which few or no performance issues are identified: these customers kept in mind the performance of the application when designing the application architecture. At these engagements, the root causes of most of the application problems were related to load or application server configuration—the applications had very few problems.

This chapter formalizes the methodology you should implement to ensure the performance of your application at each stage of the application development, QA, and deployment stages. I have helped customers implement this methodology into their organizations and roll out their applications to production successfully.

Performance in Architecture

The first step in developing any application of consequence is to perform an architectural analysis of a business problem domain. To review, application business owners work with application technical owners to define the requirements of the system. Application business owners are responsible for ensuring that when the application is complete it meets the needs of the end users, while application technical owners are responsible for determining the feasibility of options and defining the best architecture to solve the business needs. Together, these two groups design the functionality of the application.

In most organizations, the architecture discussions end at this analysis stage; the next step is usually the design of the actual solution. And this stage is where the architectural process needs to be revolutionized. Specifically, these groups need to define intelligent SLAs for each use case, they need to define the life cycles of major objects, and they need to address requirements for sessions.

SLAs

As you may recall from earlier in this book, an intelligent SLA maintains three core traits. It is

- Reasonable

- Specific

- Flexible

An SLA must satisfy end-user expectations but still be reasonable enough to be implemented. An unreasonable SLA will be ignored by all parties until end users complain. This is why SLAs need to be defined by both the application business owner and the application technical owner: the business owner pushes for the best SLAs for his users, while the application technical owner impresses upon the business owner the reality of what the business requirement presents. If the business requirement cannot be satisfied in a way acceptable to the application business owner, then the application technical owner needs to present all options and the cost of each (in terms of effort). The business requirement may need to be changed or divided into subprocesses that can be satisfied reasonably.

An intelligent SLA needs to be specific and measurable. In this requirement, you are looking for a hard and fast number, not a statement such as "The search functionality will respond within a reasonable user tolerance threshold." How do you test "reasonable"? You need to remove all subjectivity from this exercise. After all, what is the point in defining an SLA if you cannot verify it?

Finally, an intelligent SLA needs to be flexible. It needs to account for variations in behavior as a result of unforeseen factors, but define a hard threshold for how flexible it is allowed to be. For example, an SLA may read "The search functionality will respond within three seconds (specific) for 95 percent of requests (flexible)." The occasional seven-second response time is acceptable, as long as the integrity of the application is preserved—it responds well most of the time. By defining concrete values for the specific value as well as the limitations of the flexible value, you can quantify what "most of the time" means to the performance of the application, and you have a definite value with which to evaluate and verify the SLA.

Note Although you define specific performance criteria and a measure of flexibility, defining either a hard upper limit of tolerance or a relative upper limit is also a good idea. I prefer to specify a relative upper limit, measured in the number of standard deviations from the mean. The purpose of defining an SLA in this way is that on paper a 3-second response time for 95 percent of requests is tolerable, but how do you address drastically divergent response time, such as a 30-second response time? Statistically, this should not be grossly applicable, but it is a good safeguard to be aware of.

An important aspect of defining intelligent SLAs is tracking them. The best way to do this is to integrate them into your application use cases. A use case is built from a general thought, such as "The application must provide search functionality for its patient medical records," but then the use case is divided into scenarios. Each scenario defines a path that the use case may follow given varying user actions. For example, what does the application do when the patient exists? What does it do when the patient does not exist? What if the search criterion returns more than one patient record? Each of these business processes needs to be explicitly called out in the use case, and each needs to have an SLA associated with it.

The following exercise demonstrates the format that a proper use case containing intelligent SLAs should follow.

USE CASE: PATIENT HISTORY SEARCH FUNCTIONALITY

Use Case

The Patient Management System must provide functionality to search for specific patient medical history information.

Scenarios

Scenario 1: The Patient Management System returns one distinct record.

Scenario 2: The Patient Management System returns more than one match.

Scenario 3: The Patient Management System does not find any users meeting the specified criteria.

Preconditions

The user has successfully logged in to the application.

Triggers

The user enters search criteria and submits data using the Web interface.

Descriptions

Scenario 1:

1. The Patient Management

2. . . .

Scenario 2:

3. . . .

Postconditions

The Patient Management System displays the results to the user.

SLAs

Scenario 1: The Patient Management System will return a specific patient matching the specified criteria in less than three seconds for 95 percent of requests. The response time will at no point stray more than two standard deviations from the mean.

Scenario 2: The Patient Management System will return a collection of patients matching the specified criteria in less than five seconds for 95 percent of requests. The response time will at no point stray more than two standard deviations from the mean.

Scenario 3: When the Patient Management System cannot find a user matching the specified criteria, it will inform the user in less than two seconds for 95 percent of requests. The response time will at no point stray more than two standard deviations from the mean.

The format of this use case varies from traditional use cases with the addition of the SLA component. In the SLA component, you explicitly call out the performance requirements for each scenario. The performance criteria include the following:

- *The expected tolerance level*: Respond in less than three seconds.

- *The measure of flexibility*: Meet the tolerance level for 95 percent of requests.

- *The upper threshold*: Do not stray more than three standard deviations from the observed mean.

With each of these performance facets explicitly defined, the developers implementing code to satisfy the use case understand their expectations and can structure unit tests accordingly. The QA team has a specific value to test and measure the quality of the application against. Next, when the QA team, or a delegated performance capacity assessor, performs a formal capacity assessment, an extremely accurate assessment can be built and a proper degradation model constructed. Finally, when the application reaches production, enterprise Java system administrators have values from which to determine if the application is meeting its requirements.

All of this specific assessment is possible, because the application business owner and application technical owner took time to carefully determine these values in the architecture phase. My aim here is to impress upon you the importance of up-front research and a solid communication channel between the business and technical representatives.

Object Life Cycle Management

The most significant problem plaguing production enterprise Java applications is memory management. The root cause of 90 percent of my customers' problems is memory related and can manifest in one of two ways:

- Object cycling

- Loitering objects (lingering object references)

Recall that object cycling is the rapid creation and deletion of objects in a short period of time that causes the frequency of garbage collection to increase and may result in tenuring short-lived objects prematurely. The cause of loitering objects is poor object management; the application developer does not explicitly know when an object should be released from memory, so the reference is maintained. Loitering objects are the result of an application developer failing to release object references at the correct time. This is a failure to understand the impact of reference management on application performance. This condition results in an overabundance of objects residing in memory, which can have the following effects:

- Garbage collection may run slower, because more live objects must be examined.

- Garbage collection can become less effective at reclaiming objects.

- Swapping on the physical machine can result, because less physical memory is available for other processes to use.

Neglecting object life cycle management can result in memory leaks and eventually application server crashes. I discuss techniques for detecting and avoiding object cycling later in this chapter, because it is a development or design issue, but object life cycle management is an architectural issue.

To avoid loitering objects, take control of the management of object life cycles by defining object life cycles inside use cases. I am not advocating that each use case should define every `int`, `boolean`, and `float` that will be created in the code to satisfy the use case; rather, each use case needs to define the major application-level components upon which it depends. For example, in the Patient Management System, daily summary reports may be generated every evening that detail patient metrics such as the number of cases of heart disease identified this year and the common patient profile attributes for each. This report would be costly to build on a per-request basis, so the architects of the system may dictate that the report needs to be cached at the application level (or in the application scope so that all requests can access it).

Defining use case dependencies and application-level object life cycles provides a deeper understanding of what should and should not be in the heap at any given time. Here are some guidelines to help you identify application-level objects that need to be explicitly called out and mapped to use cases in a dependency matrix:

- Expensive objects, in terms of both allocated size as well as allocation time, that will be accessed by multiple users

- Commonly accessed data

- Nontemporal user session objects

- Global counters and statistics management objects

- Global configuration options

The most common examples of application-level object candidates are frequently accessed business objects, such as those stored in a cache. If your application uses entity beans, then you need to carefully determine the size of the entity bean cache by examining use cases; this can be extrapolated to apply to any caching infrastructure. The point is that if you are caching data in the heap to satisfy specific use cases, then you need to determine how much data is required to satisfy the use cases. And if anyone questions the memory footprint, then you can trace it directly back to the use cases.

The other half of the practice of object life cycle management is defining when objects should be removed from memory. In the previous example, the medical summary report is updated every evening, so at that point the old report should be removed from memory to make room for the new report. Knowing when to remove objects is probably more important than knowing when to create objects. If an object is not already in memory, then you can create it, but if it is in memory and no one needs it anymore, then that memory is lost forever.

Application Session Management

Just as memory mismanagement is the most prevalent issue impacting the performance of enterprise Java applications, HTTP sessions are by far the biggest culprit in memory abuse. HTTP is a stateless protocol, and as such the conversation between the Web client and Web server terminates at the conclusion of a single request: the Web client submits a request to the Web server (most commonly `GET` or `POST`), and then the Web server performs its business logic, constructs a response, and returns the response to the Web client. This ends the Web conversation and terminates the relationship between client and server.

In order to sustain a long-term conversation between a Web client and Web server, the Web server constructs a unique identifier for the client and includes it with its response to the request; internally the Web server maintains all user data and associates it with that identifier. On subsequent requests, the client submits this unique identifier to identify itself to the Web server.

This sounds like a good idea, but it creates the following problem: if the HTTP protocol is truly stateless and the conversation between Web client and Web server can only be renewed by a client interaction, then what does the Web server do with the client's information if that client never returns? Obviously, the Web server throws the information away, but the real question relates to how long the Web server should keep the information.

All application servers provide a session time-out value that constrains the amount of time user data is maintained. When the user makes any request from the server, the user's time-out is reset, and once the time-out has been exceeded, the user's stateful information is discarded. A practical example of this is logging in to your online banking application. You can view your account balances, transfer funds, and pay bills, but if you sit idle for too long, you are forced to log in again. The session time-out period for a banking application is usually quite short for security reasons (for example, if you log in to your bank account and then leave your computer unattended to go to a meeting, you do not want someone else who wanders by your desk to be able to access your account). On the other hand, when you shop at Amazon.com, you can add items to your shopping cart and return six months later to see that old book on DNA synthesis and methylation that you still do not have time to read sitting there. Amazon.com uses a more advanced infrastructure to support this feature (and a heck of a lot of hardware and memory), but the question remains: how long should you hold on to data between user requests before discarding it?

The definitive time-out value must come from the application business owner. He or she may have specific, legally binding commitments with end users and business partners. But an application technical owner can control the quantity of data that is held resident in memory for each user. In the aforementioned example, do you think that Amazon.com maintains everyone's shopping cart in memory for all time? I suspect that shopping cart data is maintained in memory for a fixed session length, and afterward persisted to a database for later retrieval.

As a general guideline, sessions should be as small as possible while still realizing the benefits of being resident in memory. I usually maintain temporal data describing what the user does in a particular session, such as the page the user came from, the options the user has enabled, and so on. More significant data, such as objects stored in a shopping cart, opened reports, or partial result sets, are best stored in stateful session beans, because rather than being maintained in a hash map that can conceivably grow indefinitely like HTTP session objects, stateful session beans are stored in predefined caches. The size of stateful session bean caches can be defined upon deployment, on a per-bean basis, and hence assert an upper limit on memory consumption. When the cache is full, to add a new bean to it, an existing bean must be selected and written out to persistent storage. The danger is that if the cache is sized too small, the maintenance of the cache can outweigh the benefits of having the cache in the first place. If your sessions are heavy and your user load is large, then this upper limit can prevent your application servers from crashing.

Performance in Development

Have you ever heard anyone ask the following question: "When developers are building their individual components before a single use case is implemented, isn't it premature to start performance testing?"

Let me ask a similar question: When building a car, is it premature to test the performance of your alternator before the car is assembled and you try to start it? The answer to this question is obviously "No, it's not premature. I want to make sure that the alternator works before building my car!" If you would never assemble a car from untested parts, why would you assemble an enterprise application from untested components? Furthermore, because you integrate performance criteria into use cases, use cases will fail testing if they do not meet their performance criteria. In short, performance matters!

In development, components are tested in *unit tests*. A unit test is designed to test the functionality and performance of an individual component, independently from other components that it will eventually interact with. The most common unit testing framework is an open source initiative called JUnit. JUnit's underlying premise is that alongside the development of your components, you should write tests to validate each piece of functionality of your components. A relatively new development paradigm, Extreme Programming (www.xprogramming.com), promotes building test cases prior to building the components themselves, which forces you to better understand how your components will be used prior to writing them.

JUnit focuses on functional testing, but side projects spawned from JUnit include performance and scalability testing. Performance tests measure expected response time, and scalability tests measure functional integrity under load. Formal performance unit test criteria should do the following:

- Identify memory issues

- Identify poorly performing methods and algorithms

- Measure the coverage of unit tests to ensure that the majority of code is being tested

Memory leaks are the most dangerous and difficult to diagnose problems in enterprise Java applications. The best way to avoid memory leaks at a code level is to run your components through a *memory profiler*. A memory profiler takes a snapshot of your heap (after first running garbage collection), allows you to run your tests, takes another snapshot of your heap (after garbage collection again), and shows you all of the objects that remain in the heap. The analysis of the heap differences identifies objects abandoned in memory. Your task is then to look at these objects and decide if they should remain in the heap or if they were left there by mistake. Another danger of memory misuse is object cycling, which, again, is the rapid creation and destruction of objects. Because it increases the frequency of garbage collection, excessive object cycling may result in the premature tenuring of short-lived objects, necessitating a major garbage collection to reclaim these objects.

After considering memory issues, you need to quantify the performance of methods and algorithms. Because SLAs are defined at the use case level, but not at the component level, measuring response times may be premature in the development phase. Rather, the strategy is to run your components through a *code profiler*. A code profiler reveals the most frequently executed sections of your code and those that account for the majority of the components' execution times. The resulting relative weighting of hot spots in the code allows for intelligent tuning and code refactoring. You should run code profiling on your components while executing your unit tests, because your unit tests attempt to mimic end-user actions and alternate user scenarios. Code profiling your unit tests should give you a good idea about how your component will react to real user interactions.

Coverage profiling reports the percentage of classes, methods, and lines of code that were executed during a test or use case. Coverage profiling is important in assessing the efficacy of unit tests. If both the code and memory profiling of your code are good, but you are exercising only 20 percent of your code, then your confidence in your tests should be minimal. Not only do you need to receive favorable results from your functional unit tests and your code and memory performance unit tests, but you also need to ensure that you are effectively testing your components.

This level of testing can be further extended to any code that you outsource. You should require your outsourcing company to provide you with unit tests for all components it develops, and then execute a performance test against those unit tests to measure the quality of the components you are receiving. By combining code and memory profiling with coverage profiling, you can quickly determine whether the unit tests are written properly and have acceptable results.

Once the criteria for tests are met, the final key step to effectively implementing this level of testing is automation. You need to integrate functional and performance unit testing into your build process—only by doing so can you establish a repeatable and trackable procedure. Because running performance unit tests can burden memory resources, you might try executing functional tests during nightly builds and executing performance unit tests on Friday-night builds, so that you can come in on Monday to test result reports without impacting developer productivity. This suggestion's success depends a great deal on the size and complexity of your environment, so, as always, adapt this plan to serve your application's needs.

When performance unit tests are written prior to, or at least concurrently with, component development, then component performance can be assessed at each build. If such extensive assessment is not realistic, then the reports need to be evaluated at each major development milestone. For the developer, milestones are probably at the completion of the component or a major piece of functionality for the component. But at minimum, performance unit tests need to be performed prior to the integration of components. Again, building a high-performance car from tested and proven high-performance parts is far more effective than from scraps gathered from the junkyard.

Unit Testing

I thought this section would be a good opportunity to talk a little about unit testing tools and methods, though this discussion is not meant to be exhaustive. JUnit is, again, the tool of choice for unit testing. JUnit is a simple regression-testing framework that enables you to write repeatable tests. Originally written by Erich Gamma and Kent Beck, JUnit has been embraced by thousands of developers and has grown into a collection of unit testing frameworks for a plethora of technologies. The JUnit Web site (`www.junit.org`) hosts support information and links to the other JUnit derivations.

JUnit offers the following benefits to your unit testing:

- *Faster coding*: How many times have you written debug code inside your classes to verify values or test functionality? JUnit eliminates this by allowing you to write test cases in closely related, but centralized and external, classes.

- *Simplicity*: If you have to spend too much time implementing your test cases, then you won't do it. Therefore, the creators of JUnit made it as simple as possible.

- *Single result reports*: Rather than generating loads of reports, JUnit will give you a single pass/fail result, and, for any failure, show you the exact point where the application failed.

- *Hierarchical testing structure*: Test cases exercise specific functionality, and test suites execute multiple test cases. JUnit supports test suites of test suites, so when developers build test cases for their classes, they can easily assemble them into a test suite at the package level, and then incorporate that into parent packages and so forth. The result is that a single, top-level test execution can exercise hundreds of unit test cases.

- *Developer-written tests*: These tests are written by the same person who wrote the code, so the tests accurately target the intricacies of the code that the developer knows can be problematic. This test differs from a QA-written one, which exercises the external functionality of the component or use case—instead, this test exercises the internal functionality.

- *Seamless integration*: Tests are written in Java, which makes the integration of test cases and code seamless.

- *Free*: JUnit is open source and licensed under the Common Public License Version 1.0, so you are free to use it in your applications.

From an architectural perspective, JUnit can be described by looking at two primary components: `TestCase` and `TestSuite`. All code that tests the functionality of your class or classes must extend `junit.framework.TestCase`. The `test` class can implement one or more tests by defining `public void` methods that start with `test` and accept no parameters, for example:

```
public void testMyFunctionality() { ... }
```

For multiple tests, you have the option of initializing and cleaning up the environment before and between tests by implementing the following two methods: `setUp()` and `tearDown()`. In `setUp()` you initialize the environment, and in `teardown()` you clean up the environment. Note that these methods are called between each test to eliminate side effects between test cases; this makes each test case truly independent.

Inside each `TestCase` "test" method, you can create objects, execute functionality, and then test the return values of those functional elements against expected results. If the return values are not as expected, then the test fails; otherwise, it passes. The mechanism that JUnit provides to validate actual values against expected values is a set of `assert` methods:

- `assertEquals()` methods test primitive types.

- `assertTrue()` and `assertFalse()` test Boolean values.

- `assertNull()` and `assertNotNull()` test whether or not an object is null.

- `assertSame()` and `assertNotSame()` test object equality.

In addition, JUnit offers a `fail()` method that you can call anywhere in your test case to immediately mark a test as failing.

JUnit tests are executed by one of the `TestRunner` instances (there is one for command-line execution and one for a GUI execution), and each version implements the following steps:

1. It opens your `TestCase` class instance.

2. It uses reflection to discover all methods that start with "test".

3. It repeatedly calls `setUp()`, executes the test method, and calls `teardown()`.

As an example, I have a set of classes that model data metrics. A metric contains a set of data points, where each data point represents an individual sample, such as the size of the heap at a given time. I purposely do not list the code for the metric or data point classes; rather, I list the JUnit tests. Recall that according to one of the tenets of Extreme Programming, we write test cases before writing code. Listing 5-1 shows the test case for the `Metric` class, and Listing 5-2 shows the test case for the `DataPoint` class.

Listing 5-1. *DataPointTest.java*

```java
package com.javasrc.metric;

import junit.framework.TestCase;
import java.util.*;

/**
 * Tests the core functionality of a DataPoint
 */
public class DataPointTest extends TestCase
{
  /**
   * Maintains our reference DataPoint
   */
  private DataPoint dp;

  /**
   * Create a DataPoint for use in this test
   */
  protected void setUp()
  {
    dp = new DataPoint( new Date(), 5.0, 1.0, 10.0 );
  }
```

```java
/**
 * Clean up: do nothing for now
 */
protected void tearDown()
{
}

/**
 * Test the range of the DataPoint
 */
public void testRange()
{
  assertEquals( 9.0, dp.getRange(), 0.001 );
}

/**
 * See if the DataPoint scales properly
 */
public void testScale()
{
  dp.scale( 10.0 );
  assertEquals( 50.0, dp.getValue(), 0.001 );
  assertEquals( 10.0, dp.getMin(), 0.001 );
  assertEquals( 100.0, dp.getMax(), 0.001 );
}

/**
 * Try to add a new DataPoint to our existing one
 */
public void testAdd()
{
  DataPoint other = new DataPoint( new Date(), 4.0, 0.5, 20.0 );
  dp.add( other );
  assertEquals( 9.0, dp.getValue(), 0.001 );
  assertEquals( 0.5, dp.getMin(), 0.001 );
  assertEquals( 20.0, dp.getMax(), 0.001 );
}

/**
 * Test the compare functionality of our DataPoint to ensure that
 * when we construct Sets of DataPoints they are properly ordered
 */
public void testCompareTo()
{
  try
  {
```

```
      // Sleep for 100ms so we can be sure that the time of
      // the new data point is later than the first
      Thread.sleep( 100 );
    }
    catch( Exception e )
    {
    }

    // Construct a new DataPoint
    DataPoint other = new DataPoint( new Date(), 4.0, 0.5, 20.0 );

    // Should return -1 because other occurs after dp
    int result = dp.compareTo( other );
    assertEquals( -1, result );

    // Should return 1 because dp occurs before other
    result = other.compareTo( dp );
    assertEquals( 1, result );

    // Should return 0 because dp == dp
    result = dp.compareTo( dp );
    assertEquals( 0, result );
  }
}
```

Listing 5-2. *MetricTest.java*

```
package com.javasrc.metric;

import junit.framework.TestCase;
import java.util.*;

public class MetricTest extends TestCase
{
  private Metric sampleHeap;

  protected void setUp()
  {
    this.sampleHeap = new Metric( "Test Metric",
                                  "Value/Min/Max",
                                  "megabytes" );
    double heapValue = 100.0;
    double heapMin = 50.0;
    double heapMax = 150.0;
```

```
    for( int i=0; i<10; i++ )
    {
      DataPoint dp = new DataPoint( new Date(),
                                    heapValue,
                                    heapMin,
                                    heapMax );
      this.sampleHeap.addDataPoint( dp );
      try
      {
        Thread.sleep( 50 );
      }
      catch( Exception e )
      {
      }

      // Update the heap values
      heapMin -= 1.0;
      heapMax += 1.0;
      heapValue += 1.0;
    }
  }

  public void testMin()
  {
    assertEquals( 41.0, this.sampleHeap.getMin(), 0.001 );
  }

  public void testMax()
  {
    assertEquals( 159.0, this.sampleHeap.getMax(), 0.001 );
  }

  public void testAve()
  {
    assertEquals( 104.5, this.sampleHeap.getAve(), 0.001 );
  }

  public void testMaxRange()
  {
    assertEquals( 118.0, this.sampleHeap.getMaxRange(), 0.001 );
  }

  public void testRange()
  {
    assertEquals( 118.0, this.sampleHeap.getRange(), 0.001 );
  }
```

```
  public void testSD()
  {
    assertEquals( 3.03, this.sampleHeap.getStandardDeviation(), 0.01 );
  }

  public void testVariance()
  {
    assertEquals( 9.17, this.sampleHeap.getVariance(), 0.01 );
  }

  public void testDataPointCount()
  {
    assertEquals( 10, this.sampleHeap.getDataPoints().size() );
  }
}
```

In Listing 5-1, you can see that the DataPoint class, in addition to maintaining the observed value for a point in time, supports minimum and maximum values for the time period, computes the range, and supports scaling and adding data points. The sample test case creates a DataPoint object in the setUp() method and then exercises each piece of functionality.

Listing 5-2 shows the test case for the Metric class. The Metric class aggregates the DataPoint objects and provides access to the collective minimum, maximum, average, range, standard deviation, and variance. In the setUp() method, the test creates a set of data points and builds the metric to contain them. Each subsequent test case uses this metric and validates values computed by hand to those computed by the Metric class.

Listing 5-3 rolls both of these test cases into a test suite that can be executed as one test.

Listing 5-3. *MetricTestSuite.java*

```
package com.javasrc.metric;

import junit.framework.Test;
import junit.framework.TestSuite;

public class MetricTestSuite
{
  public static Test suite()
  {
    TestSuite suite = new TestSuite();
    suite.addTestSuite( DataPointTest.class );
    suite.addTestSuite( MetricTest.class );
    return suite;
  }
}
```

A TestSuite exercises all tests in all classes added to it by calling the addTestSuite() method. A TestSuite can contain TestCases or TestSuites, so once you build a suite of test cases for your classes, a master test suite can include your suite and inherit all of your test cases.

The final step in this example is to execute either an individual test case or a test suite. After downloading JUnit from www.junit.org, add the junit.jar file to your CLASSPATH and then invoke either its command-line interface or GUI interface. The three classes that execute these tests are as follows:

- junit.textui.TestRunner

- junit.swingui.TestRunner

- junit.awtui.TestRunner

And as these package names imply, textui is the command-line interface and swingui is the graphical interface. awtui provides a batch interface to executing unit tests. You can pass an individual test case or an entire test suite as an argument to the TestRunner class. For example, to execute the test suite that we created earlier, you would use this:

```
java junit.swingui.TestRunner com.javasrc.metric.MetricTestSuite
```

Unit Performance Testing

Unit performance testing has three aspects:

- Memory profiling

- Code profiling

- Coverage profiling

This section explores each facet of performance profiling. I provide examples of what to look for and the step-by-step process to implement each type of testing.

Memory Profiling

Let's first look at memory profiling. To illustrate how to determine if you do, in fact, have a memory leak, I modified the BEA MedRec application to capture the state of the environment every time an administrator logs in and to store that information in memory. My intent is to demonstrate how a simple tracking change left to its own devices can introduce a memory leak.

The steps you need to perform on your code for each use are as follows:

1. Request a garbage collection and take a snapshot of your heap.

2. Perform your use case.

3. Request a garbage collection and take another snapshot of your heap.

4. Compare the two snapshots (the difference between them includes all objects remaining in the heap) and identify any unexpected loitering objects.

5. For each suspect object, open the heap snapshot and track down where the object was created.

■**Note** A memory leak can be detected with a single execution of a use case or through a plethora of executions of a use case. In the latter case, the memory leak will scream out at you. So, while analyzing individual use cases is worthwhile, when searching for subtle memory leaks, executing your use case multiple times makes finding them easier.

In this scenario, I performed steps 1 through 3 with a load tester that executed the MedRec administration login use case almost 500 times. Figure 5-2 shows the difference between the two heap snapshots.

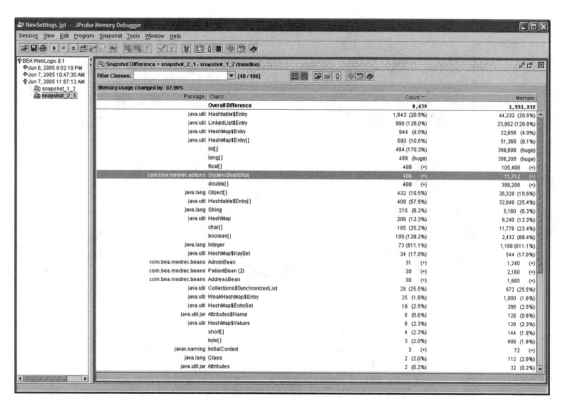

Figure 5-2. *The snapshot difference between the heaps before and after executing the use case*

Figure 5-2 shows that my use case yielded 8,679 new objects added to the heap. Most of these objects are collection classes, and I suspect they are part of BEA's infrastructure. I scanned this list looking for my code, which in this case consists of any class in the com.bea.medrec package. Filtering on those classes, I was interested to see a large number of com.bea.medrec.actions. SystemSnapShot instances, as shown in Figure 5-3.

■**Note** The screen shots in this chapter are from Quest Software's JProbe and PerformaSure products.

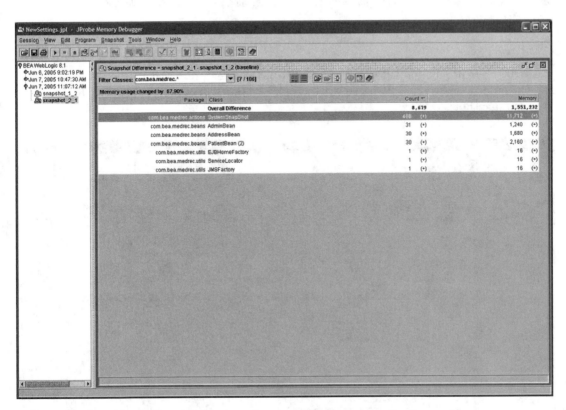

Figure 5-3. *The snapshot difference between the heaps, filtered on my application packages*

Realize that rarely is a loitering object a single simple object; rather, it is typically a subgraph that maintains its own references. In this case, the SystemSnapShot class is a dummy class that holds a set of primitive type arrays with the names timestamp, memoryInfo, jdbcInfo, and threadDumps, but in a real-world scenario these arrays would be objects that reference other objects and so forth. By opening the second heap snapshot and looking at one of the SystemSnapShot instances, you can see all objects that it references. As shown in Figure 5-4, the SystemSnapShot class references four objects: timestamp, memoryInfo, jdbcInfo, and threadDumps. A loitering object, then, has a far greater impact than the object itself.

Next, let's look at the referrer tree. We repeatedly ask the following questions: What class is referencing the SystemSnapShot? What class is referencing that class? Eventually, we finally find one of our classes. Figure 5-5 shows that the SystemSnapShot class is referenced by an Object array that is referenced by an ArrayList that is finally referenced by the AdminLoginAction.

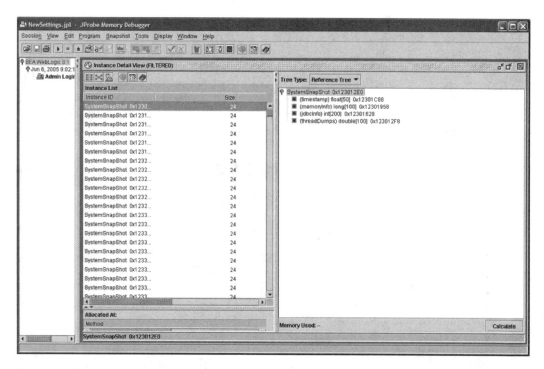

Figure 5-4. *The SystemSnapShot class references four objects: timestamp, memoryInfo, jdbcInfo, and threadDumps.*

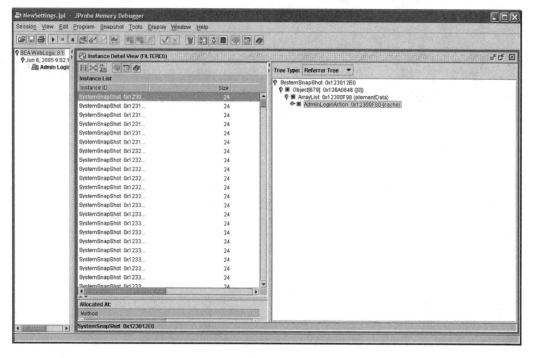

Figure 5-5. *Here we can see that the AdminLoginAction class created the SystemSnapShot, and that it stored it in an ArrayList.*

Finally, we can look into the `AdminLoginAction` code to see that it creates the new `SystemSnapShot` instance we are looking at and adds it to its cache in line 66, as shown in Figure 5-6.

You need to perform this type of memory profiling test on your components during your performance unit testing. For each object that is left in the heap, you need to ask yourself whether or not you intended to leave it there. It's OK to leave things on the heap as long as you know that they are there and you want them to be there. The purpose of this test is to identify and document potentially troublesome objects and objects that you forgot to clean up.

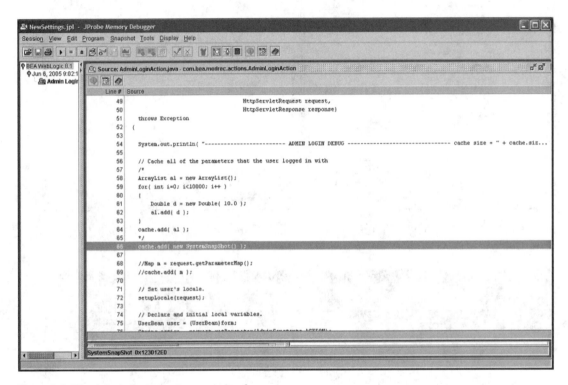

Figure 5-6. *The AdminLoginAction source code*

Code Profiling

The purpose of code profiling is to identify sections of your code that are running slowly and then determine why. The perfect example I have to demonstrate the effectiveness of code profiling is a project that I gave to my Data Structures and Algorithm Analysis class—compare and quantify the differences among the following sorting algorithms for various values of n (where n represents the sample size of the data being sorted):

- Bubble sort

- Selection sort

- Insertion sort

- Shell sort

- Heap sort

- Merge sort

- Quick sort

As a quick primer on sorting algorithms, each of the aforementioned algorithms has its strengths and weaknesses. The first four algorithms run in $O(N^2)$ time, meaning that the run time increases exponentially as the number of items to sort, N, increases; specifically, as N increases, the amount of time required for the sorting algorithm to complete increases by N^2. The last three algorithms run in $O(N \log N)$ time, meaning that the run time grows logarithmically: as N increases, the amount of time required for the sorting algorithm to complete increases by $N \log N$. Achieving $O(N \log N)$ performance requires additional overhead that may cause the last three algorithms to actually run slower than the first four for a small number of items. My recommendation is to always examine both the nature of the data you want to sort today and the projected nature of the data throughout the life cycle of the product prior to selecting your sorting algorithm.

With that foundation in place, I provided my students with a class that implements the aforementioned sorting algorithms. I really wanted to drive home the dramatic difference between executing these sorting algorithms on 10 items as opposed to 10,000 items, or even 1,000,000 items. For this exercise, I think it would be useful to profile this application against 5,000 randomly generated integers, which is enough to show the differences between the algorithms, but not so excessive that I have to leave my computer running overnight.

Figure 5-7 shows the results of this execution, sorting each method by its cumulative run time.

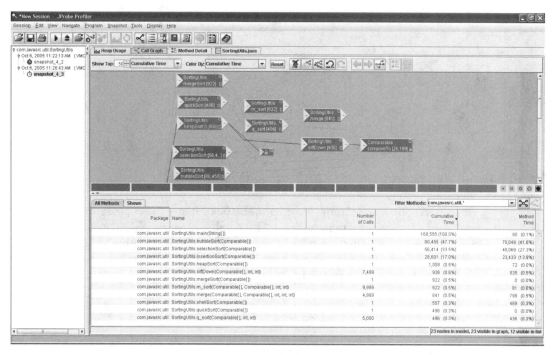

Figure 5-7. *The profiled methods used to sort 5,000 random integers using the seven sorting algorithms*

We view the method response times sorted by cumulative time, because some of the algorithms make repeated calls to other methods to perform their sorting (for example, the `quickSort()` method makes 5,000 calls to `q_sort()`). We have to ignore the `main()` method, because it calls all seven sorting methods. (Its cumulative time is almost 169 seconds, but its exclusive method time is only 90 milliseconds, demonstrating that most of its time is spent in other method calls—namely, all of the sorting method calls.) The slowest method by far is the `bubbleSort()` method, accounting for 80 seconds in total time and 47.7 percent of total run time for the program.

The next question is, why did it take so long? Two pieces of information can give us insight into the length of time: the number of external calls the method makes and the amount of time spent on each line of code. Figure 5-8 shows the number of external calls that the `bubbleSort()` method makes.

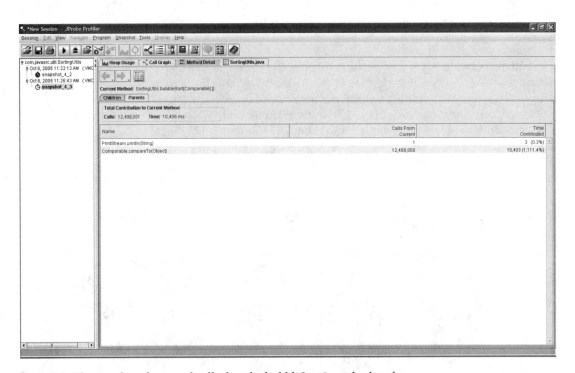

Figure 5-8. *The number of external calls that the bubbleSort() method makes*

This observation is significant—in order to sort 5,000 items, the bubble sort algorithm required almost 12.5 million comparisons. It immediately alerts us to the fact that if we have a considerable number of items to sort, bubble sort is not the best algorithm to use. Taking this example a step further, Figure 5-9 shows a line-by-line breakdown of call counts and time spent inside the `bubbleSort()` method.

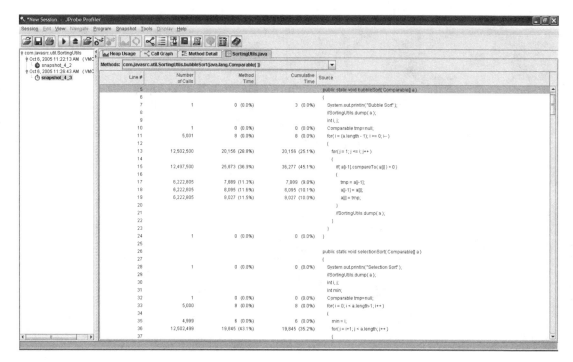

Figure 5-9. *Profiling the bubbleSort() method*

By profiling the bubbleSort() method, we see that 45 percent of its time is spent comparing items, and 25 percent is spent managing a for loop; these two lines account for 56 cumulative seconds. Figure 5-9 clearly illustrates the core issue of the bubble sort algorithm: on line 15 it executes the for loop 12,502,500 times, which resolves to 12,479,500 comparisons.

To be successful in deploying high-performance components and applications, you need to apply this level of profiling to your code.

Coverage Profiling

Identifying and rectifying memory issues and slow-running algorithms gives you confidence in the quality of your components, but that confidence is meaningful only as long as you are exercising all—or at least most—of your code. That is where coverage profiling comes in; coverage profiling reveals the percentage of classes, methods, and lines of code that are executed by a test. Coverage profiling can provide strong validation that your unit and integration tests are effectively exercising your components.

In this section, I'll show a test of a graphical application that I built to manage my digital pictures running inside of a coverage profiler filtered according to my classes. I purposely chose not to test it extensively in order to present an interesting example. Figure 5-10 shows a class summary of the code that I tested, with six profiled classes in three packages displayed in the browser window and the methods of the JThumbnailPalette class with missed lines in the pane below.

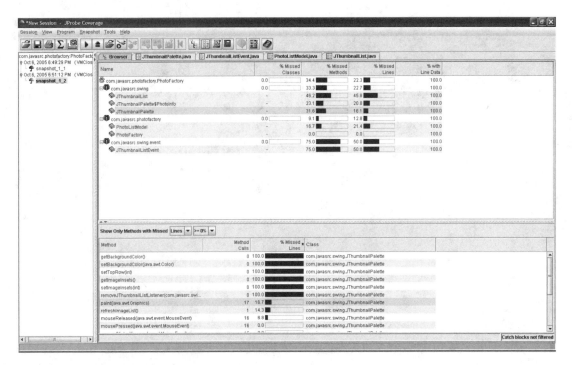

Figure 5-10. *Coverage profile of a graphical application*

The test exercised all six classes, but missed a host of methods and classes. For example, in the JThumbnailPalette class, the test completely failed to call the methods getBackgroundColor(), setBackgroundColor(), setTopRow(), and others. Furthermore, even though the paint() method was called, the test missed 16.7 percent of the lines. Figure 5-11 shows the specific lines of code within the paint() method that the test did not execute.

Figure 5-11 reveals that most lines of code were executed 17 times, but the code that handles painting a scrolled set of thumbnails was skipped. With this information in hand, the person needs to move the scroll bar, or configure an automated test script to move it, to ensure that this piece of code is executed.

Coverage is a powerful profiling tool, because without it, you may miss code that your users will encounter when they use your application in a way that you do not expect (and rest assured, they definitely will).

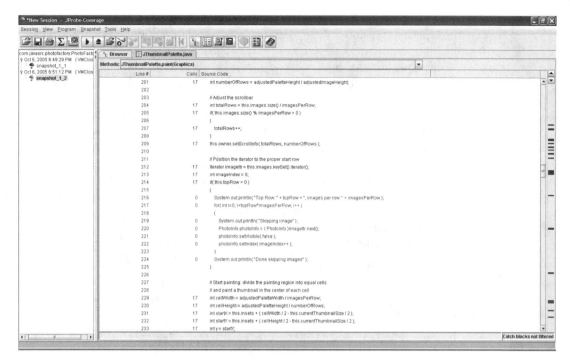

Figure 5-11. *A look inside the JThumbnailPalette's paint() method*

Performance in Quality Assurance

The integration of components usually falls more on development than on QA, but the exercise usually ends at functional testing. Development ensures that the components work together as designed, and then the QA team tests the details of the iteration's use cases. Now that your use cases have performance criteria integrated, QA has a perfect opportunity to evaluate the iteration against the performance criteria. The new notion that I am promoting is that an application that meets all of its functional requirements but does not satisfy its SLAs does not pass QA. The response by the QA team should be the same as if the application is missing functionality: the application is returned to development to be fixed.

Performance integration testing comes in two flavors:

- Performance integration general test

- Performance integration load test

QA performs the integration general test under minimal load; the amount of that load is a subset of the expected load and defined formally in the test plan. For example, if the expected load is 1,500 simultaneous users, then this test may be against 50 users. The purpose of this test is to identify any gross performance problems that might occur as the components are integrated. Do not run a full-load test, because in a failed full-load test it may be difficult to identify the root cause of the performance failure. If the load is completely unsustainable, then all aspects of the application and environment will most likely fail. Furthermore, if the integrated application cannot satisfy a minimal load, then there is no reason to subject it to a full load.

After the application has survived the performance integration general test, the next test is the performance integration load test. During this test, turn up the user load to the expected user load, or if you do not have a test environment that mirrors production, then use a single JVM scaled down appropriately. For example, if you are trying to support 1,500 users with four JVMs, then you might send 400 users at a single JVM. Each use case that has been implemented in this integration is tested against the formal use case SLAs. The performance integration load test is probably the most difficult one for the application to pass, but it offers the ability to tune the application and application server, and it ensures that the performance of the application stays on track.

Balanced Representative Load Testing

Probably the most important aspect of performance tuning in integration or staging environments is ensuring that you are accurately reproducing the behavior of your users. This is referred to as *balanced representative load testing*. Each load scenario that you play against your environment needs to represent a real-world user interaction with your application, complete with accurate think times (that is, the wait time between requests). Furthermore, these representative actions must be balanced according to their observed percentage of occurrence.

For example, a user may log in once, but then perform five searches, submit one form, and log out. Therefore the logon, logoff, and submission functionalities should each receive a balance of one-eighth of the load, and the search functionality should receive the remaining five-eighths of the load for this transaction. If your load scripts do not represent real-world user actions balanced in the way users will be using your application, then you can have no confidence that your tuning efforts are valid. Consider this example if the actions were not balanced properly (say each action receives one-fourth of the load). Logon and logoff functionalities may be far less database-intensive than search functionality, but they may be much heavier on a JCA connector to a Lightweight Directory Access Protocol (LDAP) server. Tuning each function equally results in too few database connections to service your database requests and extraneous JCA connections. A simple misbalance of respective transactions can disrupt your entire environment.

There are two primary techniques to extracting end-user behaviors: process access log files or add a network device into your environment that monitors end-user behavior. The former is the less exact of the two but can provide insight into user pathways through your Web site and accurate think times. The latter is more exact and can be configured to provide deeper insight into customer profiling and application logic.

Production Staging Testing

Seldom will your applications run in isolation; rather, they typically run in a shared environment with other applications competing for resources. Therefore, testing your applications in a staging environment designed to mirror production is imperative. As the integration test phase is split into two steps, so is the production staging test:

- Performance production staging general test

- Performance production staging load test

The general test loads the production staging environment with a small user load with the goal of uncovering any egregiously slow functionality or drained resources. Again, this step is interjected before performing the second, full-load test, because a full-load test may completely break the environment and consume all resources, thereby obfuscating the true cause of performance issues. If the application cannot satisfy a minimal amount of load while running in a shared environment, then it is not meaningful to subject it to excessive load.

Identifying Performance Issues

When running these performance tests, you need to pay particular attention to the following potentially problematic environmental facets:

- Application code

- Platform configuration

- External resources

Application code can perform poorly as a result of being subjected to a significant user load. Performance unit tests help identify poorly written algorithms, but code that performs well under low amounts of user load commonly experiences performance issues as the load is significantly increased. The problems occur because subtle programmatic issues manifest themselves as problems only when they become exaggerated. Consider creating an object inside a servlet to satisfy a user request and then destroying it. This is no problem whatsoever for a single user or even a couple dozen users. Now send 5,000 users at that servlet—it must create and destroy that object 5,000 times. This behavior results in excessive garbage collection, premature tenuring of objects, CPU spikes, and other performance abnormalities. This example underscores the fact that only after testing under load can you truly have confidence in the quality of your components.

Platform configuration includes the entire environment that the application runs in: the application server, JVM, operating system, and hardware. Each piece of this layered execution model must be properly configured for optimal performance. As integration and production staging tests are run, you need to monitor and assess their performance. For example, you need to ensure that you have enough threads in the application server to process incoming requests, that your JVM's heap is properly tuned to minimize major garbage collections, that your operating system's process scheduler is allotting enough CPU to the JVM, and that your hardware is running optimally on a fast network. Ensuring proper configuration requires a depth of knowledge across a breadth of technologies.

Finally, most enterprise-scale applications interact with external resources that may or may not be under your control. In the most common cases, enterprise applications interact with one or more databases, but external resources can include legacy systems, messaging servers, and, in recent years, Web services. As the acceptance of SOAs has grown, applications can be rapidly assembled by piecing together existing code that exposes functionality through services. Although this capability promotes the application architect to an application assembler, permitting rapid development of enterprise solutions, it also adds an additional tier to the application. And with that tier comes additional operating systems, environments, and, in some circumstances, services that can be delivered from third-party vendors at run time over the Internet.

The first step in identifying performance issues is to establish monitoring capabilities in your integration and production staging environments, and record the application behavior while under load. This record lists service requests that can be sorted by execution count, average execution time, and total execution time. These service requests are then tracked back to use cases to validate against predefined SLAs. Any service request whose response time exceeds its SLA needs to be analyzed to determine why that's the case. Figure 5-12 shows a breakdown of service requests running inside the MedRec application. In this 30-second time slice, two service requests spent an extensive amount of time executing: GET /admin/viewrequests.do was executed 12 times, accounting for 561 seconds, and POST /patient/register.do was executed 10 times, accounting for 357 seconds.

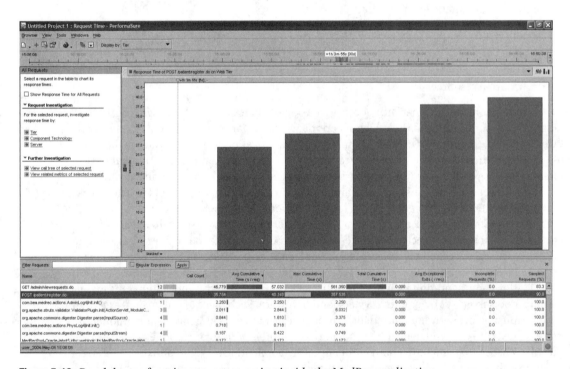

Figure 5-12. *Breakdown of service requests running inside the MedRec application*

As shown in Figure 5-13, looking at the average exclusive time for each method that satisfies the POST /patient/register.do service request, the HTTP POST at the WebLogic cluster consumed on average 35.477 seconds of the 35.754 total service request average, which is important because the request passed quickly from the Web server to the application server, but then waited at the application server for a thread to process it. The remainder of the request processed relatively quickly.

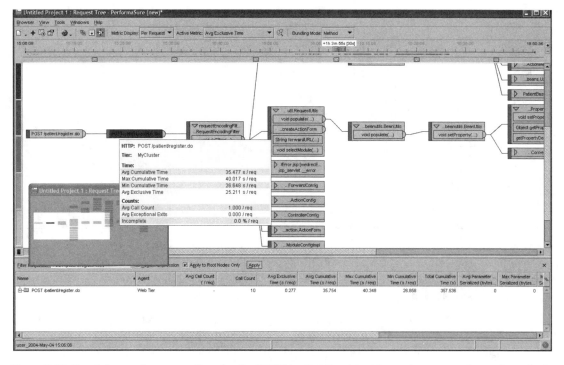

Figure 5-13. *Breakdown of response time for the POST /patient/register.do service request for each method in a hierarchical request tree*

Figure 5-14 shows a view of the performance metrics for the application server during this recorded session. This screen is broken into three regions: the top region shows the heap behavior, the middle shows the thread pool information, and the bottom shows the database connection pool information.

Figure 5-14 confirms our suspicions: the number of idle threads during the session hit zero, and the number of pending requests grew as high as 38. Furthermore, toward the end of the session, the database connection usage peaked at 100 percent and the heap was experiencing significant garbage collection.

This level of diagnosis requires insight into the application, application server, and external dependency behaviors. With this information, you are empowered to determine exactly where and why your application is slowing.

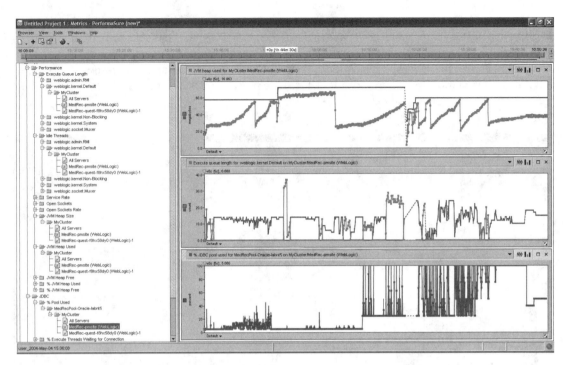

Figure 5-14. *Performance metrics for the application server during this recorded session*

Summary

In this chapter, you learned how to integrate proactive performance testing throughout the development life cycle. The process begins by integrating performance criteria into use cases, which involves modifying use cases to include specific SLA sections that include performance criteria for each use case scenario. Next, as components are built, performance unit tests are performed alongside functional unit tests. These performance tests include testing for memory issues, and code issues, and the validation of the coverage of tests to ensure that the majority of component code is being tested. Finally, as components are integrated and tested in a production staging environment, application bottlenecks are identified and resolved.

In the next chapter, we'll look at a formal performance tuning methodology that allows you to maximize your tuning efforts by tuning the application and application server facets that yield the most significant improvements. By the end of the next chapter, you'll be empowered to bring your application and environment to within 80 percent of their ideal configuration, regardless of your deployment environment.

CHAPTER 6

███

Performance Tuning Methodology

"I have been reading about performance tuning on our application server vendor's Web site, and it looks so complicated. There are all of these ratios that I need to watch and formulas to apply them to. And which ones are the most important? What's going on with this?"

John was getting frustrated with his tuning efforts. He had his team implementing the proactive performance testing methodology that I helped him with, but the concept of the by-the-book performance tuning was evading him.

"Don't let those ratios fool you—there is a much better approach to performance tuning. Let me ask you, when you take your car in for service, does the service technician plug your car into a computer and tell you what's wrong with it, or does he ask you to describe your problems?"

"Well of course he asks me about my problems, otherwise how would he know where to start looking? A car is a complicated machine," John replied.

"Exactly. There are so many moving parts that you wouldn't want to look at each one. Similarly, when tuning an enterprise application, we want to look at its architecture and common pathways to optimize those pathways. When we step back from application server ratios and focus on what the application does and how it uses the application server, the task becomes much easier." From the look on his face, I could see that he got it. He saw that the focus of tuning should be on the application, not on abstract ratios that he did not understand.

Performance Tuning Overview

Performance tuning is not a black art, but it is something that is not very well understood. When tasked with tuning an enterprise Java environment, you have three options:

- You can read through your application server's tuning documentation.

- You can adopt the brute-force approach of trial and error.

- You can hire professional services.

The problem with the first approach is that the application server vendor documentation is usually bloated and lacks prioritization. It would be nice to have a simple step-by-step list of tasks to perform that realize the most benefit with the least amount of effort and the order in which to perform them, but alas, that does not exist. Furthermore, when consulted on best practices of tuning options, application server vendors typically advise that the optimal config- uration depends on your application. This is true, but some general principles can provide a strong starting point from which to begin the tuning process.

The second approach is highly effective, but requires a lot of time and a deep understanding of performance measurements to determine the effect of your changes. Tuning is an iterative process, so some trial and error is required, but it is most effective when you know where to start and where you are going.

The final approach, paying someone else to tune your environment for you, is the most effective, but also the most expensive. This approach has a few drawbacks:

- It is difficult to find someone who knows exactly how to handle this task.

- Unless knowledge transfer is part of the engagement, you are powerless when your application changes; you become dependent on the consultant.

- It is expensive. Talented consultants can cost thousands of dollars per day and expect to provide at least two or three weeks' worth of services.

If you decide to go this route, when you're looking for a reliable and knowledgeable resource, consider the consultant's reputation and referrals. Look for someone who has worked in very complicated environments and in environments that are similar to yours. Furthermore, you want an apples-for-apples tuner: do not hire a WebSphere expert to tune WebLogic. These programs are similar but idiosyncratically different.

In addition, always include knowledge transfer in the engagement statement of work. You do not want to be dependent on someone else for every little change that you make in the future. Keep in mind, though, that it is a good idea to re-engage a proven resource for substan- tial changes and for new applications. Encourage your team to learn from the consultant, but do not expect them to be fully trained by looking over someone's shoulder for a couple of days.

The cost of a consultant's services may be high, but the cost of application failure is much higher. If you are basing your business and your reputation on an application, then a $50,000 price tag to ensure its performance is not unreasonable. Perform a cost-benefit analysis and a return on investment (ROI) analysis, and see if the numbers work out. If they do, then you can consider hiring a consultant.

One alternative that I have neglected to mention is to befriend an expert in this area and ask him to guide your efforts. And that is the focus of this book and in particular this chapter. In this chapter, I share with you my experience tuning environments ranging from small, isolated applications to huge, mission-critical applications running in a complex shared environment. From these engagements, I have learned what always works and best practice approaches to performance tuning. Each application and environment is different, but in this chapter I show you the best place to start and the 20 percent of tuning effort that will yield 80 percent of your tuning impact. It is not rocket science as long as someone explains it to you.

Load Testing Methodology

Before starting any tuning effort, you need to realize that tuning efforts are only effective for the load that your environment is tuned against. To illustrate this point, consider the patient moni- toring system that I have alluded to in earlier chapters. It is database intensive in most of its functionality, and if the load generator does not test the database functionality with enough load, then you can have no confidence that your configuration will meet the demands of users when you roll out the application to production.

With that said, how do you properly design your load tests? Before the application is deployed to a production environment and you can observe real end-user behavior, you have no better option than to take your best guess. "Guess" may not be the most appropriate word to describe this activity, as you've spent time up-front constructing detailed use cases. If you did a good job building the use cases, then you know what you expect your users to do, and your guess is based on the distribution of use cases and their scenarios.

In the following sections, we'll examine how to construct representative load scenarios and then look at the process of applying those load scenarios against your environment.

Load Testing Design

Several times in this book I have emphasized the importance of understanding user patterns and the fact that you can attain this information through access log file analysis or an end-user monitoring device. But thus far I have not mentioned what to do in the case of a new application. When tuning a new application and environment, it is important to follow these three steps:

1. Estimate

2. Validate

3. Reflect

The first step involves estimating what you expect your users to do and how you expect your application to be used. This is where well-defined and thorough use cases really help you. Define load scenarios for each use case scenario and then conduct a meeting with the application business owner and application technical owner to discuss and assign relative weights with which to balance the distribution of each scenario. It is the application business owner's responsibility to spend significant time interviewing customers to understand the application functionality that users find most important. The application technical owner can then translate business functionality into the application in detailed steps that implement that functionality.

Construct your test plan to exercise the production staging environment with load scripts balanced based off of the results of this meeting. The environment should then be tuned to optimally satisfy this balance of requests.

■**Note** If your production staging environment does not match production, then there is still value in running a balanced load test; it allows you to derive a correlation between load and resource utilization. For example, if 500 simulated users under this balanced load use 20 database connections, then you can expect 1,000 users to use approximately 40 database connections to satisfy a similar load balance. Unfortunately, linear interpolation is not 100 percent accurate, because increased load also affects finite resources such as CPU that degrade performance rapidly as they approach saturation. But linear interpolation gives you a ballpark estimate or best practice start value from which to further fine-tune. In Chapter 9 I address the factors that limit interpolation algorithms and help you implement the best configurations.

After deploying an application to production and exposing it to end users, the next step is to validate usage patterns against expectations. This is the time to incorporate an access log file analyzer or end-user experience monitor to extract end-user behavior. The first week can be used to perform a sanity-check validation to identify any gross deviations from estimates, but depending on your user load, a month or even a quarter could be required before users become comfortable enough with your application to give you confidence that you have accurately captured their behavior.

User requests that log file analysis or end-user experience monitors reveal need to be reconstructed into use case scenarios and then traced back to initial estimates. If they do match, then your tuning efforts were effective, but if they are dramatically different, then you need to retune the application to the actual user patterns.

Finally, it is important to perform a postmortem analysis and reflect on how estimated user patterns mapped to actual user patterns. This step is typically overlooked, but it is only through this analysis that your estimates will become more accurate in the future. You need to understand where your estimates were flawed and attempt to identify why. In general, your users' behavior is not going to change significantly over time, so your estimates should become more accurate as your application evolves.

Your workload as an enterprise Java administrator should include periodically repeating this procedure of end-user pattern validation. In the early stages of an application, you should perform this validation relatively frequently, such as every month, but as the application matures, you will perform these validation efforts less frequently, such as every quarter or six months. Applications evolve over time, and new features are added to satisfy user feedback; therefore, you cannot neglect even infrequent user pattern validation. For example, I once worked with a customer who deployed a simple Flash game into their production environment that subsequently crashed their production servers. Other procedural issues were at the core of this problem, but the practical application here is that small modifications to a production environment can dramatically affect resource utilization and contention. And, as with this particular customer, the consequences can be catastrophic.

Load Testing Process

If you want your tuning efforts to be as accurate as possible, then ideally you should maintain a production staging environment with the same configuration as your production environment. Unfortunately, most companies cannot justify the additional expense involved in doing so and therefore construct a production staging environment that is a scaled-down version of production. The following are three main strategies used to scale down the production staging environment:

- Scale down the number of machines, but use the same class of machines

- Scale down the class of machines

- Scale down both the number of machines (size of the environment) as well as the class of machines

Unless financial resources dedicated to production staging are plentiful, scaling down the size of an environment is the most effective plan. For example, if your production environment maintains eight servers, then a production staging environment with four servers is perfectly accurate to perform scaled-down tuning against. A scaled-down environment running the same class of machines (with the same CPU, memory, and so forth) is very effective because you can understand how your application should perform on a single server, and depending on the size, you can calculate the percentage of performance lost in interserver communication (such as the overhead required to replicate stateful information across a cluster).

Scaling down classes of machine, on the other hand, can be quite problematic. In many cases, it is necessary—for example, consider a production environment running in a $10 million mainframe. Chances are that this customer is not going to spend an additional $10 million on a testbed. When you scale down classes of machine, then the best your load testing can accomplish is to identify the relative balance of resource utilizations. This information is still interesting because it allows you to extract information about which service requests resolve to database or external resource calls, the relative response times of each service request, relative thread pool utilization, cache utilization, and so on. Most of these values are relative to each other, but as you deploy to a stronger production environment, you can define a relative scale of resources to one another, establishing best "guess" values and scaling resources appropriately.

To perform an accurate load test, you need to quantify your projected user load and configure your load tester to generate a graduated load up to the projected user load. Each step should be graduated with enough granularity so as not to oversaturate the application if a performance problem occurs.

Wait-Based Tuning

I developed the notion of *wait-based tuning* by drawing from two sources:

- Oracle database tuning theory

- IBM WebSphere tuning theory

I owe a debt of thanks to an associate of mine, Dan Wittry, who works in the Oracle tuning realm. Dan explained to me that in previous versions of Oracle, performance tuning was based upon observing various ratios. For example, what is the ratio of queries serviced in memory to those loaded from disk? How far and how frequently is a disk head required to move? The point is that tuning a database was based upon optimizing performance ratios. In newer releases of the Oracle database, the practice has shifted away from ratios and toward the notion of identifying wait points. No longer do we care about the specifics of performance ratio values; we're now concerned with the performance of our queries. Chances are that a database serving content well will maintain superior performance ratios, but the ratios are not the primary focus of the tuning effort—expediting queries is.

After reading through tuning manuals for IBM WebSphere, BEA WebLogic, Oracle Application Server, and JBoss, I understood well the commonalities between their implementations and the similarity between application server tuning and database tuning: a focus on performance ratios. While IBM addressed performance ratios, it traveled down a different path: where in an application can a request wait? IBM identified four main areas:

- Web server

- Web container

- EJB container

- Database connection pools

Furthermore, IBM posed the supposition that the best place for a request to wait is as early in the process as possible. Once you have learned the capacities of each wait zone, then allow only that number of requests to be processed; force all others to wait back at the Web server. In general, a Web server is a fairly light server: it has a very tight server socket listening process that funnels requests into a queue for processing. Threads assigned to that queue examine the request and either forward it to an application server (or other content provider) or return the requested resource. If the environment is at capacity, then it is better for the Web server to accept the burden of holding on to the pending request rather than to force that burden on the application server.

Tuning Theory

IBM's paradigm provides better insight into the actual performance of an application server and makes as much sense as Oracle's notion of wait points. The focus is on maximizing the performance of an application's requests, not on ratios.

Equipped with these theories, I delved a little further into the nature of application requests as they traverse an enterprise Java environment and asked the question, Where in this technology stack can requests wait? Figure 6-1 shows the common path for an application request.

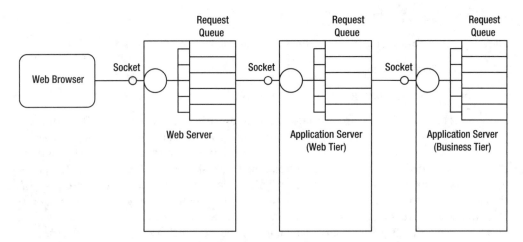

Figure 6-1. *Common path an application request follows through a Java EE stack*

As shown in Figure 6-1, requests travel across the technology stack through request queues. When a browser submits a Web request to a Web server, the Web server receives it through a listening socket and quickly moves the request into a request queue, as only one thread can listen on a single port at any given point in time. When that thread receives the request, its primary responsibility is to return to its port and receive the next connection. If it processed requests serially, then the Web server would be capable of processing only one request at a time—not very impressive. A Web server's listening process would look something like the following:

```
public class WebServer extends Thread {
...
 public void run() {
   ServerSocket  serverSocket = new ServerSocket( 80 );
   while( running ) {
     Socket s = serverSocket.accept();
     Request req = new Request( s );
     addRequestToQueue( req );
   }
 }
}
```

While this is a very simplistic example, it demonstrates that the thread loop is very tight and acts simply as a pass-through to another thread. Each queue has an associated thread pool that waits for requests to be added to the queue to process them. When a request is added to the queue, a thread wakes up, removes the request from the queue, and processes it, for example:

```
public synchronized void addRequestToQueue( Request req ) {
   this.requests.add( req );
   this.requests.notifyAll();
}
```

Threads waiting on the request's object are notified, and the first one there accepts the request for processing. The actions of the thread are dependent on the request (or in the case of separation of business tiers, the request may actually be a remote method invocation). Consider a Web request against an application server. If the Web server and application are separated, then the Web server forwards the request to the application server and the same process repeats. Once the request is in the application server, then the application server needs to determine the appropriate resource to invoke. In this example, it is going to be either a servlet or a JSP file. For the purpose of this discussion, we will consider JSP files to be servlets.

■**Note** JSP files are convenient to build because in simple implementations you are not required to create a web.xml file containing <servlet> and <servlet-mapping> entries. But in the end, a JSP file will become a servlet. The JSP file itself is translated into an associated .java servlet file, compiled into a .class file, and then loaded into memory to service a request. If you have ever wondered why a JSP file took so much time to respond the first time, it is because it needs to be translated and compiled prior to being loaded into memory. You do have the option to precompile JSP files, which buys you the ease of development of a JSP file and the general performance of a servlet.

The running thread loads the appropriate servlet into memory and invokes its service() method. This starts the Java EE application request processing as we tend to think of it. Depending on your use of Java EE components, your next step may be to create a stateless session bean to implement your application's transactional business logic. Rather than your having to create a new stateless session bean for each request, they are pooled; your servlet obtains one from the pool, uses it, and then returns it to the pool. If all of the beans in the pool are in use, then the processing thread must wait for a bean to be returned to the pool.

Most business objects make use of persistent storage, in the form of either a database or a legacy system. It is expensive for a Java application to make a query across a network to persistent storage, so for certain types of objects, the persistence manager implements a cache of frequently accessed objects. The cache is queried, and if the requested object is not found, then the object must be loaded from persistent storage. While caches can provide performance an order of magnitude better than resolving all queries to persistent storage, there is danger in misusing them. Specifically, if a cache is sized too small, then the majority of requests will resolve to querying persistent storage, but we added the overhead of checking the cache for the requested object, selecting an object to be removed from the cache to make room for the new one (typically using a least-recently used algorithm), and adding the new object to the cache. In this case, querying persistent storage would perform much better. The final trade-off is that a large cache requires storage space; if you need to maintain too many objects in a cache to avoid *thrashing* (that is, rapidly adding and removing objects to and from the cache), then you really need to question whether the object should be cached in the first point.

Establishing a connection to persistent storage is an expensive operation. For example, establishing a database connection can take between a half a second and a second and a half on average. Because you do not want your pending request to absorb this overhead on each request, application servers establish these connections on start-up and maintain them in connection pools. When a request needs to query persistent storage, it obtains a connection from the connection pool, uses it, and then returns it to the connection pool. If no connection is available, then the request waits for a connection to be returned to the pool.

Once the request has finished processing its business logic, it needs to be forwarded to a presentation layer before returning to the caller. The most typical presentation layer implementation is to use JavaServer Pages (JSP). As previously mentioned, using JSP can incur the additional overhead of translation to servlet code and compilation, if the JSPs are not precompiled. This up-front performance hit can impact your users and should be addressed, but from a pure tuning perspective, JSP compilation does not impact the *order of magnitude* of the application performance: the impact is observed once, but there is no further impact as the number of users increases.

Observing the scenario we have been discussing, we can identify the following wait points:

- Web server thread pool

- Application server or tier thread pool

- Stateless session bean or business object pool

- Cache management code

- Persistent storage or external dependency connection pool

You can feel free to add to or subtract from this list to satisfy the architecture of your application, but it is a good general framework to start with.

Tuning Backward

The order of wait points is as important as what they are waiting on. IBM's notion of sustaining waiting requests as close to the Web server as possible has been proven to be a highly effective tuning strategy. It is better to queue requests in a business logic–lite tier so as to minimize the impact on the business tier. Furthermore, if the request has already sequestered a Web server thread and it is not ready for processing, then why should we sequester an application server thread and database connection as well? If we do, then we'll add additional burden upon the business tier, and the pending request will not get processed faster anyway.

The approach of forcing requests to wait at the appropriate application point is to open all wait points until the one at the end of the tube saturates. Scale down the saturated resource until it no longer saturates—this is its capacity. For example, if an application server instance can service only 50 database requests per second, then you want to send through only enough requests to generate at most 50 database requests per second; any more requests will simply queue up at the database.

Now that the limiting wait point is identified, tune the application backward by tightening down each wait point to facilitate only the capacity of the limiting wait point. Continue with this exercise until you reach the Web server request queue. If your load is significantly more than the capacity of your limiting wait point, then you might want to configure your Web server to redirect to a "Try your request again later" page.

CASE STUDY: DEPARTMENT OF EDUCATION

I visited the Department of Education for a specific state under the following situation. Once per year the governor of that state announces that school report cards are in and urges parents to log on to the state government's Web site to see how their child's school compared to the rest of the schools in the county and state. The site's traffic patterns are unique: three days per year the load is close to that of Yahoo!, and the rest of the year the site sits virtually idle. My role was to determine the capacity of the application and environment to determine the appropriate cutoff values to set. The customer and I performed an abbreviated version of the tuning exercise described in this section to meet the state's deadline, but in the end it was highly successful.

The point of this story is that once you understand the capabilities of your environment, your Web server can throttle your load to push through only the amount of load you can support. You would rather ask someone to try again later than allow all of your users to suffer, right?

JVM Heap

Although we will discuss heap garbage collection in depth in the next chapter, it is worth noting here that it's probably the biggest wait point in any untuned Java EE environment. The application server and all of its applications run inside of the JVM heap. The Java memory model is such that unreachable objects are eligible to be discarded by a garbage collection process. Garbage collection can run in one of two modes: minor or major. *Minor* collections run relatively quickly and inexpensively, whereas *major* collections typically freeze all code running in the JVM. Furthermore, while minor collections run quickly (usually under a tenth of a second), major collections can take much longer (I have seen some take up to ten seconds to run).

Because all application requests run inside a JVM and are subject to a garbage collection process, your tuning efforts may be fruitless with an untuned heap. In my opinion, tuning memory can have the biggest impact of any tuning effort you perform.

Wait-Based Tuning Conclusions

Rather than focus on performance ratios that infer the health of an application, your tuning efforts should be focused on the application itself. The process is defined as follows:

1. Walk through the application architecture and identify the points where a request could potentially wait.

2. Open all wait points.

3. Generate balanced and representative load against the environment.

4. Identify the limiting wait point's saturation point.

5. Tighten all wait points to facilitate only the maximum load of the limiting wait point.

6. Force all pending requests to wait at the Web server.

7. If the load is too high, then establish a cutoff point where you redirect incoming requests to a "Try your request again later" page. Otherwise, add more resources.

I have effectively implemented this type of tuning exercise at customer sites, and the results have far surpassed my previous efforts of maximizing performance ratios. It is a more difficult and time-consuming exercise, but the results are superior and worth it.

Tuning Example

Tuning a Java EE environment is a difficult exercise to convey in print, but I'll try to illustrate the general process this section by describing the environment I'm tuning at each stage:

*   The state of relevant performance metrics (wait points)

*   The state of heap garbage collections

*   CPU utilization of relevant servers

Figure 6-2 shows a typical medium-sized production environment. The environment consists of two Apache Web servers configured to distribute load across four WebLogic servers running on two separate physical machines and communicating with two clustered Oracle instances.

The environment shown in Figure 6-2 represents the minimum requirements for a high-availability topology: two Web servers (in case one crashes), two physical WebLogic machines, and two databases. In Chapter 8, we'll delve deeper into the benefits of running multiple JVMs on the same physical machine, but for now it suffices to say that doing so can improve performance and resource utilization. The projected utilization for this environment is 2,000 simultaneous users.

Table 6-1 describes the initial configuration for this environment.

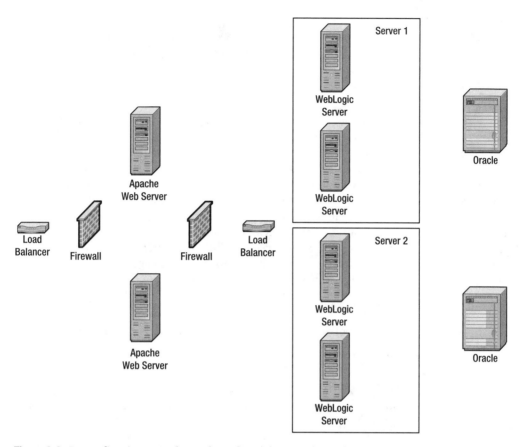

Figure 6-2. *By configuring two physical machines for each logical enterprise tier (Web tier, business/application tier, and database tier), high availability can be more easily attained.*

Table 6-1. *Initial Configuration of the Example Tuning Environment*

Metric	Value
Web server threads	150
Web server CPUs	2
Web server memory	4GB total memory
Application server threads	50
Application server database connections	30
Application server entity bean cache size	500
Application server heap	1GB
Application server CPUs	2
Application server memory	4GB
Database CPUs	2
Database memory	4GB

> ■**Note** Each of the values in Table 6-1 is defined for each physical machine. For example, two Web server CPUs means that there are two CPUs per Web server. Figure 6-2 shows two physical Web servers, so four total CPUs are dedicated to the two Web server instances.

The application is an MVC architecture utilizing stateless session beans for business processes and a small set of entity beans for transactional persistence and caching.

I configured my homegrown load tester to climb up to 1,000 users over 20 minutes and then added 50 additional users every 5 minutes. Graduating this load ensures I'm able to identify resource bottlenecks as they occur—increasing the load too rapidly may saturate the environment and mask the true nature of performance problems.

In addition to configuring the environment and the load tester, we can install monitoring software on the operating system of each machine, performance monitoring software on the application server, and tag-and-follow code instrumentation that traces requests from the HTTP server to the application server and finally records the length of calls to the database. We're looking for the following key items here:

- Thread pool utilization and pending requests for each thread pool

- Database connection pool utilization and requests waiting for a connection

- Entity bean caches

- Stateless session bean pools

- Application bottlenecks (to determine if there is anything I can tune in the environment to allow more application throughput)

The sections that follow analyze the testing iterations.

Iteration #1

The first iteration climbed up to 1,200 users before grossly exceeding its SLAs. Table 6-2 lists the observed performance metrics of the sample environment for the first iteration of wait-based performance tuning.

Table 6-2. *Performance of the Sample Environment for Iteration #1*

Metric	Value
Database CPUs	40 percent utilization
Application server CPUs	20 percent utilization
Database connection pool	100 percent utilization
Threads waiting for a connection	10 pending threads
Application server threads	100 percent utilization
Application server pending requests	20 pending requests
Entity bean cache hit ratio	40 percent
Web server thread utilization	50 percent

In this configuration, the Web server is sending significant load to the application server, to the point where the application server uses all of its threads and causes 20 requests to wait. If we look a little deeper, we see that the application server database connection pools are at 100 percent utilization and ten threads are waiting for a database connection; the database connection pool is maxed out and this is what is causing requests to wait.

The next question we need to ask is, Is this the capacity of the database (meaning that we should harden our application servers to limit database load and push pending requests back to the Web server), or does our database have more capacity? In this case, the database CPU is only at 40 percent and can support additional load. Therefore, let's increase the database connection pool size to force more load into the database.

The entity bean cache hit ratio is only 50 percent, meaning that half of our calls to entity beans require a database query. If we can increase this hit ratio (by increasing the size of the cache to service more requests from memory), then we will take additional burden off of the database.

Finally, to validate the effect of these metrics on our application, the tag-and-follow code instrumentation reported two primary wait points in most service requests:

- Application server internal Web server (for example, HTTP GET /…)

- JDBC call to getConnection()

When requests wait at the application server's internal Web server, or in other words, when there's a significant amount of time between when the application server receives the request and when it invokes the appropriate servlet, then the application server is waiting for an execution thread to process the request. If calls to getConnection() take an excessively long time, the request asked the database connection pool for a connection, but all connections were in use, hence it had to wait for a connection to be returned to the pool.

From this analysis, we implement the changes shown in Table 6-3 and test again.

Table 6-3. *New Configuration for the Sample Environment for Iteration #1*

Metric	Value
Database connection pool	60
Application server thread pool	100
Entity bean cache size	1000

The additional database connections should push more load to the database, the increase in application server threads should drive even more load to the database, and the change to the entity bean cache should reduce the number of database calls. Together, these changes should increase the utilization of the application server and database, and hence increase the throughput of the application.

Iteration #2

In the second iteration, the load climbed to 1,800 users before exceeding its SLAs. Table 6-4 lists the observed performance metrics for the second iteration of wait-based performance tuning.

Table 6-4. *Performance of the Sample Environment for Iteration #2*

Metric	Value
Database CPUs	70 percent utilization
Application server CPUs	50 percent utilization
Database connection pool	100 percent utilization
Threads waiting for a connection	10 pending threads
Application server threads	100 percent utilization
Application server pending requests	20 pending requests
Entity bean cache hit ratio	80 percent
Web server thread utilization	75 percent

In this configuration, the Web server continues to send significant load to the application server, and the application server again uses all of its threads and causes ten requests to wait. Looking at the database connection pools, we see that the application server database connection pools are at 100 percent utilization and ten threads are waiting for a database connection.

The database CPU utilization is now up to 70 percent utilization, so there is still some additional capacity we can force out of it. Therefore, let's increase the database connection pool size to force more load into the database.

The entity bean cache hit ratio is at 80 percent, meaning that the majority of calls to entity beans do not require a database query. This is an adequate hit ratio; we may try to increase it later, but it is fine for initial tuning efforts.

The tag-and-follow code instrumentation reported the same two wait points in most service requests:

- Application server internal Web server

- JDBC call to getConnection()

From this analysis, we implement the changes shown in Table 6-5 and test again.

Table 6-5. *New Configuration for the Sample Environment for Iteration #2*

Metric	Value
Database connection pool	90
Application server thread pool	120

The additional database connections should push even more load to the database, and the increase in application server threads should drive more load through the application to the database. Our hope is to increase the utilization of both the database and application server.

Iteration #3

In the third iteration, the load climbed to 2,200 users before exceeding its SLAs, and then performance degraded substantially. Table 6-6 lists the observed performance metrics for the third iteration of wait-based performance tuning.

Table 6-6. *Performance of the Sample Environment for Iteration #3*

Metric	Value
Database CPUs	95 percent utilization
Application server CPUs	40 percent utilization
Database connection pool	100 percent utilization
Threads waiting for a connection	20 pending threads
Application server threads	100 percent utilization
Application server pending requests	40 pending requests
Entity bean cache hit ratio	80 percent
Web server thread utilization	85 percent

In this configuration, the Web server continues to send significant load to the application server, and the application server again uses all of its threads and causes 40 requests to wait. Looking at the database connection pools, we see that the application server database connection pools are at 100 percent utilization and 20 threads are waiting for a database connection.

The database CPU utilization is now up to 95 percent, so it has become saturated and cannot effectively process requests. Therefore, let's decrease the database connection pool size to try to bring the CPU utilization down; at 95 percent utilization, all queries are slow.

The entity bean cache hit ratio stayed around 80 percent, meaning that the majority of calls to entity beans do not require a database query.

The tag-and-follow code instrumentation reported the same two wait points in most service requests:

- Application server internal Web server

- JDBC call to getConnection()

From this analysis, we implement the changes shown in Table 6-7 and test again.

Table 6-7. *New Configuration for the Sample Environment for Iteration #3*

Metric	Value
Database connection pool	75
Application server thread pool	100

The decrease in database connections should reduce the stress on the database (allowing for better throughput), and the decrease in application server threads should reduce the number of threads waiting for a database connection.

Iteration #4

In the fourth iteration, the load climbed to 2,200 users before exceeding its SLAs, and then performance degraded gradually. Table 6-8 lists the observed performance metrics for the fourth iteration of wait-based performance tuning.

Table 6-8. *Performance of the Sample Environment for Iteration #4*

Metric	Value
Database CPUs	85 percent utilization
Application server CPUs	80 percent utilization
Database connection pool	100 percent utilization
Threads waiting for a connection	5 pending threads
Application server threads	100 percent utilization
Application server pending requests	10 pending requests
Entity bean cache hit ratio	80 percent
Web server thread utilization	85 percent

In this configuration, the Web server continues to send significant load to the application server, and the application server again uses all of its threads and causes ten requests to wait. Looking at the database connection pools, we see that the application server database connection pools are at 100 percent utilization and five threads are waiting for a database connection.

The database CPU utilization is now at 85 percent, which is optimal—the database can efficiently satisfy its requests and at the same time is neither underutilized nor overutilized.

The entity bean cache hit ratio stayed around 80 percent, meaning that the majority of calls to entity beans do not require a database query.

Because we have found the capacity of the database to service the application, it is time to harden the application server thread pools to stop threads from waiting for database connections and then reduce the Web server threads to hold requests at the Web server.

From this analysis, we implement the changes shown in Table 6-9 and test again.

Table 6-9. *New Configuration for the Sample Environment for Iteration #4*

Metric	Value
Web server threads	125
Application server thread pool	90

We hope that decreasing the number of application server threads will allow for the highest application throughput, but reduce the number of threads waiting for database connections. Furthermore, by reducing the number of Web server threads that handle application server requests, we hope to throttle the load at the Web server and avoid application server saturation.

Iteration #5

In the fifth iteration, the load climbed to 2,200 users before exceeding its SLAs, and then performance degraded gradually. Table 6-10 lists the observed performance metrics for the fifth iteration of wait-based performance tuning.

Table 6-10. *Performance of the Sample Environment for Iteration #5*

Metric	Value
Database CPUs	85 percent utilization
Application server CPUs	85 percent utilization
Database connection pool	95 percent utilization
Threads waiting for a connection	0 pending threads
Application server threads	90 percent utilization
Application server pending requests	0 pending requests
Entity bean cache hit ratio	80 percent
Web server thread utilization	85 percent

The environment looks beautiful under this configuration:

- The database CPU is running at 85 percent utilization, which is optimal when the application is under stress.

- The application server CPU is at 85 percent utilization, with 90 percent of its threads in use, indicating it is well utilized and not oversaturated.

- Database connection pool utilization is at 95 percent, with no pending threads, which means we are sending enough threads into the application server to properly utilize the database, but not enough to cause threads to wait.

- The Web server thread utilization is good—well used yet not oversaturated.

Although we did not perform a formal capacity assessment, we can see from this exercise that the approximate capacity of our application running in this environment is 2,200 users. If we need to support additional load, we either add additional hardware or tune the application, the database, or the database queries. Simple changes to the application to reduce database calls can have significant impact on the capacity of the application. For example, if we can reduce the number of queries that a single request spawns from ten to five, then the database's capacity to support the application increases substantially. The load capacity is not necessarily reflective of the performance of the database; rather, it's reflective of the ability of the database to service the application. If the application abuses the database, then performance will suffer.

Application Bottlenecks

At a high level, enterprise Java performance problems can occur in one of four categories:

- Application code

- Platform

- External dependency

- Load

A performance problem can occur inside of application code as the result of slow-running algorithms, memory utilization, or simply the response of the application to increased load or changes to usage patterns. For example, code may run well under low load and a controlled set of data, but when the load increases or the quantity of data increases substantially, then performance problems may manifest. As we saw in the last chapter, using bubble sort to sort 100 objects functions well, but when subjected to 5,000 objects, bubble sort falls apart. This is an application code issue, but it manifests itself only under load.

The platform includes the entire technology stack upon which your Java application runs: the application server, JVM, operating system, hardware, and network. The bottom line is that numerous performance tuning parameters across the technology stack can dramatically affect the performance of your application.

A Java EE application would be fairly useless if it did not interact with some kind of external dependency. External dependencies include databases, legacy systems, and any other system that your application interacts with, such as Web services or proprietary servers. Each external dependency has a communication mechanism (usually a connection pool) that if not configured properly can cause serious performance problems.

When application code is tuned, the platform is properly configured, the external services are running optimally, but the environment is not responding acceptably, then the application business logic simply cannot support the given load. Each Java EE environment has a capacity that it can support before becoming saturated. At this point, the only solution is to add additional hardware resources or restructure the environment. For example, a single Linux box running JBoss has a finite load that it can support, and if it is subjected to more load, then it will undoubtedly fail.

The key to properly diagnosing application bottlenecks is to first triage the performance problem to determine whether the root cause is the application code, platform, external dependency behavior, or load. You accomplish this by implementing a depth of monitoring technologies across your entire application environment, including Web servers, application servers, the database, external dependencies, operating systems, firewalls, load balancers, and network communication pathways. If you can isolate the problem to application code, then the common problems can be categorized as one of the following:

- Poor algorithms

- Memory utilization or object life cycles

- Programmatic contention

Poor algorithms manifest themselves through slow-running methods. The best way to find slow-running methods is by implementing a tag-and-follow monitoring solution. The analysis of an application running with this level of monitoring identifies slow-running service requests, which can be expanded down to the method level to identify offending methods. You are looking for a slow-running method in the call path that is not waiting for any resource (a thread, a database connection, and so on), is not executing a database query, and does not make an external call to another server. In other words, you want to identify methods that are actually using the application server CPU for an inordinate amount of time, as illustrated by Figure 6-3.

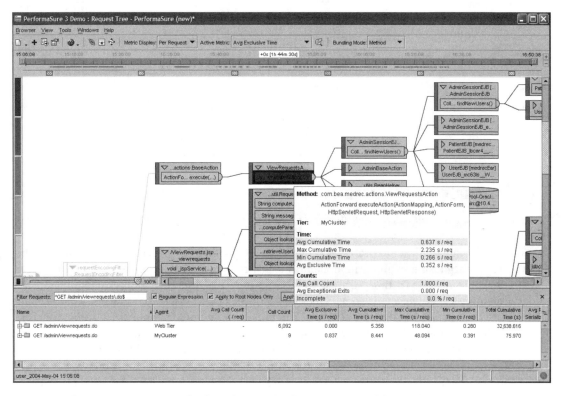

Figure 6-3. *The executeAction() method is taking a significant amount of the total processing time for the GET /admin/viewrequests.do service request.*

After slow-running service requests have been identified and it's determined that the root cause is a slow-running method, the resolution plan is to replay the service request inside of a code profiler that will identify the line or lines of code contributing most to the problem. If the performance of the method is unacceptable, then the code needs to be refactored and tuned for better performance. For example, Figure 6-4 shows the code for the bubble sort algorithm running inside of a code profiler, revealing that the poor performance relates to the sheer number of comparison calls (it is making nearly 12.5 million object comparisons).

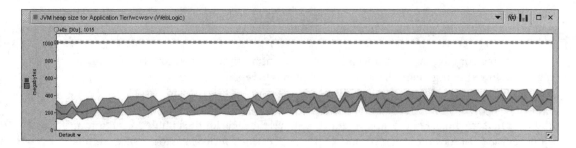

Line #	Number of Calls	Method Time	Cumulative Time	Source
5				public static void bubbleSort(Comparable[] a)
6				{
7	1	0 (0.0%)	3 (0.0%)	System.out.println("Bubble Sort");
8				//SortingUtils.dump(a);
9				int i, j;
10	1	0 (0.0%)	0 (0.0%)	Comparable tmp=null;
11	5,001	8 (0.0%)	8 (0.0%)	for(i = (a.length - 1); i >= 0; i--)
12				{
13	12,502,500	20,156 (28.8%)	20,156 (25.1%)	for(j = 1; j <= i; j++)
14				{
15	12,497,500	25,873 (36.9%)	36,277 (45.1%)	if(a[j-1].compareTo(a[j]) > 0)
16				{
17	6,222,805	7,889 (11.3%)	7,889 (9.8%)	tmp = a[j-1];
18	6,222,805	8,095 (11.6%)	8,095 (10.1%)	a[j-1] = a[j];
19	6,222,805	8,027 (11.5%)	8,027 (10.0%)	a[j] = tmp;
20				}
21				//SortingUtils.dump(a);
22				}
23				}
24	1	0 (0.0%)	0 (0.0%)	}
25				
26				public static void selectionSort(Comparable[] a)
27				{
28	1	0 (0.0%)	0 (0.0%)	System.out.println("Selection Sort");
29				//SortingUtils.dump(a);
30				int i, j;
31				int min;
32	1	0 (0.0%)	0 (0.0%)	Comparable tmp=null;
33	5,000	8 (0.0%)	8 (0.0%)	for(i = 0; i < a.length-1; i++)
34				{
35	4,999	6 (0.0%)	6 (0.0%)	min = i;
36	12,502,499	19,845 (43.1%)	19,845 (35.2%)	for(j = i+1; j < a.length; j++)
37				{

Figure 6-4. *Poor algorithms can be identified by running suspect application code inside a code profiler.*

Memory utilization problems can be difficult to identify, especially if they are subtle. The key to diagnosing an application memory leak is to observe the performance of the heap over a significant period of time, such as several hours to several days depending on how apparent the memory leak is. Objects will be created and destroyed in the heap as a natural result of a running application, but the key indicator that differentiates a potential memory leak from normal behavior is the *valleys* in the heap. If the values of the valleys consistently increase, then there is a portion of memory that the garbage collector is not able to reclaim, which indicates a potential memory leak. Figure 6-5 displays a sample heap exhibiting a potential slow memory leak.

Figure 6-5. *Over time in a heap with a slow memory leak, the number of valleys increases.*

Only by observing the pattern of increasing heap valleys can you discern that you have a memory leak. Eventually this behavior will lead to an application server crash, or if the leak is inside a session object, the garbage collector may be able to reclaim memory before a crash.

Once you have detected a potential memory leak, the next step is to tie back memory utilization to service requests and determine what service request(s) is leaking memory. Without a clear indication of what service requests are leaving additional objects in the heap after they complete, tracking down a memory leak is a nearly insurmountable task because the only way to identify the root cause of a memory leak is to replay each service request inside a memory profiler and manually look at objects left in the heap. Then, with your business domain expertise, you can assess whether these objects do in fact need to be in memory or if they are causing the leak. Without narrowing down memory leaks to a subset of service requests, you are forced to manually examine each service request in your entire application inside a memory profiler. And then, if the memory leak is subtle, you may still miss it. Depending on the size of your application, this task could be impossible.

The two most common culprits of leaking memory are objects for which a reference is inadvertently left inside a collection class and the amount of data stored in HTTP session objects. To avoid these problems, always explicitly remove an object from a collection class rather than nullifying your local reference to it and examine the life cycles of each object stored in your sessions—in other words, properly manage object life cycles. It is also advisable to try to define discrete units of work within the context of a single method, because when the method exits, all method-level variables will be eligible to be reclaimed by the garbage collector.

The final issue that commonly affects application code performance is programmatic contention. Under low load, contention and synchronization are not issues, but as load increases, minor problems can become major problems. If 2,000 users are frequently accessing your application, then it is only a matter of time before thread deadlock or request time-outs occur.

The following steps summarize the process of diagnosing code issues:

1. Triage the problem to determine whether the issue is in the application, platform, or external dependency. Your monitoring tool needs to provide deep monitoring across a breadth of technologies.

2. Through tag-and-follow code instrumentation, identify slow-running service requests and determine if they are slow as a result of an application server resource (a wait point) or a slow-running method. Similarly, if you are detecting memory leaks, identify the offending service requests.

3. Replay offending service requests inside a profiler (code profiler or memory profiler) and find the problematic code.

4. Refactor the code.

Identifying and resolving application bottlenecks is not difficult if you have the appropriate set of monitoring tools to help you pinpoint the problem. Without these tools, you are diagnosing blindly and your chances of success are limited.

Summary

To implement a formal performance tuning methodology, you need to do the following:

- Get to know your users. Discern their usage patterns through either an end-user experience monitor or an access log analyzer.

- Build test scripts that mimic end-user patterns.

- Identify potential wait points in your application technology stack, open all wait points to force load to the limiting resources, and then harden each wait point to allow only enough traffic to effectively use the weakest limiting resource.

- Identify application code issues through tag-and-follow code instrumentation, replay offending requests inside a code or memory profiler, and refactor poorly performing code.

In this chapter, we focused on setting up a proper testing environment and explored the concept of wait-based tuning. In the next chapter, we'll examine tuning the application server engine itself, regardless of the architecture of the applications running in them. We'll look at the infrastructure that each application server must provide in order to satisfy the Java EE 5 specification and how to best tune each.

CHAPTER 7

■ ■ ■

Tuning an Application Server

"Okay, I get it. We tune based on wait points, but it sounds like a long process. What I'm looking for is some low-hanging fruit. Are there a handful of things I can tune to quickly realize some real benefits right now?" John was not the most patient man, and with his CEO breathing down his neck, he did not have time to waste.

I let a small smile escape my lips as I listened to John's query. "Yes, there are a few things you can do that almost always improve performance. Let me share a story with you. I was called out by a customer to troubleshoot an application server that was crashing every two days. I spoke with the customer and learned that aside from the crash, they were experiencing less-than-optimal performance. I asked a couple questions about their configuration and noticed some things about their heap. I gave them some generic settings that I like to use as good 'best practice' starting points for memory tuning, and then I dove into troubleshooting their crashes. A couple of days later, we found the cause of their crashes, but the customer pulled me aside and told me that he noticed three different things about their environment since I made the memory changes:

- They were playing synthetic transactions against their application and alerting on slow requests: while they usually received half a dozen alerts per day, now the alerts had completely gone away.

- They had been experiencing CPU spikes on their application server machines several times a day, and those were completely gone.

- Their users had actually called to tell them that the performance was noticeably better."

"All of that from some generic heap settings?" John asked with a perplexed yet excited look.

"You got it. It is my supposition that there are four primary things you can tune to get within 80 percent of the optimal performance of almost any enterprise Java environment. The remaining 20 percent is fine-tuning that you want to address, but within an hour I can get you the 80 percent."

"Preach on, brother, I want to hear this stuff!"

Tuning individual application servers differs from vendor to vendor, but supporting the Java EE 5 specification requires basic continuity across vendors. Equipped with the knowledge of what an application server is required to do, I assert that you can effectively tune an application server to within 80 percent of its optimal performance by configuring these core services. The remaining 20 percent of application server fine-tuning represents vendor-specific optimizations on top of its standards implementation. In this chapter, we analyze the core infrastructure of an application server and discuss best practices for tuning configurations and evaluations.

Application Server Requirements

Before looking at the services that an application server must provide, let's take a step back and review the core architecture of an application server's infrastructure. Following a client request through an application server is the best way to visualize it.

As Figure 7-1 illustrates, an application server must listen on a socket for incoming requests. When a request is received, it accepts the request and places it into a request queue for processing. The application server then returns to its socket to listen for more requests. This very tight loop runs until the application server is terminated: receive a request, place it in a request queue, receive the next request, and so on.

The queue that the request is placed in may differ from vendor to vendor; common queue allocations are by request type (for example, Web requests, Simple Object Access Protocol [SOAP] requests, Remote Method Invocation [RMI] requests) or configurable by application functionality. Regardless of the implementation, each queue has an associated thread pool that removes the request from the queue to processes it. The size of this thread pool places an upper limit on the number of simultaneous actions that the application server can perform and represents one of the core tuning metrics we will consider.

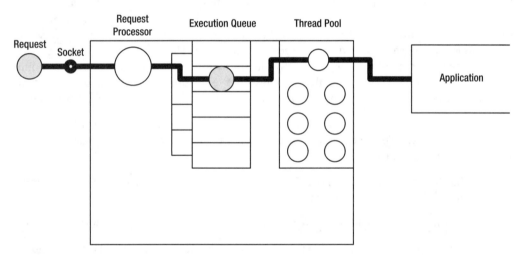

Figure 7-1. *The execution path of a request*

In a Web-based application, the thread first determines the servlet that should handle this request. If the servlet is in memory, it passes the request information to its service() method; if it is not in memory, then it loads the servlet, initializes it, and passes the request to it. The servlet then executes the application and business logic, which in a formal Java EE application might resolve to a call to a stateless session bean (which implements business processes). In order to gain access to a stateless session bean, the servlet must query the application server's Java Naming and Directory Interface (JNDI) registry to locate the bean and request an instance from its stateless session bean pool. If a bean is available, a bean instance is returned immediately; otherwise, the servlet waits until a bean is available.

Stateless session beans are designed to implement business processes and interface with a persistent object model. Many other objects in the persistent object model are cached for efficiency: if objects will be reused on subsequent requests, then serving them from memory is faster than making a round-trip to a database or mainframe. These objects cannot be pooled like stateless session beans, because they represent specific object data. For example, if you request a specific person, a different person will not suffice—you need that requested person and only that person.

This introduces a caching infrastructure with a specific memory footprint and capacity. The purpose of introducing an upper capacity is to eliminate the need to load your entire database into memory, but rather keep active data in memory and cycle items through your cache to best service your requests. If the stateless session bean requests an object that is in the cache, then that object is immediately returned to it, but if it is not, then an existing object needs to be selected and removed from the cache. The new object can then be loaded from persistent storage, inserted into the cache, and a reference to it returned to the stateless session bean.

The data object is loaded from persistent storage through some type of connection, either a JDBC connection, when talking to a database; a JCA connection, when talking to an external system; or a synchronous JMS conversation, when talking to most mainframes. Each of these connections is expensive to open, so application servers create a pool of them on start-up. The pool can be configured to grow and shrink as necessary, but always within a hard upper limit. This upper limit controls the maximum number of simultaneous requests that can interact with persistent storage. This limit is another key tuning metric.

When the stateless session bean has completed its interaction with its data objects, the results of its business processes are returned to the servlet that invoked it (through whatever infrastructure is in place). The servlet then places these results into an HTTP request and forwards the request to the appropriate JSP for presentation. The JSP extracts the results and builds the resultant HTML document to return to the client.

The scenario just described has nearly limitless variations, but the key things to identify follow:

- A thread pool contains threads that service requests.

- A caching infrastructure supports data objects to reduce network and database traffic.

- A connection pool provides connections to persistent storage and external dependencies.

Each of these pieces provides an opportunity for a request to wait: it can be waiting for a thread to process it for an object to be returned to the cache or for cache management overhead, or for a connection to persistent storage. The theory of wait-based tuning, which we explored in the last chapter, is to discover all places in your application where a request can wait and either eliminate the waiting (if possible) or control where a request waits.

All of this request processing infrastructure runs inside of a JVM. The JVM is incredible technology, because it allows us to write generic code and deploy it to any operating system and hardware infrastructure for which a JVM has been built. One of the most revolutionary concepts that JVMs introduced was JVM-managed memory. Because memory architectures differ across operating systems and hardware platforms, Java architects and developers needed an abstraction to underlying memory, but we derived, as an additional benefit, the introduction of the garbage collector. Regardless of implementation, the core tenet of garbage collection is that the JVM maintains a process that periodically gathers unreachable objects and frees the memory that they are occupying. An *unreachable object* is an object that no reachable object has a reference to; for example, if you create an Integer and then set your reference to it to null, then that Integer becomes unreachable and eligible for garbage collection.

Garbage collection runs in one of two modes, depending on what it is trying to accomplish: minor and major. *Minor collections* run quickly and do not cause the JVM to stop processing its threads, whereas *major collections* run slowly and do stop the JVM from processing its threads. A major garbage collection is sometimes referred to as a *stop-the-world collection*. If your JVM frequently runs major garbage collections, then how well your application and application server are tuned matters little, because the JVM is frozen during the garbage collection.

Tuning the JVM heap can yield the most dramatic performance improvements of any of your tuning efforts, which is why the customer mentioned at the start of this chapter was taken aback by the improvements resulting from a simple 20-minute conversation.

Biggest Bang: Quickly Grabbing the 80 Percent

Application servers are complicated pieces of software with a considerable number of moving parts. By repeatedly tuning application servers by all application server vendors, I have gained insight into where tuning efforts are best spent. This section explains the techniques I have employed to provide the biggest bang for my tuning efforts. Depending on the nature of your application, your mileage may vary; for example, this section will better benefit an e-commerce store than an application heavily dependent on messaging, but these recommendations are valid generally.

Tuning the JVM Heap

Each JVM vendor has a different memory management implementation and garbage collection strategy, which have benefits and drawbacks. Before delving into specific JVM implementations, looking first at the role of garbage collection, as well as the nature of memory leaks, is beneficial.

The JVM views objects in the heap in one of two states: reachable or unreachable. This determination is made by performing a *reachability test*. The reachability test begins by examining a set of objects known as the *root set*. The root set is a dynamically growing and shrinking set of objects that fall into one of two categories:

- Static objects

- Objects directly created by all running threads

Static objects are created as the created classes are loaded into the JVM and exist in the heap outside the context of any individual thread. Running threads create objects as they invoke methods, create method local variables, and so forth. To simply illustrate the dynamic nature of the root set, Listing 7-1 shows the source code for a single-threaded Java SE application.

Listing 7-1. *Examining the Root Set Contents of the MyClass Application During Execution*

```
01: public class MyClass {
02:   public static final Integer n = new Integer( 10 );
03:     public Integer square( Integer i ) {
04:         int result = i.intValue() * i.intValue();
05:         return new Integer( result );
06:   }
07:   public static void main( String[] args ) {
```

```
08:   MyClass m = new MyClass();
09:    Integer i = new Integer( args[ 0 ] );
10:    i = m.square( i );
11:  }
12:}
```

Processing begins when a thread is created, and the JVM asks it to execute the MyClass.main() method. Before invoking line 8, the static variable n is created and added to the root set. When the main() method is executed, the args String array is added to the root set. After line 8 is executed, the root set contains n, args, and m, and line 9 adds i.

Line 8 invokes m's square() method, moving the processing thread to line 3. When i is passed into the square() method, it is already in the root set and hence not added, but internally it now has a reference count of two: it is referenced by the main() method as well as the compute() method. Line 4 adds result to the root set, and then as soon as the compute() method returns, it is promptly removed from the root set. An interesting note about line 5 is that it creates a new anonymous Integer object which is added to the root set inside line 5 and removed as the method completes. On line 10, i is assigned to the new Integer; it is worth noting that the thread just orphaned the previous Integer that i pointed to, decreasing its reference count to zero and making that memory eligible for garbage collection.

When line 11 is executed and the main() method completes, i, m, and args are all removed from the root set, leaving only n in memory. As long as the class is in memory, n stays in memory, which in this case corresponds to the end of the application processing on line 12. Table 7-1 shows the contents of the root set for each line of code as the application is processed.

Table 7-1. *Root Set Contents for Each Line of Code in the MyClass Example*

Line	Root Set Contents
1	Empty
2	n
7	n, args
8	n, args, m
9	n, args, m, i
3	n, args, m, i
4	n, args, m, i, results
5	n, args, m, i, results, anonymous Integer
10	n, args, m, i
11	n
12	n

When garbage collection runs, it performs the reachability test by starting at each object in the root set and finding all objects that the root set objects can see. Then it finds all objects that those objects can see, and so on. For each object that the garbage collector finds, it *marks* the object, which in most cases means setting a bit on the memory occupied by that object. After it has exhausted its root set and found all objects in the heap that are reachable, it *sweeps* the memory. In this process, it walks through the heap memory and deallocates the memory for all objects that are not marked. This deallocation leaves the heap fragmented, so this process is usually followed by a *compaction* of the heap to attempt to free contiguous memory blocks. In general this process is referred to as *mark and sweep* or sometimes *mark-sweep-compact*.

A traditional C++ memory leak occurs when memory is allocated and dereferenced before it is deallocated. Java eliminates this type of memory leak by executing the reachability test, as illustrated in Figure 7-2.

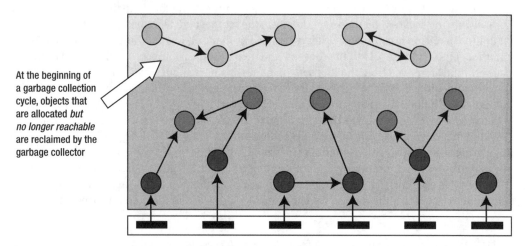

At the beginning of a garbage collection cycle, objects that are allocated *but no longer reachable* are reclaimed by the garbage collector

Figure 7-2. *The Java garbage collector eliminates C++-style memory leaks by performing a reachability test.*

Starting from the root set, the reachability test classifies objects into one of two categories: reachable and unreachable. But there is a significant amount of talk about Java memory leaks, so you might ask how those can occur. In order to understand Java memory leaks, we need to consider a third category: live. Figure 7-3 illustrates this additional state.

In Figure 7-3, Java objects to which we inadvertently maintain lingering references are leaked. All variables in Java are references to their respective objects in memory, so reference management becomes an issue. When you create a local method variable, its reference will automatically be deleted when the method exits; this is true for all code blocks, not just method bodies. One traditionally problematic area for Java programmers is the use of collections classes.

Collections classes are data structures containing object references, such as arrays, hash tables, and trees. You can add objects to these collection classes, and the collection class organizes them based on their functionality: for example, a HashMap stores its objects in a hash table for very fast lookups, whereas a TreeMap stores its objects in a tree, which supports object sorting and dynamic memory sizing.

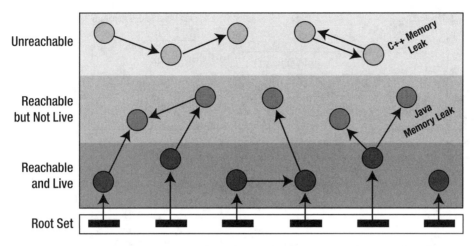

Figure 7-3. *Java memory leaks occur when object references are not destroyed for objects that will not be used again.*

Listing 7-2 demonstrates a leaked object contained in an ArrayList.

Listing 7-2. *Leaking an Object Using a Collections Class*

```
public class LeakExample {
  private ArrayList list = new ArrayList();
  public void add( Object o ) {
    list.add( o );
  }
  public void remove( int index ) {
    Object o = list.get( index );
    o = null;
  }
}
```

The problem with Listing 7-2 is that the remove() method retrieves the object at the specified index by calling the ArrayList's get() method, which does not remove the object from the ArrayList, but rather returns a reference to the object. After o is created, the object has two references (the ArrayList and o), and setting o to null dereferences only the second reference, but the first reference (maintained by the ArrayList) is still alive. Destroying that reference does not, in fact, destroy the object; the only proper way to destroy the object is to explicitly tell the collection to remove it. This reference mismanagement is illustrated in Figure 7-4.

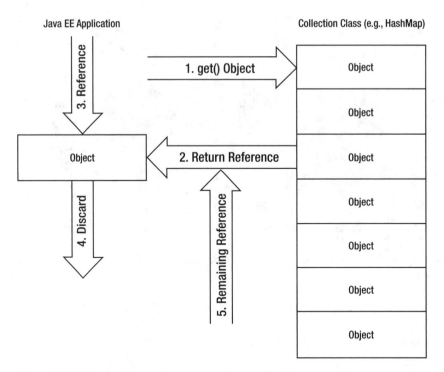

Figure 7-4. *Reference mismanagement using a collection*

While a single, small object left in memory may not hurt your application, as load is substantially increased and small objects are orphaned in the heap at a rate of several per second, then it is only a matter of time before your application server crashes. I hope this example illustrates that a seemingly innocent mistake can have significant consequences.

Sun JVM

The Sun JVM was the first JVM implementation and is arguably the most commonly used, followed closely by the IBM JVM. The Sun JVM operates under the premise that short-lived objects are created and destroyed very quickly. As such, it implements a generational heap, shown in Figure 7-5.

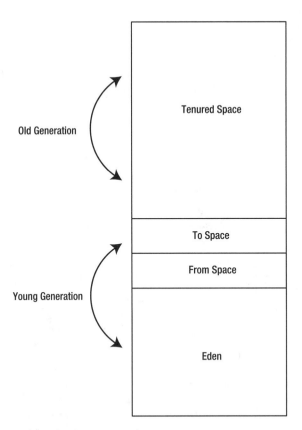

Figure 7-5. *The Sun JVM heap*

The Sun JVM heap is divided into two parts: the *old generation*, sometimes called the *tenured space*, and the *young generation*, sometimes called the *new space*. The young generation is further subdivided into three partitions: *Eden* and two survivor spaces, called the *From space* and the *To space*. Objects are created in Eden. When Eden is full, live objects are copied to the From space; when Eden is full again, objects in the from space are copied to the To space; and finally, if the object survives when Eden is full, the object is moved to the old generation. Figure 7-6 illustrates the pathway that objects follow as they survive through garbage collections.

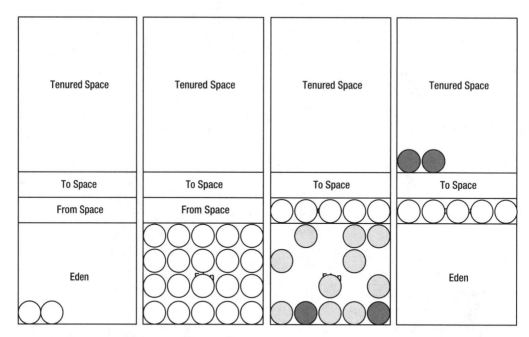

Figure 7-6. *Objects' pathways through garbage collection*

Java object instances are created in the young generation's Eden space. When enough objects have been created to fill up Eden, then the garbage collector runs a minor garbage collection, sometimes referred to as a *copy collection*. In this minor collection, the garbage collector examines objects in Eden: it removes objects with no references and copies live objects from Eden to the From space until the From space is full. In this way, very short-lived objects will die in Eden while the surviving subset of objects moves to the From space; we are guaranteed to free at least the number of bytes that comprise the contents of Eden and the From space. When Eden again becomes full, live objects in the From space are copied from the From space to the To space, in theory. In practical implementations, the JVMs maintain a pointer to the survivor spaces and each time a minor collection runs, the JVM simply changes the pointers (the From space becomes the To space). When Eden again becomes full, then any objects that are still alive in the To space are retired or tenured (copied) to the old generation. These minor collections are very fast and efficient, usually ranging from tenths of a second to hundredths of a second, depending on the size of the heap, and JVM thread processing is not halted during these collections.

When the young generation is full, and the garbage collector needs to free memory, then it performs a major garbage collection. This is a stop-the-world collection that freezes all running threads in the JVM and performs the reachability test. The reachability test results in the marking of live objects in the heap that is followed by a sweep of dead objects and an optional compaction to defray the heap. This mark-and-sweep collection is an extremely processor-intensive operation that can range in duration from a few tenths of a second to several seconds; I have seen some last upwards of 10 to 15 seconds. Therefore, regardless of how well you tune the performance of your application, frequent major garbage collections can destroy your end-user experience. The hope of this generational strategy is that moving objects around in the young generation gives short-lived objects ample time to die, and to free memory, before being tenured to the old generation. Over time, truly long-lived objects will stay alive in the old generation while short-lived objects will be cleaned up in the young generation with a relatively inexpensive garbage collection.

Figure 7-5 is drawn in the proportions that I have observed to yield the best performance: the young generation is a little less than half of the heap, and the survivor spaces are about 1/8 of the young generation. Unfortunately, because JVMs are designed to support a vast array of application types, the default configuration is far from ideal for enterprise applications supporting hundreds of simultaneous users. The default configuration varies by operating system, but in general, the young generation is too small, usually either 32MB or 64MB, and the survivor spaces are only allocated 1/34 of the young generation, which is between a little less than 1MB and a little less than 2MB. The result is that under heavy user loads, short-lived objects are prematurely tenured and therefore require a major collection to reclaim them; this premature tenuring of objects short-circuits the initial strategy of the garbage collector. Recall that when Eden is full, it is not freed all at once, but rather in chunks at least the size of the survivor space. Therefore, we could maintain a 2GB heap, but conceivably have to run garbage collections for every megabyte that is created.

As the JVM is started, you are empowered to resize the young generation as well as Eden and the survivor ratios. As you will recall from Chapter 6, my preference as a starting point, which has been proven to be effective for me in every Sun environment I have tuned, is to size the young generation to be a little less than half the size of the heap, but not much less. According to the JVM specification, making the young generation greater than half of the heap negates its ability to perform a copy collection and results in a mark-and-sweep for minor collections. I also prefer to size the survivor ratios to be somewhere between 1/6 and 1/10 the size of Eden, but I always start with 1/8.

I receive criticism with this recommendation from some, but I stand behind the idea of pinning the size of the heap and the young generation. My rationale is that the worst time to allocate memory is when you need it: if you are ever going to need 1GB of memory then take the start-up hit and allocate it on start-up. The primary criticism I receive is that a larger heap requires more time to perform garbage collections, but I counter that with the following observations:

- Minor collections may be impacted in the order of hundredths of seconds, but these collections do not freeze the heap, and the observed application throughput is negligibly affected.

- Major collections may take longer to run, but properly tuning the heap can greatly minimize their frequency.

- Any benefit in performance from an initially smaller heap will be obliterated by poor performance later when the heap allocates additional memory.

The configuration parameters for setting the heap size are shown in Table 7-2.

Table 7-2. *Sun JVM Heap Settings*

Parameter	Description
−XmxNNNm	Maximum size of the heap, where *NNN* represents the size of the heap, and *m* represents the units (m=megabytes, g=gigabytes)
−XmsNNNm	Minimum size of the heap, which I suggest should be equal to the maximum size
−XX:MaxNewSize=*NNN*m	Maximum size of the young (or new) generation
−XX:NewSize=*NNN*	Minimum size of the young (or new) generation
−XX:SurvivorRatio=*n*	Size of the survivor spaces as a ratio of its relationship to the size of Eden

The survivor ratio is a strangely configured value with formulas detailing its computation, but here is an explanation that I have found most meaningful: each survivor space receives one unit, while Eden receives the number of units specified by the survivor ratio. For example, setting the survivor ratio to 6 means that Eden receives 6 units while each of the two survivor spaces receives 1 unit, so each survivor space receives 1/8 of the young generation. A ratio of 6 equates to 1/8, 8 equates to 1/10, and so on.

The following are examples of how I would recommend initially configuring a 1GB and 2GB heap, respectively:

```
-Xmx1024m -Xms1024m -XX:MaxNewSize=448m -XX:NewSize=448m -XX:SurvivorRatio=6
-Xmx2048m -Xms2048m -XX:MaxNewSize=896m -XX:NewSize=896m -XX:SurvivorRatio=6
```

There are two ways that you can assess the health of your heap: visually and quantitatively. To assess visually, you need to take a snapshot of the usage of your heap on a regular time interval, such as every second (even if you later aggregate every 30 seconds and display the average, minimum, and maximum for the aggregate), and plot the results in a graphing tool such as Microsoft Excel. Figure 7-7 shows an example of a well-tuned heap, in which the heap has reached a steady state where objects are created and destroyed in the young generation, as evidenced by the lack of major garbage collections, while Figure 7-8 shows a poorly tuned heap, which performs frequent major garbage collections.

As illustrated by Figure 7-7, objects are created in the heap until the heap reaches a steady state. A steady state is evidenced by the heart monitor–style graph of a limited oscillation around a relatively straight line. This type of heap behavior is your goal in your heap tuning efforts. This graph is starkly contrasted by the abysmal behavior of the heap in Figure 7-8. This heap climbs almost limitlessly until it reaches about 95 percent of the heap's capacity, and then it performs a long and tedious major garbage collection—and then it starts the behavior over again!

Heap Usage

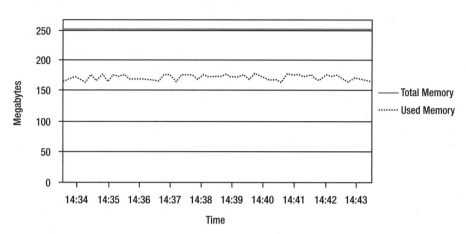

Figure 7-7. *A well-tuned heap*

Heap Usage

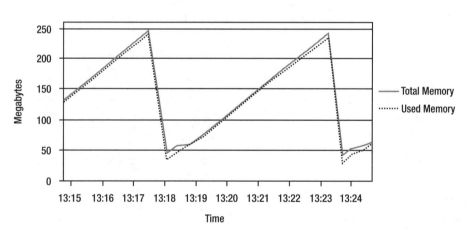

Figure 7-8. *A poorly tuned heap*

■**Note** I visited a customer who had previously implemented much of the heap tuning discussed in this section after a visit from their application server vendor consultant. The application vendor claimed that this level of tuning was not required of modern JVMs (those variations later than 1.3.x), so the vendor consultant removed the customer's tuning efforts. Performance was lacking, so I was called in, and when I observed the behavior of their 3GB heap, I saw a perfect example of Figure 7-8: their heap climbed over several minutes to almost 3GB and then a whopping 2.7GB was reclaimed by a major garbage collection, and the procedure repeated. I added the aforementioned "unnecessary" parameters back to their heap configuration, and the heap better resembled Figure 7-7. And thankfully the customer's performance problems disappeared!

The second way to assess the health of your heap is quantitatively, and the best low-overhead way to gather this information is through verbose garbage collection logs. Enabling verbose garbage collection logs can impact the performance of your JVM by 5 percent or more, but in my opinion, the benefit strongly outweighs the cost, at least initially. Verbose garbage collection and its level of logging are controlled by the parameters in Table 7-3; note that this list is not exhaustive, but includes the options that I have found to be most beneficial.

Table 7-3. *Verbose Garbage Collection Parameters*

Parameter	Default Value	Description
-verbose:gc	false	Enables verbose garbage collection
-Xloggc:filename	false	Prints garbage collection information to a log file
-XX:+PrintGCDetails	false	Prints garbage collection details, such as the size of the young and old generations before and after the garbage collection, the size of the total heap, the time length of the garbage collection in both generations, and the size of objects promoted at every garbage collection
-XX:+PrintGCTimeStamps	false	Adds timestamp information to garbage collection details
-XX:+PrintHeapAtGC	false	Prints detailed garbage collection information, including heap occupancy before and after garbage collection
-XX:+PrintTenuringDistribution	false	Prints object aging or tenuring information, which helps you tune the sizes of the generations, Eden, and the two survivor spaces
-XX:+PrintHeapUsageOverTime	false	Prints heap usage and capacity with timestamps
-XX:+PrintTLAB	false	Print thread local allocation buffers (TLAB) information

Listing 7-3 shows some sample verbose garbage collection log outputs, from which you can read the type of garbage collection that was performed: GC means minor, and Full GC means major. You can also read the amount of memory that was reclaimed and the duration of the garbage collection.

Listing 7-3. *Sample Verbose Garbage Collection Log Output*

```
Options: -verbose:gc -Xloggc:gc.log
33.357: [GC 25394K->18238K(130176K), 0.0148471 secs]
33.811: [Full GC 22646K->18501K(130176K), 0.1954419 secs]
```

The time listed to the left of each entry reports the time of the collection, in seconds, relative to the start of the application server. Note that while the major garbage collection was fast in this case, it was still over ten times slower than the previous minor collection.

■**Note** The `-Xloggc:filename.log` option overrides the `-verbose:gc` option, including it by default and making its explicit inclusion unnecessary. For clarity I include it, so that it reads explicitly that verbose garbage collection is enabled.

Listing 7-4 shows the change to the garbage collection output as the result of adding the `-XX:+PrintGCDetails` start-up option to the JVM.

Listing 7-4. *Sample Verbose Garbage Collection Log Output with –XX:+PrintGCDetails Enabled*

```
Options: -verbose:gc -Xloggc:gc.log -XX:+PrintGCDetails
19.834: [GC 19.834: [DefNew: 9088K->960K(9088K), 0.0126103 secs]
            16709K->9495K(130112K), 0.0126960 secs]
20.424: [Full GC 20.424:
        [Tenured: 8535K->10032K(121024K), 0.1342573 secs]
              13847K->10032K(130112K),
        [Perm : 12287K->12287K(12288K)], 0.1343551 secs]
```

Listing 7-4 adds additional information to the garbage collection log entries to provide details about changes to the generational spaces. The `DefNew` space refers to the entire young genera-tion (Eden plus the two survivor spaces) and reports the change details: the young generation shrank from 9,088KB (its total capacity) to 960KB, in 0.0126103 seconds. The entire used heap (the young generation and the old generation) changed from 16,709KB to 9,495KB, from a total available heap of 130,112KB. Using these numbers, we can learn something about the total number of bytes occupied by objects that were tenured as a result of this garbage collection. The entire heap size before the collection was 16,709KB, of which the young generation occu-pied 9,088KB, meaning that the old generation occupied the remaining 7,621KB of memory. After the garbage collection, the entire heap size was 9,495KB, of which the young generation is only maintaining 960KB, leaving 8,535KB in the old generation. Therefore, 914KB of data was tenured as a result of this garbage collection.

The full garbage collection may initially appear strange to you because the tenured (old) generation increased in size from 8,535KB to 10,032KB, an increase of 1,497KB, while the entire heap dropped from 13,847KB to 10,032KB, an overall decrease of 3,815KB. How can this be? Full garbage collections perform the reachability test on the entire heap to free all unreachable objects in the heap (in both the old and new generations). All reachable objects in the entire heap are marked, and then dead objects are swept away. The compaction stage moves all live objects into the old generation, leaving an empty Eden and survivor spaces.

There are two things to look for when analyzing these logs: the frequency and the duration of garbage collections. Ideally, you would like to minimize frequency as well as duration, but in reality, you have to create objects in your application. Therefore the best behaving heaps are those with more frequent minor collections, indicating that objects are being appropriately cleaned up. Measure the frequency of major collection, since frequent major collections indicate an impacted heap. To assess the impact of major collections, compute the sum of the durations over a relative time interval, and this sum represents how long your application was waiting for garbage collection. If you have not tuned your heap, this number should scare you.

In a tuning environment, you may want to enable the -XX:+PrintHeapAtGC verbose garbage collection option; it adds significant overhead that you do not want to incur in production, but in a test environment, it's incredibly valuable in helping you fine-tune your new generation sizes. An example of a verbose garbage collection log entry with this setting is shown in Listing 7-5.

Listing 7-5. *Verbose Garbage Collection Log Entry with the –XX:+PrintHeapAtGC Parameter Enabled*

```
Options: -verbose:gc -Xloggc:gc.log -XX:+PrintGCDetails -XX:+PrintHeapAtGC
18.645: [GC  {Heap before GC invocations=16:
Heap
 def new generation   total 9088K, used 9088K [0x02a20000, 0x033f0000, 0x05180000)
  eden space 8128K, 100% used [0x02a20000, 0x03210000, 0x03210000)
  from space 960K, 100% used [0x03210000, 0x03300000, 0x03300000)
  to   space 960K,   0% used [0x03300000, 0x03300000, 0x033f0000)
 tenured generation   total 121024K, used 7646K [0x05180000, 0x0c7b0000, 0x22a20000)
   the space 121024K,   6% used [0x05180000, 0x058f7870, 0x058f7a00, 0x0c7b0000)
 compacting perm gen  total 11264K, used 11202K [0x22a20000, 0x23520000, 0x26a20000)
   the space 11264K,  99% used [0x22a20000, 0x23510938, 0x23510a00, 0x23520000)
No shared spaces configured.
18.646: [DefNew: 9088K->960K(9088K), 0.0120705 secs]
        16734K->9509K(130112K) Heap after GC invocations=17:
Heap
 def new generation   total 9088K, used 960K [0x02a20000, 0x033f0000, 0x05180000)
  eden space 8128K,   0% used [0x02a20000, 0x02a20000, 0x03210000)
  from space 960K, 100% used [0x03300000, 0x033f0000, 0x033f0000)
  to   space 960K,   0% used [0x03210000, 0x03210000, 0x03300000)
 tenured generation   total 121024K, used 8549K [0x05180000, 0x0c7b0000, 0x22a20000)
   the space 121024K,   7% used [0x05180000, 0x059d95c0, 0x059d9600, 0x0c7b0000)
 compacting perm gen  total 11264K, used 11202K [0x22a20000, 0x23520000, 0x26a20000)
   the space 11264K,  99% used [0x22a20000, 0x23510938, 0x23510a00, 0x23520000)
No shared spaces configured.
} , 0.0122577 secs]
18.993: [Full GC {Heap before GC invocations=17:
Heap
 def new generation   total 9088K, used 5170K [0x02a20000, 0x033f0000, 0x05180000)
  eden space 8128K,  51% used [0x02a20000, 0x02e3caf0, 0x03210000)
  from space 960K, 100% used [0x03300000, 0x033f0000, 0x033f0000)
  to   space 960K,   0% used [0x03210000, 0x03210000, 0x03300000)
 tenured generation   total 121024K, used 8549K [0x05180000, 0x0c7b0000, 0x22a20000)
   the space 121024K,   7% used [0x05180000, 0x059d95c0, 0x059d9600, 0x0c7b0000)
 compacting perm gen  total 12288K, used 12287K [0x22a20000, 0x23620000, 0x26a20000)
   the space 12288K,  99% used [0x22a20000, 0x2361ffa8, 0x23620000, 0x23620000)
No shared spaces configured.
```

```
18.993: [Tenured: 8549K->10035K(121024K), 0.1333924 secs]
               13720K->10035K(130112K),
        [Perm : 12287K->12287K(12288K)]
Heap after GC invocations=18:
Heap
 def new generation   total 9152K, used 0K [0x02a20000, 0x03400000, 0x05180000)
  eden space 8192K,    0% used [0x02a20000, 0x02a20000, 0x03220000)
  from space 960K,     0% used [0x03220000, 0x03220000, 0x03310000)
  to   space 960K,     0% used [0x03310000, 0x03310000, 0x03400000)
 tenured generation   total 121024K,
 used 10035K [0x05180000, 0x0c7b0000, 0x22a20000)
    the space 121024K,   8% used [0x05180000, 0x05b4cc20, 0x05b4ce00, 0x0c7b0000)
 compacting perm gen  total 12288K, used 12287K [0x22a20000, 0x23620000, 0x26a20000)
    the space 12288K,  99% used [0x22a20000, 0x2361ffa8, 0x23620000, 0x23620000)
No shared spaces configured.
} , 0.1335890 secs]
```

Listing 7-5 shows the state of each part of the heap before and after the garbage collection. You can see memory move from Eden to the From space, from the From space to the To space, and from the To space to the old generation. Furthermore, the second entry shows the change in memory allocation during a major garbage collection.

With this information you can determine whether your young generation is large enough, as well as whether your survivor spaces are behaving appropriately. The key thing is that most objects in the To space should never make it to the old generation; if many do, then most likely you need to increase the size of the survivor spaces. If, however, minor collections are running excessively slowly, then you can decrease the size of the survivor spaces, as this will increase the frequency of garbage collection. To fine-tune the size of the survivor spaces, keep decreasing the size of the survivor spaces in small increments until short-lived objects are becoming tenured to the old generation, and then back up a step or two. In general practice, this fine-tuning is not necessary, but if you are trying to squeeze every bit of performance out of your heap, this can yield a measurable improvement.

Before leaving the Sun JVM heap, one more region needs to be addressed that you probably observed in the verbose garbage collection logs: the *permanent space*. The permanent space exists in the JVM process memory, but does not impact the heap size. For example, setting a new size takes memory away from the old generation, but modifying the permanent generation does not take memory away from any part of the heap, or the –XmxNNN value. The heap contains object instances, but in order for the JVM to create an instance, it must first open the class file and read its bytecode. When it reads the bytecode, it stores the class in process memory inside the permanent generation. This class is then used to create heap instances, analogous to a rubber stamp that stamps a picture or template of that class on the heap and returns a reference to it to the caller.

It is called the permanent space, or *permanent generation*, because in JVMs prior to 1.4, class files could never be unloaded from process memory: once they were in memory they remained permanently until the JVM exited. In 1.4 and later versions of the JVM, Sun abstracted this behavior by using the –noclassgc JVM option: if this option is enabled, then classes are never unloaded from the permanent space, and if it is not enabled, then the JVM has the option of unloading classes when it needs memory.

The permanent generation should not be ignored, because you need enough memory allocated to it to hold all classes in all of your applications—and this includes JSPs. Recall that a JSP is, in actuality, a servlet: a JSP is translated to servlet source code, then compiled to a servlet class file, and subsequently loaded into the permanent space in the process memory. If your application uses JSPs heavily, you may wish to increase the size of the permanent generation. In practice, I have seen permanent generations with 128MB values at most companies and one as great as 512MB, although that was excessive as they maintained nearly 10,000 large JSPs. The following options enable you to change the size of the permanent generation:

```
-XX:MaxPermSize=NNNm
-XX:PermSize=NNNm
```

■**Caution**   The `-noclassgc` option is positioned as a performance tuning enhancement option, but it can yield some unwanted results. I was visiting a customer who had an unexplained out-of-memory error crashing their application servers: the heap appeared underutilized, but they observed a slew of garbage collections that inevitably led to an out-of-memory error. They were running an old 1.3 JVM, so I recommended that they upgrade to the latest version of their application server that used a 1.4 JVM. The customer followed my advice and upgraded, but when they did, instead of their application servers crashing every three days, the servers were crashing three times a day! Upon deep investigation, we found that they now had a smaller permanent generation, and that the application server vendor's consultant had enabled the `-noclassgc` option, which caused their JVM to behave exactly as it did with the 1.3 JVM (only worse, because the consultant also shrank their permanent space). The JVM noticed that it was out of permanent space, so it attempted to reclaim memory the only way that it knew how—by running a major garbage collection. The `-noclassgc` option stopped the JVM from reclaiming memory, so the garbage collection was ineffectual. But when the garbage collection completed, the JVM still observed that it was out of memory, so it tried again, and again, and again. This explains how an underutilized heap could fall into a pit of repeated major garbage collections leading to its ultimate demise. I increased the size of their permanent generation to 512MB and disabled the `-noclassgc` option, and all of the customer's crashes stopped.

IBM JVM

The IBM JVM implements its object creation and garbage collection life cycles differently than the Sun JVM. The primary difference is that its default garbage collection scheme is not generational; instead, it implements a mark-sweep-compact (stop-the-world) garbage collection strategy in which all, or a subset of, these phases are performed as needed on the entire heap. Objects are allocated as follows: when an object is created, a block of memory is attained from the heap to hold the object. If a large enough block of memory is not available, then a garbage collection is performed to free up memory. If a large enough block of memory is still not available, then the heap is expanded to satisfy the request until the maximum heap size is reached, and the memory manager throws an out-of-memory exception. The JVM implements hoards of optimizations to streamline finding the next free block of memory and determine the ideal location for objects.

When the heap does not have available memory, the garbage collector performs the same reachability test discussed earlier in the chapter as its mark phase. It then sweeps out the garbage, or unreachable objects, from the heap. The space left between chunks of used memory can be reused for other objects, but because the IBM JVM allocates memory in 512-byte blocks, any free space smaller than 512 bytes becomes unusable and is referred to as *dark matter*. The only way to reclaim dark matter is to perform a heap *compaction*. The memory manager only performs a heap compaction if it cannot allocate a large enough block of memory to satisfy the request; again the smallest permissible block of memory is 512 bytes. The JVM rarely performs heap compaction, because heap compaction is expensive and complicated. The compaction phase not only moves objects, but also must move object references: it must ensure that all references to a moved object still refer to that object. To further complicate the process, some objects cannot be moved, such as objects that are explicitly *pinned* in a Java Native Interface (JNI) call and objects that are referred to directly by operating system registers. These objects must be identified and not moved during the compaction. Finally, the IBM JVM uses the memory address of an object as its hash value, so it must track whether an object's hash value has been requested, and if so, it must retain that hash value for the object in its new location. If it does not retain this value, then you could conceivably put an object into a HashMap and never be able to find it again.

The process of sizing an IBM heap is also different from sizing a Sun heap. While I recommend pinning a Sun heap (setting its minimum and maximum values to be the same), doing so with the IBM heap would not be wise, because garbage collection would be delayed until the heap reaches its maximum size. This delay would result in a very long-running garbage collection and, considering the nature of object life cycles in Java EE applications, long-lived objects would be interspersed with short-lived objects. This interspersion would result in the sweeping away of short-lived objects, creating a very fragmented heap of long-lived objects, which in turn would cause a lengthy compaction phase. The better approach is to size the initial heap small, so that long-lived objects can be created and moved to the beginning of the heap in quick compaction phases. Once the heap reaches its maximum size, then most long-lived objects (such as caches and pools) will exist at the beginning of the heap; short-lived objects will be at the end of the heap, so that they can be more easily cleaned up through a mark and sweep, thus avoiding a compaction altogether.

To determine the appropriate initial size of your heap, allow your application server to start up your application without any load. This amount of memory represents the initial overhead that must be created every time the environment starts and is a good initial value. The initial value is defined, then, through the minimum heap size option, -Xms.

The default target memory usage for your heap is 70 percent, so the heap attempts to maintain 30 percent free memory, firing off garbage collections and expanding the heap when it reaches 70 percent usage. If you observe that at 70 percent usage, garbage collection occurs too frequently, then this value can be decreased by increasing the free space target; for example, increase the target to 40 percent free heap through the -Xminf parameter: -Xminf0.4. In my experience, the best performance results from maintaining between 30 and 40 percent of free memory in the heap at any given time. Start with the default of 30 percent targeted free space and observe the frequency of garbage collection through verbose garbage collection logs. If garbage collection occurs too frequently, then increase the percentage of free memory.

If you increase the minimum target free space to 0.4 and garbage collection is still occurring too frequently, then increasing the amount by which the heap is expanded is a good idea. By default, the garbage collector expands the heap enough to satisfy the requested object allocation and restore the minimum target free space value, but this amount is governed by a minimum expansion size of 1MB. So regardless of how much memory is needed, the heap will expand by at least 1MB. In a production environment, this value is far too small and should be increased. You do need to balance the concept of inducing more frequent but short-running garbage collections with the frequency of heap expansions, but in general, a heap expansion of 20MB to 50MB is not unreasonable. The value can be set using the -Xmine parameter; for example, -Xmine50M creates a 50MB expansion size.

The time that a garbage collection takes to complete its mark, sweep, and optional compaction phases are referred to collectively as *pause time*. The verbose garbage collection logs can help you determine your pause time, and if it is too great, the IBM JVM provides an option to mitigate pause time. The -Xgcpolicy option controls the internal behavior of the garbage collector and can be told to optimize either throughput or pause time. If pause times are too great, passing the JVM the -Xgcpolicy:optavgpause value will better normalize garbage collection pause times, but at an estimated cost of 5 percent reduction in throughput. In order to optimize pause time, the garbage collector implements a feature called *concurrent marking*. Before the heap is full, a concurrent phase starts, in which the garbage collector asks each thread to scan its own stack. It then starts a low-priority background thread that traces through live objects in each stack and then employs each application thread to record and update changes to traced objects. When the heap runs out of memory and needs to perform a garbage collection, the mark phase is already complete, leaving only the sweep and the optional compact phases to run.

■**Note** Concurrent marking is somewhat analogous to what we used to do just prior to performing an annual inventory in a retail store. Inventory was performed once a year to physically count each object in the store to reconcile actual inventory with our database inventory. It would be literally impossible to count each item in a large retail store in a single night, so we started counting items a couple of weeks before. Once a group of items had been counted, then the sale of one of those items would be recorded; we monitored the delta only, so we did not need to recount the entire group when we sold one item. In this analogy, the background thread is the initial inventory counter, and we, the sales consultants, are the application threads that record changes to the inventory that we make. When time for inventory arrives (or for garbage collection to run), then we only need to reconcile our changes and record our results. This was the only way we were able to leave the store before daylight!

In summary, here are my recommendations for tuning the IBM JVM parameters:

1. Set the initial heap size (-Xms) to the size of the steady state of the heap after the application server starts, which can be determined through the verbose garbage collection logs.

2. Set the maximum heap size (-Xmx) to ensure that the heap used during load is approximately 70 percent of the maximum.

3. Observe garbage collection frequency, and if it is too frequent, then increase the target free space (-Xminf) to between 30 and 40 percent.

4. Increase the minimum expansion size (-Xmine) from 1MB to between 20MB and 50MB and observe the frequency of garbage collection. If it's too frequent, then increase this value; if it's less frequent but the pause time is too long, then decrease this value.

5. If your pause time is sporadic, then normalize it by enabling concurrent mark (-Xgcpolicy:optavgpause).

For more information about tuning the IBM JVM, refer to the following URL:

`http://www-128.ibm.com/developerworks/java/jdk/diagnosis`

Note The IBM JVM provides a new argument, -Xgcpolicy:gencon, that causes the JVM to use generational garbage collection, but at the time of this writing I have not encountered any customer production environments using this option. Although my internal tests yield favorable results, I hesitate to recommend it until the long-term performance implications can be properly assessed.

Tuning Thread Pools

Because thread pools define an upper limit on the number of simultaneous actions that an application server can configure, properly tuning thread pools can have a significant effect on performance. Choosing the appropriate starting value is a daunting task, but as a guideline, consider the number of users your application supports, calculate a realistic think time (the time between application requests), and combine that with the average response time per request. For example, if your application supports 1,000 users with an average 20-second think time and an average response time of 5 seconds, then on average you would need 250 threads: every 20 seconds each user makes a request that occupies 5 seconds of thread usage, or each user is using a thread 25 percent of his time in your application. 25 percent of 1,000 is 250.

Unfortunately this type of computation is never this straightforward, but with proper monitoring you can *guess* at a ballpark figure. You can determine the effectiveness of your thread pool settings in two ways:

- Thread pool metrics

- Throughput

The thread pool metrics that are important in determining effectiveness are the thread pool usage and pending requests. In the average case, you want to keep thread pool usage at or below 80 percent with no pending requests. This percentage gives you a comfortable buffer for peak periods. If, on the other hand, you observe thread pool usage at or above 90 percent and see frequent pending requests, then thread pools are too small.

One caveat exists in defining thread pool sizes this way: each application server instance has a capacity, and as soon as you exceed it, performance degrades. The best way to determine the thread capacity of your application server is to generate balanced and representative user load against your application server while monitoring application throughput. Throughput is a measure of units of work accomplished in a specific time period, such as requests committed per second. As the number of threads increases, the throughput will increase, because you are doing more work at a given time, but you eventually reach a point where throughput levels off and then degrades. This degradation results from thread context switching impacting the actual work that the threads are accomplishing.

The tuning process, therefore, is to define a starting value by analyzing the number of users, think time, and average response time, and then load test your environment with balanced and representative requests. Capture the throughput and gradually increase the number of threads until throughput levels off and starts degrading, and then tune the threads back down to the point just prior to the throughput leveling off. If increasing your initial settings immediately causes throughput to decrease, then decrease the number of threads while the throughput increases, levels off, and then decreases—the start of the decrease is the optimal thread pool setting to maximize request throughput.

■**Note**   This tuning approach is not in conflict with the wait-based tuning methodology presented in the previous chapter. Rather, this tuning approach is directly impacted by wait points and should be performed after tuning all wait points between the thread pool wait point and its dependent resources. Consider that throughput will always suffer if threads are waiting on anything.

Tuning Connection Pools

Enterprise applications seldom maintain all business functionality in memory; rather they interact with external resources. Establishing a connection to an external resource is an expensive operation; therefore the best performance for interacting with external connections is to establish a connection pool and share connections. If the application server does not have enough external dependency connections, then threads must wait on the connection pool for a connection to be returned by another thread.

There are two primary metrics to read when determining the effectiveness of connection pools:

- Connection pool usage

- Number of execution threads waiting for a connection

Ideally, you want to maintain a usage at or below 80 percent with no waiting threads for average usage patterns, leaving a buffer to support peak usage or a change in usage patterns.

The final thing to consider when tuning connection pools is that most define a range of connections; you can set a minimum, maximum, and growth rate. Be sure that the minimum number of connections supports at least the average usage pattern, because even if the pool can grow to support the usage, if a connection is not available then your application will take the performance hit for establishing the connection. Setting the maximum value is not sufficient to tune a connection pool.

Tuning Caches

Marc Fluery once wrote an article entitled "Why I Love EJBs," in which he made the claim that the entity bean cache provides an order of magnitude better performance than accessing a database across a network. Although EJB 3.0 has experienced significant performance enhancements since Fluery wrote that article, EJB persistence schemes still benefit from internal caches, and therefore his comments are still accurate. Caches can provide incredible performance enhancements to enterprise applications, but if they are not sized properly, then they can introduce new bottlenecks.

Traditional caches maintain a collection of objects in memory for rapid access. Each cache has a finite size that defines exactly how many objects are allowed in memory at any given point in time. If the size of the cache is not large enough to maintain the number of frequently accessed objects in the cache, then the overhead to maintain the cache eliminates the benefits that you draw from the cache itself. Consider the process for serving an item that is not currently in a full cache: select an item to remove from the cache (usually using a least recently used algorithm), remove it (which may require persisting it back to a database or file store), load the new object from the database, insert the item into the cache, and finally return the object back to the caller. Removing an item from the cache is referred to as *passivating* the object. Monitor and track the passivation rate of your cached objects to determine how frequently the aforementioned procedure is performed. If the passivation rate is high, then the size of the cache needs to be increased. But if you observe that the cache is growing too large, then you need to consider whether or not the object should really be cached or if you should manually query the database for the object upon request.

■**Note** I was at a customer site that implemented the persistence of documents using entity beans. The problem discovered after deep analysis was that the entity bean hit count was near zero, the miss ratio was near 100 percent, and the passivation rate was high. I analyzed the customer's access logs to calculate how frequently individual documents were requested. I learned that in a given hour, over 7,000 different documents were requested, with fewer than five duplicate requests. In order to support these documents in a cache, the cache would have to hold those 7,000 objects. With a request for duplicate document every couple hours, the memory overhead required to maintain those documents yields almost no value. My recommendation was to completely remove the cache.

Fine-tuning: Realizing the Remaining 20 Percent

While tuning the JVM heap, thread pools, connection pools, and caches represents 80 percent of the performance benefits, fine-tuning the remaining 20 percent is important for maximizing the performance of the existing infrastructure. This section presents the remaining performance tuning metrics that yield measurable improvements.

Tuning EJB Pools

Stateless session beans and message-driven beans are maintained in a pool. They are pooled and not cached, because when you use objects that do not maintain state between invocations, you do not need to obtain the same object instance on subsequent invocations—any object will do. As a very loose analogy, consider leaving a store with your family: you want your children, not someone else's (therefore your children would be cached), but you can purchase your items from any cashier (therefore cashiers would be pooled).

By default most application servers tune EJB pools well, but if your application has specific requirements for specific beans, these pools represent another wait point. Similar to the behavior of JDBC connection pools, if a stateless session bean is requested, and the pool does not have one available, then the requester must wait for a bean to be returned to the pool before it can complete its business process. Therefore when load testing your system, be aware of the stateless session bean pool behavior. If the usage is at or near 100 percent, and bytecode instrumentation determines that calls to the stateless session bean's home interface's `create()` method are taking a long time to run, then the pool is a wait point in your application. You need to remove the wait point by increasing the pool size. On the other hand, if the pool usage is very low, and the minimum number of beans in the pool is rarely or never reached, then you might want to consider reducing the pool size, or at least the initial and minimum sizes.

Precompiling JSPs

In many instances, you hear people refer to servlets and JSPs as being the same objects, and when a JSP is loaded into memory, those people are right. Although a JSP file looks remarkably similar to an HTML document, application servers treat them completely differently. For example, consider the following two code snippets: Listing 7-6 presents an HTML document and Listing 7-7 presents a similar JSP file.

Listing 7-6. *myhtml.html*

```
<html>
<head><title>My HTML Page</title></head>
<body>
Hello, HTML!
</body>
</html>
```

Listing 7-7. *myjsp.jsp*

```
<html>
<head><title>My JSP Page</title></head>
<body>
Hello, JSP!
</body>
</html>
```

These documents look similar, but when you drop them into a Java EE WAR file and deploy it, the application server treats them as follows:

- The HTML file is directly returned to the caller.

- The JSP file is translated into a servlet source code file. That source code file is then compiled into a class file; the class file is loaded into memory; an instance of that class is created on the heap; and the new servlet's `service()` method is invoked.

So although renaming an HTML document to have a JSP extension morphs it into a JSP page, its behavior is dramatically different. An exercise that I very much enjoy performing with my students in my servlets and JSP class is looking at the intermediate source code that the translator generates. Listing 7-8 shows a readable sample of what this resultant servlet may look like.

Listing 7-8. *Sample Servlet Source Code Generated from a JSP File*

```
...
public void service( HttpServletRequest req, HttpServletResponse res ) {
  PrintWriter out = res.getWriter();
  out.println( "<html><head><title>My JSP Page</title></head>" +
               "<body>Hello, JSP!</body></html>" );
  ...
}
```

Although this code is a gross simplification of the true resultant file, you would not be surprised to look at these files yourself and see this simple out.println() call somewhere in the middle of the resultant servlet. Looking at these intermediate files is such a powerful tool that I routinely utilize this in teaching students how to write JSPs. Considering all of the nuances of the JSP specification can be a little overwhelming, but seeing the results of the various options makes it crystal clear. For example, the following code snippet:

```
<% Integer n = new Integer( 10 ); %>
<%=n%>
```

is translated in the servlet to the following:

```
Integer n = new Integer( 10 );
out.println( n.toString() );
```

And this code:

```
<jsp:getProperty name="mybean" property="name" />
```

is translated in the servlet to the following:

```
out.println( mybean.getName() );
```

This example is a great learning exercise, but you may be wondering what it has to do with performance. Obviously, returning static content in an HTML file is much faster than generating a JSP file that writes the information back to the client, but the real issue is that when each JSP file is requested, it must pass through these translation and compilation phases before it can be loaded into system memory to create an instance in the heap. Translation and compilation are expensive operations, so many application servers provide the ability to precompile your JSP pages on or prior to deployment. For example, Tomcat provides access to the Jasper JSP Engine through an ant task that you can employ to precompile your JSP files. Precompiling will eliminate the translation and compilation phases when a user hits a JSP file for the first time.

Although not precompiling JSP files can have a huge impact on the performance of your application, I opted to put it in the fine-tuning category for the simple reason that it only affects the first user that accesses the page. Once the JSP has been compiled and loaded into memory the first time, it is served from memory on subsequent invocations.

Tuning the JMS

In applications with limited or no messaging, JMS tuning is unproductive, but the situation is different for applications that heavily rely on JMS. JMS is only a specification; the underlying implementation differs from vendor to vendor, and most application server vendors allow you to plug in your choice of JMS implementations. JMS operates in two modes: point-to-point messaging and publish/subscribe messaging. When using *point-to-point messaging,* one process puts a message on a JMS destination (a queue), and another process removes the message from the destination. When using *publish/subscribe messaging,* a message producer publishes a message to a JMS destination (a topic), and all subscribers to that destination receive the message.

There are two primary facets of JMS tuning:

- Container tuning

- Message delivery tuning

Some JMS containers impose limitations on the number of messages and/or bytes that can reside in a JMS destination at a given time. The limitations' purpose is to minimize the impact of the JMS server on your application server heap—if the JMS server consumes a significant amount of heap memory, then it impacts the effectiveness of garbage collection and, in the worst case, can lead to out-of-memory errors. If you are heavily using JMS, then you need to ensure that these size limits are properly managed. The JMS server needs to hold enough messages so as not to reject new incoming messages, but JMS consumers need to remove messages fast enough to mitigate memory issues.

JMS defines levels of reliability for message delivery, and your choice of reliability will be a balance between business requirements and performance. Messages can be defined to be persistent or nonpersistent: a *persistent message* ensures that a message is delivered once and only once to a message consumer, whereas a *nonpersistent message* only requires that a message be delivered at most once to a message consumer. A persistent message is more reliable and can withstand a JMS provider failure, but it does so at a greater performance cost.

The JMS 1.1 specification recommends, for the highest level of assurance that a message has been properly produced, reliably delivered, and accurately consumed, that a persistent message should be produced from within one transaction and consumed within another transaction from a nontemporary queue or a durable subscriber. The point is that if you want to guarantee that your messages are properly delivered to your consumers and receive an acknowledgment, it will cost you. Compare your business requirements to these options and configure your message delivery and transactional constraints to meet your business requirements with the least performance overhead.

Understanding Servlet Pooling and the Impact of Non-Thread-safe Servlets

By default, servlets run in a thread-safe fashion, meaning that multiple threads can access a single servlet at the same time. The main property of a *thread-safe servlet* is that, in the context of servicing a request, it does not rely on any stateful information maintained in the servlet itself. For example, you store a user's information in an HttpSession object rather than in a servlet member variable, because if two threads store their respective users' information in the same servlet member variable, they are going to overwrite each other. If you require that your servlet support only a single thread at a time, you can force the container to enforce this requirement by marking your servlet as implementing the `javax.servlet.SingleThreadModel` marker interface. This interface has been deprecated as of the Servlet API 2.4 and should no longer be used and for good reason—it creates an additional wait point in your application.

The reason to mention this tuning option is that if you ever see `SingleThreadModel` in your servlet code, then the code needs to be refactored to ensure that it is thread-safe and that the `SingleThreadModel` demarcation is removed. Non-thread-safe servlets require servlets to be pooled, which increases memory overhead, and they introduce another wait point that you need to tune, so do not use them.

Tuning Prepared Statement Caches

Prepared statements are interesting enhancements to Java EE applications: they parameterize JDBC calls to accomplish both SQL statement precompilation and reuse. The concept is to prepare the statement once with parameterized values and then reuse it on subsequent calls, rather than execute similar SQL statements repeatedly against a database. For example, the following statements can be converted to prepared statements:

```
SELECT * FROM users WHERE user_id = 1;
SELECT * FROM users WHERE user_id = 2;
SELECT * FROM users WHERE user_id = 3;
```

Instead, these statements can be rewritten as follows:

```
SELECT * FROM users WHERE user_id = ?;
```

From a Java programming perspective, instead of executing this statement from a `java.sql.Statement`, execute it from a `java.sql.PreparedStatement`. The following code:

```
Statement stmt = conn.createStatement();
ResultSet rs = stmt.executeQuery( "SELECT * FROM users WHERE user_id=1" );
```

then changes to the following:

```
PreparedStatement ps = conn.prepareStatement(
                "SELECT * FROM users WHERE user_id=?" );
ps.setInt( 1, 1 );
ResultSet rs = ps.executeQuery();
```

The JDBC driver maintains these prepared statements in its own cache, and when it sees a call to `prepareStatement()`, it first checks to see if it has the precompiled statement before going to the database to compute a database explain plan for it (which defines how the database is going to execute the query). As always, the sizing of the cache is very important, because while a properly sized cache can dramatically improve performance, a poorly sized cache can dramatically hinder performance. Even a small cache imposes the overhead of checking the cache, making the trip to the database to prepare the statement, and then managing the cache (selecting a candidate to remove from the cache to make room for the new statement). If you see a high prepared statement discard rate on your prepared statement cache, then its size should be increased, but you need to be cognizant of the memory requirements for maintaining the cache.

To further complicate things, each JDBC connection maintains its own prepared statement cache, so the memory requirement for the prepared statement cache is multiplied by the number of database connections. For example, if your prepared statement cache is sized to hold 100 prepared statements, and you have 50 database connections, then you are potentially putting 5,000 prepared statements in memory at one time. Therefore this value needs to be carefully adjusted, especially for database-intensive applications. Tune this value to the lowest possible value that minimizes the prepared statement discard rate.

Configuring Advanced JDBC Options

Tuning JDBC is not limited to container settings such as connection pools and prepared statement caches, but also includes deployment options that manage the concurrency models between database connections reading from and writing to the same data in a database. Concurrency management is implemented through the notion of a transaction: a transaction has a rich history that was initially applied to relational databases and characterized using the acronym ACID. An ACID transaction is defined as having the following characteristics:

- *Atomicity*: A transaction is said to be atomic, or treated as a single unit, when either all actions must complete or the entire transaction is aborted. A partially successful atomic transaction does not exist; it is either completely successful or a total failure.

- *Consistency*: A consistent transaction either creates a new and valid state in the database when it succeeds or returns all data to its original state upon failure, as if the transaction never occurred.

- *Isolation*: A transaction is isolated when it ensures that actions performed inside a transaction are not visible to other transactions until after the transaction is committed.

- *Durability*: A transaction is durable when all changes that it makes and successfully commits to a database are permanent, and therefore will survive system failures.

JDBC has mimicked much of the ACID transaction functionality, but has also opened up transactional behavior to your control, so that, given your business requirements, you can optimize transactional performance. A full ACID transaction is expensive to manage, and in some business cases, you do not need your transactions to be fully ACID and would benefit from the database being a little lax in your transactional requirements. JDBC exposes this control by defining transaction isolation levels.

The JDBC 4.0 specification defines transaction isolation levels as specifying "what data is 'visible' to statements within a transaction. They greatly impact the level of concurrent access by defining what interaction, if any, is possible between transactions against the same target data source."[1] And it places possible transaction interactions into three categories:

- Dirty reads

- Nonrepeatable reads

- Phantom reads

---

1. Sun Microsystems, Inc., *JDBC 4.0 Specification: JSR 221* (December 2005), p. 54. Also available online at http://jcp.org/aboutJava/communityprocess/pr/jsr221/index.html.

A *dirty read* occurs when a transaction is allowed to see uncommitted changes to data, for example, if a change is made to data inside one transaction that is visible to other transactions before the changes are committed to the database. A dirty read means that if the transaction modifying the data rolls its transaction back and reverts the data back to its state before it started, then other transactions may be operating against incorrect data.

A *nonrepeatable read* occurs when one transaction reads a row of data, another transaction modifies that row, and then the first transaction rereads the row and finds a different value. In this case, after a transaction reads data from the database, it has no guarantee that the data is still when it's used.

A *phantom read* occurs when one transaction reads all rows from a table that satisfy a WHERE condition, then another transaction adds a new row that satisfies the WHERE condition, and finally the first transaction requeries the table and is able to see the new *phantom* row.

In order to determine how a database connection treats data in light of these three transactional interaction categories, JDBC defines five transaction isolation levels, shown in Table 7-4.

Table 7-4. *JDBC Transaction Isolation Levels*

Isolation Level	Description
TRANSACTION_NONE	Indicates that the driver does not support transactions and is therefore not a JDBC-compliant driver
TRANSACTION_READ_UNCOMMITTED	Allows transactions to see uncommitted changes to the data, meaning that dirty reads, nonrepeatable reads, and phantom reads are possible
TRANSACTION_READ_COMMITTED	Indicates that any changes made inside a transaction are not visible outside the transaction until the transaction is committed, which prevents dirty reads, but not nonrepeatable reads and phantom reads
TRANSACTION_REPEATABLE_READ	Disallows dirty reads and nonrepeatable reads, but permits phantom reads
TRANSACTION_SERIALIZABLE	Specifies that dirty reads, nonrepeatable reads, and phantom reads are not permitted, thus a serializable transaction is fully ACID-compliant

As the transaction isolation level increases from the least restrictive (TRANSACTION_NONE) to the most restrictive (TRANSACTION_SERIALIZABLE), it increases the database overhead and hence degrades performance. You need to carefully evaluate your business requirements against these transaction isolation levels and choose the least restrictive level that meets those business requirements.

Summary

This chapter has provided a great deal of tuning information that can be applied generically across application server vendors. It began by reviewing the Java EE 5 specification and deriving the requirements for an application server to sufficiently implement this specification. From these requirements, it identified tuning configuration parameters and weighted their significance in terms of performance impact.

I proposed that for the majority of Java EE applications, 80 percent of their performance capabilities can be met by tuning the following four parameters: heap configuration, thread pools, connection pools, and caches.

Finally, we turned our attention to the remaining 20 percent of fine-tuning options, including sizing EJB pools, precompiling JSPs, tuning JMS parameters, understanding servlet pooling, tuning prepared statement caches, and configuring advanced JDBC options.

In the next chapter, we look toward high-performance deployment options and answer the following questions: How do you scale a tuned application server instance? Should you implement clustering? How should you lay out your hardware? And how should you separate your logical tiers?

CHAPTER 8

■ ■ ■

High-Performance Deployments

"There's still one thing that I don't understand," said John, with a gleam of concern in his eyes. "What's that?" I asked.

"Well, I can tune my application and my application server, but how do I deploy them? I have heard some people say that I need to scale my application and other people say that I need to cluster it. They mention vertical and horizontal scaling and clustering. What is best? And, most important, how do I do it?" While John's tone was inquisitive, I could sense his frustration with the amount of outside information he was being fed.

"Deployments can be tricky," I replied. John had touched on a point that I hold very close to my heart, as I have been burned before by faulty deployments—the best application can be brought to its knees if the deployment is faulty. "First off, while scaling and clustering are related, they are not mutually exclusive. Scalability is governed by your availability requirements: you scale based upon the percentage of the time you need your application available to your users. Clustering, on the other hand, is governed by your failover requirements: you cluster based upon the way your users are affected by application server outages.

"Next, vertical scaling and clustering refers to installing multiple application server instances on a single machine, while horizontal scaling and clustering refers to installing multiple application server instances on multiple machines.

"Again, scaling and clustering are not mutually exclusive, and the best choice is usually a combination of the two. Let me walk you through the details . . ."

Deployment Overview

When developing an application according to the methodology presented in this book, you choose the optimal design patterns to meet your business requirements; introduce performance criteria into use cases; iteratively test the performance of your components in unit testing, integration testing, and production staging testing; and perform a capacity assessment to understand what load your application can reasonably support and specifically how your environment responds when that load is exceeded. Meanwhile, you tune your application and application server using the wait-based tuning approach to uncover both application and application server bottlenecks. Finally, you harden your application servers to maximize request throughput and move waiting requests to the most appropriate location. At this point, you have a good understanding of your application and application server capabilities, and the next step is to plan your deployment.

Depending on the nature of your application and the requirements of your business, the deployment can be simple or extremely complex. You should consider the following three criteria when planning your deployment strategy:

- Expected user load

- Availability requirements

- Failover requirements

Your *expected user load* dictates the hard requirements for the minimum number of hardware and software servers you need, which is closely related to the results of your capacity assessment. Note, however, that if one server can service 500 simultaneous users, it does not necessarily follow that two servers can service 1,000 simultaneous users. Other variables (discussed later in this chapter) complicate the math ever so slightly.

You should next determine your application's *availability requirements*, or the percentage of time your application needs to be functional. For example, an e-commerce site's availability requirements are extremely high. This type of site may demand 99.99 percent availability, meaning that the maximum tolerable downtime is approximately 53 minutes per year. An intranet application may have much looser requirements: it might be used every day from 8:00 AM to 5:00 PM, which facilitates easy application server restarts in the evening when necessary. Furthermore, if the intranet application is not available, a simple restart may be adequate. These are the two extremes, and your organization probably falls somewhere between them. Keep your availability requirements in mind as you read through this chapter.

Failover requirements are slightly different from availability requirements. Availability requirements dictate how much of the time your application needs to be available, whereas failover requirements define the impact of application server outages on your users. As you will see later in this chapter, you can configure multiple application servers inside the context of a cluster to behave as one logical unit, and when one instance goes down, its traffic can be redistributed across the remaining servers.

But failover begs the question, How is the user impacted? Is this transition from one application server instance to another seamless to the user, or is the user required to log on to the system again and start work over? While the former case is obviously ideal, it can significantly impact application performance, so you need to evaluate this requirement against your business requirements. In the previous example, an e-commerce company may be required to make the transition seamless. Consider what you would do if you connected to your favorite e-tailer, browsed for an hour, put 15 items into your shopping cart, and then unexpectedly all of your selections were lost. Would you feel confident in this vendor? Price notwithstanding, would you continue to frequent this e-tailer's site? In the intranet example, asking users to log on again may be acceptable, but clearly the same does not hold true for an e-commerce site. Again, it all depends on your business requirements.

The purpose of this chapter is to equip you with the knowledge to configure your hardware and software environments to best suit your users' requirements. To this end, we'll examine your high availability and failover requirements to determine the best performing deployment.

Formal Deployment Topology

Most high-performance deployments configure multiple application server instances to service their requests, and place a load balancer between the application servers and the users to distribute requests appropriately. In some cases, this configuration is adequate, but in the context of best practices and defining the optimal deployment methodology I am promoting, this section defines the various logical tiers that compose an enterprise Java environment. Feel free to combine logical tiers into single units when appropriate to your environment.

Figure 8-1 shows a breakdown of the logical tiers that make up an enterprise Java environment.

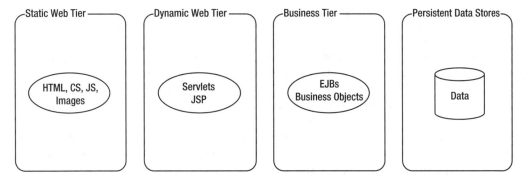

Figure 8-1. *An enterprise Java environment contains a static Web tier, a dynamic Web tier, logical business tiers, and back-end persistent data stores.*

Figure 8-1 shows the logical separation of functionality into the following tiers:

- Static Web tier

- Dynamic Web tier

- Business tier(s)

- Persistent data stores

The static Web tier is facilitated by your Web server. This tier is responsible for serving static content such as HTML pages, style sheets, and images. A request for a static resource should not disturb the rest of your environment and hence should be allocated its own resources. If the request requires dynamic Web content, then it can be forwarded to the next tier.

The dynamic Web tier holds all of your servlets and JSPs. Its purpose is to generate dynamic responses based upon the nature of a request. If it can serve its content from either a cached resource or a direct computation, then it can return the response directly to the user. Otherwise, it forwards the request to the appropriate business tier.

The business tier is responsible for implementing business logic and managing data persistence. There are two reasons to provide it with its own resources:

- If the Web tier can return the response without interacting with the business tier, then it does not disrupt requests that require business tier interactions.

- In hybrid environments with both Web and non-Web clients, the business tier can have multiple entry points. You do not want your non-Web clients needlessly affecting the performance of the Web tier.

The business tier also manages data persistence through the data persistence scheme that you choose. Regardless of the implementation, your business objects will undoubtedly need to interact with a transactional data object model. There is a distinct logical separation between business logic objects and business data objects, but they are so tightly coupled in practical implementations that physically separating them into their own tiers usually degrades performance beyond any benefit you might gain by separating them.

Finally, the persistent data stores represent your databases and legacy systems. These are implemented by anything that provides storage and retrieval capabilities. In any production deployment, you should strive to physically separate data stores from your application business tier. Consider the impact of interrupting your business processing with the movement of a read/write head on your hard drive to seek an additional block of data, or the impact of re-indexing a table. Databases are well optimized to perform these operations, but not on the same machine that is running your application server.

The best deployment strategy is to separate each tier into distinct application server instances, which may or may not reside on the same physical machine. Furthermore, it is best to have multiple application server instances working together to satisfy requests to each tier. Figure 8-2 shows this deployment strategy.

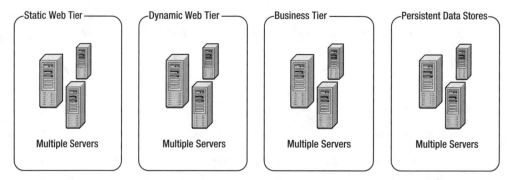

Figure 8-2. *Deploying multiple application server instances to service each logical tier*

As you can see in Figure 8-2, each logical tier can be serviced by multiple application server instances. This has two benefits:

- More servers can service more load.

- Availability is enhanced. If one instance goes down, then its load can be redistributed across the remaining instances.

The physical separation of tiers introduces some additional complexity in tuning because as you increase the number of thread pools, you introduce additional wait points. But as you tune your environment, you will learn that this separation actually provides much greater control of your tuning capabilities. This separation alludes to the core precept in the wait-based tuning hardening phase: requests should wait at the appropriate place. For example, a request being serviced directly by the dynamic Web tier should not take resources away from the business tier, as it would slow down the business tier and affect the performance of the entire application.

Software Clusters

Now that you have physically separated tiers appropriately to satisfy your business domain, you next need to determine how you are going to address failover. When an application server crashes or is restarted, such as for maintenance, is user session information preserved, or is the user forced to re-create it (for example, by logging on again or redoing previous activities)?

If you require application failover or user session information to be preserved when an application server goes down, then the solution is to configure application server instances to run inside a cluster. When application servers run in a cluster, they work together to service requests as one logical unit. Furthermore, each application server is configured to replicate its session information to one or more secondary application server instances. Different implementations are available that vary from replicating to a single secondary server to replicating to all servers in the cluster, and your choice of implementation depends on how much risk you are willing to tolerate. Replicating to all servers is the least risky approach, but it incurs the most overhead. In practical terms, replicating to a single secondary server that resides on a separate physical machine suffices for 90 percent of use cases. It enables your application to be resilient to application server outages as well as hardware failures.

Figure 8-3 illustrates replicating a primary server to a single secondary server. In this scenario, server 1 replicates to server 3, and server 2 replicates to server 4. This is the most efficient configuration because it is resilient to application server crashes and hardware failure, but at the cost of maintaining data to a single application server instance.

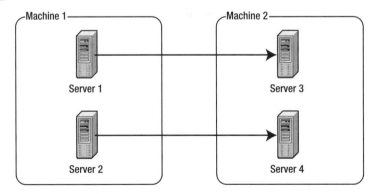

Figure 8-3. *Replicating a primary server to a single secondary server*

Figure 8-4 illustrates replicating a primary server to all other servers (as secondary servers). In this scenario, all servers replicate to all other servers—for example, server 1 replicates to server 2, server 3, and server 4. While this is the most resilient form of failover (no matter what application server or machine fails, the failure is not apparent to the user), it is also the most expensive in terms of performance.

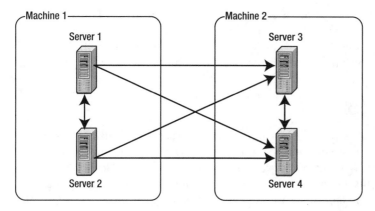

Figure 8-4. *Replicating a primary server to all other servers (as secondary servers)*

The technical steps that the failover process implements are defined as follows:

1. The load balancer is configured using *sticky sessions*, meaning that it sends a user back to the same server instance every time.

2. Whenever a session object is updated, the primary server sends the updated session object across the network to the secondary server.

3. If the primary server is not available, then subsequent requests are sent to the secondary server.

4. The secondary server now becomes the primary server. It selects a new secondary server of its own and replicates its session information to its secondary server.

This process obviously incurs additional overhead in transmitting session information across the network, but it allows your users to cleanly fail over from one server to another. As servers go up and down, your users are not affected.

Technical Requirements

To facilitate failover and clustering, your session information must be serializable. *Serialization* is the process of writing or reading an object to or from a stream. For example, you can serialize your object to disk through an OutputStream and subsequently rebuild the object by reading it through an InputStream. In technical terms, an object must be marked serializable by implementing the marker interface java.io.Serializable. A *marker interface* is an interface that has no methods and exists only to label a class as participating in a specific role. Although java.io.Serializable is a marker interface, it is a special interface type, with default methods that facilitate the physical reading and writing of the object from and to a stream, specifically the following:

```
private void writeObject( java.io.ObjectOutputStream out ) throws IOException
private void readObject( java.io.ObjectInputStream in ) throws IOException
```

The default implementation persists each of the object's nonstatic and nontransient fields. *Static* fields are JVM specific (similar to global variables), and, by definition, *transient* fields are purposely not persisted. If your application requires any custom functionality in these methods, you can override them in your own serializable class. You can always gain access to the original functionality inside the overridden method by invoking the `out.defaultWriteObject()` and `in.defaultReadObject()` methods, respectively.

In addition to implementing the `java.io.Serializable` interface, your nonstatic and nontransient fields must be either primitive types (for example, `int`s or `float`s) or serializable themselves (implementing the `java.io.Serializable` interface and adhering to the same set of standards).

If you attempt to deploy an application to a cluster that maintains nonserializable session information, then you will most likely receive a run-time error or unexpected behavior. An example of unexpected behavior is when you test failover and it may appear not to work at all—for example, when your users fail over they are required to log in to the application again—but the root of the problem is in the session serialization, not in the failover configuration. As a result, you may see an entry in your log files that alludes to attempting to serialize a nonserializable object.

Architecting Clusterable Applications

Once you've satisfied the technical requirements, you can conceivably fail over any amount of session information from one server to another, but in practice you need to understand your sessions and decrease the quantity of information stored in your sessions. The quantity of data stored in your sessions directly impacts your cluster's performance because the session data must be transferred between primary and secondary application server instances.

To further complicate matters, the granularity of session objects can have a direct impact on the quantity of data transferred between machines. Consider storing a configuration object in a user's session object that occupies approximately 1MB of memory. Modifying a single integer in that object marks it as dirty, and the entire 1MB object must be transferred across the network to the server's secondary server(s). On the other hand, while sending a single integer is more efficient than sending a 1MB object, managing 2,000 individual object attributes is not sustainable. So you need to establish a balance between manageability and performance.

Because you need to meticulously scrutinize every byte of data stored in your sessions, I suggest following these guidelines when defining session attributes:

- Store in sessions temporal information, such as navigation information (where did I come from? What steps did I follow to get here? Where am I going?), and ensure that it is cleaned up appropriately when the active business process is complete.

- Store paging indices or iterators, but never in the objects themselves.

- Store a handle to a stateful session bean that maintains the user's session information.

The last guideline may be a point of contention for some, but there is a good reason behind it: most production performance problems that result in application server crashes are `OutOfMemoryError` errors. My experience has demonstrated that the biggest cause of `OutOfMemoryErrors` in enterprise Java applications is the presence of a large number of heavy sessions; sessions impact memory requirements in direct proportion to the number of users in your application, including phantom users lingering for the duration of your session time-out. Stateful session beans are maintained in a cache with a predefined and specific upper limit governing exactly the number of beans allowed in memory at any one time. When the cache is full and a new bean is added to the cache, then an existing bean must be selected to be removed from the cache (usually using a least recently used algorithm) and subsequently persisted to permanent storage to make space for the new bean. If the cache is sized too small, then this selection and persistence process will begin to negatively impact application performance; cache management overhead can negate the benefits of using a cache in the first place. But if the cache is sized appropriately to support the typical number of active users in your application, then you draw the following two benefits:

- Phantom users will quickly disappear from the in-memory cache to make room for active users, reducing the memory requirements for inactive users.

- Regardless of load, the maximum memory requirements to support user sessions will decrease.

If phantom users return, their session information is not lost; rather, it only needs to be reloaded from permanent storage. This is a reasonable trade-off between session memory management and usability: users that stay inactive for too long retain their state, but require additional load time to obtain their state information when they return.

If the load increases dramatically beyond the size of the cache, then application response time will degrade as a result of the cache management, but the application server will avoid an out-of-memory error condition. This is certainly not ideal, but degraded response time is better than no response.

In summary, when architecting clusterable applications, you need to store as little information in user sessions as possible. If the session size still results in memory stress, then consider moving session information into a stateful session bean and sizing the cache appropriately to support as many active users as you can without negatively impacting the performance of your application server heap.

Horizontal and Vertical Clusters

Software clusters come in two forms: horizontal clusters and vertical clusters. *Horizontal clustering* involves deploying clustered application server instances on different physical machines. *Vertical clustering* involves deploying multiple application server instances on the same physical machine. Each approach has its own benefits, and the best implementation is a combination of the two.

Horizontal clustering provides resilience to hardware failure in addition to the standard support for load balancing and failover. When defining your clusters, you always want to have clustered application servers residing on at least two different machines because hardware failure is not something that is within your control, even with the best preparations and plans. I know that hardware is becoming increasingly more resilient and is far more dependable than software, but imagine a tech mistakenly unplugging the wrong network cable—how can you recover from that?

Vertical clustering provides additional failover benefits and minimizes the effects of restarting an application server, because additional application server instances are supporting your application. For example, if you have two application server instances—one running on each of two machines—and one fails, then you have reduced your application capacity by 50 percent. But if you have two application server instances running on both machines (four application server instances total), then when one fails or needs to be restarted, your application capacity is reduced by only 25 percent.

Vertical clustering surprisingly adds another benefit that you might not initially consider: it provides better utilization of system resources. When you purchase a big, beefy machine to support your application server, the nature of the operating system limits the ability of a single process to adequately make use of all system resources. IBM published a study a few years back that substantiated this concept and determined that two or more processes can better utilize the CPU and physical memory than a single process. There is definitely a point of diminishing returns when you have too many processes running and competing for system resources, but as a general guideline consider defining one application server instance for every two CPUs. More processes may cause excessive context switching, while fewer may not be able to effectively use all of the CPUs.

To discover the optimal number of application server instances for your environment, begin by defining one application server instance per two CPUs, load test, and measure both the system utilization and the throughput of your applications. Then add an additional application server instance on the machine, load test again, measure the system utilization and application throughput, and compare these results to the first test. Under expected load, was the CPU load better utilized without being saturated? Did the application throughput increase? If the answer to both questions is yes, then the added application server instance helpf performance of your application; otherwise, the additional instance hurt the performance and should be removed. Depending on the CPU load, you may wish to continue this exercise until you reach a point where performance degrades—back off one application server instance and this is your ideal configuration. The target CPU utilization for your applications running under expected load should be between 75 and 85 percent.

Disaster Recovery

Before leaving the topic of software clusters, I want to examine a statement that Oracle CEO Larry Ellison made to the world in his 2001 Comdex keynote address a couple of years ago regarding the resilience of Oracle 9i to everything from hardware failure to natural disasters. Java EE was architected for resilience through clustering, and the proper deployment can ensure the level of resilience that you require. When Larry Ellison colorfully articulated that Oracle 9i could survive hardware failure, he was referring to horizontal scaling. When he claimed that Oracle 9i could survive natural disasters, he was referring to the creation of a horizontal cluster in which application servers fail over to other application servers residing in a different physical data center, potentially across the country or across the globe.

The point is that if you require 99.999 percent availability and need to be able to withstand the loss of a complete data center, this is possible using Java EE. The key is to establish horizontal clusters that span all of your data centers—if a data center is lost, then your users are redirected to their secondary servers in an alternate data center. But before establishing this level of resilience, be sure that you need it, because it is incredibly expensive to transfer user session information to one or more secondary servers across the Internet whenever a user makes a request.

The appropriate way to implement this approach is as follows:

1. Remove menial information from user sessions, such as page history, to ensure that a session is replicated only when a significant event has occurred.

2. Minimize session footprints so that when session information must be replicated across servers, the quantity of information is minimal.

Then configure your cluster as you normally would, but ensure that a primary application server's secondary server resides in an alternate data center. Some application servers may offer different deployment options to better optimize this process, but this is the theory upon which this level of resilience is built, as illustrated in Figure 8-5.

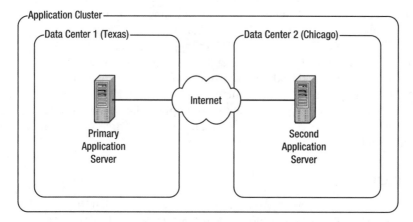

Figure 8-5. *Implementing application resilience with failover across data centers*

Because replicating session information across the Internet is expensive, one strategy that I have seen employed by several large customer sites is the introduction of the following compromise: when an application server crashes within a data center, then the user's session information must fail over to an alternate server, but when an entire data center is lost, then the user's session information is lost. It is a fairly rare occurrence that an entire data center is lost, and requiring your users to log on again may not be unreasonable in this case. This implementation involves the creation of two (or more) separate clusters, one residing at each data center, as illustrated in Figure 8-6. By adding the caveat that failovers are not permissible across data centers, the overhead required to replicate session information is significantly reduced.

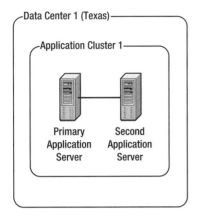 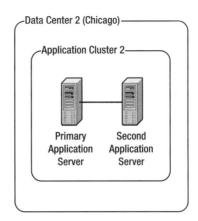

Figure 8-6. *Implementing application resilience with two (or more) separate clusters, one residing at each data center*

Implementing two different clusters that persist to the same database can be a complicated configuration that typically requires a more restrictive data source configuration. If you maintain data objects in a cache in your cluster, and one of your items is changed in another cluster, then you have no way of knowing that your object is stale. The most common configuration I have seen is a hardening of user distribution to ensure that a specific user is always referred to a specific data center and a set of scheduled database synchronizations and cache invalidations. The result is that your data may be stale for up to a specified period of time (for example, your data may be guaranteed to be no more than 30 minutes stale), but when configuring high-availability applications you need to make a significant number of trade-offs to improve performance. Remember that you can always create cross–data center clusters and ensure the integrity of your data, but this comes at a performance cost.

Realizing the Logical Configuration

Logically you want to separate tiers by functionality, and, as you realize this configuration, you want to create at least two instances of each logical tier. You want at least two Web servers, two application server instances, and two database instances. Furthermore, when separating the dynamic Web tier from business tiers, you want at least two instances of each, because when you configure the environment with two nodes at each tier, scaling to address additional requirements is relatively straightforward: add the new instance and add it to the cluster (or to the domain manager if not clustered). Establishing such an environment from the onset and configuring your application components to work in this environment early will save you pain if you are forced to scale later. Figure 8-7 illustrates this concept.

To implement this configuration from a physical perspective, start by scaling tiers horizontally and then vertically in order to make your servers resilient to both application server and machine failures. For example, if you install four application server instances on the same machine, and that machine fails, then you lose all of the servers. But if you install two servers on each of two machines, then you still have four instances, but a hardware failure will not bring down your application.

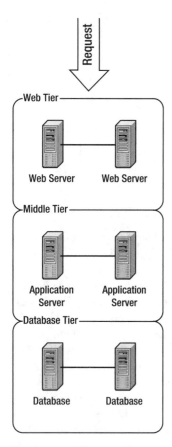

Figure 8-7. *Defining at least two instances to support each tier makes scaling easier later.*

Finally, depending on your financial resources, try to keep your Java EE tiers physically separated: at least two machines horizontally and vertically clustered (or scaled) in the dynamic Web tier, and at least two in the business tier, as illustrated in Figure 8-8.

In summary, the best layout is both vertical and horizontal scaling defined at each tier. If your failover requirements necessitate clusters, then define replication across physical machines.

■**Note** The configuration described in this section works for standard environments, but the game starts to change when using very large machines. In the case of very large machines, such as mainframes with hordes of CPUs, the machine is typically broken into logical partitions: you assign a certain amount of memory and a number of CPUs to a logical partition, and that acts as a virtual machine in and of itself. Once these logical partitions have been established, the aforementioned guidelines are applicable with the caveat that you cannot scale horizontally physically, only logically. But in reality, these machines rarely crash, and you can be reasonably confident that your application is safe.

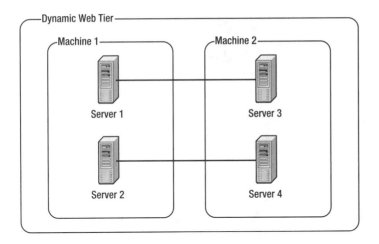

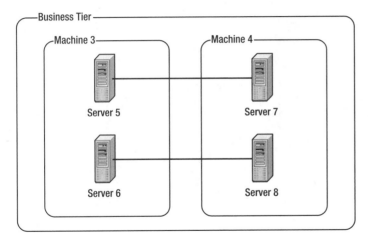

Figure 8-8. *The dynamic Web tier and the business tier each consist of four application server instances running on two physical machines, with replication being sent between machines.*

Hardware Infrastructure

Hardware configurations are virtually limitless. Figure 8-9 attempts to summarize visually what I have seen most commonly in the field.

As a request is received, it passes through a firewall to a load balancer that distributes the request across a collection of Web servers. The load balancer is best configured with *sticky sessions*, meaning that once a user makes a request and is forwarded to an application server, the user is forever directed to the same application server. This helps ensure both that a user's session information is always valid and never caught in between replicated servers and that the user is never redirected to a server that does not have the user's information.

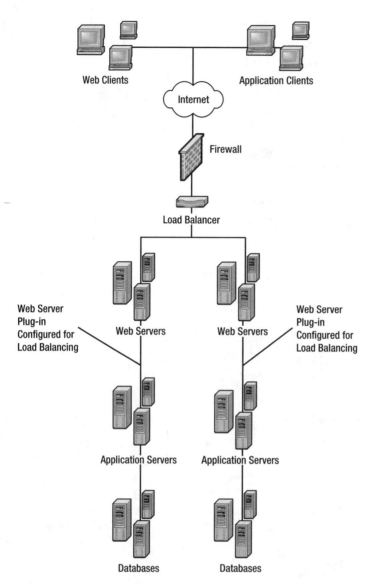

Figure 8-9. *A typical production environment*

The Web servers typically are configured using an application server software plug-in to balance the requests destined for an application server to the appropriate application server. The Web server plug-in should also be configured to use sticky sessions, because sending the same user to the same Web server—but not to the same application server—defeats the purpose of making sessions sticky. In some environments, Web servers are separated from application servers by another firewall, but not always. When making this decision, you need to consider how secure your business tier needs to be: if someone hacks into your Web server, do you need to stop the intruder there, or are security measures at the Web server sufficient? Inserting a firewall between your Web and application servers is a good idea for security, but it adds additional overhead to your requests as well as additional responsibilities to your workload to manage and maintain it. If you are working with users' personal and/or financial information, then I would consider a firewall placed between the Web and business tiers essential. But if you are only displaying the contents of an online catalog or maintaining a message forum, then the urgency to do so is reduced.

As previously mentioned, application servers can be broken down into a dynamic Web tier and a business tier, each equipped with its own set of hardware and software servers. In the case of a cluster, each tier should access a consistent primary business server and fail over appropriately. This will help mitigate the load.

Finally, as requests are made against the database, these requests need to be properly load balanced. Fortunately, in large environments, this is handled for you by your database clustering software. And for small environments, database clustering is too expensive to be feasible, so load balancing is accomplished by refactoring your data model to allow data to be maintained in distinct database instances.

Load Testing Strategy

Before closing this chapter, we'll revisit the different performance testing phases. In development, we implement performance unit tests; in integration and QA, we implement a performance integration test and a performance integration load test; and in the production staging environment, we implement a production staging performance test and a production staging performance load test. Remember when implementing production staging tests that your deployment strategy must be represented in your production staging environment.

It is not sufficient to load test your application running in a shared environment with other applications competing for resources without implementing the same tier breakdown in your deployment strategy. Requests spend time traveling between tiers and passing through firewalls, so for the highest degree of confidence, be sure to create a production staging environment that resembles your production environment. Ideally, you would maintain a production staging environment that either mirrors production or is a stripped-down version of production. For example, if you have six application server instances in your business tier in production, two might suffice in production staging. But testing your entire application server on the same machine or missing any of its tiers reduces confidence as applications are rolled out to production.

As a general rule, when scaling down a production environment to create a staging environment, scale down the environment proportionally. For example, if you have four Web servers and eight application servers, then production might have two Web servers and four application servers. If you drop down to two Web servers and two application servers, you will find it difficult to extrapolate the behavior of the Web servers when forced to spread the load between two servers (each) instead of one.

Summary

A high-performance deployment strategy depends on expected user load, availability require-ments, and failover requirements. The expected load defines the number of simultaneous users you need to support and thus directly impacts the number of servers in your environ-ment. Availability requirements dictate how much time your application needs to be available. Failover requirements define the impact of application server outages on your users. Equipped with this information, you can scale your application vertically and horizontally to satisfy the expected user load and meet availability SLAs while implementing clusters to satisfy failover requirements.

A well-planned deployment strategy can save you countless hours and help you avoid sleepless nights. It can give you confidence that your application can handle whatever curveballs your users send its way.

In the next chapter, we'll look at the process of performing a capacity assessment against a production staging environment that adheres to our deployment strategy.

CHAPTER 9

Performance and Scalability Testing

"I sent my architect on a tuning mission following the wait-based tuning approach that you showed us. We decided to scale both vertically and horizontally inside a cluster, carefully choosing our replication strategy. So now how do I set my expectations for the environment?"

John took a step that I was hoping that he would. He recognized that, while tuning efforts and deployment planning exercises improve the performance of your applications, they do nothing to instill you with confidence until after you have run performance and scalability tests and can support the effectiveness of your efforts with hard numbers.

"That is a very good question. Remember when we talked about the behavior of an application when it is exposed to an increasing user load?"

"Do you mean the response time, utilization, and throughput graph?" John asked.

"Exactly," I replied. "As user load increases, the system is required to do more, so resource utilizations increase; the application performs more work, so throughput increases; and thread contexts switch, so response time is marginally affected. But there is a point where resources saturate, causing the system overhead to hinder application performance, reduce throughput, and finally increase the response time exponentially." Whenever I describe this graph (see Figure 9-2) without any props, my arms move in upward curves and crosses, which are meaningless to anyone who has not seen the graph before. Luckily John knew exactly what I was talking about and tolerated my flapping arms.

"Yes, that graph scares me, because when things start going bad, they go bad very quickly!"

"Yes, so the key to attaining confidence in your tuning efforts and deployment planning exercises is to run performance and scalability tests. And the final goal in running these tests is overlaying your performance metrics on top of such a graph. In the end, you can state with confidence the number of users your application can support while meeting SLAs and how it behaves afterward. Let me show you the strategies I employ to perform these tests."

Performance and scalability testing are crucial to the successful deployment of your applications. You can design solid applications, test each component individually, test the integrated solution, and even test your applications in a production staging environment, but until you discover the limits of your environment, you will never attain sufficient confidence that your application can meet the changing needs and expectations of your users.

Here's a coarse comparison: back in 1997, I bought a 1995 Mazda RX7 (the Batmobile-looking car). It is a high-performance sports car boasting acceleration from 0 to 60 mph in less than five seconds and a top speed of over 160 mph. It corners fast and handles incredibly, but it has a limitation referred to as "unpredictable oversteer"—it can take corners very fast, but once you pass a certain threshold, the car's behavior is unpredictable. Shortly after buying the car, I took my friend Chris for a ride, and we discovered that threshold. I approached a tight corner, and instead of letting off the gas, I accelerated. The car performed two 360-degree spins before coming to a (thankfully) safe stop. Needless to say, Chris and I needed to take another short trip around the neighborhood to restart our hearts, but I never pushed the car past the limit that I discovered.

Let's bring this back to performance and scalability testing: you may be comfortable with the performance of your application in general and even with its performance at your current or projected usage, but until you discover its breaking point, you will always experience uncertainty every time marketing runs another promotion or a new, high-profile customer endorses your application. The key to attaining this confidence is to perform the following tasks:

- Assess the performance of your application at expected load.

- Determine the load that causes your application to exceed its SLAs.

- Determine the load that causes your application to reach its saturation point and enter the buckle zone.

- Construct a performance degradation model from expected usage to exceeded SLAs to saturation point.

With this information in hand, you will be well equipped to project the effects of changes in usage patterns on your environment and intelligently recommend environment changes to your CIO.

Performance vs. Scalability

The terms "performance" and "scalability" are commonly used interchangeably, but the two are distinct: *performance* measures the speed with which a single request can be executed, while *scalability* measures the ability of a request to maintain its performance under increasing load. For example, the performance of a request may be reported as generating a valid response within three seconds, but the scalability of the request measures the request's ability to maintain that three-second response time as the user load increases.

Scalability asks the following questions about the request:

- At the expected usage, does the request still respond within three seconds?

- For what percentage of requests does it respond in less than three seconds?

- What is the response time distribution for requests that do not respond within three seconds?

If you recall from Chapter 5, an SLA is defined by the following three key criteria:

- It is specific.

- It is flexible.

- It is reasonable.

The "specific" value measures the performance of a single request: the request must respond within three seconds. The "flexibility" value, however, measures the scalability of the request: the request must respond within three seconds for 95 percent of requests and may fluctuate, at most, one standard deviation from the mean.

The strategy is to first ensure the performance of a request or of a component and then test the request or component for scalability. Ensuring the performance of a request or of a component depends on where your application is in the development life cycle. Optimally, you want to implement proactive performance testing in the development phase of your application, which includes developing unit tests using a unit testing framework, like JUnit, and implementing code profiling, memory profiling, and coverage profiling against those unit tests.

From code profiling, you want to watch for the following three key things:

- Poorly performing methods

- Methods invoked a significant number of times

- Classes and methods that allocate an excessive number of objects

The purpose of code profiling is to identify any egregiously slow algorithms or methods that are creating a surplus of objects; for example, trying to sort 1 million items using a bubble sort algorithm can result in up to 10^{12} object comparisons, which could take minutes or hours to execute.

When implementing memory profiling, you look for the following two things:

- Loitering objects

- Object cycling

Loitering objects, also referred to as *lingering object references*, are unwanted objects that stay in the heap after the end of a use case. They reduce the amount of available heap memory and typically are tied to one or more requests, so they are leading the heap down a path to its ultimate demise. Another side of memory mismanagement is *object cycling*, or the rapid creation and destruction of objects in the heap. While these objects do not linger in the heap and consume permanent resources, they force the garbage collector to run more frequently and hence hinder performance.

Finally, *coverage profiling* establishes the level of confidence you have in your unit tests. The coverage profiler tells you each condition that was and was not executed for every line of code. If you test the functionality and performance of your code in unit tests, and your coverage is high, then you can feel comfortable that your code is solid. On the other hand, if your coverage is low, then you can have very little confidence in your test results.

Chapter 5 details how to use each of these performance profiling tools and how to interpret the results. If you jumped right to this chapter, I suggest you review the material in Chapter 5 before investigating performance problems.

Thus far we have been looking at the bottom-up approach to performance tuning from an application's inception. This approach is great in theory, and you can definitely apply it in the *next* project, but what do you do today? Luckily, we can apply similar principles with a top-down approach. I hope that you have a production staging environment that you can test against, but if not, you can capture performance data from a running production environment.

■**Note** Configuring a diagnostic tool to run in a production environment can be a tricky task, but depending on the tool itself, its impact on the environment can be mitigated. The core factors that can help you mitigate the impact of such a tool in production are configuring filters, increasing aggregate sampling intervals, and bundling components. Filters allow you to capture only the requests you are interested in (in some cases, you may need to record several iterations of data with different filters to capture all interesting data). Call traces are aggregated at a specific interval, and increasing this interval reduces the workload on the data correlator (for example, aggregate data every 1 or 2 minutes, rather than every 10 or 30 seconds). To isolate poorly performing components, sometimes bundling related code packages together into individual components and returning a single value, rather than reporting method-by-method data, can provide valuable information at lesser overhead. You will need to spend significant time with your performance diagnostic tools and tool vendors to determine the best approach to recording detailed information in a live production environment.

The process is to record detailed, method-level performance information against your environment while it is subjected to load. From this data, you want to extract the following information:

- What are the slowest running requests?

- What are the most frequently executed requests?

- From these requests, what are the hot paths through the requests?

- What are the hot points in those hot paths?

- Are the performance problems code issues, configuration issues, or external dependency issues?

Examine each slow request and determine why it is slow: is it a slow method, a slow database call, or an environment threading or memory issue? If you can identify the problem as being code related, then examine the offending methods. If the performance issues still evade you, then examine the offending methods inside a code profiler by replaying the problematic requests against your profiled environment and examining the offending methods line by line. Continue this process until all major code bottlenecks have been resolved.

To fine-tune your application, identify requests and/or methods that are executed frequently. Try to find methods that you have a chance of tuning; for example, your application may call StringBuffer.append() millions of times, but you cannot improve its performance. (Actually, in this case, you want to find out why the method is being called so many times and substantially reduce that if possible.) Shaving a few milliseconds off of a frequently executed method can yield dramatic improvements in application performance.

All performance issues not related to your code need to be investigated on their own; for example, database issues need to be evaluated in a database diagnostic tool. Your Java EE information should provide you with problematic contexts such as SQL statements and the call path that generated the undesirable behavior.

The goal is to resolve as many performance bottlenecks as possible prior to performing a capacity assessment. While a capacity assessment can help you tune your environment, tuning is only the secondary goal—the primary goal is to determine the maximum load you can support while meeting your SLAs and establish a degradation model for your application once SLAs are violated.

Capacity Assessment

The purpose of a capacity assessment is to identify the following key data points:

- The response time of your requests at expected usage

- The usage when the first request exceeds its SLA

- The usage when the application reaches its saturation point

- The degradation model from the first missed SLA to the application's saturation point

A capacity assessment should be performed against your production staging environment, but only after you have verified that your application can sustain expected usage through a performance load test. The capacity assessment is the last test performed at the end of an iteration or prior to moving the application to production. Your production staging environment should mirror your production environment, if possible, or be a scaled-down version of it; otherwise, the results of the capacity assessment are of little value.

Graduated Load Tester

The key tool that empowers you to perform a capacity assessment is a *graduated load tester*. A graduated load tester is configured to climb to your expected usage in a regular and predefined pattern and then increase load in graduated steps. The purpose behind this configuration is to allow you to capture and analyze performance metrics at discrete units of load. The behavior of graduated load generation is illustrated in Figure 9-1.

Graduated step sizes need to be thoughtfully chosen: the finer their granularity, the better your assessment will be, but the longer the test will take to run. You can usually find a good compromise between the test run time, the analysis time, and the granularity of the steps; it varies from application to application, but as a general rule, I configure these steps to be about 5 percent of the expected load. For example, if you need to support 500 simultaneous users, then your graduated step might start at 25 users. Graduated steps are required because of the nature of enterprise applications, as Figure 9-2 illustrates.

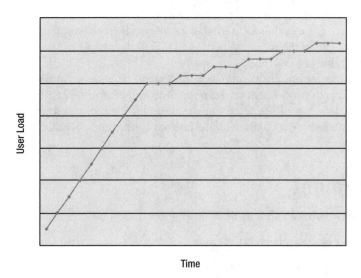

Figure 9-1. *A graduated load test*

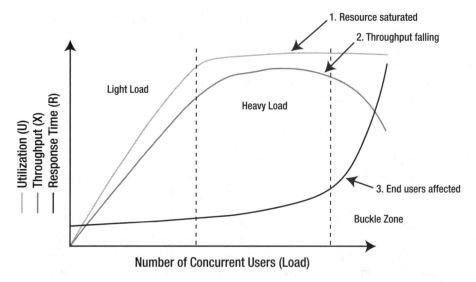

Figure 9-2. *A loaded enterprise application follows this typical pattern.*

As the number of users (load) increases, the system utilization naturally increases, because you need more resources to do more work. Likewise the throughput increases, because as you are sending more work to the application, it is performing more work. When the load becomes too heavy for the environment to support, then resources become saturated, which manifests in excessive CPU context switching, garbage collections, disk I/O, network activity, and so on.

These manifestations result in a decline in request throughput, which means that requests are left pending and response time increases. If the load continues to increase when the system is in this state, then the response time performance degrades exponentially. The point at which performance time degrades is referred to as the *saturation point*, or, more colorfully, the *buckle zone*.

Capacity Assessment Usage Mappings

The capacity assessment attempts to map the behavior of your environment to the graph shown in Figure 9-2. Therefore, at the end of the capacity assessment, you should be able to construct a graph similar to Figure 9-3.

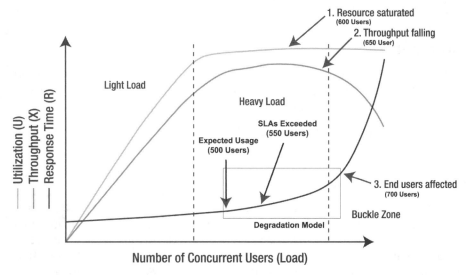

Figure 9-3. *In this test, we successfully satisfied our expected users, and we have a buffer before we start exceeding SLAs.*

Figure 9-3 illustrates that the application is successfully satisfying its 500 expected users, but at 550 users the application starts exceeding its SLAs, showing that we have a 10 percent user buffer that can be supported. The buffer percentage represents your comfort zone for your application—if your load never moves outside of your buffer, even during peaks, then you can sleep well at night. You should strive to maintain approximately a 25 percent buffer to allow for marketing promotions or any other significant increase in traffic. A buffer greater than 40 percent is typically too large, because it means that you are maintaining additional hardware and software licenses that really are not needed.

■Note Although a 25–40 percent buffer is generally ideal, you need to analyze your usage patterns to determine what is best for your environment. If your usage patterns are very volatile, then you might want a larger buffer, but if you are running an intranet application with a fixed maximum load, a smaller buffer may be sufficient.

The environment's resources start to become saturated at 600 users, and by 650 users the request throughput degrades substantially. User requests begin backing up in thread pools and finally at the socket level, and by 700 users, the application has entered the buckle zone. Once the application is in the buckle zone, the only option is to stop accepting requests and allow the application to process all pending requests. But in reality, at this point, the only feasible answer is to begin restarting application servers to manually flush out user requests.

The user response time, resource utilizations, and the request throughput between the expected usage point and the buckle zone can be used to construct a degradation model. The degradation model explicitly identifies the support buffer and response time patterns. The purpose of constructing a degradation model is to allow your CIO to determine when to acquire additional hardware and software resources. For example, if usage patterns are increasing month-over-month in an identified trend, and a degradation model identifies that within 12 weeks end-user SLAs will be violated, then a strong case is presented for acquiring additional resources.

Measurements

Before configuring your graduated load tester and firing load at your environment, you need to put the tools in place to gather the appropriate measurements to assess the various states of your environment. In the previous section, we identified three categories of metrics:

- Resource utilization

- Throughput

- Response time

The executive summary of your capacity assessment may state simply that at 600 users resources became saturated, but the detailed resource analysis is going to report far more than a simple saturation point metric. We look at a variety of resources in a capacity assessment and identifying the limiting resources is important. For example, if the application is CPU-bound, meaning that the core resource that becomes saturated and brings down the application is the CPU, then adding additional RAM may not be very helpful. You need to configure each relevant resource with monitoring tools and record its behavior during the capacity assessment.

Throughput, the second category of metrics, is defined simply as work performed over a period of time. In a transactional application, requests committed per second is a common measure of throughput, and in some environments, I have used the load tester's recording of successful requests processed per second as a measure of throughput. Your choice of measurement is not as important as the fact that throughput is recorded consistently.

Finally, response time can be measured in terms of single requests, business transactions that are a composite of requests, or a combination of the two. The most effective measure of response time that I have observed has been a high-level recording of business transactions with the ability to drill deeper into the individual requests that comprise the business transaction. But in the end, you are measuring your response times against your use case SLAs, so be sure that your measurements are consistent.

Resource Utilization

The most common resource measured is CPU utilization, because it always increases in direct proportion to the user load: more requests made against the system require more CPU resources to process them. But you need to capture other important metrics, namely the following:

- Physical memory utilization

- Operating system disk I/O rates

- Operating system thread/process utilization

- Application server thread pool utilization

- Application server connection pool utilization

- Application server heap utilization and garbage collection rates (frequency and duration)

- Application server cache and pool utilizations

- Messaging system utilizations

- External dependency profiles (databases, legacy systems, Web services, and so forth)

- Network traffic sent between application nodes

The analysis of CPU utilization is pretty straightforward: under 80 percent utilization means that the CPU is not under serious duress, but as it increases from 80–95 percent, the entire system begins to suffer. If the CPU becomes pinned at 95–100 percent utilization, then it is going to have difficulties processing anything in a timely manner.

The key to physical memory analysis is identifying anything that is being swapped out to disk. Virtual memory and swapping are manageable on your desktop client, but you know that as soon as your operating system's memory requirements exceed the amount of physical memory that you have, your computer becomes less and less responsive. The same thing happens on a server, only the manifestations of the conditions are much more severe for your end users. Throughout the capacity assessment, you need to record physical and virtual memory usage as well as paging rates: high physical and virtual memory usages combined with increased paging rates signify physical memory saturation.

Disk I/O rates represent how much data is being read from and written to the hard disk. Disk reads and writes are expensive relative to reading and writing to physical memory, and typically, high disk I/O rates mean that caching has not been configured optimally. For example, when you make a request from a database, its data resides on the file system, but it maintains frequently accessed data in memory caches. If the database is properly tuned, it should be serving the majority of its requests from a cache, rather than having to read from the file system to satisfy every request.

Different operating systems define their threading strategies differently, but regardless of the implementation, the operating system controls its applications' access to the CPU. The operating system's ability to maximize the use of its CPUs needs to be analyzed: if the threading configuration prohibits the maximum use of its CPUs, then the environment can be thread or process bound. For example, in older Linux threading models, each thread was represented by a new process, so the Linux maximum process configuration limited the maximum number of threads an application server could use. On the other hand, Solaris allows a single process to maintain its own internal threads, but only through the configuration of multiple processes can the operating system's CPUs be fully utilized. Tracking application server thread utilization is not sufficient for a capacity assessment; you need to track the operating system's threads as well.

When a request is received by an application server, it is placed into an execution queue that is processed by a thread from the designated application server's thread pool. If the application server is out of threads, then the request will sit waiting in the execution queue for a thread to process it. If the application server thread utilization approaches 100 percent and pending requests are waiting in the execution queue, then the environment is bound by the number of application server threads. Of course, this value must be evaluated in the context of the entire system. For example, if the application server thread pool utilization is at 100 percent with pending requests, and the operating system CPU is at 40 percent, then the thread pool size should be increased. But if the application server thread pool is at 100 percent, and the CPU became pinned at 100 percent 30 seconds earlier, then the CPU bottleneck caused the request backup. All of these components are tightly integrated, and your job is to uncover the root cause of bottlenecks.

Most applications access a database or some other external dependency, such as a legacy system. Rather than establishing a new connection to the external dependency each time that the application needs to interact with it, the preferred implementation is to create a pool of connections to it (either a JDBC or JCA connection pool). If your application server is processing a request that depends on a connection from a connection pool, and no connection is available, then the processing thread must wait for a connection to become available. If you recall Chapter 6, where we explored the concept of wait-based tuning, application server wait points represent application server metrics that you need to monitor and analyze during a capacity assessment—the same principles established in Chapter 6 apply here as well.

The application server heap can significantly degrade performance as load increases if it is not configured properly. While performing the capacity assessment, you want to observe the heap utilization and the garbage collection rate. As load increases, the rate of temporary object creation and destruction increases, which adds additional burdens on the garbage collector. If these objects are created and destroyed faster than the garbage collector can reclaim them, then the garbage collector will have to freeze all threads in the JVM while it performs a full mark and sweep (and optionally compact) garbage collection. During this time, nothing is processing, and all of your SLAs may be compromised.

Session storage requirements also can affect heap performance under load. If each session requires 1MB of memory, then each additional user will consume an additional 1MB of memory—700 users require 700MB of memory. These storage requirements are a strong reason to keep sessions light, but depending on your business requirements, doing so may not be an option. Therefore, you need to monitor the heap growth throughout the capacity assessment and potentially increase the heap size to meet the application requirements.

Application server caches and pools can become wait points in your application call stacks, because as requests obtain objects from caches and pools, they may have to wait for the objects to be returned. The wait time can be mitigated by proper sizing and management algorithms (such as using a least-recently-used caching algorithm), and your capacity assessment will identify if these caches or pools are causing your waits. Look for cache thrashing (high passivation rates) and threads waiting on pools to detect this condition.

Many applications make significant use of messaging, either for asynchronous processing or as a communication mechanism between Java EE and legacy systems (IBM shops tend to do this a lot). You need to ensure that messages are passing through the messaging server quickly and efficiently without being rejected. The configuration parameters for tuning a message server will differ from vendor to vendor, but some common things to look at are message and/or byte utilizations and message throughput. If the messaging server resides on its own physical machine, then you need to watch all operating system statistics and internal messaging thread pools.

The same operating system– and domain-specific metrics need to be observed for all external systems that your application interacts with, such as databases, legacy systems, and internal Web service providers. Consider that each technology your application interacts with is built on top of a technology stack that has the potential to cripple the capacity of your application. Your goal is to identify the potential wait points in those various technology stacks, capture relevant metrics during a capacity assessment, and analyze their behavior as it relates to your application.

Finally, one of the most important metrics that can yield significant insight into the capacity of your environment is network traffic, including communication and latency. Every remote call that you make has the potential to disrupt the performance of your application, and the impact increases in proportion to your load. And depending on the number of network hops that a request makes, the impact may not compare one to one with the user load. For example, if the majority of requests pass from a load balancer, to a Web server, to an application server Web tier, to an application server business tier, and finally to a database, then a single request to the Web server resolves to three additional network hops. Therefore 500 simultaneous requests resolve to 1,500 network calls, which can dramatically affect the performance of your environment.

In order to perform a valid capacity assessment, you need to capture metrics on each machine in your environment related to the application servers, operating system, external dependencies, messaging, and network communications, as Figure 9-4 illustrates.

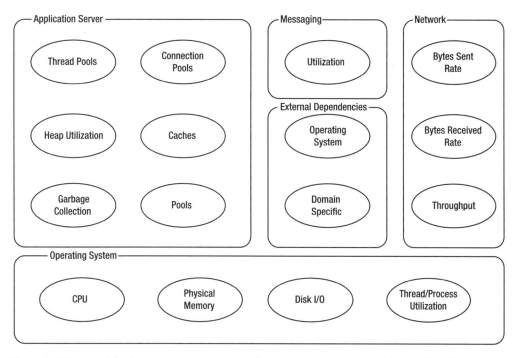

Figure 9-4. *Some of the key metrics that you need to capture on each machine during the capacity assessment*

Building a Capacity Assessment Report

The capacity assessment report serves the following two purposes:

- The communication mechanism to express the capacity of an environment

- A historical marker to assess the impact of application changes

First and foremost, the capacity assessment identifies the capacity of a given environment. It must clearly state the performance of the environment under expected or projected usage and the maximum capacity of the environment while maintaining SLAs. For example, it might summarize performance information by stating that at the expected 500 users, the average response time is 20 percent below defined SLAs, and the environment can support a maximum of 550 users before violating SLAs. Furthermore, the capacity analysis provides models from which hardware and software forecasts can be constructed.

The secondary purpose of the capacity assessment is to establish historical performance markers against which future application releases can be compared. Quantifying the impact of software enhancements against a known baseline is important, so that as your applications evolve, you know what features helped and hindered performance. At the end of each capacity assessment, you should compare the results to previous capacity assessments and add them to your Capacity Assessment Report.

The Capacity Assessment Report is composed of the following components:

- Executive summary

- Test profile

- Capacity analysis

- Degradation model

- Impact analysis

- Final analysis and recommendations

This section reviews each component of a Capacity Assessment Report and defines the articles that should be included in each.

Executive Summary

The executive summary is the overview of the capacity assessment, suitable to be presented to an IT manager or CIO. The executive summary should convey the pertinent results with minor substantiation, but not with the same level of detail the capacity analysis will provide. In general, your CIO will be very interested in the results themselves, but much less interested in many of the details that informed your conclusions. And those details are examined elsewhere in the report for review by any interested party.

Specifically, the executive summary needs to include the following information:

- *Performance of the environment at the expected usage*: This should be presented by stating the expected usage along with the average difference, minimum difference, and maximum difference (as percentages) between the use case SLAs and observed response times at the expected load.

- *Load at the time that the first use case SLA was violated*: Note that use cases are defined in terms of a specific value, a measure of flexibility, and a hard upper limit, which is usually defined in terms of standard deviations from the mean. This definition means that your results do not report that the SLA has been violated on a single incidence but rather when the violation exceeds the level of flexibility.

- *The resource saturation point, including the resources being saturated*: Rather than reporting that resources are saturated at 600 users, reporting that at 600 users the environment became CPU-bound as the Web tier CPU became saturated is more valuable.

- *The end user experience fail point*: This point is where the request response time begins increasing at an exponential rate, and it highlights the point of no return that can only be resolved by an application server restart.

- *A graph*: The graph, similar to Figure 9-3, visually summarizes the preceding four bullet points.

- *An overview of the impact analysis results*: The overview primarily focuses on capacity differences, either as improvements or degradations of supported load.

As with the executive summary of any report, the emphasis should be on the results of the analysis with minimal supporting evidence; the body of the document provides all necessary supporting evidence. The goal is for you to quickly convey your results to the reader.

Test Profile

The test profile describes the load test scripts and load tester configurations used to perform the capacity assessment. This description is valuable, because it establishes the context for which the capacity assessment is valid. If product management provides you with a collection of usage profiles and asks you to first tune the environment and then perform a capacity assessment against the environment, your ability to successfully perform these tasks is only as valid as the usage profiles. By adding a detailed test profile, you gain the benefit of a peer review process—the production management team, as well as your peers, can analyze the nature of your capacity assessment and provide feedback as to why the test may or may not necessarily yield valid results.

Specifically, the test profile should answer the following questions:

- What use cases were executed?

- What was the balance between use cases?

- What was the frequency of each use case?

- What was the specific configuration for each use case, such as think-time settings, image downloads, and so on?

- What was the load testing profile, such as the ramp-up period and pattern, graduated step sizes, load duration, and so forth?

- How were the physical and logical servers configured in the test environment?

- What was the monitoring profile? For example, what was monitored and at what level?

The test profile serves both as a historical marker for the test context and as a point for later validation against actual production usage. After the application is running in production, validating user patterns against the test profile and the observed behavior against expected behavior makes a very good exercise. This exercise can help you refine your future estimates.

Capacity Analysis

The capacity analysis presents your findings, with all of the details to support your conclusions. This section supplies all supporting evidence in graphs and detailed textual analysis of the graphs. It should begin by presenting the same graph displayed in the executive summary and providing a more detailed overview of your conclusions. The sections following the initial graph detail the behavior of the environment at each critical point in the graph, including sections for the environment behavior at the following times:

- Expected load

- The SLA violation point

- The saturation point

- The buckle zone

Each section should include a table presenting a summary of the behavior of each use case at the expected load. A sample is presented in Table 9-1. Your assessment might introduce the table by explaining, "At the expected load of 500 users, the following behavior was observed."

Table 9-1. *Sample Use Case Summary*

Use Case	SLA Ave	SLA Dist	SLA Max	Actual Ave	Actual Dist	Actual Max	Actual SD	Actual 2xSD	Delta Resp Time Buffer
Login	4 sec.	95%	6 sec.	3.2 sec.	97%	4.7 sec.	1.2 sec.	2.0 sec.	20%
Search	3 sec.	95%	5 sec.	2.6 sec.	96%	4.0 sec.	0.6 sec.	1.0 sec.	13.3%
Input Claim	7 sec.	95%	10 sec.	5.5 sec.	98%	9 sec.	2.0 sec.	3.0 sec.	21.4%
Summary									18.2%

The Use Case Summary columns are defined in Table 9-2.

Table 9-2. *Use Case Summary Column Definitions*

Column	Description
Use Case	The use case name or number being presented.
SLA Ave	The SLA's "specific" value, or the average maximum value for the defined distribution.
SLA Dist	The SLA's "flexibility" value, or the percentage of requests that must fall below the average in order for the use case to uphold its SLA.
SLA Max	The maximum value permissible for any request, the hard limit (or relative limit if working in standard deviations) that if exceeded immediately causes an SLA violation.
Actual Ave	The average observed response time for the use case.
Actual Dist	The observed percentage of requests below the average SLA value.
Actual Max	The maximum observed response time for the use case.
Actual SD	The standard deviation of observed response times.
Actual 2xSD	Two standard deviations of the observed response times.
Delta Resp Time Buffer	The response time buffer percentage. This is a measure of the buffer that the use case has between the observed average response time and the SLA average response time. It roughly identifies the amount that the use case can grow before it is in danger of violating its SLA.

In addition to providing information about the use cases, these sections should also present summary information about pertinent resources. From a Java EE perspective, this information is going to include CPU utilization, heap utilization, garbage collection rates, thread pool utilization, pending requests, connection pools, caches, and request throughput.

These four sections present a snapshot of the state of use case response times, resource utilization, and throughput. The conclusion of each section should include an analysis of the raw data, including articles required to substantiate your conclusions. For example, you can include charts and graphs, numerical analysis of the presented data, historical capacity assessment data, and so on.

Degradation Model

While the capacity analysis sections provide detailed information with snapshots captured at specific points in the assessment, the degradation model reports the entire assessment in a timeline. It identifies trends in response time and resource utilization data throughout the assessment, but its primary focus is on the segment between the expected load and the buckle zone.

The degradation model contains a considerable number of graphs, illustrating the following information:

- Use case response times

- Utilization of each relevant resource

- Application throughput

Each of these graphs should be overlaid with the following identified performance zones:

- Expected usage to SLA violation point

- SLA violation point to resource saturation point

- Resource saturation point to buckle zone

The purpose of this section is to identify not only the behavior of use cases at various user loads, but also why performance issues arise. For example, if the Login use case degrades at 550 users and exceeds its SLA, is it because of an external dependency, the application server CPU utilization, a database connection pool, a database call, or an application server thread pool? Domain knowledge of your environment and your applications empowers you to be able to correlate metrics and derive accurate conclusions in this section of the Capacity Assessment Report. When I am on-site with customers, I spend a considerable amount of time interviewing them to learn the following:

- What technologies are they using (for example, servlets, JSP, stateless session beans, entity beans, JMS)?

- What design patterns have they employed and where?

- What does a whiteboard sketch of the path of a typical request through the application look like?

- What objects are cached, and what are those objects used for?

- What objects are pooled?

- How is the environment configured (for example, thread pools, the heap, and connection pools)?

- What is their network topology?

- What external systems are their applications interacting with and through what communication mechanisms?

Through this interview process I "cheat": I anticipate where performance problems might occur, so that when I analyze the customer's environment and see them occur in the capacity assessment, I have a strong idea about what metrics to check for relevant correlations. Without this information, constructing an accurate degradation model is difficult at best.

Impact Analysis

Once a capacity assessment has been performed against a Java EE environment, it should be saved for future comparisons; these performance comparisons are explored in the impact analysis. The impact analysis identifies the differences between two or more capacity assessments with the primary intent of quantifying the impact of code changes against system capacity.

If your organization is mature enough to routinely perform capacity assessments throughout the development of an application, then the impact analysis can be mostly automated, because it tracks performance differences between response times and resource utilizations for the same use cases and very similar, if not identical, test scripts. But if you are like most companies for whom performing a formal capacity assessment on each significant iteration is not feasible and who reserve capacity assessments for released code, then the task is a little more daunting and requires deep, domain-specific analysis. In this case, the summary of the impact analysis should be performed using response time buffer percentages. Recall that the response time buffers measure the percentage difference between the observed performance at a specific user load and the SLA. With this measurement, you can assess the performance of application functionality at specific user loads and determine whether a particular functional element degraded or improved in a subsequent release; you measure the degradation or improvement against the SLA defined for that functionality. If the SLA is renegotiated as a result of new or changed functionality, then an altered response time will not skew the impact analysis.

The purpose of the impact analysis is to identify the following:

- General capacity impact of code changes, including the performance at the expected load, the SLA violation point, the resource saturation point, and the buckle zones

- Specific degradations and improvements of use cases

- Specific degradations and improvements in resource utilizations

The sample Capacity Assessment Report later in this chapter provides additional details about the impact analysis.

Analysis and Recommendations

The analysis and recommendations section provides a conclusion to the Capacity Assessment Report. As such, it summarizes the findings again, but includes information about the impact of the findings on the business process and provides recommendations. It attempts to answer the following questions:

- What is the performance at the current or expected load?

- What load can the environment support and still satisfy SLAs?

- At what point does the environment need to be upgraded?

- What is the nature of that upgrade? Should it add more application server instances, or modify application server configurations (heap size, thread pools, connection pools, and so on)?

- At what point does the environment require additional hardware?

If you have any insight into seasonal patterns, marketing promotions, or any other trending information that will affect user load, this information should be summarized or referenced here to justify your recommendations with forecasted behavior.

Sample Capacity Assessment Report

Excerpts from the various sections of a Capacity Assessment Report follow. An actual Capacity Assessment Report may be 20 to 50 pages or more in length, so this sample attempts to reproduce each major section and include at least one major item in each section. You can fill in the remaining components with performance observations relevant to your environment.

Executive Summary

In this capacity assessment, the Acme Buy High, Sell Low stock application was evaluated in a mirrored production environment for performance. The expected user load for this application is 500 users, and the observations extracted from the test are illustrated in Figure 9-5.

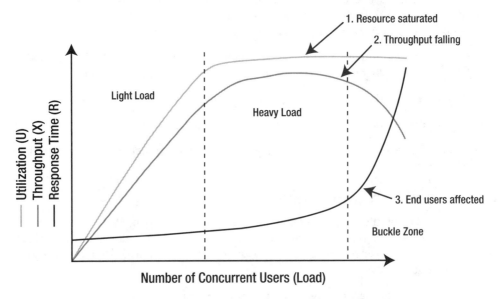

Figure 9-5. *The Buy High, Sell Low environment's behavior as load increases*

Figure 9-5 can be summarized by the following observations:

- At the expected user load of 500, all use cases satisfy their SLAs.

- The first SLA violation is observed at 550 users.

- The environment's saturation point occurs at 600 users.

- The environment enters the buckle zone at 700 users.

Use cases currently maintain an average response time buffer of 19.24 percent and based upon current trend analysis, this will dissipate rapidly over the next three months. My estimates suggest that the current environment will be in violation of its SLAs within five months. The test results indicate that the environment is CPU-bound and requires additional application server hardware to mitigate the five-month degradation point.

The performance of the Buy High, Sell Low application has degraded with the release of version 2.0. The average response time degradation is 12 percent, and the average resource utilization at expected load has increased by 7 percent. Throughput at expected usage has likewise degraded by 10 percent. The maximum capacity has decreased from 650 users to 550 users, a degradation of 15.3 percent.

I recommend additional hardware resources for addition to the environment while the source code is examined to identify the root of the performance degradation.

Test Profile

The capacity assessment was implemented using in-house load testing technology exercising the use cases shown in Table 9-3.

Table 9-3. *Test Profile*

Use Case	Distribution Weight
Login	0.1
Add Stock	0.1
Historical Query	0.2
Historical Graphing	0.2
Stock Discovery	0.2
Profile Management	0.2

The load test was configured to ramp up linearly over 30 minutes to the expected user load of 500 users. The test then implemented a graduated step sized at 25 users to ramp up over 5 minutes and hold for 5 minutes before initiating the next step.

Test Script Configurations

The following section summarizes the test script configurations. It includes detailed information about the primary use case scenario and summarizes the scenario distributions.

Login

The primary scenario for this use case is the successful login of a user with a valid username and a valid password. The steps for this scenario are summarized as follows:

Request	Think Time	SLA Ave	SLA Flexibility	SLA Maximum
GET /stock/index.html	10 sec.	3 sec.	95%	5 sec.
POST /stock/login.do	End	5 sec.	95%	8 sec.

with the following scenario distribution:

Scenario	Distribution
Successful Login	94.5%
Valid username, invalid password	5%
Invalid username	0.5%

Test Platform Topology

The test platform consisted of six physical machines:

- Two Web servers
- Two application servers
- Two database servers

Two application server instances run on each physical application server, totaling four application server instances. Figure 9-6 illustrates this topology.

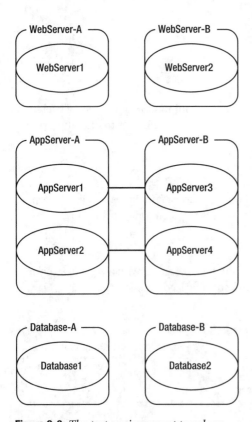

Figure 9-6. *The test environment topology*

The test environment includes clustering with AppServer1 using AppServer3 as its secondary server, AppServer2 using AppServer4 as its secondary server, and vice versa. In this way, the environment is resilient not only to application server instance failure, but also to hardware failure. This configuration adds additional performance overhead, but it meets the predefined availability and failover requirements.

Monitoring Configuration

The monitoring employed during this capacity assessment was configured to poll operating system, database, Web server, and application server statistics after every minute. The load tester was responsible for recording the overall request response times, while light bytecode instrumentation was employed to report tier-level response times. The bytecode instrumentation was not configured to record method-level statistics.

Capacity Analysis

This section presents the observations and conclusions derived in this capacity assessment.

Expected Usage

The expected usage for the Buy High, Sell Low application is 500 users. Table 9-4 reports a summary of the use case behavior at the expected load.

Table 9-4. *Use Case Summary at Expected Usage*

Use Case	SLA Ave	SLA Dist	SLA Max	Actual Ave	Actual Dist	Actual Max	Actual SD	Actual 2xSD	Delta Resp Time Buffer
Login	8 sec.	95%	13 sec.	6.2 sec.	97%	9.7 sec.	1.2 sec.	2.0 sec.	22.5%
Add Stock	10 sec.	95%	14 sec.	8.5 sec.	97%	12 sec.	2.0 sec.	3.2 sec.	15%
Hist Query	10 sec.	95%	14 sec.	8.2 sec.	96%	12 sec.	2.2 sec.	3.5 sec.	18%
Hist Graph	12 sec.	95%	16 sec.	10.1 sec.	98%	14.2 sec.	1.8 sec.	2.2 sec.	15.8%
Stock Disc	8 sec.	95%	12 sec.	6 sec.	99%	8.2 sec.	1.5 sec.	2.0 sec.	25%
Profile Mgmt	12 sec.	95%	16 sec.	9.7 sec.	95.5%	15 sec.	2.5 sec.	5 sec.	19.16%
Summary									19.24%

The SLA Violation Point

The SLA violation point for the Buy High, Sell Low application occurred at 550 users. Table 9-5 reports a summary of the use case behavior at the SLA violation point.

Table 9-5. *Use Case Summary at the SLA Violation Point*

Use Case	SLA Ave	SLA Dist	SLA Max	Actual Ave	Actual Dist	Actual Max	Actual SD	Actual 2xSD	Delta Resp Time Buffer
Login	8 sec.	95%	13 sec.	7.8 sec.	92%	12 sec.	2.2 sec.	4.0 sec.	Violation
Add Stock	10 sec.	95%	14 sec.	9.5 sec.	95%	13.7 sec.	2.0 sec.	3.9 sec.	5%
Hist Query	10 sec.	95%	14 sec.	8.9 sec.	96%	13 sec.	2.9 sec.	3.9 sec.	11%
Hist Graph	12 sec.	95%	16 sec.	11.1 sec.	91%	15.8 sec.	2.8 sec.	3.2 sec.	Violation
Stock Disc	8 sec.	95%	12 sec.	7.4 sec.	95%	10 sec.	2.5 sec.	3.0 sec.	7.5%
Profile Mgmt	12 sec.	95%	16 sec.	10.2 sec.	94%	15.7 sec.	2.5 sec.	5 sec.	Violation
Summary									50% Violation

The Saturation Point

The saturation point for the Buy High, Sell Low application occurred at 600 users. Table 9-6 reports a summary of the use case behavior at the saturation point.

Table 9-6. *Use Case Summary at the Saturation Point*

Use Case	SLA Ave	SLA Dist	SLA Max	Actual Ave	Actual Dist	Actual Max	Actual SD	Actual 2xSD	Delta Resp Time Buffer
Login	8 sec.	95%	13 sec.	12.8 sec.	22%	37 sec.	6.2 sec.	12.0 sec.	Violation
Add Stock	10 sec.	95%	14 sec.	19.5 sec.	14%	32.7 sec.	8.0 sec.	12.9 sec.	Violation
Hist Query	10 sec.	95%	14 sec.	18.9 sec.	34%	23 sec.	3.9 sec.	4.9 sec.	Violation
Hist Graph	12 sec.	95%	16 sec.	17.1 sec.	33%	25.8 sec.	4.8 sec.	3.2 sec.	Violation
Stock Disc	8 sec.	95%	12 sec.	15.4 sec.	27%	18 sec.	6.5 sec.	3.0 sec.	Violation
Profile Mgmt	12 sec.	95%	16 sec.	20.2 sec.	42%	27.7 sec.	5.5 sec.	5 sec.	Violation
Summary									100% Violation

The Buckle Zone

The buckle zone for the Buy High, Sell Low application occurred at 700 users. At this point, all use cases exceeded their SLA average values for greater than 80 percent of requests.

Degradation Model

The aggregate use case response time degradation model is shown in Figure 9-7. The aggregate response time degradation model plots the average response time buffer percentage against the user load.

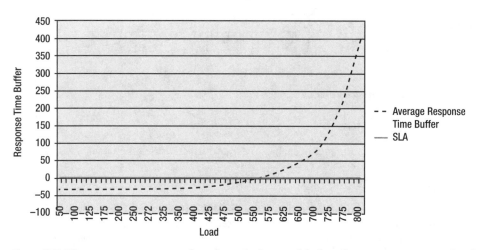

Figure 9-7. *The aggregate response time degradation model plots the average response time buffer against user load. In this case, the average response time buffer percentage hits zero at a user load of 550 users.*

The response time buffer follows nearly an exponential pattern and crosses SLA boundaries at 550 users, so once the SLA is violated, the system can only sustain 100 to 125 users until the application is deemed completely unusable by the users. "Unusable" is defined as response times that exceed their buffer by more than 50 percent.

The environment is primarily bound by CPU utilization in the application server tier. Figure 9-8 displays an aggregate of all CPUs present in the application server tier, and in this figure, you can plainly see that CPU utilization is trending upward.The application server tier CPU aggregate, shown in Figure 9-8, illustrates that by 650 users, the CPU spikes at over 90 percent and then continues to increase, staying over 95 percent utilization at 725 users. The alarming component of Figure 9-8 is the near linear increase of CPU utilization to user load. A linear increase indicates that if the application cannot be refactored to reduce CPU utilization, then tuning efforts are always going to be battling CPU limitations.

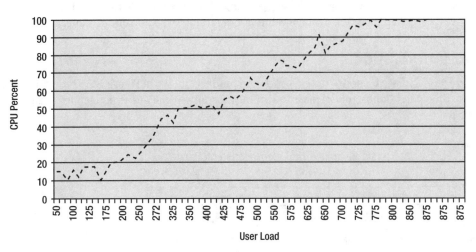

Figure 9-8. *The application server tier CPU aggregate*

Use Case Degradation Model

This section presents the performance of each use case performed during the capacity assessment.

Use Case: Login

Figure 9-9 illustrates the performance of the Login use case throughout the capacity assessment.

The response time for the Login request stayed relatively steady below the four-second mark until reaching about 500 users; it experienced a couple spikes above four seconds up until this point, but nothing sustained or in violation of the flexibility of the use case's SLA. Consistent with the observed degradation patterns, after the user load exceeded 550 users, the response time started to increase significantly.

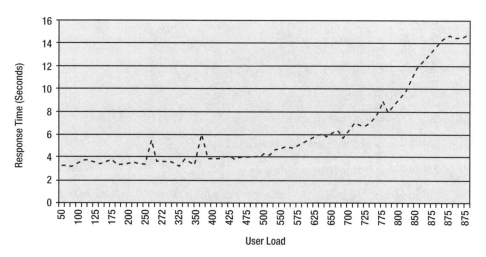

Figure 9-9. *The response time for the Login use case*

Resource Degradation Model

The Buy High, Sell Low application is CPU-bound primarily on the application server tier. Figure 9-8 shows the aggregate CPU utilization for the two machines running in the application server tier.

This section details the performance of each component in each tier as observed during the capacity assessment.

■Note This section, the largest in the Capacity Assessment Report, contains performance graphs for all physical machines, internal servers, and network interactions. Pick the resources that are relevant for your environment and combine multiple related metrics on the same graph. The point of this section is to illustrate the degradation of resources over user load, and to record the behavior of resources for historical impact analysis. Therefore this section reports resources that degrade as well as resources that do not.

Web Tier

Insert graphs of the Web servers, including the following:

- CPU utilization

- Physical memory utilization

- Process memory utilization

- Request throughput

- Thread pool utilization

Application Tier

Insert graphs of the application server machines and instances, including the following information:

- CPU utilization

- Physical memory utilization

- Process memory utilization

- Application server instance heap utilization and garbage collection rates

- Application server instance thread pool utilizations

- Application server instance pool utilizations

- Application server instance cache counts of activation/passivation, hits, and misses

Database Tier

Insert graphs of the database machine and performance information, including the following information:

- CPU utilization

- Physical memory utilization

- Process memory utilization

- Disk I/O rates

- Cache hit/miss counts

Network

Insert graphs that display the response time and load between all servers against user load.

Impact Analysis

The performance of the Buy High, Sell Low application has degraded with the release of version 2.0. The average response time degradation is 12 percent, and the average resource utilization at expected load has increased by 7 percent. Throughput at expected usage has likewise degraded by 10 percent. The maximum capacity has decreased from 650 users to 550 users, a degradation of 15.4 percent.

Figure 9-10 illustrates the impact of the version 2.0 code against the version 1.1 code.

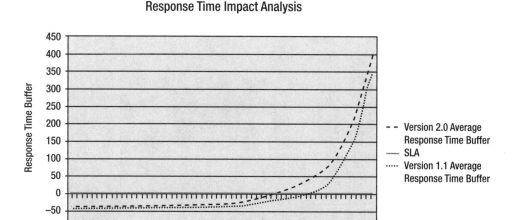

Figure 9-10. *The response time impact analysis*

The growth patterns between the two response time buffers are similar, but version 2.0 code crosses the SLA violation point at 550 users while the version 1.1 code crosses the SLA violation point at 650 users. This pattern shift represents a degradation in overall application capacity of 15.4 percent.

The resource utilization of both code versions was CPU-bound, but version 2.0 code degraded sooner than the previous version, as illustrated in Figure 9-11.

Continue to add resource degradation graphs for relevant resources in your capacity analysis, and where relevant, include graphs illustrating the performance differences between unchanged use cases. For example, if the login functionality did not change between versions, and the performance degraded, then calling out resource utilization differences in the impact analysis is important. However, if the functionality dramatically changed, such as swapping a text file for an LDAP server for user validation upon login, then a direct comparison of response times is not particularly useful to include (unless, of course, this comparison was requested). When functionality changes significantly, the best option is to compare the response time buffers between the application versions: is the new login functionality (with its new SLA) satisfying its SLA as well or better than the previous version?

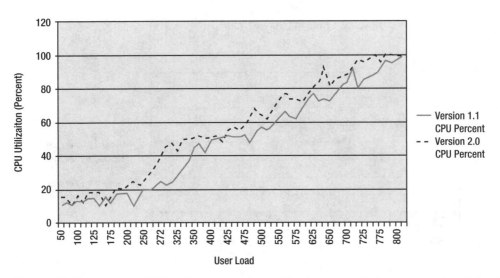

Figure 9-11. *The aggregate CPU utilizations at the application server tier between versions 1.1 and 2.0 of the Buy High, Sell Low application demonstrate that version 2.0 makes heavier use of its CPUs at lower user load than version 1.1.*

■**Note** Many times the code functionality between major versions of an application is significantly different, so a deterministic impact analysis is impossible to perform. In these cases, performing the impact analysis is still beneficial, but focus on comparing the response times and resource utilizations of the expected usage of the new version against the response time and resource utilizations of the expected usage of the previous version. Figure 9-10 plots the average response time buffers rather than request response times to focus on that comparison—the average response time buffer value is relative to each use case's SLA. You may need to add this disclaimer to your impact analysis: "The impact analysis reports the differences between the performance of an enterprise environment executing two sets of application code functionality against their individual performance criteria; it does not necessarily reflect a direct response time impact."

Final Analysis and Recommendations

At the current user load of 500 users, all use cases are satisfied, and the environment can support an additional 50 users. This represents a 10 percent user buffer, which by industry standards is too low: the optimal user buffer for a volatile application like the Buy High, Sell Low application is anywhere between 25 and 40 percent.

The primary factor impeding the performance of the application is the CPU utilization of servers running in the application server tier. Therefore, either the addition of CPUs to existing servers in this tier or of a new physical machine is recommended.

Furthermore, the latest version of the application uses and saturates the CPU faster than the previous version; therefore, analyzing in a code-profiling tool the use cases identified as being problematic in the use case degradation model is recommended to determine the root of the performance changes.

Summary

This chapter discussed the difference between the concepts of performance and scalability: performance measures the speed with which a single request can be executed, while scalability measures the ability of a request to maintain its performance under increasing load. It also outlined the strategy of ensuring performance before testing for scalability. This strategy led to a detailed exploration into the ultimate scalability test—the capacity assessment. A capacity assessment identifies the following key points about your environment:

- Its performance at expected load

- The load that causes it to violate its SLAs

- The load that causes the environment to become saturated

- The load that forces the environment into the buckle zone

Equipped with the correct load testing strategy and monitoring tools, we explored how to ascertain this information and assemble it into a formal Capacity Assessment Report.

In the next chapter, we explore performance assessments that occur more frequently and are used to diagnose performance issues and validate the accuracy of capacity assessments.

PART 3

■■■

Performance Management in Production

CHAPTER 10

Java EE Performance Assessment

"Now that our application is in production and not crashing, I can finally relax," John sighed. It had been several months of hard work rebuilding his application and environment.

"Not quite yet," I replied. "Now you need to validate that your environment is in fact behaving as you expect it to."

"So what do you recommend that I do?" John queried.

"I recommend that you periodically perform a Java EE performance assessment. This assessment will reveal the performance of your application requests, your environment configuration, and your external dependencies."

"But how is that different from a capacity assessment?"

"Well, a capacity assessment is done to, among other things, determine how much load will cause your environment to break," I responded. "A performance assessment is done to determine how your application is performing in your production environment. You wouldn't want to break production now, would you?" This is the key difference between the purposes of a capacity assessment and a performance assessment: a capacity assessment identifies the limitations of an environment, whereas a performance assessment identifies the current performance of an environment.

"Of course not. What do I need to get started?" asked John.

"You are going to need some monitoring tools and a strategy to gather performance information from those tools without disrupting your end users' experience. Let's get started."

Whereas a capacity assessment is performed rather infrequently, such as at the conclusion of a significant iteration or just prior to the production rollout of a new version of an application, a Java EE performance assessment is performed frequently as part of a proactive plan to improve the performance of your applications. The purpose of a performance assessment is to identify performance bottlenecks or simply as a mechanism to proactively tune an application. For example, I once worked with a customer in the telecommunications industry to set up a weekly process to identify the company's top five slowest SQL statements and top five slowest service requests. The person I worked with managed the system administration group, which in this particular organization included database administrators, and he wanted a constant set of tasks that his team could be working on when not troubleshooting issues. Whenever members of this group had breaks in their work schedules, they would start working on bringing down their "top fives."

While a performance assessment is typically conducted against a production environment, if balanced and representative load can be generated against a production staging environment, then it can be conducted there. The difference between recording information from a production staging environment and recording from a production environment is that when recording information from a production environment, a strategy to minimize the impact on production environment end-users must be employed. Consider that you always affect a system by observing it, and the impact of observing the system needs to be mitigated so that your users do not experience a performance degradation and you do not affect the system so much that it skews your observations (for example, by producing false positives). In the case of the aforementioned telecommunications company, we implemented a staged approach to capture live production data with minimal impact on the end-user experience.

In this chapter, we discuss the reasons for and strategies behind building a Java EE performance analysis report. We start off by taking a closer look at the benefits of performance assessments.

Performance Assessment Benefits

Why do we need to run Java EE performance assessments? Isn't a capacity assessment enough? What benefits do performance assessments offer?

These common questions I hear from customers when I help them implement a full performance management plan are quite valid: why should they dedicate time and resources to an activity unless they can realize substantial profit from it? To address these questions, you need to assess the health of your enterprise Java environment for the following reasons:

- You cannot make any assumptions about the capabilities of your enterprise Java environment until you have tested it.

- As the saying goes, an ounce of prevention is worth a pound of cure—by assessing your environment prior to deployment, you can prevent unwanted issues from arising after the application goes live.

- You cannot have confidence in your capacity assessment until you have validated it.

The first point is straightforward: have you ever developed and deployed an application without testing its performance? You can develop an application with appropriate design patterns and best practices, but until you subject it to a load test while monitoring it with byte-code instrumentation, all you can do is hope for the best. Rather, you need to identify and resolve application, platform, and dependency bottlenecks before deploying the application.

I apologize for the cliché in the second point, but it is 100 percent true with respect to application performance: *spending one week performance testing your application and identifying and resolving bottlenecks prior to deployment is better than spending one hour resolving a production performance issue while your users wait.* A performance assessment is the formal mechanism employed to guide tuning efforts.

Regarding the third point, when your application moves from a production staging environment into production, your capacity assessment is put to the test. Considering that you are required to build your capacity assessment from a load testing tool and a set of load scripts, you still require validation that your load tests accurately represent actual end-user behavior. Two simultaneous approaches to validating the accuracy of your capacity assessment are as follows:

- Examine access logs or your end-user experience monitor and analyze usage patterns against load scripts.

- Run a performance assessment to discover the actual end-user experience and the behavior of environment resources.

It is only by combining the information gathered from user logs with the actual behavior of your environment that you can truly feel comfortable with the accuracy of your capacity assessment.

In summary, the benefits performance assessments offer are tuning the performance of your application and validating that your tests and expectations are in line with reality.

Performance Assessment Overview

This section outlines the performance assessment stages: prerequisites, process, and analysis.

Prerequisites

Before starting a performance assessment, you need to satisfy some prerequisites for your assessment to be valuable:

- *Formally defined SLA*: You need a formally defined SLA to accurately assess if a request is performing as expected. Without a formally defined SLA, your assessment is essentially a stab in the dark—the best you can do is assume that because a service request is taking a long time to run that it is problematic, without knowing how the request is supposed to respond.

- *Application monitoring*: You need to implement application monitoring in the form of bytecode instrumentation to isolate performance problems. It is not enough to learn that your application—or even a specific request—is not performing as expected, unless you can properly isolate the cause of the performance problem.

- *Application server monitoring*: Application server monitoring identifies the performance of application server resources such as heap management and garbage collection, thread pools, and connection pools to enable you to identify if application server tuning can help the performance of your application.

- *Resource monitoring*: Outside the application, you need to monitor the performance of operating system resources such as server CPUs, disk I/O rates, and network communications, in addition to external resources such as databases and legacy systems. Without this level of monitoring, application performance anomalies may be miscategorized as application code issues.

- *Preproduction requirements*: If you are implementing a performance assessment against a preproduction or production staging environment, then you need a representative subset of production as well as appropriate load to test your application against. You can only tune an application to the way that your users use it; if your load is not balanced and representative of actual end-user behavior, then you cannot have confidence that you have identified performance bottlenecks.

Once you understand the expected performance of your application, put the proper monitoring frameworks in place, build a representative production staging environment, and have an accurate load generation tool, then you are ready to begin your performance assessment.

Process

The implementation process of a performance assessment for a preproduction environment and for a live production environment is different. In a preproduction environment, you maintain control of the load, the user ramp-up time, and the user behavior, whereas in a production environment, the user maintains control of these factors. Furthermore, in a preproduction environment you are free to generate as much load on the system as necessary, including monitoring overhead, but in a production environment, you want to gather valuable information without your users noticing performance degradations.

The latter sections of this chapter describe the best-practice strategies for obtaining performance information, both from a preproduction environment and a production environment. But regardless of how you capture the data, the goal is to obtain performance statistics at each relevant point in your environment, including statistics from inside your application, while users (either synthetic or real) are actively using your application.

Analysis

With performance statistics in hand, your goal is to transform this raw data into derived business values. For example, a saturated thread pool with pending requests is a raw value, but the interpretation that pending requests equates to waiting users, and hence the degradation of service request response times can be applied as a business value to your company, for example: "The result of the undersizing of this thread pool is that business processes cannot satisfy their SLAs, which puts the company in violation of its contractual obligations."

Sometimes people—especially technical people—get caught up in low-level details, without taking the time to understand the business implications. In the past, I have spent time implementing features that are cool, but do not satisfy consumer demand, and I have spent time tuning complicated functionality that is seldom accessed. But as the Java EE system administrator, you need to understand both the technical implications of performance statistics and how those implications affect your company's business processes. Furthermore, you need to be able to articulate the business process implications in a performance assessment report to your superiors, to provide them with enough information to make business-level decisions (for example, whether functionality ABC takes priority over functionality XYZ).

Interpreting raw statistics and assessing their impact on business process is somewhat of an art and is dependent on your specific application and environment. In this chapter, I provide general guidelines detailing how to interpret direct metrics as well as how to interpret the implications of abnormal application behavior, or indirect metrics. Through this analysis you can accurately assess the health of your enterprise environment.

Mitigating Performance Overhead

As mentioned earlier, by merely observing a system, we affect its behavior. As such, every monitoring tool needs facilities to control the level of observable impact it subjects its environment to. As a precursor to learning about preproduction and production monitoring strategies, it is important to understand what affects performance monitoring overhead, so this section explores some common configuration options that can mitigate performance overhead in two distinct areas:

- Platform recording

- Application recording

Platform Recording

Platform recording includes the entire layered technology stack upon which a Java EE application runs, specifically the following:

- Application server

- JVM

- Operating system

- Hardware

Typically when you record platform metrics, you use a tool to capture periodic snapshots of the current state of the platform, including such metrics as the number of threads in use and the number of database connections in use. The tool then presents summaries of multiple snapshots, sometimes in graphs, from which you can assess the health of the various platform components. For example, knowing that during a one-hour test session the minimum number of threads in use was 7 and the maximum number of threads in use was 48, out of a total of 50, might lead you to increase the thread pool size to provide enough of a buffer to satisfy usage peaks.

Statistically speaking, capturing performance metrics in this snapshot fashion provides a representative view into the performance of a platform component. But the accuracy of the representation depends wholly on the length of the recorded session and the interval upon which the metrics are captured. For example, capturing performance metrics every 5 minutes over a 1-week period is sufficient to provide an accurate representation of the platform behavior. But capturing performance metrics every 5 minutes for a 30-minute recorded session hardly yields conclusive results. In a 1-week period, 5-minute samples will converge on the representative behavior, but in a 30-minute period, a finer granularity of sampling is required.

Therefore, the sampling interval needs to be appropriately chosen to mitigate performance overhead: you need to balance the granularity of samples between performance overhead and usefulness of the captured data. Ensure that you are capturing information that will help you tune the platform, while not bringing the platform to its knees in the process.

The amount of data captured in a snapshot likewise affects the performance overhead of monitoring. For example, if a snapshot includes the entirety of an application server's JMX registry, then capturing this information even every minute adds significant burden to the application server. To mitigate this impact on performance overhead, employ the following strategies:

- Gather configuration information less frequently than run-time information.

- Consistently gather cursory or summary information, but gather detailed information only once it has been requested.

The first point is straightforward. For example, the maximum number of threads that can exist in a thread pool is not going to change very often; therefore, you do not need to gather that information on each sample. But be warned that what initially may appear to be configuration metrics may in actuality change more frequently than you would expect. Growable thread pools are a prime example of this. There is a difference between the maximum number of threads that can exist in the thread pool at any given time and the total number of threads that currently exist. In the past, this has led to some confusion when I observed thread pool usage spike to over 150 percent: the thread pool usage was defined as the number of threads in use divided by the total number of threads, but the total number of threads changed as the thread pool grew. So while the total number of threads appeared to be a configuration parameter, it was a dynamic value that needed to be sampled more frequently than it was.

The second point sounds good in theory, but it is difficult to use in practice, especially in a performance analysis report. The reason in interactive monitoring applications is that when you expand a node or drill down into a detailed metric, you usually want to see the graph prepopulated with at least the last several minutes of data. And by definition, the detailed information is obtained when it is requested, thereby negating this expected behavior. The reason that this is not possible when building a performance analysis report is that the analysis is typically performed after the fact, when it is too late to capture detailed information. The final solution may be to integrate a strong analysis engine that can dynamically capture detailed information when specific conditions occur, but at the time of this writing tools with this characteristic do not exist. Depending on your requirements, this effort to reduce monitoring overhead may be possible, but you do need to realize the implications.

The final configuration that can impact monitoring overhead is ingrained in your monitoring tool: how does it obtain its performance information? Is it touchless, or is it through a mechanism installed on your application server? A touchless architecture has been a real selling point that has some benefits: you spend time up front configuring your monitoring tool, but then by specifying connection information, you can connect to any application server instance (or administration server). Typically you need to match up remote protocol library versions, but once that is accomplished, you can easily connect to any server or cluster in your environment. The alternate architecture is to first deploy some communication mechanism (such as a servlet) to the environment and then point your monitoring tool at the servlet. Each server that you want to monitor needs to have this servlet deployed to it, but then the monitoring tool does not need any remote protocol libraries; it works over standard HTTP.

From this description, it may sound as though the touchless architecture is less intrusive in your environment because you do not need to deploy any code to it. But recall Chapter 4, where we implemented performance measurements by writing a servlet that read the JMX registry and returned the requested data. It required several calls to obtain even a small subset of information. In a touchless architecture, monitoring software can obtain information in one of two ways: bulk calls and individual remote calls.

The bulk mechanisms return more data than you are necessarily interested in and still require a plethora of remote calls. Neglecting to obtain information in bulk results in more remote calls than you can count. Either way, the network overhead and processing overhead required to handle the remote calls severely impacts the performance overhead of a touchless architecture.

The traditional architecture is to deploy a servlet to the application server instances and then make calls to it. In this architecture, the servlet can make all of the calls locally and return all pertinent information in a single network call. To mitigate the performance impact, it can return raw metrics and allow the calling program to derive values from the raw metrics, but the point is that it is all accomplished with a single HTTP call. Again, you are required to deploy an additional Web application to your environment in order to implement such an architecture.

Application Recording

Application recording involves bytecode instrumentation that traces requests as they happen, so application recording overhead cannot be mitigated by adjusting the time of snapshots. A snapshot of running methods would be almost worthless, but a list of processed requests with their associated call traces aggregated for a specific time interval is incredibly valuable. Therefore, the strategies we employ to mitigate performance overhead when recording application requests are more complicated. They fall into the following categories:

- Sampling percentage

- Sampling period/aggregate period

- Filters

- Level of detail

- Custom components

I discuss each category in the sections that follow.

Sampling Percentage

Bytecode instrumentation differs from metric recording in that while metric recording can be performed at regular intervals by taking snapshots (for example, capturing at a specific time how many threads are in use or how many database connections are open), processed requests must be captured when they occur and aggregated at specific intervals. Therefore, your byte-code instrumentation tool should be configurable for the percentage of requests to trace as well as the interval to aggregate request information (that is, report how many times each request, class, and method was executed, and their average, high, and low response times). The higher the percentage of requests traced and the more frequent the aggregate period, the greater the performance overhead. But the higher the percentage of requests traced and the more frequent the aggregate period, the easier it is to accurately isolate a single request for troubleshooting. As with all performance tuning options, it is a balance between overhead and quality of data.

Sampling Period/Aggregate Period

In addition to configuring the percentage of requests to sample, you need to configure the time period in which to aggregate those samples. Capturing and storing every request is unwieldy from a storage perspective when you can glean significant insight by aggregating those samples over a time period and reporting back the average response time, maximum response time, execution count, and so on. The configuration of this time period, however, can greatly affect the overhead inflicted on the environment. For example, aggregating performance information every ten seconds requires more frequent computations than aggregating performance information every minute. But the trade-off is that if an individual request performs poorly, it is easier to find and analyze it if the aggregate period is small.

Filters

Filters control what requests or request patterns are recorded. For example, to record all requests into the myapp Web context, you would configure a filter to record all requests matching /myapp/* and exclude all others. Filters can be used to greatly reduce the number of requests that are traced and hence have the biggest impact on performance monitoring overhead. It is common to write a performance analysis report for a single application, and this is possible by implementing filters.

Level of Detail

The level of detail configures whether the tool captures full call stacks at the method level, only significant components, or simply requests. The finer the level of detail, the greater the overhead.

Method-level recordings provide complete call stacks from an HTTP request, through application classes and methods, and to back-end dependencies such as databases, offering the finest level of detail and the best information, but at the highest overhead.

Component recordings, or boundary recordings, can aid you in identifying poorly performing parts of your application. A typical component recording breaks down how much time each request spent in the Web tier, Web architecture (such as Struts), EJB tier, JDBC calls, and so forth.

Finally, request-level recordings provide an overview of all requests executed during a recording, the number of times they were executed, and their minimum, maximum, and average response times. Request-level recordings are good for identifying candidates for method-level recordings in subsequent tests.

Custom Components

Custom components group classes and/or packages together into a black box: the call enters the black box, does some "stuff," and then either returns or makes calls out of the black box. The tool captures and records the response time of the entire black box, but does not provide detailed call traces for it. Good candidates for custom components are third-party libraries.

For example, if you use JDOM to parse your XML files, it suffices to know the overall contribution of JDOM to response time—you do not need to know the intricacies of where JDOM is spending all of its time. After all, if you find a performance problem (which is still visible by using the custom component), it does not do you any good to isolate the root cause of the problem, because you cannot change the code. Of course, if you are a nice person, then you can isolate the problem and report back the root cause to the development community to enhance the product in the future, but the root cause of a JDOM problem does not belong in your performance analysis report.

Preproduction Strategy

We start performance analysis in preproduction because ideally, if you can reproduce user load, preproduction is the best environment to test in. Here, you can subject the environment to as much load and overhead as is required to identify performance issues. For your testing efforts to be effective, you need to do a little bit of legwork first, including the following:

- Preparing the production environment

- Assessing usage patterns

- Evaluating critical mass

- Determining user load

- Recording metrics

We examine each task in more detail in the sections that follow.

Preparing the Production Environment

You need to prepare either a mirrored or scaled-down version of your production environment to test against. From a mirrored environment, you can assess the exact behavior of your production environment without requiring extrapolation, but from a scaled-down version, you will have to extrapolate the performance of the preproduction environment to the production environment. As a general rule here, as with everything in your job, make your work as easy as possible! Unless it is completely unavoidable, do not try to test an application in JBoss on a single-CPU Intel machine running Linux when the application is destined to be deployed to WebLogic on a quad-processor Sun machine running Solaris. Doing so will make your extrapolations synthetic and error-prone.

The best strategy is to attempt to make the extrapolations as linear as possible. To do this, try to build a test environment with the same class of machines as in your production environment and with an evenly divisible number of machines and/or CPUs. For example, if your production environment consists of eight machines in the application server tier, then two of the same machines could suffice in your preproduction environment. Furthermore, if your production environment has eight CPUs in each machine, then two or four might suffice in preproduction (it's trickier to extrapolate performance projections about CPUs than the number of machines). The point is that if you scale down the number of machines and CPUs evenly, then your extrapolations will be easier to perform and less error-prone.

■**Note** When you read "linear" here, keep in mind that there is no such thing as true linear extrapolation in enterprise environments. While one machine may service 200 users, it does not necessarily mean that two machines can service 400 users, because with a second machine you have potentially introduced additional state replication across your network as well as remote resource references (such as accessing a cached entity bean residing on a different machine).

Extrapolation is a difficult process, especially when network communications are involved, and there is no single reliable formula to help you, because the variables that impact scalability include your availability and failover implementations, replication strategy, replicated object size, hardware and network configuration, and mix and configuration of horizontal *and* vertical servers. In practice, you can derive this extrapolation value with your own tests and be equipped to more accurately estimate through scaled-down observations than with any formula I could provide you.

Assessing Usage Patterns

After you have set up your preproduction environment, the next major task you are faced with performing is a usage pattern assessment, to understand what your users are doing and in what balance they are doing it. The usage pattern assessment again refers to identifying balanced and representative requests; your tuning efforts are only as good as the load you send against your environment. Balanced and representative requests were required for performance tuning and capacity assessments and they are also required for performance assessments inside a preproduction environment. Without balanced and representative requests you may waste time tuning code that is seldom executed, and you might miss code that experiences significant performance issues when subjected to usage patterns that do not match your tests. Access log analyzers and user experience monitors can help you understand users' behaviors.

Web servers can be configured to record all requests made against them, and typically these requests are stored in a file named access.log, although the storage location can vary among vendors. An access log analyzer can parse this log file and display the top requests as well as report the frequency of each request. From this analysis, you can better design your load scripts to mimic your end users' behavior. The difficulty that parsing access logs presents is that access logs report only URL requests and not parameters passed to those URLs—in other words, access logs are not application aware; they are only URL aware.

User experience monitors, on the other hand, are physical devices that sit on your network and watch requests as they happen in real time. Typically, you can preconfigure them with knowledge about your application so they're able to identify application functionality as opposed to simply reporting URLs. Another difference between access logs analyzers and user experience monitors is that access logs do not typically report request response times, but user experience monitors do. Not only do user experience monitors report response times, but also they can be configured to fire alerts (for example, send e-mails or even launch application processes) when SLAs are exceeded.

It is worth noting that access log analyzers are mostly used by marketing departments to identify user demographics and behavior as well as assess the efficacy of marketing dollars. An access log analyzer attempts to answer the following questions:

- What path did the user get to a particular page?

- What types of advertising, such as banners, have been effective?

- What part of the country/world is the user located?

- What are the most popular pages/documents on the site?

Therefore, with respect to assessing user behavior, you do not need the most expensive log analyzer—you really need only answers to the following questions:

- What are the top pages being viewed?

- In what order are users visiting pages? (You determine this by tying together user requests by IP address and aggregating log entries into approximate transactions.)

- What are the average think times between requests within a transaction?

- What are the average think times between transactions?

- What is the average load (requests per time period/simultaneous requests)?

- What is the peak load?

Most of these questions can be answered using a good parser if you cannot afford a commercial access log analyzer offering. Extracting the desired information from the access logs is a nontrivial undertaking, but not overwhelming.

Evaluating Critical Mass

With balanced and representative requests, you next need to determine the critical mass of your application. In other words, you need to know what amount of load and/or what amount of time causes your application to create all of the components, fill all the pools, and generate typical caching behavior that it is representative of your production environment. You can learn a lot from watching your application achieve critical mass, but the performance assessment is primarily concerned with the behavior of your application once critical mass has been achieved.

Configure your load tester to ramp up and cause the application to reach critical mass before recording performance information. Failure to do so may cause you to spend time investigating performance anomalies that only occur on start-up, such as the compilation of a JSP. In this case, the solution is to precompile the JSP, but if you are capturing performance information, the aggregated response time value may be skewed by the compilation time and send you on a fruitless tuning effort.

Determining User Load

You need to size the amount of load against the environment to closely resemble your production traffic (scaled down to your preproduction environment, of course). When implementing a performance assessment, it is not crucial that your load match exactly, but you need to fall within an acceptable range. If your production load is about 500 users and you test with 400, your results should be fine, but if you test with 50, then your test results cannot be completely trusted.

Some performance issues only manifest under significant load, such as the impact of session sizes and the creation of temporary objects. For example, maintaining a 1MB session may not present a problem with 50 users, but with 500 it can quickly eat up your heap. Likewise, creating a handful of objects to satisfy 50 users (with appropriate think times) may allow plenty of time for garbage collection, but objects for 500 users may flood the application and force premature object tenuring, increasing the frequency and duration of major garbage collections. The point is that a lot of unexpected events can happen when an application is subjected to load, so when performance testing your application, you must do so under load.

Recording Metrics

Because you are recording in a preproduction environment, the best strategy is to capture as much meaningful data as you can. This means that you should record application server and operating system statistics at a fine-grained interval—for example, every minute or even every 30 seconds—and you should record detailed application metrics using bytecode instrumentation. You can employ other strategies to minimize the overhead of application-level monitoring, but typically they can be omitted in a preproduction environment.

■**Tip** You might need to reduce overhead when your application is simply too large (with too many classes or too large of a call tree), or when you are testing only a subset of an application (you can inadvertently reduce overhead by simply not monitoring classes and requests that you are not interested in).

The following common strategies can help you isolate problematic sections of code, even when overhead is not an issue:

- *Filters*: Only record requests that you are interested in and filter everything else out.

- *Custom components*: When integrating external libraries or code your requests interact with, but that you have no interest in seeing detailed call traces for, you can roll calls in these classes or packages into black boxes referred to as custom components.

The purpose of implementing filters and custom components is to narrow the scope of user requests that you have to review to assess the health of your application. Considering the sheer size of an enterprise application, performance tuning can be a daunting task, and if you can eliminate items that you do not care about and have no control over, you can reduce the overall amount of data you analyze and more efficiently identify real problems.

Production Strategy

While the goal in the preproduction strategy is to obtain a reasonably detailed level of information about the components and requests you are interested in, production recording adds the caveat that you do not want to noticeably impact the end-user experience. When you gather information from a production environment, performance impact must take precedence over level of detail. As you will see, you can still gather a similar level of detail, but in a staged approach.

Before diving directly into production, let's consider the two primary reasons for recording real-life users as they are executing an application:

- Production behavior cannot be reproduced in a preproduction environment.

- We want to gain a true understanding of end-user behavior.

Obtaining these real-life user behaviors is important because most customer sites that I visit maintain large enterprise environments, so when a performance issue occurs, it is very difficult to reproduce it in a controlled environment because of the sheer number of moving pieces. In this situation, there are two strategies:

- Record user requests from production and replay them in a controlled environment.

- Jump into production to diagnose the problem.

Regarding the first strategy, new tools are emerging that can record live production usage and replay it against another environment, such as a test or preproduction environment. Because of their newness, though, these tools have not been widely adopted.

Most companies opt for the second strategy of diagnosing the problem in production. If production usage cannot be reproduced in a preproduction environment, then tuning efforts against a preproduction environment are not fruitful—you can only tune your application to the user load it is subjected to.

In this section, you'll learn how to mitigate the performance impact of monitoring in a production environment and look at the following topics:

- Identifying the best time intervals to record data

- Choosing the correct subset of your production environment to monitor

- Recording production data using a staged approach

- Configuring the recording to compute metrics effectively

Recording at the Right Intervals

The first consideration when recording live production data is when to record it. The target is to identify a period of time within a day or a week with average user load, when users are performing actions representative of their typical behavior. For example, in the case of an intranet application that requires users to log on in the morning, perform daily activities, and log off before they leave, the login and logoff hours of the day are less representative of the majority of user actions—a user logs in once but may generate a couple dozen reports throughout the day. Therefore, recording a 30-minute session with users logging in may distort your tuning efforts, causing you to spend too much time tuning seldom-used functionality while missing true performance tuning opportunities.

An access log analyzer or user experience monitor can help you pinpoint the best opportunities during the day or week to capture average user activities. The time period you are looking for is when the user load is average—you do not want a dramatically under- or overutilized time. If the application is underutilized, then you risk missing problems that only manifest under load; if the application is overutilized, then you run the risk that the monitoring overhead may negatively affect end users' experience.

The ideal time period exhibits the following characteristics:

- Eighty percent or more of the most frequently executed requests are being performed.

- User load is within one standard deviation of the mean user load.

The key to effectively identifying this time period is to perform historical analysis of your log files or user experience monitor over a significant time period. Although the analysis of a single day's activity may reveal a seemingly ideal recording period, you can only confirm that period as ideal after looking at the entire week or even the entire month. When implementing proactive tuning measures, you want to ensure that you choose the appropriate recording time window to maximize your tuning efforts.

■**Note** Although in the big picture, choosing the correct recording interval is required to maximize tuning efforts, I have never let this point be a sticking point for me. Most companies know approximately when user activity is representative of typical behavior, so while I am sure to later validate the interval as representative, I follow the lead of the companies I'm working with and record and analyze data at the intervals they identify.

Environmental Subsets

Depending on your application and resource utilization levels, monitoring overhead can dramatically impact production application performance. And if the impact is observable to your users, then it is too much! In addition, consider the size of your enterprise environment: how many servers do you have in your application server tier? Do you have a load balancer configured to distribute the load evenly?

■**Note** While observable monitoring overhead is typically classified as "too much overhead," if the system is under severe stress, then the additional overhead is acceptable if it provides information that can lead to the resolution of the performance problem. If a server is going to crash in 15 minutes and you make it crash in 5 minutes instead, but you capture detailed information about why it crashed, then crashing it sooner is worth it!

A technique I often use to reduce monitoring overhead, given the fact that the size of the environment is large and the load balancer should be equally distributing the user load, is to record detailed data from a subset of the environment. For example, the telecommunications company I mentioned at the beginning of the chapter that wanted to capture the top five performance bottlenecks configured the detailed monitoring to record from a single server in their 32-server environment. Their environment was configured with 32 identical machines (spread across two data centers), with load balancers evenly distributing the load, so any individual server should be representative of the actual end-user activity.

Recording from an environment subset serves several purposes:

- Reduces the impact of monitoring overhead

- Provides representative data, but reduces the quantity of data to sift through

- Results in less error-prone configurations

The first point addresses the perceived impact of monitoring overhead. I will provide detailed information later in this chapter about how to reduce the actual overhead, but this point relies on the fact that only a subset of users will be affected by the test.

The second point may not be instantly obvious, but given identical hardware and software configurations, and considering that a single server is representative of what is happening on each server, why do you need additional data? If application code bottlenecks are occurring at a single point, then it does not matter if you see one occurrence of the problem or one hundred occurrences—you have found the problem. You still need to monitor the environment with production load to identify problems that may be load dependent, but less data that is still representative is quicker to navigate.

The best analogy I can use to convey the concept relates to statistical surveys. When you read the results of a survey stating that 35 percent of the population believes XYZ, do you know how the survey company arrived at this value? Did the survey company interview the entire population? No—it interviewed enough people to generate a representative subset of the population and extrapolated the results to the rest of society. The survey challenges are to identify a representative subset of society (for example, it's not a good idea to conduct an interview in front of a hot dog stand, asking people who just bought lunch there if they like hot dogs) and interview enough people to generate statistically relevant data. Similarly, your load balancer helps ensure that each server is a representative subset of the application behavior, and depending on the size of your environment, one or two servers may suffice to be statistically relevant.

Furthermore, every server that you are monitoring sends data to your monitoring solution, so the amount of load that the monitoring solution must organize can quickly become overwhelming. Basic metrics are one thing, but detailed bytecode instrumentation can be expensive to manage. When 20 application servers each send hundreds of call stack 40 or 50 methods deep to the monitoring solution, the monitoring solution's hardware and databases can grow overwhelmed and fall behind recording the information. Keep monitoring as simple as possible.

The final point is moot once the environment is configured, but realistic in practice: the more servers you configure, the higher the chances of human error. Furthermore, if a single error removes one server from your test, does that mean that your test becomes invalid? It is much easier to choose a representative subset.

Staged Recording

What do you do if you employ every mechanism to reduce the impact of monitoring overhead and it is still too high? The solution I have implemented in dozens of environments is to stage the recording into two primary phases:

1. Cursory recording

2. Detailed recordings

The *cursory recording* is a lightweight recording that records at a minimum request information such as request name, response times, and call counts, and at most records component-level information, breaking a request down into its major components such as Web server called servlet X that called EJB Y that executed the JDBC query Z. The purpose of this cursory recording is to learn what parts of your application you want additional information about. Specifically, you want to answer the following questions:

- What service requests are exceeding their SLAs?

- What service requests are particularly slow (even if not exceeding their SLAs)?

- What service requests are contributing the most time to the application? (These make good proactive tuning targets.)

- Which components are being routinely accessed that are either performing well or that you have no ability to tune?

Take the information that you derive from the cursory recording and configure one or more *detailed recordings*. The detailed recordings should be configured to filter out all requests except for the identified requests; in busy environments, I try to limit each detailed recording to five requests. The detailed recordings capture full call stacks through bytecode instrumentation to direct you to the root cause of their performance hot points. This collection of detailed recordings will be analyzed in the performance analysis report.

If your monitoring tool has the ability to capture component or boundary data in the cursory recording, then in addition to configuring filters to isolate identified requests, you can create custom components that do not report the inner workings of specified classes or packages. In this scenario, performance overhead is reduced and the instrumentation reports less information by excluding information that you are not interested in. As an example, consider Apache Struts. When you build a Struts application, you implement your business functionality inside action classes, and Struts handles the application and navigation logic. If you were to create a custom component that wraps the package `org.apache.struts`, then the instrumentation would report something like the following:

1. The Web server received a request for `GET /myapp/myaction.do`.

2. The Web server forwarded the request to Struts.

3. Struts forwarded the request to your servlet's `service()` method.

4. `service()` called `X.method()`, and so on.

The point is that the internal workings of the Struts servlet would be hidden from your recorded data. It's sufficient to say that after the Web server forwarded the request to the Struts front controller servlet, the servlet did "a bunch of stuff" and then eventually invoked your action. The recording still reports the amount of time the request spent inside of Struts, but excludes the inner workings between the initial invocation and the call to your action class.

Metric Recording

When you record metrics in a production environment, monitoring overhead dictates the level of detail you can obtain. Consider the following when configuring bytecode instrumentation recordings parameters that limit overhead:

- Number of samples

- Sampling period/aggregate period

- Filters

- Level of detail

- Custom components

When recording in a production environment using a staged approach, the initial component-level recording should be configured to record enough samples as to not overload the servers it is monitoring. This may mean that a large number of samples are skipped, but primarily what you are interested in during the first component phase is a list of candidates for which you will capture detailed information in subsequent recordings. In the subsequent detailed recordings, you have filtered out the majority of requests and are only looking at a handful of requests. Therefore, the monitoring tool should be configured to capture as many samples as possible.

The sampling period, or timeframe that we aggregate request summaries, is always problematic in production environments because of the added load it subjects the application server to. In the first component-level recording phase, diagnostics will be localized to identifying candidates for additional information, so the sampling period can be configured very coarsely, such as every five minutes. In subsequent phases, when you perform detailed recordings on a filtered subset of requests, diagnosing performance problems is the primary goal, so the sampling period should be finer. Depending on the resource utilizations of your production environment, you can entertain values ranging from 30-second samples to 2-minute samples. Typically I use 1-minute samples in production, just to be safe.

In the staged approach that you implement when recording in production, the component recording implements minimal filtering (you might filter a specific application, but in general you want to see as many requests as possible), but the detailed recordings make extensive use of filters. A detailed recording may filter out (exclude) all requests except for four or five specifically named requests.

By definition, the component-level recording uses the component level of detail, while the detailed recording uses a detailed, or method, level of recording.

Finally, create custom components for all third-party libraries that your application uses. You might want more detailed information about a third-party library when recording in a preproduction environment, but in a production environment you want to obtain as much valuable information as possible, but with minimal performance monitoring overhead. Your performance analysis report can include callouts to the contributions of third-party libraries to request response times, but identifying the root cause of third-party performance problems in a production environment offers no real benefits.

Metric Analysis

At this point, you should have obtained performance metrics about both your platform and your application, from either a preproduction staging environment or a live production environment. Regardless of where you obtained the information, the real challenge is in analyzing the data and assigning meaningful business values to it. In this section, we'll break down the analysis of performance metrics into the following categories and discuss how to interpret those metrics:

- *Environment*: This section reviews the environment upon which the application server runs, including the operating system and JVM.

- *Application server*: Here you'll review the performance of application server–specific metrics and how your application interacts with them.

- *Application*: In this section, you'll examine the performance of your application, focusing on identifying the hot path through a slow request as well as the hot point within the hot path. Also, you'll learn about the principles of wait-based tuning to reveal implicit configuration issues that manifest through application behaviors.

- *SQL report*: Because most enterprise applications interact with a database, it is important to identify poorly performing SQL code, as it impacts the application. In this section, you'll also look at properly tuning prepared statement caches.

Environment

For the purposes of this discussion, the *environment* is the platform that hosts the application server, including the underlying hardware, operating system, and JVM. Specifically from an analysis perspective, I want to focus on three primary performance metric categories in the sections that follow:

- Heap performance

- CPU utilization

- Process memory utilization

You can review many metrics with respect to the environment, but these three metrics have the biggest impact on your tuning efforts—I always check the previously listed metrics when constructing a performance analysis report.

Heap Performance

Java EE applications run inside a JVM process, which provides a memory heap in which all object instances exist. Every object that your application creates is first loaded into process memory, an instance of it is created in the heap, and a reference to it is returned to your application. Your application interacts with that object, and when the object is no longer required, your application deletes the reference to it, making the object eligible for garbage collection. The JVM maintains a garbage collector thread that, depending on your JVM vendor and configuration, periodically cleans up memory occupied by unreferenced objects. Because of this tight interaction between your application, application server, and JVM, the behavior of the JVM can greatly affect the performance of your application.

You have three primary considerations when analyzing the performance of a heap:

- Heap utilization

- Heap growth pattern

- Garbage collection behavior

Regardless of the JVM vendor, your application will need a certain amount of memory to hold all of its objects. The typical behavior is that the heap climbs steadily until it reaches a steady state. Temporary objects are created and destroyed, but in general the heap remains relatively flat. Figure 10-1 shows a heap that has already reached its steady state.

You can read Figure 10-1 as follows:

- The heap size is represented by the flat line at the top of the figure and is 800MB.

- The average heap usage is the solid line inside the shaded region. It ranges between 250MB and 350MB.

- The shaded region represents the range of the heap during a sample interval. The minimum heap averaged approximately 150MB and the maximum heap averaged approximately 400MB.

The utilization of this heap climbs to about 450MB at its peak (on an almost regular basis), which is 56 percent of the total heap size. If this recorded session is representative of typical usage patterns, then the heap size could potentially be reduced—it is best to keep the heap utilization at about 70 percent for typical usage patterns, as this provides room for additional usage but is not wasteful.

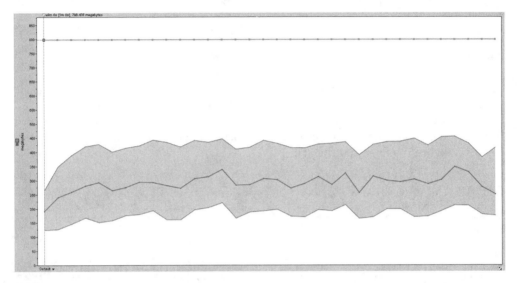

Figure 10-1. *A heap that has reached its steady state*

A heap's growth pattern measures the slope of the heap's minimum values after it reaches a steady state. An increasing slope may indicate a memory leak, whereas a flat or decreasing slope could indicate that the garbage collector is able to reclaim the same or more objects than are created. A flat slope does not necessarily indicate that your application doesn't have a memory leak, but it does indicate a decreased probability of a memory leak. In a 30-minute session, the growth pattern may or may not be conclusive, but if you analyze the same metric over a few days or a week, then you can extract some strong conclusions about the likelihood of a memory leak. The slope of Figure 10-1 is flat, which is interpreted in a performance analysis report as indicating a low probability of a memory leak, but a longer test is required for a conclusive answer.

In contrast to the behavior demonstrated in Figure 10-1, Figure 10-2 shows a slowly increasing heap.

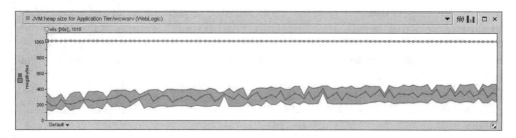

Figure 10-2. *This heap appears to have a slow memory leak.*

At first glance the heap in Figure 10-2 appears healthy: it is at its steady state with an average utilization below 40 percent and a range of 150MB. But when you closely examine the minimum values for each sample and plot a line through those values, the resulting line displays a visibly increasing slope. Note the darker line in Figure 10-3, which approximates the closest straight line through the minimum value points.

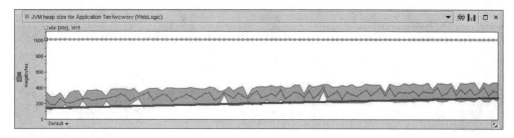

Figure 10-3. *The line plots a straight path through the minimum values and reveals that the slope is definitely increasing.*

As you can see in Figure 10-3, the slope of the minimum values for each heap sample is in fact increasing, which indicates a slow memory leak. The term "slow memory leak" means that the application is leaking memory either through very small objects or only on specific requests that are less frequently invoked. The next step in identifying the root cause of this memory leak is to determine which requests were being executed at the time of the recording and replay those requests in a memory profiler.

While the heap in Figure 10-1 is fairly healthy, a point of concern is that the range of the heap during each one-minute interval is 250MB, or almost 32 percent of the heap's size. If this is a high-traffic site, then a 250MB range is perfectly acceptable, but if the traffic is relatively low, then I would advise the application developers to chase down potentially cycled objects. A large period range is an indirect indication that garbage collection may be running excessively and its impact may be observable. Figure 10-4 displays garbage collection metrics (rate and overhead) for the heap in Figure 10-1.

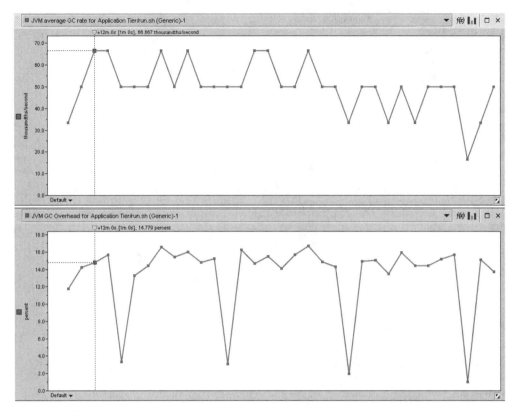

Figure 10-4. *Graphs showing the average garbage collection rate and the garbage collection overhead for the heap shown in Figure 10-1*

The rate of garbage collection is measured in thousandths of occurrences per second, which after conversion to minutes resolves to the top points being four occurrences per minute and the bottom point being one occurrence per minute. Depending on the nature of the application, this may or may not be a problem, but over one-third of the samples showed garbage collections occurring every 15 seconds. This recording was measured against a Sun heap, so we can further break down the data into rates of garbage collection in the new generation and the old generation, as shown in Figure 10-5.

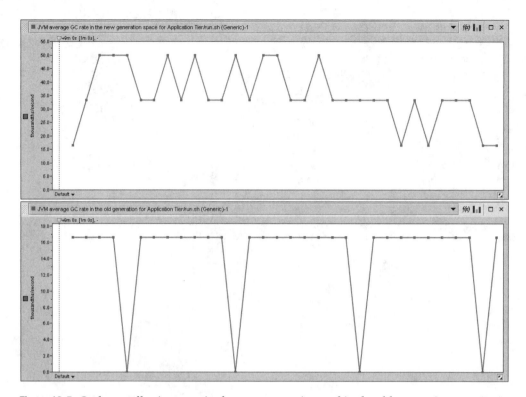

Figure 10-5. *Garbage collection rates in the new generation and in the old generation*

Figure 10-5 shows that the majority of garbage collections occurred in the young generation, with at most one per minute occurring in the old generation. New, or young, generation garbage collections are referred to as *minor* collections and occur against a running heap; old generation garbage collections are referred to as *major* collections and require the heap to be frozen in order to run (these are also called *stop-the-world* garbage collections). While major garbage collections occur relatively infrequently in relation to minor collections, it is still a point of concern that they are occurring as frequently as once per minute. For a large heap (1GB–2GB or larger), a major garbage collection can take several seconds to run, so your heap should be configured to minimize these occurrences. In a well-tuned heap and a solid application, major garbage collections should occur at most a couple times per day; in a well-tuned heap for an average application, you can still reduce this rate to once or twice per hour.

The second graph in Figure 10-4 displays the overhead that the garbage collector is inflicting on the system. An average overhead of approximately 15 percent is too high for an average environment and indicates the heap needs to be tuned. Chapter 7 discussed the strategies employed to tune both the Sun and IBM JVM heaps.

Aside from using a monitoring tool to assess the health of garbage collection, you can gain valuable information at about a 5 percent overhead by using the JVM's -verbose:gc option.

In addition, the -XX:+PrintGCDetails option provides details about the changes in heap partitions, and the -XX:+PrintGCTimeStamps option prints the time of garbage collection occurrences relative to the start of the JVM. With these options, you can generate a log file from which you can extract the garbage collection rate, time, and impact. For more information, refer back to Chapter 7 and then read through Sun's "Tuning Garbage Collection with the 5.0 Java Virtual Machine" document, which you can find at the following URL:

http://java.sun.com/docs/hotspot/gc5.0/gc_tuning_5.html

CPU Utilization

CPU utilization is one of the best measures of your application's impact on its underlying hardware. What you hope to observe is a relationship between application load and CPU utilization: the CPU steadily increases as the load increases, and the CPU decreases as the load decreases. If your physical machine can support the load that it is subjected to, then you should never see the CPU utilization grow over 80 percent, but if the CPU is consistently over 85 or 90 percent, one of the following two conditions is true:

- Your application is too CPU intensive and needs to be refactored.

- Your environment simply cannot support the load it is being subjected to.

The easy solution to this condition is to add additional CPUs or new machines to your environment, but this is expensive, in terms of both hardware costs and software licensing costs. A more time-consuming option, but one that is better in the long term, is to analyze your application components inside a code profiler and refactor the code sections that are performing poorly.

However, if you observe periodic CPU spikes—for example, a machine that averages 30 percent CPU utilization unexpectedly spikes to 90 to 100 percent utilization, and returns back to 30 percent utilization—then this behavior can be categorized as either an effect of garbage collection or an application anomaly.

Whenever a stop-the-world garbage collection occurs, the CPU spikes significantly, usually pinning itself at 100 percent until the garbage collection completes. Therefore, whenever you observe a CPU spike, check for a correlation with an occurrence of a major garbage collection. If you find no correlation between a CPU spike and an occurrence of a major garbage collections, and the CPU utilization is associated with the Java application server process (by looking at the CPU utilization of the application server's "java" process), then it is possible that you have detected a problematic piece of application code.

In this situation, the strategy is to identify the requests that were running during the CPU spike (if you do not have a tool to help you identify these requests, you can find the information by parsing access logs) and replay those requests against your application running in a code profiler. Your code profiler should allow you to profile your application using elapsed time (including blocked threads and waits) or CPU time. To detect a method or application subgraph that is abusing the CPU, set this configuration option to "CPU time" and find the top offending methods and lines of code that occurred during each request candidate.

■**Note** The difference between *elapsed time* and *CPU time* may initially be confusing. Here is an example that highlights the difference: consider a method that checks a queue and then sleeps for 30 seconds. In an elapsed recording, this method would report that it spent 30.01 seconds to complete, while in the CPU recording, it would report only the 0.01 second, because it did not have the CPU while sleeping. Both metrics are interesting to observe: the elapsed time reports the perceived run time for a method (if the tested code is not a background process, then the reported time is the amount of time that a user had to wait for this functionality to complete), whereas the CPU time reports the amount of time that a method had the CPU.

In summary, here are the steps I recommend following when evaluating the health of an environment's CPUs:

1. Observe the CPU utilization during the recording. Check whether the CPU is climbing normally or spiking.

2. Determine whether CPU spikes (if any) are associated with garbage collections.

3. If CPU spikes are not associated with garbage collection, then identify the methods and lines of code that were running during the spike.

Process Memory Utilization

The operating system process memory for the JVM process includes the heap as well as the permanent generation memory. The permanent generation memory is used for loading things that do not reside in the heap, such as the contents of a `.class` file that is used when constructing class instances on the heap. Examining the process memory is important to observe the following two items:

- Operating system memory constraints

- Permanent memory anomalies

With regard to the first point, the size of your JVM process will always be larger than the size of your heap due to the JVM permanent objects that it needs to manage your Java applications. Some operating systems restrict the amount of memory that a single process can occupy, so you need to be aware of how much memory your Java process is using. If the process runs out of memory, then it can crash your entire environment.

Furthermore, you need to ensure that your JVM heap is never running in a swapped capacity, meaning that the heap is running in virtual memory because not enough physical memory is available to support it. Swapping memory to disk is almost always a bad idea (from a performance perspective), but doing so in an enterprise environment is even worse.

In reference to the second point, it is important to observe the behavior of physical memory in conjunction with verbose garbage collection logs to understand the behavior of the permanent generation. The primary use of the permanent generation is to hold descriptions of classes that are used to create class instances on the heap. I mentioned in Chapter 7 an incident where my attention to process memory utilization identified a puzzling problem: the application reported that it was out of memory, but the heap utilization was at or below 50 percent utilization. If the heap had over 1GB of memory available, then how could the heap report an `OutOfMemoryError`? The answer was that although the error message appeared to be from the heap, it was actually generated by an event in the permanent space. The permanent space was full (from loading application classes), and as a new class was requested, there was no room for it, so the JVM threw an `OutOfMemoryError` and crashed. In the end, we upgraded the system to a newer JVM and subsequently enabled class unloading to solve the problem.

In summary, analyzing the performance of process memory can help you identify operating system constraints, process memory contention, and paging, and better understand the impact of the JVM's permanent generation space.

Application Server

In a performance analysis report, the platform is separated into two parts: the environment and the application server. The application server has its own category because it has so many moving points to tune. Specifically, the performance analysis report examines these components, which we'll cover in the sections that follow:

- Thread pools

- Connection pools

- Caches

- Component pools

- Message servers

- Transactions

Choose the components that are relevant in your environment. For example, if you are not using entity beans and do not have any other caching infrastructure in place, then omit that section. The amount of space dedicated to any given topic will be wholly dependent on your environment; focus on what is important to your application.

Thread Pools

When an application server receives a request, either via the Web or through RMI, it accepts the request and places it in an execution queue. Each execution queue maintains a pool of execution threads. When a request is placed in the queue, if a thread is available, then the thread processes the request, but if a thread is not available, then the request is forced to wait for a thread to become available. Analysis of the performance of a thread pool involves the following characteristics:

- Thread pool utilization

- Queue depth

- Request throughput

Regarding the first point, *thread pool utilization*, you need to carefully choose thread pool sizes, as there is a balance between system resources, request processing, and CPU saturation. The most common complaint I hear about sizing a thread pool too large is that it consumes too many system resources, and depending on your operating system and threading library, this may be true. For example, in earlier versions of Linux, each thread ran in its own process, and the operating system limited the maximum number of processes (usually to 256). With other operating systems (such as Windows, Solaris, and AIX), and with an alternate threading library in Linux, all threads run under the umbrella of a single process. So while system resources are required to support multiple threads, dormant threads do not consume CPU time and thus their impact on the system is relatively minimal.

The much greater potential danger in maintaining too many threads is that they could all be in use at once. Consider an environment that can optimally support 100 threads but maintains a thread pool with 200 threads. If 200 threads are in use, then the CPU will become saturated because it has to switch the CPU context between all 200 threads. It is far more efficient to cause requests to wait in a request queue while earlier requests are processed optimally, rather than to force too many requests into a system that cannot support them.

The second characteristic, *queue depth* (sometimes simply referred to as *pending requests*), reports the number of requests waiting in the queue to be processed. The queue depth will grow if requests are received and threads are not available to process them.

Finally, the *request throughput* is a measure of requests processed over a period of time, such as requests processed per second. In essence, the throughput tracks the capabilities of your application at the current load. Figure 10-6 shows a thread pool that is not under duress.

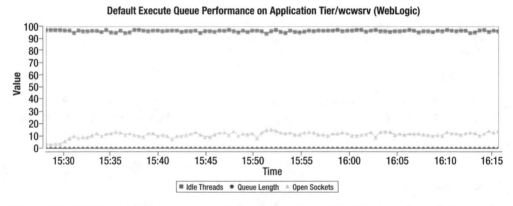

Figure 10-6. *This thread pool is not under duress. It has almost 100 idle threads at all times with no pending requests while supporting 10–20 simultaneous open connections.*

Figure 10-6 displays the following information:

- *Idle Threads*: The number of threads in the thread pool that are available to process requests

- *Queue Length*: The queue depth, or number of pending requests

- *Open Sockets*: The current number of open sockets, or simultaneous requests

The thread pool in Figure 10-6 is highly underutilized, and if the sample period is representative of average user behavior, then the thread pool could be reduced in size to limit the impact on system resources. But of course you would want to test this environment with enough load to use all those threads and see if the environment becomes saturated; this would yield a far more conclusive recommendation.

Figure 10-7 shows a thread pool under severe distress.

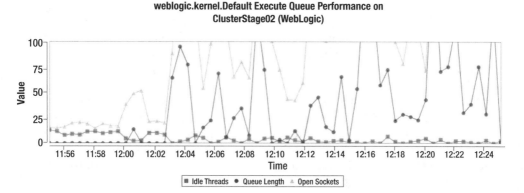

Figure 10-7. *This thread pool is under any severe duress. It has 10 or fewer idle threads, and the number of pending requests grows to above 100 several times during the test.*

The performance of the thread pool in Figure 10-7 was so bad that it broke my analysis software (that is, my homegrown analysis software, not my company's software), as some of the pending request spikes grew above 100. In this case, you need to first determine whether the system can support additional threads—in other words, is the system already saturated, or can you add additional threads without saturating it? If the system is saturated, then the environment needs additional CPUs or physical machines. But if the system is not saturated, then the size of the thread pool should be increased.

Here are some guidelines to follow when you analyze thread pools:

- The thread pool usage should not grow above 80 percent for any significant percentage of time.

- There should not be any pending requests. Periodic occurrences of five or fewer waiting threads is acceptable, but anything more should trigger a critical alert. (Setting a threshold of five requests avoids catching in-flight requests that are added to a request queue but removed *almost* instantly by a live thread, meaning that the snapshot is taken between the time the request is added to the queue and a thread pulls it off of the queue.)

- If the number of waiting pending requests grows to the size of the thread pool, then issue a fatal alert. At this point, the thread pool is saturated and can recover only if the user load diminishes.

- Compare the number of open sockets to the size of the thread pool. If there is a huge discrepancy, such as twice as many open sockets as threads, then advise the user that the size of the thread pool may need to be increased.

- Review the behavior of the request throughput against load (open sockets). If there is a point where the load increases but the throughput decreases, then chances are your thread pools are saturated.

Connection Pools

To communicate with a database or other external resource, an application needs to obtain a connection to that resource. When communicating with databases, applications use JDBC connections, and when communicating with other resources, applications use either a JCA connection or a proprietary connection. Regardless of the type of connection, creating a connection is usually an expensive operation, so rather than creating the connection every time a request needs one, application servers implement connection pools that create connections ahead of time and make them available to any request that needs one. Requests obtain a connection from a connection pool, use it, and return the connection back to the connection pool when finished.

A connection pool greatly improves the performance of applications by removing the connection creation time, but if the connection pool is empty, it can represent a bottleneck in the request call stack. In some cases, a request can wait for a connection to be returned to a connection pool longer than it would take to create another connection, so it's important to accurately assess the health of connection pools. Two primary metrics used to analyze the performance of a connection pool are as follows:

- Connection pool utilization

- Execute threads waiting for a connection

These metrics are somewhat analogous to the thread pool analysis of utilization and queue depth: what is the percentage of connections in use and are any threads (requests) waiting for a connection?

Figure 10-8 shows a healthy JDBC connection pool.

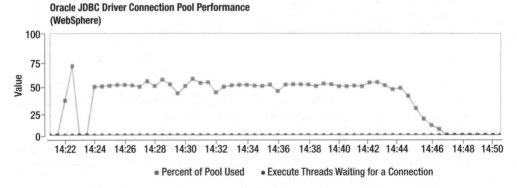

Figure 10-8. *A healthy connection pool*

The performance of the connection pool in Figure 10-8 is what we all strive for:

- Peak usage at approximately 70 percent

- Average usage between 50 and 70 percent

- No execute threads waiting for a connection

During your analysis of connection pools, here are some guidelines to follow:

- The peak usage should not grow above 80 percent for any significant period of time. Keeping pool usage below 80 percent allows your application to absorb changes in usage patterns.

- The average usage should be in the range of 50 to 70 percent. If the average usage is below 50 percent, then you want to decrease the size of the pool because you are holding on to too many unused resources; if the average usage is above 70 percent, then you want to increase the size of the pool because changes in usage patterns could significantly impact the performance of your application.

- No threads should be waiting for connections. Periodic occurrences of five or fewer waiting threads are acceptable, but anything more should trigger a critical alert.

- If the number of waiting threads grows to the number of connections in the pool, then issue a fatal alert. The database connection pool is saturated and can recover only if the user load diminishes.

Caches

A few years ago, Marc Fleury, the founder of JBoss, published a blue paper entitled "Why I Love EJBs" in which he postulated that the entity bean cache delivers a level of magnitude better performance by servicing requests out of memory than accessing a database across the network. He is completely right, and his postulation can be applied to any caching infrastructure: anytime you can service a request directly from memory rather than make a network call, performance will improve. But as with all performance enhancements, caches need to be tuned appropriately.

A cache works in the following way: when a request needs an object, it first checks the cache, and only if the object is not available does the request make the network call to obtain the object remotely. In an EJB framework, this caching mechanism is encapsulated for you: you ask the Entity Manager for a bean, and it either serves it from cache or makes a remote call. Caches are a finite size, so to keep the cache current, and hence effective, the cache attempts to keep the most heavily accessed and recent objects in memory. When the cache receives a request for an object not currently in memory, it performs the following steps:

1. Checks for the object in the cache

2. Loads the object by making a remote call (for example, to a database) because the object is not in the cache

3. Runs an algorithm against the cache (usually a least recently used algorithm) to select an object to remove from the cache to make room for the new object

4. Removes the selected object from the cache (depending on your persistence scheme this may require a write back out to the database)

5. Adds the new object to the cache

6. Returns a reference to the object to the caller

If the cache is sized too small and this process occurs frequently, then the cache is said to be *thrashing*, meaning the caching infrastructure is spending more time managing the cache then servicing requests. The size of the cache has to be large enough to minimize thrashing, but remain cognizant of its memory requirements. If the only way to reduce thrashing is to size the cache unusually large, then you need to consider whether the object should be cached at all. I have been at customer sites where I have told the customer that objects are not being accessed frequently enough to justify a cache and they *should* request those objects from a database every time they are needed. For example, one customer maintained documents in an entity bean cache, but when the cache was sized at 1,000 beans, they had a 100 percent miss count. By parsing access logs it was determined that in an hour 7,000 different documents were being requested, and the average time between requests for the same object was over an hour. In order to satisfy these requests from cache with a minimum amount of thrashing, they would require a cache that held more than 5,000 objects. This simply is not practical, so I advised them to forego their cache altogether.

When analyzing the performance of a cache, consider the following performance metrics:

- *Passivation count*: The removal of an object from the cache

- *Activation count*: The addition of an object to the cache

- *Passivation rate*: The rate that objects are removed from the cache (for example, objects removed per second)

- *Activation rate*: The rate that objects are added to the cache (for example, objects added per second)

- *Hit count*: The number of requests satisfied by the cache

- *Miss count*: The number of requests not satisfied by the cache

When a cache is being populated, its hit count will be zero and its activation rate will be high, but when the application has reached its steady state and the cache is populated, then these metrics are valuable. Usually to avoid start-up anomalies, we analyze the miss count as a percentage (miss count divided by number of requests) and the passivation rate in relation to the size of the cache. The metrics are interpreted as follows:

- If the miss count averages greater than 30 percent, then the cache is not effective and should be resized.

- If the miss count averages greater than 60 percent, then the cache is really not effective and its objects should be evaluated to see whether they warrant a cache.

- If the miss count averages above 90 percent, then the objects most likely should not be cached.

- If the passivation rate per relative time period (I usually choose one minute) is greater than 50 percent of the size of the cache, then the cache is not effective. This depends to a large extent on load, because a cache can be ineffective with a passivation rate that is 1 percent the size of the cache if the cache is not being accessed frequently. The point is to identify how quickly the cache is turning over relative to user load.

Component Pools

Stateless EJB components such as stateless session beans and message-driven beans are maintained in a pool to avoid creating and destroying them on a per-request basis. They are implemented this way for the same reason that JDBC connections are maintained in a pool: it is more efficient to check an object out of a pool than to create it. Being similar to connection pools, component pools are analyzed using the same metrics:

- Pool utilization

- Requests waiting for an object

And as before, the analysis is defined as follows:

- The peak usage should not grow above 80 percent for any significant period of time.

- The average usage should be in the range of 50 to 70 percent.

- No threads should be waiting for connections. Periodic occurrences of five or fewer waiting threads are acceptable, but anything more should trigger a critical alert.

- If the number of waiting threads grows to the number of connections in the pool, then issue a fatal alert. The component pool is saturated and can recover only if the user load diminishes.

Typically, the default application server component pool sizing is sufficient, but it is something specific that should be checked in a performance analysis report.

Note Component pool sizing presents a theoretical problem, but in practice it is not very problematic. Components are not as expensive to create as database connections and are usually small in size, so application server vendors typically size them very large (for example, I have seen some sized to 1,000, and others can grow indefinitely). To put component pool tuning in perspective, I have to tune database connection pool sizes during almost all tuning engagements, but I have never had to adjust the size of a component pool.

Message Servers

Message servers are interesting in enterprise environments: they are either not used at all or used very cursorily, or they are an integral part of an application technology stack. In the former, they appear to facilitate asynchronous business processes, such as sending confirmation e-mails. In the latter, they usually appear as integration mechanisms between systems, typically integrating an application server with a mainframe application. The metrics involved in analyzing the performance of message servers are as follows:

- Message and/or byte upper threshold (If an upper threshold constrains how many messages or how many bytes can reside in the message server at any given time, then what is it?)

- Current number of messages/bytes in the message server

- Number of messages rejected from the message server

Built-in message servers that ship with application servers usually only allow you to tune the capacity of the message server. If you are using such a server, you need to ensure that messages are not being rejected, so observe the following values:

- If the message server averages over 80 percent of its capacity, then you should issue a critical alert that its capacity needs to be increased.

- If the message server averages over 95 percent and messages are being rejected, then you should issue a fatal alert that its capacity needs to be increased.

Another consideration to evaluate is the amount of time it takes for a message to be delivered to its destination; this can be impacted by the reliability that is being assigned to the message. *Reliability* is a measure of how certain you need to be that your message is delivered to its recipient(s). If it is of the utmost importance that the message be delivered, then reliability is high, requiring the delivery to be acknowledged by the recipient. If the message delivery does not have to be guaranteed, such as a message containing a status update in which several messages will be sent every few seconds, then reliability is low because losing a message is not necessarily that important. Decreasing the level of reliability can help messages move through the message server faster.

Finally, if you are using an advanced message server, such as IBM MQSeries or the TIBCO suite of products, as an integration tool between your application and another infrastructure, then you have entirely another beast to tune. Due to the discrepancy between message server implementations, I suggest you reference the manufacturer's tuning guide for more information. But keep in mind that the tuning goal is to move messages as quickly as possible between your application and mainframe and still satisfy reliability requirements.

Transactions

Java EE provides the Java Transaction API (JTA) and Java Transaction Server (JTS), which allow you to run code inside the context of a transaction. Code that runs inside a transaction behaves as follows: if the transaction succeeds, then its changes are committed to the state of objects as well as transaction-aware resources such as databases, but if the transaction fails, then the system is returned to its state before the transaction started. This property of transactions is referred to as *atomicity*, meaning that the transaction behaves as a single atomic unit: either it all works or the system returns to its state before the transaction started.

Java EE provides explicit control over transactions or container-managed control over transactions. In Java EE 5 applications, EJB business methods can elect to participate in transactions by simply adding annotations to method headers (refer to the EJB3 specification, section 12.3.7 for additional information). The level of transaction participation can be one of the following values, specified through the `TransactionAttribute` annotation as one of the following `TransactionAttributeTypes`:

- `MANDATORY`: The method must be invoked inside a client's transaction context.

- `REQUIRED`: The method must be invoked inside a valid transaction context. If a transaction context does not currently exist, then a new one is created.

- `REQUIRES_NEW`: The method must be invoked inside a new transaction context. This method will act as its own atomic unit.

- SUPPORTS: If this method is invoked inside a transaction context, then it will participate, but it is not required to run inside a transaction context.

- NOT_SUPPORTED: This method does not participate in transactions, so if it is invoked by a method currently running inside a transaction, that transaction is suspended while this method runs.

- NEVER: This method will never run inside a transaction. Furthermore, if you call it from a method currently running in a transaction, then this method will throw an exception.

When transactions occur, either they can be committed or they can fail and roll back. From an analysis perspective, we look at commit rates, rollback rates, and the nature of rollbacks. Rollbacks can come in one of several forms, defined as follows:

- *Application rollbacks*: An application transaction has failed; this can be a normal function of the application. For example, an application that processes a survey may roll back a transaction if the user submitting the transaction is under 18 years old.

- *System rollbacks*: Something very bad happened in the application server, such as a hardware failure that causes the application server to stop responding.

- *Resource rollbacks*: A resource somehow failed—for example, the application server attempts to renew a database connection and cannot connect to the database.

- *Time-out rollbacks*: A request took too long to process, so the application server killed it and threw a time-out exception.

In a performance analysis report, these metrics are interpreted as follows:

- If the percentage of transactions rolled back is greater than 10 percent, then issue a critical alert.

- If a nonapplication rollback occurs, issue a fatal alert.

Application

Analyzing the performance of an application involves identifying slow service requests and then triaging and isolating their root causes, which we look at in the sections that follow.

Identifying Slow Service Requests

The first step is to identify slow-running service requests, which come in three flavors:

- Service requests that average slow response times

- Service requests that average acceptable response times, but experience periodic spikes in response time

- Service requests that average acceptable response times, but significantly impact the system due to the sheer number of times they are called

Your monitoring tool should provide the following information for each aggregated sample for each request that it observes during a test:

- *Average response time*: The average response time for the request during the aggregated sample

- *Maximum response time*: The maximum response time for the request during the aggregated sample

- *Call count*: The number of times the request was executed during the aggregated sample

- *Total response time*: The total time that this request spent executing during the sample (average response time multiplied by the call count)

- *Exceptional exits*: For each request during the aggregated sample, how many times it ended in an exception

- *Percent incomplete*: For each request during the aggregated sample, how many times it failed to complete within the configured time-out value

Identifying service requests that average slow response times involves sorting all requests by their average response time. Figure 10-9 displays this information for a session sorted by average response times, revealing three service requests that took longer than five seconds on average during the recording.

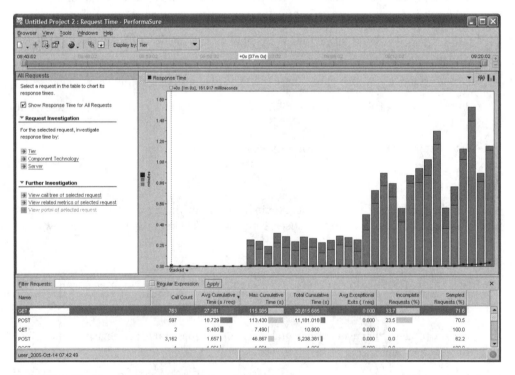

Figure 10-9. *Requests sorted by their average response times*

Figure 10-10 displays the same requests, but sorted by maximum response time. While the third request completed with an acceptable average response time (1.657 seconds), its maximum response time was almost 47 seconds. When things went bad, they went very bad!

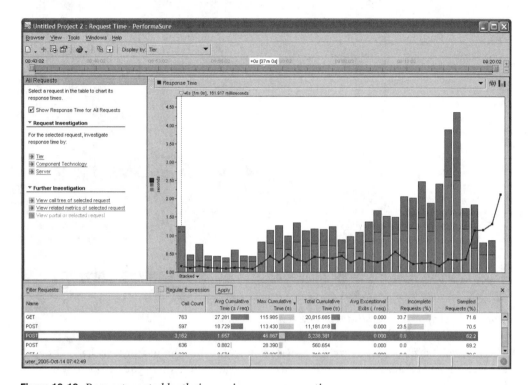

Figure 10-10. *Requests sorted by their maximum response times*

Figure 10-11 displays the same requests, but sorted by total response time. While the fourth request completes with an acceptable average response time (0.878 seconds), it is executed 1,248 times, yielding a total response time of 1,095 seconds.

Each of the aforementioned requests deserves attention and deeper diagnostics. You cannot simply look at requests that perform slowly on average; you must also include those with periodic spikes and those that significantly impact the performance of the application because of their call counts. The difference in diagnostics is that tuning average slow-running requests is a reactive process, while tuning requests with heavy impact is a proactive process to improving application quality. But as you can observe from Figures 10-9 through 10-11, there is a great deal of overlap: requests that average slow response times usually have spikes and are often called frequently.

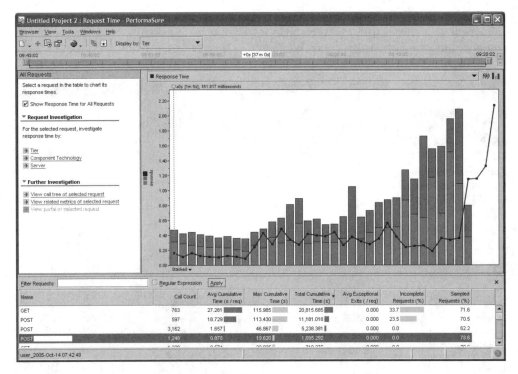

Figure 10-11. *Requests sorted by their total response times*

Once you have identified service requests that require deeper diagnostics, the next step is to view their call traces, or open them in a call tree view. From these call trees you want to determine the following:

- What is the hot path through a request?

- What is the hot point within that hot path?

The *hot path* reveals the slow path through the code: what path did the request follow from initially receiving the request to its slowest method? The *hot point* identifies the slowest method in the request. In order to identify the hot path and hot point, you need to sort the method response time data by different values:

- *Average cumulative time*: This is the amount of time spent inside of a method in addition to all methods that it called out to. Sorting by average cumulative time reveals the hot path through a request.

- *Average exclusive time*: This is the amount of time spent only in a method (and does not include any time spent in methods that it called out to). Sorting by average exclusive time reveals the hot point in a request.

Figure 10-12 shows a view of a request tree sorted by the average cumulative time.

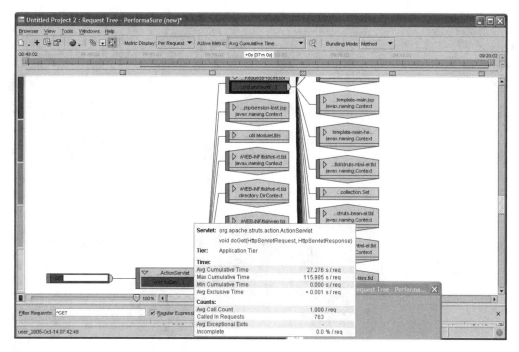

Figure 10-12. *The call tree color codes its nodes by the average cumulative time of each method.*

As Figure 10-12 illustrates, the Web server receives the request, forwards it to the Apache Struts doGet() method, which in turn calls the RequestProcessor.process() method. The pop-up window demonstrates that the doGet() method was a component of the hot path (because its average cumulative time was 27.276 seconds), but it is not a hot point (because its average exclusive time was less than 0.001 second).

Figure 10-13 shows a view of the same request tree sorted by the average exclusive time. Figure 10-13 sorts the color coding by exclusive time, revealing that the RequestProcessor. process() method spent 13.5 exclusive processing seconds of a total of 27.7 cumulative seconds. Further investigations will reveal that this is the largest hot point within the request, but another 14.2 seconds need to be accounted for.

■**Note** This is a complicated request, and the 27.7 seconds of total response time are broken into various components. The 13.5 exclusive seconds spent inside the RequestProcessor.process() method are actually a little misleading, because the org.apache.struts.action package is grouped in a custom component, so the process() method may not have taken 13.5 seconds, but 13.5 seconds elapsed inside the org.apache.struts.action package before calling out to application code.

We continue this process by identifying the next slowest node in the hot path, isolating its subtree, and finding its hot point. In this example, the next slowest method, calculateOrderTax(), accounted for almost 3 of the remaining 14.2 seconds, as shown in Figure 10-14.

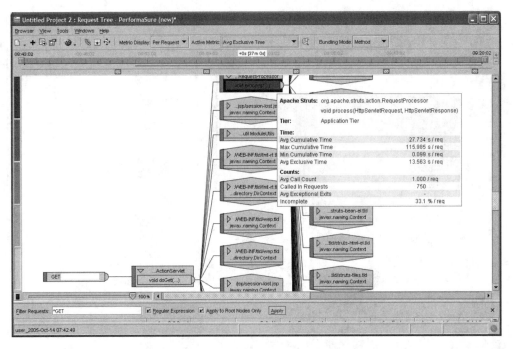

Figure 10-13. *The call tree color codes its nodes by the average exclusive time of each method.*

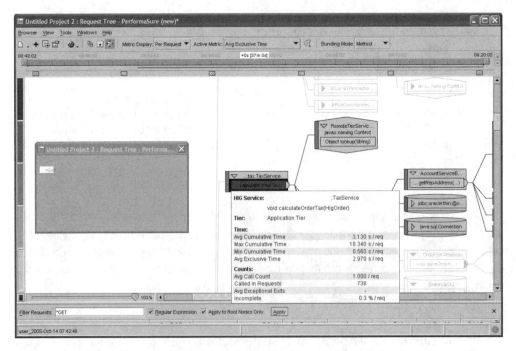

Figure 10-14. *After moving past the Struts code that is not part of the application, the next slowest point in the request was a call to calculateOrderTax().*

In the end, you will have identified a collection of offending methods, and it is your responsibility to identify why they are slow. One of the most common causes of a slow method is a call to an external dependency, such as a database. Figure 10-15 reveals that there was a SQL statement in this example that took almost 1 second to complete.

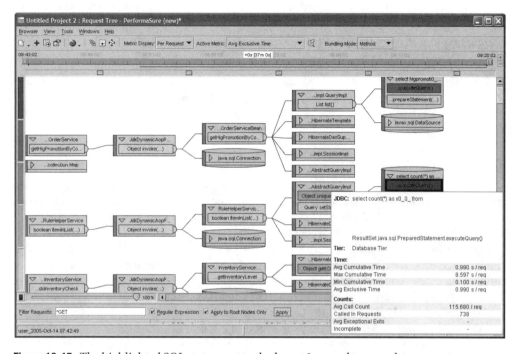

Figure 10-15. *The highlighted SQL statement took almost 1 second to complete.*

As shown in Figure 10-15, the highlighted SQL statement spent on average 0.990 seconds executing, but it is worth noting that its maximum response time was 8.597 seconds, meaning that when the request's response time executed slowly, the database contributed significantly to the overall response time. (Note that I extracted this example from a real customer application, so I excluded the customer's SQL for privacy reasons.)

Performance problems inside applications tend to have one of the following causes:

- A slow call to an external dependency.

- A method (or subgraph of a request) called an excessive number of times. The method may perform adequately each time it is called, but it is called so many times that it becomes problematic. This issue is common when building large strings; internally, string concatenations resolve to `StringBuffer.append()` method calls. The `append()` method usually completes in less than one millisecond, but when it is called 10,000 times, it becomes problematic!

- A slow method. If the problem is not the result of an external call or the sheer number of calls to a method, then the ultimate issue may simply be the method itself. When this occurs, the answer is to take the code off-line and analyze it in a code profiler to determine why it is slow.

- An environmental issue, such as a saturated thread pool or a major garbage collection.

Diagnosing Implicit Problems

When diagnosing application issues, you may inadvertently discover environmental problems. The manifestations of these problems may be initially confusing because slow response times at these points should not be possible, but once you understand that they are wait points, it all becomes clear. The sections that follow detail common interpretations of implicit problems discovered through application call tree analysis.

Thread Pool Pending Request

During the course of request analysis, you may see a request waiting at the application server's embedded Web server. This is characterized by a significant amount of time being spent in the GET /webapp/myaction.do node (or whatever the URL happens to be), which is the node that executes just prior to the servlet's process(), doGet(), or doPost() method. In theory this is impossible, because the after the Web server receives a request, it should immediately invoke the appropriate servlet, but it makes sense as soon as you realize that the request handling process places the request in a queue and it is subsequently picked up by an execute thread for processing. Any exclusive time spent in this node identifies the amount of time a request is spending in a request queue waiting for an execution thread.

On a related note, if you separate your environment into a distinct static Web tier and a dynamic Web tier by placing a Web server such as Apache or Microsoft IIS in front of your application, you can learn how much time the request spends in the Web server before being passed to the application server by looking at that node. Different monitoring tools have different solutions for they type of integration, but the tool I use, PerformaSure, has a specific Web server plug-in that records that time. Typically this pass-through is quick, so a large exclusive time in this node may be an indication that the Web server thread pool is backing up.

JDBC Connection Pool

Although you have explicit JDBC connection pool monitoring and rules to determine when all of the connections in a connection pool are in use, you can identify the same problem implicitly and learn about the requests being affected by looking at bytecode instrumentation. During the course of your application processing a request, if your application needs a database connection, it obtains that connection from the connection pool when your code calls DataSource.getConnection(). The getConnection() method is available through bytecode instrumentation, and if a connection is available in the connection pool, then it should be returned almost instantaneously. But if the request spends any significant amount of time in the getConnection() method, the connection pool does not have any available connections and is forced to wait for an available connection.

Nonprecompiled JSP

In an MVC-based Web architecture, the standard process is to implement a controller servlet that handles incoming requests. The front-controller servlet (Controller) interacts with business functions that build resultant beans (Model) containing the results of the request, and those results are forwarded to a JSP for presentation (View). In this type of environment, if the JSP is not currently compiled, when the `RequestDispatcher`'s `forward()` method is called, the application server must go through a three-step process before executing the JSP functionality:

1. It must convert the JSP to servlet source code; it builds a `.java` source code file.

2. It must compile the servlet into bytecode; it builds a `.class` file.

3. It loads the `.class` file into permanent memory and creates an instance in the heap to handle the request.

When this process occurs, from a bytecode instrumentation perspective, the `RequestDispatcher.forward()` method takes extra time to process. If the JSP is already compiled, then this method should have close to zero exclusive time, but if not, then this method can contribute greatly to the overall response time of the request.

SQL Report

The most accurate assessment of database performance health is best performed by database monitoring software, but you can learn a lot about how database queries affect the performance of Java EE applications. By using bytecode instrumentation, you can learn the following, for example:

- The number of unique SQL statements executed by an application

- A list of all SQL executed by an application

- The number of times each SQL statement was executed

- The average response time for each SQL statement

- The maximum response time for each SQL statement

- The total response time for each SQL statement

- A breakdown of the time spent in preparation, execution, and retrieval for each SQL statement

- The service requests that were affected by each SQL statement

The SQL report serves these purposes:

- Identifies problematic SQL to send to DBAs for troubleshooting

- Determines the number of unique SQL statements executed to best size the prepared statement cache

- Maps SQL statements to the requests that execute them

As you saw earlier when investigating slow-running service requests, and specifically in Figure 10-15, the problem can reside in a call to a database. In Figure 10-15, the identified slow point in that request was a call to executeQuery() passing a specific SQL statement.

This approach to identifying poorly performing SQL is reactionary: we first identify a slow-running request, then identify its hot points (some of which are SQL), and send the SQL to our DBAs for diagnosis. Another, database-centric proactive approach is to start with the SQL itself. Figure 10-16 shows a list of all SQL statements executed during a recorded session.

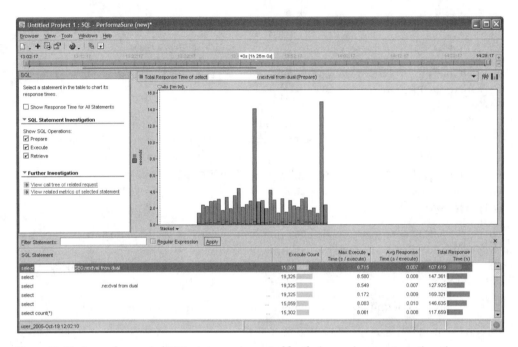

Figure 10-16. *Several executed SQL statements, sorted by their maximum execution time*

In Figure 10-16, you can see that the top statement was executed over 15,000 times, and while its average time was good (0.007 second), its maximum execution time was abysmal (8.815 seconds). From this SQL performance presentation, you can quickly identify candidates to send to DBAs for further analysis.

The list of SQL statements also reveals the number of unique statements, and from that you can better understand how to size your prepared statement cache. When you use prepared statements, each connection maintains a collection of precompiled statements to help avoid the recompilation of statements, both at the database as well as at the Java layer. These prepared statements improve performance but need to be sized carefully, as they are maintained on a per-connection basis. For example, 50 cached statements does not sound like much, but if you have 50 connections, then the impact on memory is 2,500 statements. Figure 10-17 shown a breakdown and distribution of SQL statement executions.

Figure 10-17 illustrates that there were 89 unique SQL statements executed during the recorded session, with over half of them executed five or more times. Depending on the length of the recording session, we may want to cache those statements, or at least cache those that were executed ten or more times, which in this case encompasses 33 statements. This break-down gives you confidence in your selection of the size of the prepared statement cache.

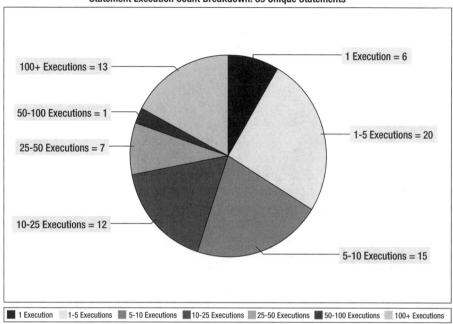

Statement Execution Count Breakdown: 89 Unique Statements

100+ Executions = 13

50-100 Executions = 1

25-50 Executions = 7

10-25 Executions = 12

1 Execution = 6

1-5 Executions = 20

5-10 Executions = 15

■ 1 Execution   1-5 Executions   ■ 5-10 Executions   ■ 10-25 Executions   25-50 Executions   ■ 50-100 Executions   100+ Executions

Figure 10-17. *A breakdown and distribution of SQL statement executions*

The final benefit provided by a Java EE SQL report is the mapping of SQL statements to the requests that execute them. This is important, because without this information you might waste time tuning a SQL statement that is executed by a noncritical component. For example, your application may maintain a background thread that builds reports and that executes slow-running SQL. In this case, tuning this SQL is not nearly as important as tuning SQL that is executed while a user waits for a request to return.

Summary

This chapter presented the rationale and strategies behind building a Java EE performance analysis report. A performance analysis report provides information about the performance of a Java EE application and environment and, more important, it provides advice about how to improve that performance.

After covering performance assessment benefits and basics, this chapter went on to divide capturing performance data into two categories: capturing data from a production staging test environment and capturing data from a live production environment. From that performance information, the main part of this chapter was spent analyzing that data and deriving the business impact of seemingly raw and unrelated data.

In the next chapter, we turn our attention to resolving production issues. You'll learn the methodology you should follow to maximize the effectiveness of your troubleshooting efforts to avoid involving parties that are not required to solve the problem at hand. The goal is to solve production problems as quickly as possible without disturbing users unnecessarily.

CHAPTER 11

■■■

Production Troubleshooting Methodology

"**I** still have something that I want you to explain to me." John had an air of confidence about him as we sat in the restaurant that night. Although I knew he wanted to get home to his family, as did I, I could tell that he understood what we had been talking about the past few weeks and had a burning question that needed to be answered by the time the server brought dessert.

"I understand the proactive approaches to building solid code, and I understand how to test my applications and environment to determine their capabilities, but I want to know how I can best solve production problems when they occur. Last month when our servers started crashing, I called in my staff and sent them searching for the problem. It was a mess! They pointed fingers back and forth, blaming each other and wasting time. In the end, I had to pull the new code and roll back the changes before my job was on the line. There has to be a better way."

John got it! He discovered one of the key tenets of performance management.

"Let me tell you, I think this is the biggest thing that I have learned in my adventures in Java tuning: troubleshooting production issues is tough, but with the right tools and the right procedures in place, the pain can be minimized," I replied. "We can quantify losses to your organization, irrespective of the application type—business-to-business, business-to-consumer, or intranet—in measurable dollars, and the only way to reduce those losses is to define and follow a formal process. Do you know what to do if there is ever a fire in your building?"

"Of course." John could tell where I was going with this. "We have planned escape routes and people—we call them fire marshals—designated to be accountable for subgroups within each floor. So if a fire does occur, we walk down one of the predefined stairwells and meet in the parking lot. The fire marshals perform a roll call, and then we can report anyone missing to the fire department. Thankfully, we haven't had more than practice drills, but yes, we know in excruciating detail what to do if a fire occurs."

"One more question," I said, hoping not to annoy him too much with these obviously leading questions. "How do you know when you have a fire?"

"If there is a fire, then the fire alarms go off, and all of the fire doors close," John responded.

"So the fire alarms are your tools, and the escape plan is your procedure. Troubleshooting production issues is similar to reacting to fires, only production issues happen much more frequently than fires, thankfully! Let me show you the tools you need to identify problems in your Java EE environment and help you define the procedures you need to implement when problems occur. But let's pick it up in the morning; here comes dessert!"

Performance Issues in Production

When a performance issue occurs in a production application, the costs can be severe, measured both in terms of the resolution costs as well as revenue loss. When an application is unavailable or underperforming, the revenue loss can be quantified in the following three categories:

- *Business-to-consumer applications*: Poor performance can lead to site abandonment and a loss of confidence in your organization.

- *Business-to-business applications*: Poor performance can lead to a loss of confidence in your technical abilities, loss of contractual revenue through violated SLAs, and in the worst case, the loss of a business partner.

- *Intranet applications*: Poor performance can lead to a loss in productivity, as your employees spend more time waiting and less time working.

The impact of this revenue loss is in direct proportion to the significance of the performance problem and the resolution time. In addition to external losses, each individual involved in troubleshooting the cause of the performance issue loses productivity. In the case of a long-running problem that is not properly managed and consumes efforts from multiple resources, the loss can be measured by delayed development schedules or changes in the scope of product delivery, which can cause a loss of competitive edge in the marketplace. For example, consider a performance problem that takes developers away from their primary development responsibilities for two weeks. The product management team now has a decision to make: is the product released on time with missing features or does the product release date slip? In the former case, your sales force may lose sales opportunities, because your competitors' products have features that you did not have time to implement while you were busy troubleshooting performance issues. In the latter case, slips in release dates may force your prospective customers to buy products from your competition.

Regardless of where you experience a loss, the loss is real and quantifiable. Therefore, reviewing the way many corporations handle production performance issues is beneficial.

Corporations all too often troubleshoot production problems by assembling a war room containing the leads of all teams. While the intent is to quickly identify the cause of the problem, the result is usually an activity I like to call a "finger-pointing face-off." The application architects point to the database administrators, who point to the system administrators, who point back at the architects. In a flurried attempt to absolve themselves of blame, these otherwise talented individuals waste valuable time and resources. Rather than being any individual's character flaw, this behavior is the result of an environment that has been cultivated by a lack of a formal production workflow process.

A formal process that everyone knows needs to be in place, so problems are rapidly and accurately triaged to the appropriate party for resolution. For example, if the problem is in the database configuration, then the application architects do not need to be involved, but if the problem is in the application code, then they very well may be involved. Only through a repeatable and proven process can resolutions be rapid and directed, downtime be minimized, and revenues saved. Again the cliché "An ounce of prevention is worth a pound of cure" applies: put the tools in place and build a problem-solving process around them before you have problems to solve.

Prerequisites

Before diving into the production support methodology, a set of monitoring tools needs to be in place if the methodology is to be effective. Without monitoring tools in place, you have no early defense system, and the first casualties of poor performance will be your users. As an analogy, consider why you have smoke detectors in your house. If a fire breaks out in the middle of the night you want to be woken up before the fire reaches your bedroom so that you can evacuate. The smoke is a leading indicator of a fire, and your smoke detector is your monitor. The same is true of enterprise applications, and from the perspective of this book, the tragedy is poor performance.

In order for your monitoring tools to be effective, they must exhibit the following qualities:

- They must monitor your environment 24×7.

- They must support intelligent alerting.

- They must exhibit a depth of monitoring across of breadth of technologies that spans, at minimum, end-user experience (both real and synthetic), application servers, and database servers.

Real-time visualization tools provide valuable insight into the internal workings and performance of your primary technologies and contribute significantly to resolution efforts, but unless you plan on maintaining three full-time shifts of highly paid workers monitoring these tools 24 hours a day, 7 days a week, you need more. Unattended 24×7 monitoring is the core requirement for any monitoring software. If a problem occurs at 2:00 AM when no one is watching the environment, the monitoring system must detect the problem and alert the appropriate party. Additionally, the monitoring system has a critical requirement to store sufficient historical detail about problems to enable postmortem diagnostics, so that reproducing production issues in a test is not always required.

While simple threshold alerting may be valuable to an individual administrator, for example, an execution queue depth of 7 is valuable to a Java EE administrator, a high-level monitoring solution that watches an entire enterprise needs deeper and more intelligent alerts. An intelligent alert acquires and correlates metrics from multiple sources and derives discernable business values from them. It answers the following question: how is this particular condition affecting users? For example, an execution queue depth of 7 alerts Java EE administrators to a backup of requests and hence a degradation in performance. If the requests still exhibit a response time buffer of 25 percent, then users are not affected, and the problem is not too severe.

Additionally, when a problem occurs that does affect end users, you need to understand how to derive the root cause. The symptoms of a response-time degradation may include missed SLAs, an aggravated queue depth, CPU spikes, and increased garbage collection pause times. Correlating these apparently disparate metrics yields the following conclusions: because the application cycles objects, garbage collections are extended, which causes CPU spikes that delay processing and cause the queue depth to increase. Identifying the root of the problem requires understanding the interaction between these components. Individually, each metric could send you down a different diagnostic pathway, but combined, they reveal the true nature of the problem. Intelligent alerts must include the ability to define rules that minimize false alarms (otherwise, administrators will either ignore the monitoring system alerts or turn them off). And finally, intelligent alerts must allow for combinational logic across various domains of technology.

An enterprise monitoring solution must also provide a depth of knowledge across a breadth of technologies. Recall that enterprise applications are composed of a series of tiers that interact to solve a business process; they may include one or more Web servers, application servers, databases, operating systems, firewalls, load balancers, messaging systems, legacy systems, Web services, and other external dependencies, as well as network devices to facilitate communications between them. With so many different technology stacks at each tier, no single individual can maintain an up-to-date mastery of them all. Therefore, your monitoring solution needs a depth of knowledge about each layer of each technology stack. For example, monitoring only the application server itself is not enough: this monitoring may point to symptoms of the problem, but without knowing with which components it interacts, the cause can be evasive. The monitor must also provide dedicated user interfaces for the separate core administration groups (for example, database administrators, application administrators, and help desk personnel); without this, these administrators will simply default to their own custom tools.

Combining these requirements, we have a 24×7, unattended monitor that provides a depth of monitoring across a breadth of technologies with intelligent alerts that rise above isolated thresholds to assess the impact of observed behavior on business processes. Mixing such a tool with a proven methodology will maximize your troubleshooting efficiency and minimize application downtime and lost revenue.

■**Note** Benjamin Franklin is often misquoted as saying "Jack of all trades, master of none." Rather he said "Jack of all trades, master of one," meaning that a cultured person knows something about everything and everything about one thing. Knowing a little about everything is great, but you should have an area of expertise, which is an area where you know all. Therefore, from a business perspective, you should understand how all of these disparate pieces fit together to solve a business problem, but you also need a specialization in one area where everyone turns to you for answers. And of course, from a personal perspective, if you are a "Jack-of-all-trades, but a master of none," you might consider what is valuable to you and find your one specialization, but we'll leave that for another discussion.

Production Support Methodology

Production support methodology is based upon configuring intelligent alerts, specific to an individual enterprise environment, and then identifying the optimal path through the support and development organizations to deliver the alert to the appropriate individual or group. The goal, met through using your triaging process, is for an alert to reach the appropriate individual or group to handle that alert without involving unnecessary groups or individuals. Meeting this goal optimizes resolution time and minimizes the impact of production issues on the organization itself, because for example, a DBA is not involved in troubleshooting an application server issue.

Roles of Support Personnel

Before following an alert through this methodology, let us meet the players:

- *Level 1 support*: Production support help desk or network operations center (NOC) personnel

- *Level 2 support*: Technology administrator

- *Level 3 support*: Application support engineer, application maintenance engineer, or performance engineer

- *Level 4 Support*: Architect or developer

The production support help desk of an NOC consists of a team of individuals responsible for identifying performance issues throughout the organization, including Java applications, application servers, databases, mainframes, operating systems, hardware, networks, load balancers, routers, firewalls, and so on. They are truly Jacks-of-all-trades and masters of both the monitoring tool and the escalation process. They have one of the best views of the entire organization's technology stack and are experts at managing their monitoring tools and triaging issues to the appropriate second tier.

Technology administrators are responsible for the performance and availability of a specific piece of the technology stack. This group includes Java EE administrators, DBAs, system administrators, network administrators, and the like. Any significant technology stack in your organization needs to have an identified administrator for that technology. In the ideal case, an individual or individuals should be dedicated to the technology administrator's role, but depending on the size of your organization, this role may be another hat that someone must wear.

As the third level of support for alerts, application support engineers are responsible for the performance of individual applications or technologies. Application support engineers can exist in any tier running code. For example, a database application support engineer maintains extensive knowledge of stored procedures and functions that are used by an application while a Java EE support engineer maintains extensive knowledge of a component or components. The point is that application support engineers have not necessarily developed the application but have detailed enough code and architecture knowledge about the application's function to fix bugs and make minor modifications to its behavior. Additionally, their job responsibility includes the ability to isolate code-level issues to the specific area in within the code, such as the method, or to identify architectural issues that require code or configuration changes.

Finally, the architect, or developer, is a member of the development team who has deep knowledge of the applications; this person may be a technical lead or technical owner of individual application components. In addition to maintaining intimate knowledge of application code, the architect also has the authority to change code or delegate the responsibility to another team member.

Note While ideally your organization should have an individual dedicated to each role, these roles can be considered "logical." For example, a single individual may fill the database administrator role (configuring tables, indexes, and so on) and the database application support engineer role (managing and maintaining the stored procedures and underlying data). The important thing is that you identify an individual in each of these areas to handle production issues.

The Production Support Workflow

When an alert is triggered, either by user feedback or an intelligent alert, it is sent to the NOC that triages the issue to the appropriate technology administrator. The issue is then either resolved or forwarded down the chain to the next level of support until the problem is resolved. Figure 11-1 provides a visual representation of the production support workflow.

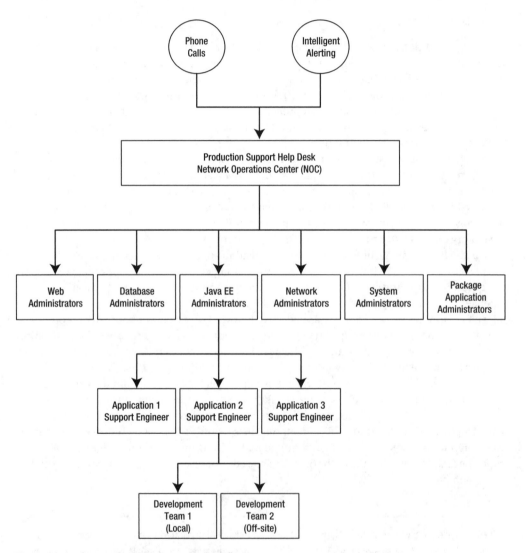

Figure 11-1. *The production support workflow*

The trigger that starts the production support workflow is either user feedback or an intelligent alert. The more intelligent and accurate your alerts are, the fewer user complaints you will receive. Being alerted to a problem by an early warning system is much better than hearing about it from your customers! An early warning system should include synthetic transactions and some mechanism for measuring real user experience on the desktops as well.

The NOC (level 1 support) receives the trigger, opens a production support case, and triages the alert to the appropriate technology administrator (level 2 support). While the NOC is responsible for triaging and tracking support cases, the technology administrator is the first tier that can attempt to resolve the problem. For example, if the issue is triaged to a specific database, then it should be forwarded to the database administrator for the offending database; to avoid another bottleneck (created by sending a database issue to all database administrators), the alert is forwarded with context to the appropriate database administrator.

The technology administrator's role is usually confined to nonapplication changes (configuration changes). For example, a database administrator can set up new indexes or move data stores to different hard drives, but unless the administrator also wears the database application support engineer hat, he or she should not change the underlying SQL code. If the technology administrator cannot resolve the issue through the configuration of the technology, then he or she identifies the offending application and forwards the alert to the appropriate application support engineer (level 3 support).

The application support engineer is a technical representative in his particular domain; for example, an application support engineer in the application tier has development experience and may have been involved in the team that originally built the application. He or she has the ability to change code to resolve issues, but if the problem is deemed architectural in nature, requires a feature modification, or simply cannot be fixed by the application support engineer, then the alert is elevated to the appropriate development team (level 4 support).

The development team may be local or off-site, but one architect or team lead should be the point of contact within the development team that the application support engineer engages for such alerts. The team lead, then, can determine who to remove from current development efforts to resolve the problem. In this tier the most visible impact on the organization can be observed: developers working either on a new project or the next version of an existing project must delay their work to resolve a production problem. This delay can impact release schedules and feature sets, which can lead to losses in competitive edge, and hence sales and revenue.

Figure 11-1 illustrates the path that a Java EE application related alert travels through the production support workflow, but other technologies follow a similar pathway. The key to optimizing this workflow is to identify each tier in your environment and determine how far each alert could conceivably travel before being resolved. Then optimize the workflow accordingly by defining roles at each major checkpoint between the NOC and that final alert recipient. These checkpoints should occur in technology locations where the issue can either be resolved by an individual or forwarded to the next tier.

Triggers

Triggers come in one of two flavors:

- User-initiated triggers

- Intelligent alerts

User-initiated triggers are particularly bad: your users observed errors or poor performance in your application before you did! If alerts are properly constructed, user-initiated triggers can be avoided. That is not to say that users will not complain, but rather you should know about the problem before they do, so that you can be working on a solution when they contact you.

Intelligent alerting is the key to staying several steps ahead of your users, but it is also the most difficult part of monitoring. The best way to build intelligent alerts is to bring together an expert from the NOC, who understands and can configure the monitoring solution, with the chief architect for the project, who maintains detailed knowledge of each tier in the technology stack. The chief architect is able to define intelligent alerts while the NOC expert can articulate those rules to the monitoring solution. Many times the chief architect finds it helpful to include representatives from various areas in the technology stack in such a discussion, as his or her vision for intelligent alerts must be substantiated by specific low-level pieces of data. As an example, the chief architect may state an alert is needed when user requests are pending, and the response time varies atypically; but the Java EE system administrator can translate that into an alert when queue depth is greater than 5, and the standard deviation of response times differs more than 25 percent from its average. The chief architect has the vision, while technology administrators have the knowledge both to advise the chief architect and realize his or her vision.

Level 1 Support

The principle responsibilities of the first level of support are to triage the alert to the appropriate technology domain and track the status of the alert throughout its life cycle. The NOC, or production support help desk, representative answers the following questions:

- How was the alert triggered?

- What technology component owns the alert?

- Are users being affected yet?

- What is the severity of the alert?

- Who is the technology administrator responsible for handling the alert?

In other words, the NOC representative must establish the context of the alert by answering each of the aforementioned questions.

The trigger of the alert is a leading factor in establishing the severity of the alert, but calling the trigger out explicitly on its own is important. Some common triggers include the following, in order of severity from lowest to highest:

- *Intelligent alerting*: These early warning alerts are identified by the monitoring solution.

- *Violated SLA*: SLAs can be evaluated through two mechanisms: passive and active. In the *passive* monitoring of SLAs, the monitoring solution watches live user requests as they occur and records metrics about those requests. In *active* monitoring, the monitoring solution generates synthetic transactions that target key points in the application. If either of these indicates that SLAs are violated, then an alert is triggered in the monitoring solution.

- *User e-mail*: One or more users can send e-mail to support indicating poor performance or the failure of a piece of functionality.

- *User phone calls*: Users are dissatisfied enough that they call support directly.

In the best-case scenario, your alerts encompass the majority of performance problems, so that your early defense system can identify them before SLAs are violated and users are affected. If a performance problem slips past your early defense system, the next catchall detection tool is your SLA monitoring. SLAs are configured to meet user requirements, so you should not receive user complaints while you are satisfying SLAs. Once SLAs are violated, users may start complaining, but if your SLA monitoring solution alerts you to the problem early enough, then you can either resolve the problem completely or at least inform users who do complain that your organization is aware of the problem and actively seek a remedy.

Note Being able tell upset users that you are already aware of the problem and seeking a solution always reflects better on your organization's technical abilities than being caught off guard. Although this does not necessarily meet their immediate needs well, consider the alternative—acting surprised that the problem occurred and asking the user to describe the symptoms. While the user may feel some degree of personalization that you are looking at his or her specific problem, the typical reaction after such a user hangs up the phone is to complain about your organization's incompetence and reflect on how you should hire him or her to solve your problems. The user response when you acknowledge the problem is either neutral, or maybe a mild annoyance, while the response when you do not know about the problem is dramatically negative. All you can do is choose the lesser of two evils!

When users trigger your alerts, then the impact is more severe, and the mechanism that they use to alert you can be an indicator of how severe the problem is: if they click a support link or send an e-mail, then there is a legitimate problem, but by the time they call your support number, they are typically irate. You still have to quickly address e-mail complaints, but the urgency is not as great as if calls are coming in!

Obviously, identifying performance problems before your users are affected is preferable, but if users do find problems for you, doing a postmortem analysis on the alert is important. Specifically, you want to identify the symptoms of the problem just prior to user complaints by looking at the historical data that your monitoring solution captured, and correlate the behavior of the system to the root cause of the problem that you discover. With any luck, you will be able to develop a new intelligent alert, so that you will be better equipped to detect this problem in the future.

In general production issues can be categorized as either *intermittent* or *persistent*. Level 1 support must be prepared to detect and triage both. Intermittent issues, while typically lower in priority than similar types of persistent issues, tend to be more challenging to capture and require monitoring technology that can be set up to trigger alerts and take actions based on advanced rules using combinations of measurements from across multiple tiers of an application environment. Additionally, the monitoring tool must store diagnostic and other details for historical diagnosis as well as trending and capacity planning.

The final activity that level 1 support must perform when responding to an alert is to open a support ticket and initiate alert tracking. This is important for the following three reasons:

- *Logging*: The support ticket is logged for other support representatives to see when they receive calls.

- *Tracking*: Tracking (that is, following a support ticket from inception to resolution) is important to ensure that it does eventually attain closure; only through tracking can support representatives determine whether an issue has already been captured.

- *Analysis*: The number of support tickets and the specific areas experiencing problems are gauges of the health of the performance of an application; an analysis of support tickets may help justify replacing an application server vendor, network devices, and so on. Additionally, this analysis will quantify improvements in mean time to resolution and other core indicators related to the organizational process and tools used for triaging production issues.

Remember that in order to learn from mistakes and optimize your production support workflow, tracking and analyzing all support issues that arise is of the utmost importance and is an ongoing process that must continually improve.

Level 2 Support

Level 2 support is composed of technology administrators, each responsible for his or her own technical stack. On the Java EE side, the Java EE administrator is the level 2 support. To review, the Java EE administrator is responsible for all application server instances, deployment topology, and configuration options; therefore, this person determines whether a particular alert is the result of an application issue or a container issue. More specifically, the Java EE administrator does the following three things:

- Determines if the long-term fix for the reported alert is application or configuration related

- Triages the alert to the appropriate application and component owner, if the problem is application related

- Determines if initiating a short-term configuration change can mitigate the impact of the alert

Determining the root of a problem is important, but determining whether a short-term solution that can mitigate the impact of the problem until a proper solution can be implemented is equally so. If only a long-term solution is considered, it may be underarchitected and poorly implemented in the interest of providing a solution to meet SLAs. For example, I have been at several customer sites where HTTP sessions were unnecessarily large, which led to poorly performing garbage collections and even out-of-memory errors. The proper solution to this session-size problem is to refactor the session implementation and associated code to reduce the amount of data stored in the session, but this refactoring is a major undertaking that could require months to implement properly. Simply identifying the core problem was not enough to both satisfy user requirements today and accurately build and test a long-term solution. Therefore, I helped them implement the following two-phase plan:

1. Configure a large heap, and spend time tuning the heap to maximize its performance to support such large sessions.

2. Perform an architecture review on their application, and set forth a plan to reduce the session size.

When application problems are identified, the problem should be triaged to the correct application and correct component. Again, the goal is to reduce the amount of time wasted by the involvement of unnecessary parties: if the problem is in the data persistence layer, then you do not need to take time away from the visualization team. But be aware that problems are usually not absolutely definitive, so you need experience, skill, and a good diagnostic tool to be able to identify offending components. And yes, performance problems can easily span multiple components, but as the Java EE administrator, you need to isolate the problem as much as you can.

■**Note** A common situation I see in the field is that companies are beginning to build new common application infrastructures consolidating numerous, separate departmental or other types of application deployments into a single, highly powered infrastructure. This facilitates common tooling, deployment, and management practices, but also presents major challenges around identifying which application and component in a large pool of applications causes a particular issue. This situation is where application- and transaction-level detailed isolation is paramount. And SOA further complicates this management problem.

Non–Java EE troubleshooting at this phase follows a similar approach: the administrator must determine if she can solve the problem or if the problem is in details outside of her control. For example, a DBA might determine that the root cause of performance problem lies inside a stored procedure that he does not own. After analyzing the explain plan, he determines that he can create additional indices to mitigate the impact of the problem. He makes the changes, and then forwards the problem to the database developer responsible for the stored procedure for the true fix. Similarly, in some packaged application environments where the application source code cannot be modified, DBAs still have the ability to configure the database to interpret bad SQL code in a more efficient way, so the ability to see that bad SQL code and automatically evaluate all possible alternatives is essential.

The important thing in level 2 support is to clearly define the person in each technology tier who is responsible for handling these problems. When the NOC staff finds a problem and triages it to a specific technology, they must have a specific individual to forward that problem to.

Level 3 Support

From a Java EE perspective, level 3 support consists of application support engineers, programmers responsible for maintaining application code and troubleshooting bugs. Development organizations typically maintain groups of developers building the next release(s) of their applications and groups that support the existing release(s). Maintaining these two distinct groups is important, because all applications have bugs, and usage patterns can never be completely anticipated; so application releases have to be supported. Each time a support issue arises, you do not want it to affect the schedule of the next release.

The application support engineer can support an entire application, a subset of components in the application, or an individual component of it, depending on the size of the application and the company. When an alert is elevated to third level support, the application support engineer must perform the following steps:

1. Determine if this issue is already known, and uncover the resolution plan: will this issue be fixed in a patch release or in a subsequent major or minor release?

2. Uncover the nature of the problem: is the problem a simple programmatic error that can be resolved by refactoring the code, or is it architectural in nature?

3. If the problem is architectural in nature or extends beyond the scope of a support request, then a change request must be submitted to the change control board, which in most organizations means forwarding the request to product management for examination.

4. If the problem can be fixed through code refactoring, then the application support engineer fixes the problem, submits a request for a patch release, and merges the changes into the change control system for inclusion into the next release of the software.

5. Finally, if the problem is well within the scope of a support request, but the application support engineer cannot solve it, then the engineer must forward it to the appropriate development team. Forwarding the request does not reflect negatively on the application support engineer, but rather indicates that the code's complexity requires the original development team to address the problem.

Note Determining the fine line between a support request and a change request can be difficult for an application support engineer. In some circumstances the determination is easy, such as a request for a new interface, but the line can quickly become blurred. For example, consider a performance problem that occurs because of the format of an internal file structure. The internal file structure may interact with a great many components in the application, and hence optimizing it may break everything else. Therefore put the request in front of product management, so that they can ask the development team for an estimate of the effort required to implement the change and evaluate the request against other priorities.

Development and product management teams tend to be at odds with one another, because the development team sees the application from a technical perspective and makes decisions based on technology, whereas production management sees the application from a business perspective and weighs the impact on current customers' license revenue and future sales. Many decisions that product management makes that seem irrational to developers are very rational once you understand external factors that impact product sales.

As application support engineers forward problems to the next level, they need to perform additional triaging and information gathering. They need to determine the offending component(s) and provide as much context as possible to the technical lead or architect of the offending component(s). Remember that any time spent in the fourth support tier can potentially impact the release schedule of the next version of the application, and hence lead to the quantifiable losses outlined previously in this chapter.

Occasionally some level of animosity exists between application support engineers and software developers working on the next release of software. I know that I felt it when I was working in each role: software developers writing new code sometimes feel superior to those maintaining code, whereas developers maintaining code feel like they are cleaning up the mess of their inferior counterparts. The resolution to this animosity requires a change in mind-set and an understanding of both roles:

- Software developers writing new code need to understand that without application support engineers, evolving the software would be a tough task.

- Software developers maintaining code need to understand that schedules and feature requirements can affect the quality of code, even when proper testing methodologies are employed.

Both groups are necessary in order for a company to be successful, and both groups have distinct skill sets that the other may or may not have. A successful company is partitioned into a set of interwoven development groups, and without each one, the company will fail.

Note In considering quality as a function of schedules, I am reminded of my time working for a computer manufacturer. Back in the mid-1990s, we were selling desktops and minitowers running DOS and Windows 3.x; we were a Japanese company operating in an American culture. We implemented our software configurations, tested them, and released them in a relatively aggressive time frame. Some of our Japanese competitors building similar systems in Japan placed great emphasis on quality control, and therefore spent months of additional time in testing. As a result, we released products faster, but our quality was lower, while they released better-quality products more slowly. Who had the competitive edge in the United States? When we were releasing systems with DOS 6.2.2, our competitors were still releasing software with DOS 5.0, so we won hands down. The lesson: competitive edge can be more important to sales than quality, of course, with some qualification. This interesting lesson opened my eyes to analyzing the market in which we operate!

Level 4 Support

Involving level 4 support has the greatest impact on your organization, but if the problem necessitates that involvement, then it must be done. Typically problems enter support level 4 through a component architect or technical lead who determines the best person or team to assess the problem. From this assessment, the technical lead balances the severity of the problem against the estimate of the effort to resolve it to propose options to the development manager. The options include the following:

- Fix the problem now.

- Fix the problem in a subsequent release.

- File the problem as a known issue that will not be fixed.

The response to a problem is a balance between the severity of the alert and the effort required to resolve it: high-severity problems must be resolved while low-severity problems may be resolved if the effort is minimal. While each problem must be evaluated on an individual basis, the quadrants in Figure 11-2 may help you determine the best option.

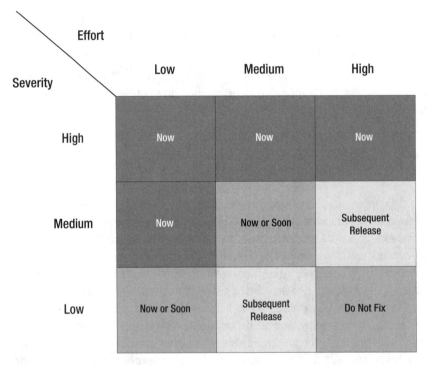

Figure 11-2. *You can use this chart as a guide to determining the response to a problem based on the severity of the alert and the effort required to resolve it.*

For example, if the severity of the problem is high, such as daily application crashes, then fixing the problem immediately may be the only viable option, regardless of the effort required to do so. But if the severity is minor, such as if 1 out of 10,000 user logins fails, then even a medium effort required to fix the problem may preclude it from ever being fixed. Again, you are balancing impacted release schedules with the severity of problems, and each decision must be made from a business perspective.

Based upon the problem assessment, if any substantial effort is required to resolve the problem, then the architect or technical lead should compile a concise problem assessment document and present it to the development manager responsible for the component. The development manager can then determine whether or not the problem will be resolved, or if the problem needs to be evaluated further. If the decision requires input from the business units, then they will be consulted; meanwhile, developers can return to their other tasks.

■**Note** Observe that I use the term "concise problem assessment document" and not "problem assessment report." The time spent building and reviewing this document can be counted toward impacted release schedules, thus you do not want to waste too much time building reports. A concise document detailing the nature and severity of the problem and the effort required to resolve it provides enough information for the development manager to decide whether or not to fix the problem, or to ask for additional information. If the problem requires major architectural changes, then a formal problem assessment report can be constructed and reviewed by the development manager and product manager to determine how and when, or if, it will be resolved.

In the end, if the problem has been labeled as a known issue not to be fixed, then the problem ticket needs to be closed and listed as such. The issue is then filed in the bug tracking system, so that if it is reported again, development does not have to be involved. The most appropriate place for the final determination of whether a subsequent problem alert is a duplicate is at the application support tier, because similar problem symptoms may not necessarily be caused by the same problem. The individuals best equipped to make this determination are the ones who elevated the problem to development in the first place.

Benefits of a Formal Production Support Methodology

From a high level, defining a formal production support methodology is relatively simple. Take the following steps:

1. Divide the support effort into tiers.

2. Assign roles to individuals in each tier.

3. At each tier, try to resolve the problem, or triage the problem and gather contextual information before escalating the problem to the subsequent tier.

The challenge is effectively implementing a tiered resolution process that is specific to your organization. Use the four-level model presented in the previous section as a guide, and adapt it to address each technology stack in your organization to yield the following benefits:

- A standardized process that eliminates confusion and leads to quicker resolution times

- Delegated roles to streamline the troubleshooting process

- Effective triaging that eliminates finger-pointing

- Minimized losses in productivity across all development tiers by involving only the required teams

A standardized process that is methodically followed each time a problem arises leads to quicker resolution times, because the forethought of the process eliminates confusion when the problem occurs. Consider fire drills again: when a fire occurs, we do not want everyone to attempt to run out of a burning building, follow the same routes, trample each other, and then assemble without any way to know who is missing. Rather, we segment groups within our company and define specific escape routes. We assign a leader for each group who is responsible for determining who is accounted for and who is missing. When a fire does occur and everyone follows the process, no one gets trampled, and everyone is accounted for.

In the production support workflow, when an application fails to respond, rather than putting together all team and technology leads in a war room to shout out theories, the individual best equipped to diagnose the application failure receives it. The process continues until the problem reaches the individual or team best equipped to resolve it, with no confusion about who is involved or about the process that each person that the problem touches is expected to follow.

By designating support roles to specific individuals at each tier, not only do you eliminate confusion, but you also minimize resistance from that individual. Deflecting blame from oneself is human nature, but when problem occurrences are methodically triaged to a particular technology or component, the individuals responsible for supporting that technology or component are more willing to respond appropriately. Furthermore, with a predetermined process to follow, they are not caught unprepared and unaware of what to do next. They were designated to be in this role and know the process to follow, so chances are they will not resist near as much as if the process did not exist. And when they do not resist the process and turn immediately to solving the problem, then the natural result is a quicker resolution.

Triaging may be the most important component to the sanity of your support team, and as a result, may significantly minimize your resolution times. Recall that the finger-pointing face-off occurs frequently, but when an intelligent alert identifies a problem and points to a component, the finger-pointing is removed. For example, either the database listener is up or it is not: the intelligent alert leaves no room for intelligible debate. There may be room for that debate in a Monty Python sketch, but now for something completely different . . .

My first foray into finger-pointing battles occurred when I was working on a large, distributed application, responsible for the front end interface. The front end interacted with our homegrown middleware technology to access the persistence layer, and during an integration phase, a functional issue halted all integration testing. Being on the front end, the manifestation of the problem was that the data was not available, and I was blamed by the middleware team. I needed two days of programming to prove that the problem was, in fact, in the middleware code. The two problems in this example were a lack of personal responsibility (finger-pointing) and a lack of monitoring insight in order to triage the problem. Deeper monitoring insight would have saved me two days of effort and shortened our integration phase.

The final internal benefit to a formal production support workflow is that only the minimal amount of internal productivity is ever lost, because only parties responsible for offending technologies are involved in the troubleshooting exercises. In my previous example, had the problem been properly triaged and handed to the middleware team, not only would the problem have been resolved quicker, but I would not have wasted two days troubleshooting the problem.

Implementing a formal production support workflow has countless benefits, but in the end, it reduces the losses outlined in the beginning of the chapter.

Summary

The effects of production performance issues on your business can be measured in terms of losses of revenue, productivity, and credibility. The only effective mechanism to minimize these losses when a performance problem occurs is implementing a formal production support workflow. By putting the appropriate tools and processes in place, you can be alerted to problems before your users and optimize problem resolution times.

This chapter serves as a guide that you can follow to optimize your production support workflow. In your organization, roles will probably overlap and boundaries between them blur, but attempt to define a stakeholder responsible for each role and plan your support strategies, much like you would plan for a fire by performing fire drills.

CHAPTER 12

■■■

Trending, Forecasting, and Capacity Planning

"**I** think I have my head around applications in production now," John stated. "I know how to assess the health of my environment and tune it, and if problems do arise, I know how to field them. I feel confident!"

I didn't want to burst his bubble, but we still needed to talk about one topic. "You've arrived at a good point, but let me ask you a question. What are you planning on doing with your environment in the future? Do you know how many users you are going to have in six months? Do you know how your environment can handle that?"

John looked a little irritated at my question, but I saw a slight gleam in his eyes as he anticipated that I was going to complete his production story. "Okay, Einstein, tell me where you're going with this."

"Three topics for you: trending, forecasting, and capacity planning. You need to know where you are, where you're going, and how you're going to arrive at the correct destination," I said.

"I've heard those terms used a lot. What is the difference between them, and how can I use them to make both my users and my boss happy?" One of the things that I really appreciated about John was his focus on the bottom line: meeting the needs of his users and his business.

"It is true that they are closely related, but there are distinct differences. Trending involves constructing models around your environment and analyzing those models against historical data with the intent to identify discernable patterns. Forecasting is the projection of trends in conjunction with business domain expertise to assess their impact on your environment. Finally, capacity planning is the analysis of forecasts on business processes and the construction of a resolution plan. The frequent analysis of your environment in this context can help ensure that your application is always meeting your SLAs, keeping both your users and your boss happy. Let me tell you more about it."

The terms "trending," "forecasting," and "capacity planning" are sometimes used interchangeably, but the following definitions show the distinctions between them:

- *Trending* is the analysis of data with the intention of identifying discernable patterns.

- *Forecasting* is the projection of those identified patterns on business growth patterns to understand the impact on business processes.

- *Capacity planning* is the response to forecasts that ensures the integrity of business processes.

More plainly stated, first we analyze data and look for trends. Next, we make projections against those trends, in combination with the knowledge of our business domain, to forecast the impact of those trends against our business processes. Finally, we respond to those forecasts by developing a plan to mitigate risk and ensure the integrity of our business processes. Trending is a science; forecasting is a methodology; and capacity planning is an art. But with a solid understanding of the activities that are performed during each, the process is not insurmountable.

Trends

Trends can be identified in almost any area in an enterprise environment, but the subset of data that we focus on in this chapter, for practical purposes, includes the following:

- Usage patterns

- Heap usage patterns

- Resource utilization patterns

- Response time patterns

When looking at usage patterns, look for changes in user behavior that may negatively affect the performance of the environment or may change the way that applications interact with their platform, requiring a retuning of the platform.

Because all objects are created in the heap, and garbage collection can freeze all threads when it runs, heap utilization and garbage collection behavior greatly affect performance. Therefore observing the behavior of the heap over time is important to ensure that as usage patterns change the heap remains optimally tuned; the optimal tuning will change to suit usage behavior.

As your application runs, it makes use of application server and system resources. Your resource usage patterns cause different behaviors in your application that affect the way that your application makes use of these resources, so tracking these resources to discern when your usage patterns cause resources to become saturated is important.

The final key trend to watch is the pattern of response time patterns. Average response times are generally tracked, but you can learn a great deal by observing the distribution of response times; variations in response times can be leading indicators of future problems. For example, while the average response time may remain relatively constant, a significant change to the standard deviation means that some users may be experiencing far from acceptable response times.

Usage Patterns

Usage patterns are tracked through both raw usage and request distribution; changes to either can disrupt the balance that you have worked so hard to establish. *Raw usage* describes the requests that users are executing, and *request distribution* means the frequency with which users are executing those requests. Recall one of the key tenets of the performance tuning methodology presented in this book: the effectiveness of your tuning efforts is only valid if your load test scripts accurately represent user behavior. For example, if your users perform actions A, B, and C, and you tune your environment to support X, Y, and Z, then you can have no confidence that your application will be able to satisfy its SLAs. Changes in usage patterns therefore affect the performance of your environment and must be captured and analyzed very carefully.

One of the more challenging parts of analyzing usage patterns is the great variation in user load and behavior throughout the day, week, and year. For example, an intranet application probably has a significant spike in load at 8:00 AM or 9:00 AM when users start the day. Furthermore, the login functionality is strongly exercised in the morning but then dies off throughout the day. In a business-to-consumer application, user load may be strongest during lunch hours and after work on a daily basis, but throughout the year, the load may spike with seasonal shoppers (for example, in the United States the consumer retail business is greatest between the Thanksgiving and Christmas holidays). And a business-to-business application may experience significant user load during normal business operation hours, but nothing over the weekend. The point is that knowing your users' individual requests is not enough—you need to identify usage peaks and abnormal behaviors and ensure that you can effectively handle them.

You can use the following two primary mechanisms for obtaining these usage patterns:

- Access logs

- User experience monitor

Most Web servers can be configured to record the URL for each requested Web page to a log file. For example, if your application is using the Apache Struts Action Framework, each piece of business functionality is partitioned into its own unique and identifiable request. Based upon the structure of your Web requests, this log file may provide you with enough information to identify business processes.

But for business functions that are not discernable from an individual request or for which a single request implements multiple business functions, you need a deeper analysis tool than simple access logs. For deeper analysis, you can obtain a user experience monitor. A *user experience monitor* is hardware (another computer) that sits on your network, very close to your load balancer, and sniffs all Web traffic as it passes to your Web servers. Because this device captures traffic as it passes across network switches, it does not inflict any performance overhead, and it can be configured to look deeper into requests than access logs to identify business functionality. For example, if your application implements a Front Controller servlet design pattern and differentiates business processes by Web parameters passed to the same request, a user experience monitor can be configured to analyze its data based on the Web parameters that you specify for that request. Furthermore, regardless of the structure of a Web request (for example, whether you can determine the functionality by the request alone or only by obtaining a deeper level request context), a user experience monitor can allow you to define business functions and processes by the requests that implement them. Access logs focus on requests, but a user experience monitor focuses on your business.

Once you have the means to identify requests and their associated business processes, you need to construct a model with that data that identifies the following information:

- Peak usage patterns

- Average usage patterns

- Service request distribution

The model needs to be hierarchical to allow you to aggregate user load over time—daily, weekly, monthly, seasonal, and annual behavior. You need to gather data for at least two or three weeks to identify daily trends, and two or three months to identify weekly trends. From this model, you want to garner a deep understanding of when your peak user loads occur and what your users are doing specifically at those times. Are users' activities during peak load the same as during average load? If so, then your tuning efforts are greatly simplified; tune your environment using load simulating peak usage, and the average case will be satisfied too. On the other hand, if your peak user load activities are not representative of average load activities, such as the case of peak user load executing a strong imbalance of searches over shopping cart management and check out functionality, then you need to tune your environment to satisfy both activities. The best strategy if your system is significantly underutilized is to generate both loads simultaneously and tune the environment. But if your environment is close to saturated, which is typical of environments that I encounter, then things are not so easy!

At this point there are two realizations that you have to make:

- I need to satisfy users at peak times.

- I need to satisfy average user patterns.

Sounds simple enough, right? In this case, performing a full tuning exercise of the environment under peak usage patterns is best. When the environment can satisfy that usage, start from that configuration and perform a full tuning exercise with the average usage patterns. Be sure not to decrease anything in the second tuning exercise that you needed to support peak users, but because you are methodically following a process, this level of tuning is attainable.

Given this background in analyzing usage patterns and tuning your environment to satisfy different usage scenarios, let's turn our attention more specifically to trending. Recall that trending is the analysis of data to identify discernable patterns. In usage pattern trending, our goal is to use significant identified changes in user behavior throughout the day, week, month, and season to follow that pattern historically. For example, if a daily pattern for an intranet application reveals that 500 users log in to your application between 7:45 AM and 8:15 AM on average, what was that daily trend last month, last quarter, or even last year? Did that pattern exist then? If so, has it changed over time? Six months ago, did the same pattern exist, but for only 300 users? Follow this analysis back through your data to see if you can quantify the changes. For example, you might determine the peak user login pattern has been experiencing linear growth week after week for the past year, with a 10 percent increase in user load every month.

The point is that you first need to define a model, or profile, for your user behavior and then trace that model's history to identify changes in it. These changes represent trends in usage patterns.

Heap Usage Patterns

Throughout this book I have been emphasizing the importance of heap tuning: your application runs inside your heap, and a poorly tuned heap can destroy the performance of your application. Therefore, generating a profile of your heap behavior and performing a trend analysis on its behavior are important. Remember that the behavior and tuning of your heap are directly related to your usage patterns: changes in usage patterns may necessitate a retuning of the heap.

The heap trend analysis that we perform includes the following:

- Heap configuration behavior

- Memory leaks

Heap configuration behavior includes both heap utilization and garbage collection behavior. Every application has a certain number of objects that it needs to maintain in memory to support its user load. This includes pooled and cached items as well as user session information. Your goal under normal load is to maintain a heap utilization of about 70 percent. This percentage provides you with enough memory to support peaks in usage but not so much that its size burdens garbage collection. Garbage collection behavior tracking includes the frequency, type, and duration of garbage collections. You want to know how frequently stop-the-world garbage collections run and how long they take. Furthermore, you want to know how frequently minor collections run and how effective they are (for example, how much memory are they able to reclaim?).

When you know the current heap utilization and the frequency and duration of each type of garbage collection, the next step is to analyze the historical performance of these metrics to identify trends. For example, three months ago the heap was at 65 percent utilization, but today it is at 80 percent utilization. Furthermore, major garbage collections were running every 30 minutes, and now they are running every 15 minutes. The pattern between these changes has been a steady linear growth in proportion to an increase in user load. In this scenario, user load has added additional overhead on the heap, and the heap needs to be resized and potentially retuned. Proactive attention to heap configuration trends can mitigate many performance problems. Your proactive analysis needs to be performed frequently and methodically.

A memory leak is one of the biggest problems in Java EE applications. Java's garbage collection eliminates standard C++-style memory leaks caused by allocating and dereferencing memory: the garbage collector reclaims all memory that has been dereferenced when it needs additional memory. Because all Java object variables are created on the stack and reference physical objects on the heap, each object has a reference count associated with it. When its reference count reaches zero, the object can be reclaimed by the garbage collector. However, if you are maintaining an inadvertent reference to an object, then the garbage collector cannot free it.

One of the biggest causes of memory leaks in Java is the misuse of Java Collections classes. A Collections class is a data structure that acts as a container for objects and, as such, defines a reference to each object. Programmers commonly retrieve an object from a Collections class, use it, and discard it when finished, thinking that the object can be garbage collected. But because they did not explicitly remove the object from the Collections class, the Collections class continues to maintain a reference to the object. In this scenario, a lingering reference to the object remains, and its memory cannot be reclaimed until the object is explicitly removed from the Collections class. Figure 12-1 illustrates this lingering object reference graphically.

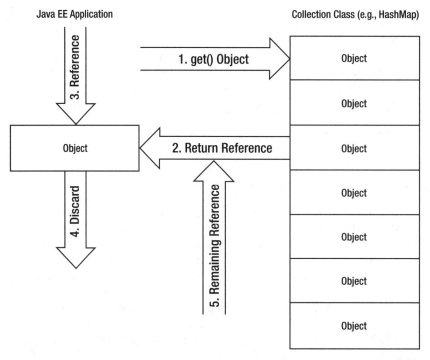

Figure 12-1. *Because the application calls get() on the Collections class, a new reference is returned to the application. When the application discards the reference, the Collections class continues to maintain its reference to the object; hence, the object cannot be garbage collected.*

Memory leaks are typically subtle and may take days or even weeks to crash an application server. In order to detect a potential memory leak, you need to analyze your heap utilization, specifically the heap utilization valleys. As objects are created and destroyed, the heap utilization oscillates, so its utilization has peaks and valleys. If the valleys are consistently increasing, then the application is allocating more memory than it is freeing, and you can draw one of the following three conclusions:

- The application is approaching its steady state, and the increasing trend is just indicative of natural growth.

- Your heap is too small to support the requirements of the application; the heap should eventually level off, but your heap is too small to do so.

- You have a memory leak.

Figure 12-2 illustrates the behavior of a heap that might be experiencing a memory leak.

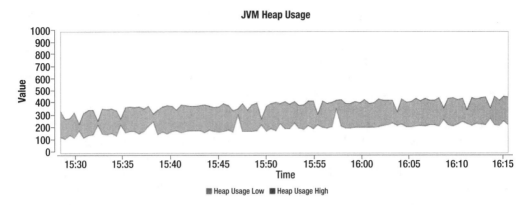

Figure 12-2. *This heap is slowly trending upward, which is evident by looking at the low usage growth pattern (the valleys).*

Figure 12-2 presents a heap that is trending upward. The shaded area shows the range of the heap while the lines demark the low and high utilization of the heap for that sampling interval. The lower mark shows the amount of heap that the JVM was able to make available to the application in the sampling interval. By observing the heap over time, you can see that the JVM is losing memory. In this situation, I would observe the heap over a much longer time interval, which can range from several hours to several weeks, depending on the behavior of the heap, to see if the heap utilization levels off or if it eventually runs out of memory.

Note If you are using a Sun JVM, you have a more definitive mechanism to detect a memory leak: analyze the growth pattern of the old generation partition of the heap. Recall that the new generation is where objects are created and short-lived objects are destroyed, while the old generation is the home for long-lived objects. Leaked objects are, by definition, long-lived, so they will consume the old generation until they exhaust the memory. Therefore, looking at the growth pattern of the old generation, rather than the entire heap, is more conclusive.

Resource Utilization Patterns

In addition to measuring heap utilization and garbage collection rates, you want to construct a model that represents your other resources. Specifically, you want to include analyses of the following metrics:

- Thread pools

- Connection pools

- Object pools

- Caches

- CPU

In addition, you should include any other significant resource in your environment. For example, several of my larger IBM WebSphere clients use the MQSeries messaging infrastructure to communicate with a mainframe. In this case, the mainframe performance and the ability of MQSeries to transfer messages between the application server and the mainframe are both key to the performance of the application. MQSeries includes performance metrics such as message time in a queue, queue depth, and thread pool utilization.

The methodology is to construct a model for each of these metrics that describes its current and historical behavior and then review the resource's history to discern any patterns. The difficult part is that you need to build daily, weekly, monthly, and annual models, and then look back at the historical data to determine if any trends exist against those models. For example, consider the following scenario, identified by analyzing the CPU utilization of an application server: every nonholiday business day over the past month, the CPU has been running at 65 percent utilization between 8:00 AM and 9:00 AM (part of the daily model). If this is the case, then how was the CPU performing three or six months ago? Furthermore, what is the pattern of behavior between six months ago and today? Does this pattern present a valid trend, or are your observations part of a monthly or annual model?

Assume that this example is an intranet application in which users log in between 8:00 AM and 9:00 AM, and for which the only annual patterns that affect user utilization are user vacations, so the fluctuations are minor. Looking back six months ago, the CPU was at 30 percent for the time period in question, and during the last six months, the staff increased by 10 percent. This type of utilization increase will have an impact on the CPU, but it should not cause CPU utilization to nearly double. The CPU utilization growth pattern was relatively flat until four months ago, when it mysteriously increased by 25 percent and gradually increased another 5 percent, until it reached its current 65 percent utilization. Looking back at changes that occurred four months ago, we learn that the authentication mechanism was upgraded from a basic, file-based authentication to an LDAP server. Furthermore, the entire staff increase occurred between four months ago and today, accounting for the additional 5 percent increase.

By defining an annual CPU utilization model, we knew that this change in behavior was not because of seasonal changes throughout the year. By defining a weekly model, we learned that CPU utilization was slightly higher on Monday and slightly lower on Friday, but the changes were global and did not change any weekly pattern. The daily model demonstrated conclusively that the 8:00 AM to 9:00 AM CPU utilization increased consistently, regardless of all other trends. And finally, the trend analysis pointed to the time frame that caused the problem.

Define the following models for each resource:

- Daily

- Weekly

- Monthly

- Annual

Daily models examine resource utilization behaviors during your standard business days. If you run an e-commerce site, then every day is a business day, but if you maintain an intranet application, then your business days might be Monday through Friday. The goals of defining this model and analyzing its historical behavior are to identify peak daily usage times and detect large-scale and global changes that affect the performance of your environment. Daily models and trends need to be carefully analyzed against business environmental factors, such as marketing activities and promotions, to determine whether model trends are the result of these factors, and hence temporary, or whether they present a long-term problem. Finally, when trying to understand the cause of a daily trend, always perform a sanity check by identifying changes in user load: more users will almost always increase resource utilization.

Weekly models examine resource utilization behaviors during the course of your standard business week. Again, the demarcation of a business week is dependent on your business. As an example, an online retailer may observe a significant increase in user load, and hence increased resource utilization, on Saturdays and Sundays when people are home from work. Or the site might experience a spike in utilization on Friday afternoons when its customers are bored at work and pass time browsing the online store. Regardless of the cause of a weekly anomaly, the goal is to identify special behavioral periods throughout the week and trace those behaviors back historically to determine any trends in that behavior.

Monthly trends, which may or may not be applicable to your environment, serve to examine resource utilization behavior during the course of a month. For example, consider the impact of paydays on an online retailer. Online retailers might have spikes in activity on the 15th and 30th of the month, on the 10th and 25th, and on every Friday (covering people paid every other Friday). If these spikes in activity exist, then you need to identify them and compare them to historical data to identify trends that may exist as results of increases in specific sets of application functionality. In the payday scenario, use of the application's catalog browsing functionality may increase a day before a payday, and online purchases may increase on the payday itself. Both of these activities execute separate paths of the application code, and thus may use resources differently: browsing may make more database queries, while purchasing may use more session space and interact with a third-party merchant for payment verification.

Finally, annual models and trends examine the behavior of resources throughout the year. They attempt to predict when user load is the highest; for example, an online retailer in the United States may experience the most load between the day after Thanksgiving and Christmas Eve. Analyzing these behaviors is important, so that you are prepared to maintain SLAs during these peak usage periods. Annual trends are typically the easiest to analyze, because the time periods are so great between events, but for the same reason, their accuracy when moving into forecasting is inconclusive if you have less than five or ten years' worth of data.

Note When time differences are too great between measurements, and you have very few measurements, forecasting is usually not fruitful. Consider this scenario: have you ever tried to start a business? To do so, you construct a business plan, and as part of that plan, you build one-year, three-year, five-year, and sometimes seven-year projections defining the future of your company. Most companies do not make it to seven years (actually, most do not make it past the first year), but if they do, their financial state in seven years is almost certainly not in line with their initial business plan projections. However, if the time difference between measurements is short with respect to the life of the company, and you have a significant number of measurements, then the forecasts can be trusted. Consider a U.S. retail company that has been in business for ten years: it can trace its Christmas season growth patterns over a decade and very accurately predict what will happen in the following year.

Analyzing resource use for trends is important because of the following specific reasons:

Thread utilization identifies the number of simultaneous requests that are being processed as well as the throughput of the application. If the thread pools are sized too large, then the system could become saturated as the CPU wastes too much time context switching between the threads. If the thread pools are sized too small, then incoming requests will have to wait for an execution thread to process them, and therefore both response time and throughput will degrade.

Connection pools control the number of simultaneous threads that can access a resource such as a database. If they are sized too large, then the resource experiences an extra burden, and the application server loses the memory required to maintain them. If they are sized too small, then execution threads may be forced to wait for a connection to be returned to the pool, and as a result, response time will degrade.

Object pools, such as stateless session bean and message-driven bean pools, face a similar dilemma. If they are too large (greater than the size of the execution thread pool), then the application server must maintain additional unused resources. If they are sized too small, then execution threads may be forced to wait for an object to be returned to the pool, and as a result, response time will degrade.

Caches can be more difficult to analyze and detect trends for, but they are incredibly important to the performance of your application. A properly sized cache can increase the performance of your application dramatically, while a poorly sized one can have the opposite effect. A cache that is sized too large can unnecessarily occupy a significant amount of memory, while a cache sized too small can thrash and add significant cache-management overhead to the response time.

The CPU is probably the easiest resource to analyze, because your process CPU utilization can be quantified by a number. During peak times, very low CPU utilization may mean that your environment is oversized, causing added expenses for excess application server licenses, support staff, hardware, hardware support licensing, network devices, and so forth. But if the CPU is saturated, then the server spends more time accomplishing less, resulting in degraded response times.

The point in analyzing these resources and identifying trends in their behavior is to ensure that your environment is currently running optimally as well as to serve as a foundation upon which to construct forecasts that predict when resource configurations need to change or when new resources need to be added.

Response Time Patterns

While we have looked at usage patterns and environmental patterns such as the heap and other resources, the most important trend to identify from a business impact perspective is the behavior of service request response times. All other trends help manage the environment in hopes of mitigating their impact on response times—they serve as early warning indicators to preserve the integrity of your SLAs.

Response time patterns should be monitored similarly to resource utilizations, but rather than creating a model that identifies outlier behavior, quantifying the weak points in the response times is more important. We look at four specific metrics with respect to response time:

- Average, or mean, response time

- Maximum response time

- Total response time

- Standard deviation

The mean response time is important to quantify, because it represents your end-user experience. But when things go wrong in the application, the response time deviation is even more important to identify, because it reveals how wrong things have gone and helps to diagnose why. The maximum response time also lets you know if you have violated any of your SLAs. The total response time for a particular time segment reveals how important that particular request is to the business—it indicates which requests have the greatest impact on your environment.

While the first three metrics are obviously important, most people tend to ignore the last one: the standard deviation of service request response time. The standard deviation tells you how much distribution of response times varies. If, for example, the average response time for a request is 4 seconds with one standard deviation of .2 seconds and two standard deviations of .5 seconds, then you know that the majority of your users are experiencing a response time between 3.5 and 4.5 seconds. On the other hand, if the average response time is 4 seconds, but one standard deviation is 2 seconds and two standard deviations equals 5 seconds, then you know that, although in general the response time is acceptable, a great number of users are experiencing poor performance. The average response time can be deceiving sometimes without knowing the distribution pattern of response times, and the standard deviation provides you with that insight.

Once you have a strong understanding of these metrics for your requests for distinct time periods, such as every hour, every day, and every week, then you are ready to perform historical analysis against these metrics over time to try to identify trends. A common situation that I encounter during these exercises is a slight degradation of response time over several months as user load increases, but an increase in the standard deviation. So while the average response time may only increase from 4 seconds to 4.5 seconds, the number of users experiencing that reasonable response is becoming fewer and fewer. Usually before the response time for a particular request degrades substantially, the distribution of response times becomes increasingly volatile.

The effective analysis of service request response times is the key to ensuring your SLAs. With the right methodologies and processes in place, you should be able to identify trends in response time and resolve their root causes before users are affected.

Forecasting

Forecasting begins by extrapolating trends to the point that they impact business functions and then applying additional business domain expertise to the trends to better understand their impact. Trending can be easily taught, and when performed frequently and methodically, it can become a very fruitful exercise, but proper forecasting can only come through experience and deep industry insight. For example, when building Java EE applications, the development team may be replacing J2EE 1.4 entity beans with Java EE 5 entity beans. The trends might extrapolate to excessive database interactions in three months, but because you know that the underlying persistence engines are substantially different between J2EE 1.4 entity beans and Java EE 5 entity beans, you do not recommend a hardware upgrade to the database to support a dying technology. You were able to make this realization, because you were communicating with development and abreast of their plan, and you were familiar with the technology.

Some of the external factors that you need to be cognizant of when forecasting trends can be summarized as follows:

- Technology changes

- Natural growth

- Targeted growth (marketing promotions, tradeshows, Webinars)

Technology changes can include upgrades to application servers, operating systems, and underlying hardware, as well as changes anywhere in the technology stack of any external dependency that the application interacts with significantly, such as a database. For the purposes of this discussion, we define *environmental technology* as major, third-party–provided or third-party–purchased technologies, such as application servers, databases, and hardware. Aside from environmental technology changes, internal technology changes must also be considered, such as the development team replacing TopLink with Hibernate or using a different logging library. These applications are considered internal technologies, because although they are provided by a third party, your applications make use of them directly, and their performance will depend greatly on your application's use of them. The distinction between internal and external technologies is not always black and white, but generally, classify infrastructure as external, and code-level technologies as internal.

When either of these changes is scheduled, it can greatly affect extrapolated trends, and as the person responsible for developing accurate forecasts, your role is to understand the impact of such technical decisions and incorporate that understanding into your forecasts. As the previous example stated, this role requires the following two things from you:

- Open communication with the technology groups in your organization, including both the development team and Information Services (IS)

- Deep industry knowledge and research into popular technologies

Natural growth, the second external factor to monitor, is a sustained increase in user load. Users may be employees hired by your company that will be using your intranet application or shoppers on your e-commerce site who become regular customers as the result of a coupon that you sent to them. The point is that natural growth denotes an increase in user load that can be expected to be sustained for the foreseeable future. Any increase in user load is going to affect the performance of your applications, and most trends begin with the extrapolation of changes based on additional users. For example, the response time of a particular request is 4 seconds with 500 users, and with a good mathematical model representing the response time patterns, we expect the same request to take 4.5 seconds with 550 users. Notwithstanding any external influences such as technology changes or marketing promotions, natural growth represents the clearest factor in establishing forecasts.

Targeted growth is characterized by short-term spikes in user load based on some event, such as a new marketing campaign, targeted promotion, tradeshow, Webinar, or seminar. When your company proactively seeks additional users, some of them may move into the natural growth bucket and become customers, but you can, nonetheless, expect a spike in user load. Therefore, you need to be cognizant of your marketing efforts as well as industry events to attempt to project their impact on your user load. Failure to do so will invalidate your extrapolated trend-based forecasts.

In summary, effective forecasting is a combination of accurate trending, open communications, and industry insight. These factors are summarized in Figure 12-3.

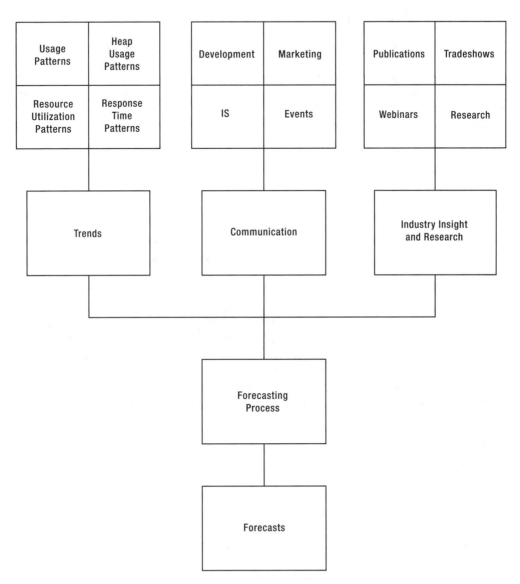

Figure 12-3. *The forecasting process accepts trends, communication, and industry insight as inputs and outputs documented forecasts.*

From Figure 12-3, you can see that trends are built from an analysis of four components: usage patterns, heap usage patterns, resource utilization patterns, and response time patterns. The transformation of trends into forecasts involves open communications with development,

IS, marketing, and events coordinators, as well as industry insight that can be attained by reviewing publications, attending tradeshows and Webinars, and your own research into technology. The results of the forecasting process are documented forecasts that will be used to feed capacity planning efforts.

Capacity Planning

Capacity planning is the reaction to forecasts to ensure the integrity of business processes. Constructing models of the behavior of your environment, analyzing historical data to identify trends, and applying communication channels and industry insight to those trends to construct forecasts would be completely fruitless if you did not take proactive measures to avoid performance failures. The actual process of capacity planning can be broken into the following three phases:

1. Analysis of forecasts

2. Capacity assessment

3. Capacity plan

Forecasts project trends in threats to your business processes, such as reporting that the current thread pool utilization is following an upward trend that will lead to a degradation of response time during the Christmas holiday season. The capacity planner must make a recommendation to the business about how to mitigate this risk and uphold SLAs during the affected period. As a result, the capacity planner may analyze the other metrics in the system, such as the CPU utilization in this case, to determine whether a simple configuration change is enough to avoid the issue or whether deeper analysis is required. Regardless of the methods employed, the result of this phase should be a plan that will be validated by a capacity assessment.

We have seen the steps that are performed by a capacity assessment, and although the mechanism is the same, the motivations behind performing a capacity assessment as a capacity planning phase differ from those behind performing the assessment to gauge the impact of forecasts on the environment. The motivations in a capacity planning phase are twofold:

- Validate the business impact of forecasts

- Test the impact of the analysis results

In other words, are the forecasts consistent with observations of the environment under specific scenarios? And can making a specific change to the system avoid the business impact?

Forecast analysis and capacity assessment validations are an iterative process, comprised of the following steps:

1. The forecast suggests that behavior A will negatively affect the performance of transactions B and C.

2. Analyze the forecast in light of the observed behavior of the capacity assessment.

3. Try configuration modifications and perform another capacity assessment.

4. If the problem is not resolved, then either upgrade the environment or go back to step 2.

At the conclusion of this exercise, a capacity plan is constructed and presented to the appropriate parties, such as the IS manager or CTO, depending on your organizational infrastructure. The capacity plan relates the impact of forecasts on the business process and provides documented suggestions to mitigate their risk. A capacity plan can be a simple document that suggests and justifies a handful of configuration changes, or it can be extremely complex, suggesting and justifying the addition of new hardware or platform upgrades. It prioritizes each potential risk, provides a resolution plan, and justifies all recommendations.

Forecast Risk Analysis

The goal of forecasting is to apply business domain expertise to trends to assess the impact of trends on the environment. Capacity planning takes that a step further and translates environmental impacts into business impacts. This planning process begins by analyzing the forecasts against input from business owners to assess the severity of the risk. For example, if a response time trend indicates that the login functionality is slowly degrading, and the forecast suggests that during next month's tradeshow it will exceed its SLA by three seconds, then it is the business owner's responsibility to prioritize its resolution. The business owner has two choices: file it as a known issue and assume responsibility for it, or request a root-cause analysis to be performed to assess the cost of mitigating the issue. In this case, the issue is determined to be in the newly added LDAP authentication code and requires a reconfiguration of the LDAP server. The cost to resolve a configuration issue is much less than that of a hardware issue; therefore the business owner recommends that the issue be resolved in this fashion.

The following is some of the information that you need to present to the business owner for the various applications affected in your analysis:

- The specific business functionality that will be affected

- The number of users that will be affected

- The degradation model for the affected functionality

You need to obtain the following information from the business owner:

- The severity of each business function that is affected

- The business impact of affected functionality on current users

- The business impact of affected functionality on future sales

And finally as you triage the problem's cause and isolate it through the appropriate support channels, you need an associated cost for resolving the problem. If it is a configuration issue that you own, then the cost will be minimal, but if the problem is caused by application code, then the cost can be severe. Finally, if the problem is caused by load, and hence requires additional resources, then the cost will be measured in terms of both direct financial cost (hardware and software licenses) and time (to integrate the new hardware into your existing environment).

With this information in hand, you are equipped to prioritize forecasted problems and recommend solutions for changes that are beyond your control. But for problems that are within your control, you may wish to perform one or more capacity assessments.

Capacity Assessment

As discussed in Chapter 9, the purpose of a capacity assessment is to identify the following key data points:

- The response time of your requests at expected usage

- The usage when the first request exceeds its SLA

- The usage when the application reaches its saturation point

- The degradation model from the first missed SLA to the application's saturation point

The process in creating a capacity assessment is to integrate a graduated load generation tool to reproduce end-user behavior at graduated steps until the environment breaks, constructing a degradation model for each request from the point that the first SLA is violated until the environment reaches its saturation point. When performing a capacity assessment as a result of a forecast, we are anticipating a specific user load performing a specific set of functionality. For example, if at a tradeshow presentation, someone reported the availability of a white paper on your Web site to 5,000 people, then you can expect an increased load in the functionality that serves white papers. Previous experience as well as industry reports might reveal that up to 20 percent of the people in attendance download white papers sometime within the week, 5 percent the following week, and then things return to normal thereafter. If this is the case, then the load scripts in the capacity assessment can be crafted to produce the anticipated load, and a capacity assessment can be constructed around that load.

This capacity assessment empowers you to execute forecasted scenarios and project their impact on your production environment. In addition the capacity assessment identifies SLA violation points, saturation points, and request and resource degradation models. Therefore in the capacity plan, the impact of the forecast can be quantified and used to justify change requests. For example, if you expect to have an additional 500 people accessing your Web site for a week after a tradeshow, and specifically searching your whitepaper archive, then you can present the scenario, including the observed behavior and degradation model of the environment under the projected load. Supporting your recommendations with hard numbers is much more powerful than with projections. As shown in Figure 12-4, applications and environments do not degrade linearly.

■**Note**   Because the degradation model is not linear, you have to be very careful when making projections. I once worked for a company that outsourced load testing in order to assess the capacity of its system. The company came back and told us that at 500 users, our response time was well below our SLA requirements, and because the company tested only one of our four machines, we could comfortably satisfy over 2,000 users. As soon as the user load increased in conjunction with a major promotion, application servers started crashing well below 800 users. I seriously question the company's testing strategy, but whatever its strategy, the organization's projections were completely off. We might have been able to support 500 users within our SLAs, but if our CPU was at 95 percent, then we had no hope of supporting an additional 50 users, let alone 1,500 more. Understanding your resource saturation point is paramount to making accurate projections.

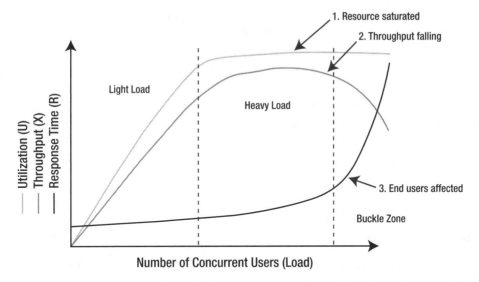

Figure 12-4. *As the number of users increases, system resource utilization and request throughput increase. But at the point in which resource utilization becomes saturated, throughput drops and response time increases exponentially.*

Capacity Plan

The capacity plan is the culmination of trending, forecasting, and analysis efforts. It summarizes identified trends, their forecasted impact on business processes, observed behaviors in a production staging environment, the cost to fix them, and your recommendations. The capacity plan is the formal mechanism used to communicate the steps that you propose to mitigate impending risks. It is composed of the following sections:

- Executive summary
- Forecast risk assessment
- Forecast risk resolution plan

Executive Summary

If the resolutions you suggest are expensive or time consuming, be assured that you will need to present your findings to someone who does not have time to read through all of the details. The information the person needs is fairly simple:

- What are the potential risks?
- How many users will be affected by the risks?
- What is the cost to resolve the risks?
- What are your recommendations?

The executive summary provides all key points covered in the report with minimal justification. Any additional justifications for the material in the executive summary that the reader needs can be found in the body of the report.

Forecast Risk Assessment

This section in the capacity plan presents the results of the forecast risk assessment that was performed earlier in the process. The main questions that you need to answer for the reader are as follows:

- What are the risks?

- What are the impacts of the risks?

- How many users will be affected by the risks?

- How will the risks affect current users?

- How will the risks affect future sales?

- What are the costs to resolve each risk?

- What are your recommendations?

For each forecast that you address, you need to answer each of the aforementioned questions. Establishing a need before proposing a solution and measuring that solution with a cost is important. Consider the example risk assessment presented in the following sidebar.

RISK 1: DEGRADED LOGIN FUNCTIONALITY

The login functionality of the Acme application is forecasted to begin significantly exceeding SLAs during next month's promotion: once the user load ramps up to current usage, then all subsequent users will be affected, accounting for 20 percent or more of our users. The impacts of this risk are as follows:

- Support calls and e-mails by existing customers

- Site abandonment by promotion targets (future customers)

This is the result of changing from a file-based basic authentication scheme to an LDAP solution. The cost to resolve this problem is a hardware upgrade to the LDAP server itself, estimated at $10,000, as well as 20 labor hours to implement the new solution. Because of the high-profile nature of this problem, it is recommended that the solution be implemented as soon as possible.

As you can see from this example, each of the main questions of the forecast risk assessment is addressed, but at a surface level. The forecast risk detailed resolution plan section will better clarify the nature of the problem and present the detailed steps required to attain the solution.

Forecast Risk Detailed Analysis

While the forecast risk assessment provides summarized information for each forecasted potential risk with a recommended resolution, the forecast risk detailed analysis provides detailed analysis of each risk, including the detailed steps required to resolve the problem.

In this example, we would replace "this is the result of changing from a file-based basic authentication scheme to an LDAP solution" with "the LDAP authentication process at the projected load saturates the CPU and causes LDAP threads to wait." And we change "a hardware upgrade to the LDAP server" to "add two additional CPUs to the LDAP server." In this capacity, the recommendation describes the exact problem, so that if approved, the resolution is not ambiguous.

Finally, the risk detailed analysis provides the deep analysis from the capacity assessment describing the exact nature of the problem and the degradation models of the binding resources and requests, which serves as justification for each recommendation.

Summary

Trending, forecasting, and capacity planning may sound similar at first, but the differences between them can be summarized as follows:

- Trending is the analysis of data with the intent of identifying discernable patterns.

- Forecasting is the projection of those identified patterns to understand the impact on business processes.

- Capacity planning is the response to forecasts to ensure the integrity of business processes.

We begin by constructing models of the behavior of various components of our environment, including usage patterns, heap usage patterns, resource utilization patterns, and response time patterns. Then we analyze those models against historical data to detect trends. We combine those trends with business domain expertise and corporate insight to forecast the impact of those trends on the environment. Finally, we compare those forecasts against business processes with application business owners to assess the forecasts' impact on end users and the costs to resolve any problems. All of this information is summarized in the capacity plan and presented to decision makers within your organization.

This chapter began by stating that trending is a science; forecasting is a methodology; and capacity planning is an art. But with the process presented in this chapter, and a little experience, successful capacity planning is very attainable.

In the next chapter, we complete the analysis of Java EE performance management in production by assembling a formal performance management plan. The performance management plan assembles the various performance-related activities discussed in this book into a cohesive performance management solution.

CHAPTER 13

■ ■ ■

Assembling a Performance Management Plan

"**L**ooks like we're about done. We've covered everything that I can think of with respect to performance management. Is there anything else you want to share with me?" John asked. He and his team had worked very hard to put into place the various methodologies we discussed, and they were back on track for success.

"Ah, yes, one last important thing," I replied. "We've talked about performance management from the inception of a product through its architecture, development, and testing; constructed high-performance deployment strategies; defined the optimal workflow to troubleshoot production issues; and even looked at trend analysis, forecasting, and capacity planning. But let's tie them all together, so I'm not leaving you with a set of disparate activities."

"You're right, that's quite a list. What do we need to build a coherent story including all of these activities?" John asked.

"Performance management is an evolving practice, and as such, I expect to see some formal standards emerge in the next couple of years, but for now you need three things: process, tracking, and analysis. You need to define what performance activities you are going to perform at every stage of your application's development and deployment life cycles, track artifacts generated at each stage, and then analyze both the performance of your applications as well as the effectiveness of your process. Or, in a single term, you need a PMP. That's a performance management plan."

"Sounds reasonable, but how big of a document is this thing going to be?"

"If only it was as easy as building a document," I began. "No, rather it is more of an infrastructure. Let me walk you through it . . ."

Formal performance management and tracking are currently undefined arts. I envision the formal definition of performance management standards and the appearance of performance management infrastructure management software emerging over the next couple of years. In the meantime, let this chapter serve as my definition of the artifacts and processes that must exist, regardless of the names and conventions that they eventually use. I realized the performance management processes explained in this chapter, and then took them to the street, so to speak—I introduced many of these performance management processes into Fortune 500 companies and refined them into what is presented in this chapter. The next steps moving forward for the industry will be to establish a standards committee for performance management and formalize its artifacts. But rather than wait years for the standards committee,

I want to include this information here, so you and your organization can start benefiting from it today!

Evolution of the Performance Management Plan

Before formally defining a performance management plan, a review all of the activities that performed in the field of performance management may be fruitful in establishing some cohesion among them. Although performance management can begin at any stage of the development life cycle, depending on the current stages of your applications, let us consider the performance management steps from application inception to production management. The following list briefly outlines these steps at each stage of the application:

- *Architecture*: Establish performance criteria and integrate those into use cases.

- *Development*: Define specific processes to test application components for performance; specifically, run unit tests using a code profiler, memory profiler, and coverage profiler.

- *QA*: Require QA to evaluate an application against performance criteria in addition to functional criteria. Furthermore, require QA to perform performance integration tests as well as performance integration load tests.

- *Production staging*: Require the performance team to perform production staging performance testing as well as production staging performance load testing, which includes scalability testing. Before passing the application over to production deployment, as well as during the last few iterations of the application development, the performance team includes performance user acceptance testing (UAT) to ensure that the application satisfies performance requirements as well as the traditional functional requirements.

- *Production deployment*: Evaluate the results of the performance integration test to optimally tune your production environment. These results include an evaluation of and planning for high-availability and failover requirements.

- *Production support*: Define performance monitoring rules and intelligent alerts to detect performance problems before they impact your users. Define processes, so that when performance problems do occur, you can quickly triage them and send them to the most appropriate party to resolve them.

- *Capacity planning*: Once an application is running in production, perform trend analyses, build forecasts combining trends with your business domain knowledge, and construct a capacity plan to ensure application performance.

A PMP needs to encompass all of these activities into a process that you can manage and track. If these activities remain disparate units of work with their own separate documents, then the process will become difficult to maintain. Rather, they need to be grouped into a larger category of performance documents under the umbrella of a PMP.

Table 13-1 lists the important artifacts to capture at each of the seven stages of the application performance life cycle.

Table 13-1. *Performance Management Artifacts*

Stage	Artifacts
Architecture	Performance criteria definition process, integration of performance criteria into use cases
Development	Performance testing process, performance unit test results
QA	Performance testing process, integration load test results
Production staging	Performance testing process, production staging load test results, capacity assessment results
Production deployment	Production deployment process, high-availability and failover requirements, scalability analysis results
Production support	Production support process, production support workflow, incident tracking
Capacity planning	Capacity planning process trend analysis, forecasting analysis, and capacity planning analysis

As you review this list of artifacts, you will notice some overlap across stages as well as some artifacts unique to various stages. Specifically, the process and performance testing process artifacts appear in multiple stages. Once the application is in production, then you see the introduction of unique artifacts, such as production deployment scalability analyses; production support workflow; and trending, forecasting, and capacity analyses. Therefore, we overlay the following five sections of the performance management infrastructure across the seven stages of the application performance life cycle:

- Performance process infrastructure

- Performance testing infrastructure

- Performance deployment infrastructure

- Production support infrastructure

- Capacity planning infrastructure

Figure 13-1 illustrates the overlay of the relationship between these five categories of artifacts and the seven performance management stages of an application's life cycle.

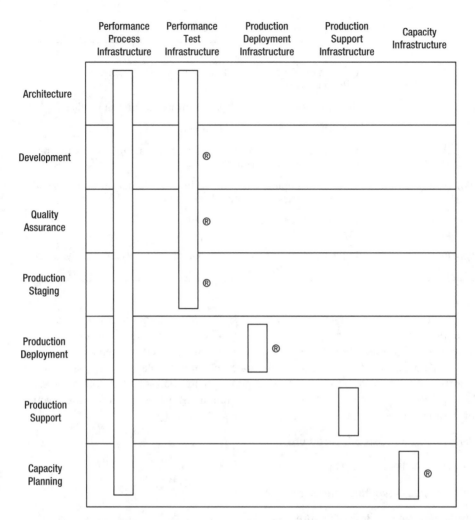

Figure 13-1. *The performance management infrastructure. The performance process infrastructure spans the entire application life cycle, the performance testing infrastructure spans the architecture through production staging phases, and the remaining infrastructures address specific niches in the application life cycle. Artifact repositories are maintained at various stages in the application performance life cycle, denoted by the ® symbols.*

One of the primary components of the performance management infrastructure is the notion of *repositories*. Repositories may be simple directory structures or version-controlled software storage applications. The point is that at various stages in the performance management process artifacts will be generated, and those artifacts need to be managed and tracked. In the ideal situation, a software infrastructure would exist to manage these artifacts and allow them to be queried to visualize the performance impact of changes. For example, if a new version of an application is released that negatively affects the capacity assessment, you should be able to trace application code changes back to changes in the results of integration performance tests and, further back, to changes in the results of individual performance unit tests. And ideally, those performance unit test reports and results can lead back to source control comments and code-level changes. By encapsulating all stages of the application performance life cycle into a single managed infrastructure, performance issues can be quickly identified and resolved, hopefully before your users ever experience them.

Performance Management Infrastructure

Therefore, we can define a *performance management plan* (PMP) as a collection of artifacts that define processes to manage the performance of an enterprise application from application inception to production management. The concept of a PMP has been lacking in the Java industry for years, which is probably why so many companies miss their production SLAs, so one of my goals is to promote the adoption of a PMP by my clients. And thus far performance teams in companies that have embraced the concept, either fully or in the part of their organization over which they have control, have found the PMP fruitful. As you read through this chapter, keep in mind that while a PMP ideally addresses your entire organization, in reality its complete adoption is difficult to achieve in a large company. Therefore, extract the parts that are relevant to your group within your company, and you will still achieve significant benefits.

The term "performance management plan" is an abstraction for what might be better termed a "performance management infrastructure," because as previously mentioned, rather than being a document, it is really a collection of artifacts. Let's now review the functions of each artifact.

The performance process infrastructure includes a performance process document that defines the organization's performance standards across the software development and deployment life cycles. For each application within the organization, it maintains application performance management documents that serve to integrate individual applications into the performance process. While the performance process document focuses on the processes that are performed at each stage of the performance management life cycle, the application performance management documents focus on application-specific implementations of that process, including schedules, artifact locations, and component owners.

The performance testing infrastructure specifies the schedules, repositories, and roles for performance testing for each application across the organization. This infrastructure includes performance unit tests, performance integration tests, performance integration load tests, production staging tests, performance staging load tests, and capacity assessments. In addition, it defines the initial loads as well as the load test loads to be executed at each stage for each application.

The performance deployment infrastructure specifies the hardware and software topologies for each deployment environment, as well as providing deployment analysis. The purpose is to track the performance of applications historically against deployment configurations.

The production support infrastructure defines the individuals in each role in the production support methodology, so during issue triaging, the owners of each component across support levels two, three, and four are unambiguous. Furthermore, the infrastructure allows you to track performance issues to their resolutions for historical analysis leading to the improvement of applications and deployment options.

The capacity planning infrastructure defines the schedules and durations for capacity planning activities, including trend analysis, forecasting, and capacity planning. It identifies the individuals or teams responsible for performing capacity planning activities for each application. Finally, it provides a repository for tracking capacity planning artifacts historically, which leads to improved quality of these artifacts across the lifetime of an environment.

Performance Management Process Document

A PMP is built around the various phases of the software development and deployment life cycles and at its core is the performance management process document. Specifically, the performance management process and artifacts are grouped into the following sections:

- Architecture

- Development

- QA

- Production staging

- Production deployment

- Production support

- Capacity planning

The architecture section of the performance management process document defines the criteria from which SLAs must be written. For example, it may state that all SLAs must provide an average response time, and that average response time must be true for 95 percent of invocations of the use case. Furthermore, at no time during a use case execution is the response time allowed to deviate greater than 50 percent over the SLA value. As in this example, the architecture section defines what SLAs in various environments must look like without defining each SLA; later, when the SLAs are written by the application technical owner and the application business owner, they know the standards to which they must adhere, so they can set specific values for their use cases and nail down deviation limits. The architecture section of the PMP process document ensures clarity when integrating performance criteria into use cases.

The development section of the performance management process document defines the performance testing requirements for each project under development. For example, it may require functional unit tests for each piece of code submitted to the source control system that exercises more than 90 percent of the components. Furthermore, it may require developers to capture performance baseline snapshots and submit a performance snapshot difference for newly submitted code. The performance snapshot difference reveals the differences in response times for the tested code (down to the line-of-code level) as well as object creation differences. The exercise of reviewing this data should be sufficient to help developers ensure the performance of their components. Ideally, the developers' performance data should be stored in a performance repository that can perform historical analysis on the developers' behalf and trace changes in performance to developer notes about changes in functionality.

The QA section of the performance management process document defines the performance testing process that QA must follow. QA procedures exist for functional testing, but they are seldom implemented for performance testing. Therefore, this section defines performance integration tests and performance integration load tests. It also defines how to measure performance and interpret and validate use case performance criteria. It emphasizes the importance of including coverage profiling against load scripts (while not under significant load) to validate that load scripts are truly testing the majority of the application code. The goal of the QA section is to provide QA team members with all of the performance management process information that they need to effectively perform their jobs.

The production staging section of the performance management process document defines the performance processes that need to be implemented when integrating an application into a shared, production-like environment. These processes include a formal definition of a production staging performance test and a production staging load test and what these tests mean specifically in the environment. This section addresses the processes employed to perform capacity assessments. For example, it may assert that the applications should be load tested using product XYZ following a normal ramp-up period to expected usage and then following a linear graduated step as defined in the Application Performance Management document(s). Furthermore, the production staging section defines the monitoring criteria for measuring resource utilization, response time, and request throughput during a capacity assessment, such as enabling the 24×7 monitoring tool without deep diagnostics enabled, to mimic production.

The production section of the performance management process document defines the production support workflow infrastructure, such as monitoring tools and alerts to be implemented, as well as the production support workflow process, which, in turn, defines the entry point of alerts and the triaging process. For example, the production performance management process may state that inputs to the support process may include user phone calls and e-mails as well as monitoring alerts. When an alert enters the system, it is directed to the help desk for triaging. Using the performance monitoring tool, the help desk representative triages the alert to the appropriate component, and after reviewing the APM document for the offending component, the alert is forwarded to the appropriate second-level support representative. This section details how the production support methodology (see Chapter 11) is implemented in each environment.

The capacity planning section defines the frequency and nature of capacity planning activities, including trend analysis, forecasting, and capacity planning. Recall that trending is the analysis of performance data to identify discernable patterns; forecasting is the projection of those patterns on the enterprise environment to understand the impact on business processes; and capacity planning is the response to forecasts to ensure the integrity of business processes. As such, these activities are not trivial and must be planned into the performance management life cycle. The capacity planning section of the PMP defines the tools to be used for capacity planning as well as the frequency and duration of the activities. For example, the capacity planning section may allocate one month of time every two quarters for the performance team to perform capacity planning activities.

The process document is application agnostic, and as its name suggests, it focuses on process details. The APM documents focus on the performance management details for individual applications.

Application Performance Management Document

Each application maintains an Application Performance Management Document (APMD) that defines application-specific participation in the PMP process. Like the PMP process document, this document is divided into sections that correspond to each phase in the application development and deployment life cycle. In many cases, the specific values for performance criteria are defined in other architecture artifacts, and in such cases, the APMD serves as a directory to locate these documents. The APMD must not duplicate much information from other architecture artifacts, because if it does, it will quickly fall out of synch with the architecture documents and lose its value.

How often in a software development project have you built architecture documents, implemented code that did not exactly follow the architecture documents, and then gone back and matched the documents to the code? Very rarely, I would guess, unless you worked in a very strict environment that demanded that you keep your documents in synch with your code. Architecture documents provide a solution to a problem, but the practicality of realizing that solution may necessitate architectural modifications. Reflecting those modifications back into the architecture documents is an arduous and tedious process that usually falls by the wayside, unless an automated tool synchronizes them on your behalf. If you were required to not only synchronize your architecture documents with your code but also your APMD with your architecture documents, there is little chance that you would do it. An out-of-synch document is worth less than the paper it is printed on (or the bytes that it occupies on your hard drive).

The APMD's architecture section explicitly names the application technical owners and application business owners for each major component or application (depending on how you break the roles down). The rationale is as follows: if a change is requested for a component, then its feasibility needs to be assessed by the application technical owner, and its applicability and impact need to be approved by the application business owner. Therefore, these people must be explicitly identified. This section also summarizes the various architectural artifacts for the application as well as where they can be found. For example, the use cases for iteration 7, with embedded performance criteria, are located in the following document:

```
\\DocumentServer\MyApplication\Architecture\Iteration 7 Use Cases.doc
```

Remember that when QA team members evaluate the application against both functional and performance criteria, they need to know the criteria with which to evaluate the application. The APMD is the first location that they will examine to determine where to find these criteria.

While the process document defines the standard toolsets and processes around development performance testing methodologies, the APMD defines the frequency of automated performance tests as well as the technology leads that will review them. For example, the APMD for an application may require that code and memory profilers be run against the code every weekend, while the coverage profiler should run every day. Furthermore, for each component, a designated lead reviews the reports every Monday morning as well as the historical performance trends of the various subcomponents. The APMD identifies specific components and subcomponents within the application and the primary parties responsible for each. Production support may use this information when triaging performance issues.

From the APMD, the QA team members need to know the performance criteria with which to evaluate the functional aspects of use cases. They also need an iteration-by-iteration breakdown of success criteria. For example, if on the first iteration of use case 13, a full pass through the entire application technology stack is not executed, the performance criteria should be evaluated accordingly. Additionally, they need to know the critical masses for the integration performance tests, specifically the user load for the performance integration test and the performance integration load test.

The production staging performance teams need to be able to collect similar information from the APMD, about user load for the production staging performance test and production staging load test. They need to know when (that is, at the conclusion of which iteration) the application will be mature enough to subject to a production staging set of performance tests. Additionally, they need an environmental breakdown of the applications that are targeted to run in the same shared environment.

The production support team members require from the APMD a hierarchical breakdown of applications that they are required to support, as well as the location of the production support workflow documentation for each application. Including this information is important, so that when a production performance issue does arise, no ambiguity exists with regard to who handles the problem when it is triaged.

Finally, during capacity planning, the performance team needs to find within the APMD a breakdown of production environments and application profiles for each environment, as well as locations of all performance architecture artifacts and performance analyses. They need to know the scheduling of capacity planning activities for each environment and application.

Performance Test Infrastructure

Though APMD comments about how specific application testing criteria overlay the process established in the process document, it largely points to the performance test plan that resides within this infrastructure. The performance test plan defines the test schedules and success criteria for performance tests as well as the user load to use for initial performance tests and performance load tests. Most important, realize that your performance test infrastructure is the backbone of all performance test efforts, and therefore is paramount to ensuring the performance of your application *before* deploying it into a production environment.

The performance test infrastructure also serves as a repository of performance test artifacts and performance test analysis reports. Refining testing methodologies and assessing the effectiveness of testing efforts are important tasks. Therefore, test results should be stored and analyzed by development, QA, and performance testing, in their respective areas. Specifically, performance unit tests should be performed at regular intervals, such as every weekend, so the automated reports should be stored in the performance test infrastructure repository and analyzed in conjunction with historical reports to determine the effect of code changes on performance. When you begin performance integration testing, their results should be similarly tracked; these results are a good indication of the effectiveness of performance unit testing methodologies. If performance unit tests consistently report satisfactory results, but during integration the application as a whole falls apart, then both the nature of the unit tests and the division of the application into components need to be analyzed. Performance unit tests should help performance, and if they do not, then you are wasting important development cycles by building performance tests and analyzing their results.

Similar analysis needs to be performed on production staging tests and capacity assessments. Performance integration tests, performance production staging tests, and capacity tests are only performed at the conclusion of a successfully integrated iteration, which means that throughout your development life cycle, you should not amass more than a couple dozen of these. With these few data points, assessing the effectiveness of your performance testing infrastructure is not difficult, and when implemented as both an intermediate step and a post-mortem follow up, it will greatly improve the delivery of your applications.

Performance Deployment Infrastructure

Deploying a Java EE application is a nontrivial task, and as such, it needs to be carefully planned, which requires a considerable amount of time and experience. Deployment must be based on quantifiable data, such as data obtained through capacity assessment analysis and scalability testing. Capacity assessments reveal the characteristics of an enterprise environment as load increases to the point of failure; as such, they reveal the resources that bind the performance of the application. The configuration of the environment should be tailored to maximize the performance of the application in light of its binding resources.

Understanding the capabilities of the environment through a capacity assessment is of paramount importance to ensuring its success in a production environment, but assessing the scalability of the environment is also important. Recall that you design and tune for performance, and test for scalability. When you complete a tuning exercise and harden an individual application server instance, you need to understand how the environment performs when you add additional hardware and/or software (application server instances). You can scale an enterprise environment in two ways: horizontally and vertically. Scale horizontally by adding additional hardware servers; scale vertically by adding additional application server instances on the existing hardware. In practical terms, the best solution is a combination of both: deploy your application to multiple application server instances, each running on multiple machines. But in order to do this, you need to understand both the capabilities of your application (capacity assessment) and the scalability of your environment (namely, how the environment performs with additional servers).

The two primary factors that affect the scalability of an enterprise environment follow:

- High-availability requirements

- Failover requirements

High-availability requirements define the percentage of time that your application needs to be available to your users. If your availability requirements are high, then you need to add redundancy to your topology. In this case, I usually recommend using multiple application server instances per machine, so that if one application server instance crashes, then you do not lose the entire machine; or using multiple machines, because if one machine fails, then you still have others.

Failover requirements define failed application server instances' impact on the users— is the users' session information preserved during an application server crash, or are the users required to re-create their environment before the crash? In the former case, you need to define an aggressive session replication strategy; in the latter case, you can gain performance during scalability with a more limited session replication strategy.

The performance deployment infrastructure tracks scalability analyses, deployment topology documents, and postmortem performance analyses of the various environments. The purpose is to assess the effectiveness of the deployment options by correlating estimations and quantifiable production performance metrics. With this information, future deployments should become increasingly more effective.

Production Support Infrastructure

The production support infrastructure includes the following:

- Production support workflow document

- Historical performance tracking repository

The production support workflow document is described in detail in Chapter 11. In this context, names and groups are assigned to each node, so that when performance issues do arise, triaging is unambiguous. Then, too, when a performance problem does occur, tracking that performance problem and identifying its resolution are important, not only for streamlining future troubleshooting efforts, but to identify problematic components. In this context, components include application code, application server configuration, JVMs, operating systems, hardware, networks, external dependencies, and the technology stack supporting any system that your application interacts with.

More than simply recording that problem A equates to resolution B, the historical performance tracking repository can help you assess the most problematic aspects of your enterprise environment. This assessment can help you choose the most appropriate components to upgrade when planning for capacity. For example, if your analysis reveals that 25 percent of all problems are network related, then when planning your upgrade pathways, a wider network is a primary consideration for upgrade; but if the problem is always in a specific application component, then that code needs to come under closer scrutiny.

As with much of the performance management infrastructure, the production support infrastructure is far more than a document, but rather a means to track and analyze performance artifacts.

Capacity Planning Infrastructure

This book has presented detailed performance activities that are performed throughout the application development and deployment life cycle and the most complicated of those tasks revolve around capacity planning activities, because trend analysis, forecasting, and capacity planning require a significant amount of data and even more experience to yield accurate results.

One advantage to these activities is that as you perform them more, you get better at performing them. But this advantage only holds true if you track your analyses and results alongside application performance assessments to evaluate the effectiveness of those analyses. Therefore, you need to capture your trend analyses, forecasting analyses, and capacity plans in a format that can be easily programmatically analyzed and compared. Separate your data from the presentation of that data: the analysis is stored in a presentation-independent form from which various outputs can be generated. The analyses of these output reports aim to identify trends impacting the business, the accuracy of forecasts, and the effectiveness of your evasive maneuvers to mitigate the impact on business processes.

PMP Life Cycle

An important aspect of the PMP is keeping it current, which includes the frequent review of its processes and their effectiveness. Performance management, like development, is an iterative process. You do not simply define it, swear by it, and blindly follow it; rather, you continually review it, keep the aspects of the PMP that are helping you, and improve the things that are not. The following truth can be applied to all methodologies: methodologies define the optimal approach to solving a problem in the ideal case. But real applications and environments are rarely ideal, and thus the principles defined in methodologies need to be flexible enough to adapt to a real-world scenario and continue to add value.

By keeping the plan up-to-date and adapting the requirements contained in it to satisfy your specific environment, you can better understand where your performance is today, where it needs to go tomorrow, and what steps you can take to ensure that it gets there.

Summary

This chapter has purposely remained very theoretical, because it presents information that needs to be formalized by a standards body, but the information is new enough that no standards body has done so yet. Therefore, rather than skip over this information, this chapter presented the nature of the data that needs to be captured to complete the task of performance management.

The core concepts behind constructing a PMP can be summarized into three categories:

- Process

- Repository (tracking)

- Analysis

You need to build detailed processes that direct your performance management efforts and remove ambiguity from your activities. You need to store performance management artifacts in repositories, so that you can track progress. Finally, you need to analyze these artifacts to improve both the quality of your applications and your performance management processes.

Tip Keep your eyes on www.javasrc.com for updates in this field. I will post regular updates as these processes and methodologies evolve.

PART 4

■■■

Tips and Tricks

CHAPTER 14

■ ■ ■

Solving Common Java EE Performance Problems

I am really going to miss my time at Acme. John is a great guy, and I thoroughly enjoyed this engagement. But I feel confident that Acme has all of the things it needs to be successful in place.

"I appreciate all of your time," John said. "But before you go, can you tell me what common performance problems to look for in my environment and how to tell the difference between them?"

"Sure!" I responded. "The main thing that I want to provide you with is a brain dump of the common things that I have encountered in my time out in the field. Many things can go wrong in an environment as complicated as yours, but as luck would have it, many problems seem to occur over and over."

"That's what I thought, but it just seems that it would take a long time to catalog those as they come in, wouldn't it?" John asked.

"A catalog of common problems is one thing that a performance tuning consultant is in the unique position to provide to you; we get called in only when there are problems. When companies have performance problems, they call me, I spend two to four weeks isolating and resolving their problems, and then I move on to the next company. This setup does not allow me to be immersed too deeply in one environment, but it does expose me to all kinds of problems! Let's get started . . ."

Java EE applications, regardless of the application server they are deployed to, tend to experience the same sets of problems. As a Java EE tuner, I have been exposed to a variety of environments and have made some observations about common problems. In this capacity, I see my role as similar to that of an automobile mechanic: you tell your mechanic that the engine is chirping; then he asks you a series of questions that guide you in quantifying the nature, location, and circumstances of the chirp. From this information, he forms a good idea about a handful of possible causes of the problem.

In much the same way, I spend the first day of a tuning engagement interviewing my clients. During this interview, I look for known problems as well as architectural decisions that may negatively affect the performance of the application. With an understanding of the application architecture and the symptoms of the problem, I greatly increase my chances of resolving the problem. In this chapter, I share some of the common problems that I have encountered in the field and their symptoms. Hopefully, this chapter can serve as a troubleshooting manual for your Java EE environment.

> ■**Note** Some of the content in this chapter is collected from material presented previously, but it is repeated here in the context of the problems being addressed. For additional information, please refer to the appropriate chapters earlier in the book.

Out-of-Memory Errors

One of the most common problems that plagues enterprise applications is the dreaded `OutOfMemoryError`. The error is typically followed by one of the following:

- An application server crash

- Degraded performance

- A seemingly endless loop of repeated garbage collections that nearly halts processing and usually leads to an application server crash

Regardless of the symptoms, you will most likely need to reboot the application server before performance returns to normal.

Causes of Out-of-Memory Errors

Before you attempt to resolve an out-of-memory error, first understanding how it can occur is beneficial. If the JVM runs out of memory anywhere in its process memory space, including all regions in the heap as well as the permanent memory space, and a process attempts to create a new object instance, the garbage collector executes to try to free enough memory to allow the new object's creation. If the garbage collector cannot free enough memory to hold the new object, then it throws an `OutOfMemoryError`.

Out-of-memory errors most commonly result from Java memory leaks. Recall from previous discussions that a Java memory leak is the result of maintaining a lingering reference to an unused object: you are finished using an object, but because one or more other objects still reference that object, the garbage collector cannot reclaim its memory. The memory occupied by that object is thus lost from the usable heap. These types of memory leaks typically occur during Web requests, and while one or two leaked objects may not crash your application server, 10,000 or 20,000 requests might. Furthermore, most objects that are leaked are not simple objects such as `Integers` or `Doubles`, but rather represent subgraphs within the heap. For example, you may inadvertently hold on to a `Person` object and that `Person` object has a `Profile` object that has several `PerformanceReview` objects that each maintain sets of data. Rather than losing 100 bytes of memory that the `Person` object occupies, you lose the entire subgraph that might account for 500KB or more of memory.

In order to identify the root of this problem, you need to determine whether a real memory leak exists or whether something else is manifesting as an `OutOfMemoryError`. I use the following two techniques when making this determination:

- Analyze deep memory statistics

- Inspect the growth pattern of the heap

The JVM tuning process is not the same for all JVMs, such as Sun and IBM, but some commonalities exist.

SUN JVM Memory Management

The Sun JVM is generational, meaning that objects are created in one space and given several chances to die before they are tenured into a long-term space. Specifically, the Sun JVM is broken into the following spaces:

- Young generation, including Eden and two survivor spaces (the From space and the To space)

- Old generation

- Permanent generation

Figure 14-1 illustrates the breakdown of the Sun heap's generations and spaces.

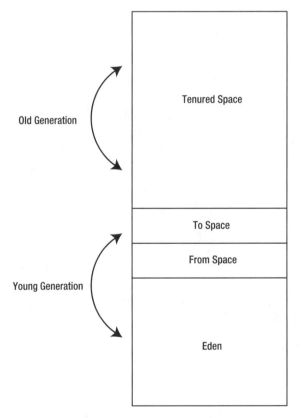

Figure 14-1. *The Sun JVM is partitioned into two major generations: the old generation and the young generation. The young generation is further subdivided into three spaces: Eden, From space, and To space.*

Objects are created in Eden. When Eden is full, the garbage collector iterates over all objects in Eden, copies live objects to the first survivor space, and frees memory for any dead objects. When Eden again becomes full, it repeats the process by copying live objects from Eden to the second survivor space, and then copying live objects from the first survivor space to the second survivor space. If the second survivor space fills and live objects remain in Eden or in the first survivor space, then these objects are tenured (that is, they are copied to the old generation). When the garbage collector cannot reclaim enough memory by executing this type of minor collection, also known as a copy collection, then it performs a major collection, also known as a stop-the-world collection. During the stop-the-world collection, the garbage collector suspends all threads and performs a mark and sweep collection on the entire heap, leaving the entire young generation empty and ready to restart this process.

Figures 14-2 and 14-3 illustrate how minor collections run.

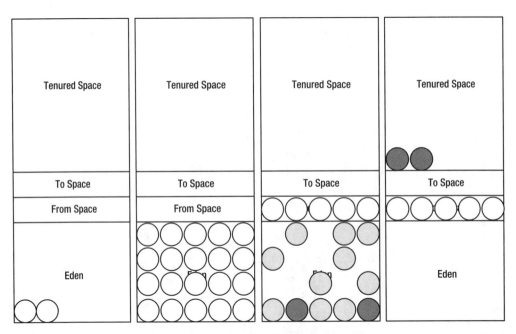

Figure 14-2. *Objects are created in Eden until it is full. Then the garbage collector traverses all objects in Eden, freeing dead objects and copying live objects to the survivor space until it is full. Live items remaining in Eden are moved to the tenured space.*

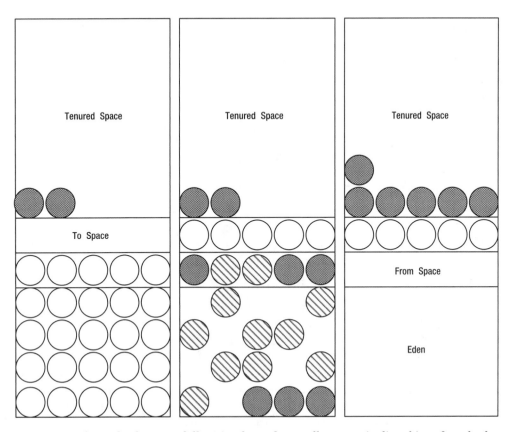

Figure 14-3. *When Eden becomes full again, the garbage collector copies live objects from both Eden and the first survivor space to the second survivor space until it is full. Remaining live objects are moved to the tenured space. The order of processing is important: the garbage collector first traverses Eden and then the survivor space; this ensures that objects are given ample opportunity to die before being tenured.*

Figure 14-4 illustrates how a major collection runs.

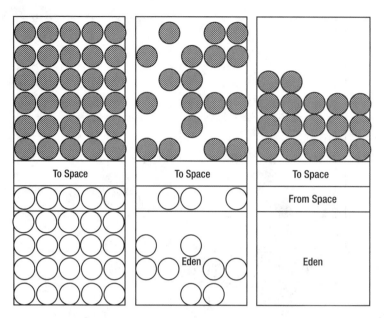

Figure 14-4. *When the tenured space becomes full, the garbage collector suspends all execution threads and performs a full mark and sweep garbage collection. It frees all dead objects and moves all live objects to a newly compacted tenured space, leaving Eden and both survivor spaces empty.*

From Sun's implementation of garbage collection, you can see that objects in the old generation can be collected only by a major collection. Long-lived objects are expensive to clean up, so you want to ensure that short-lived objects die in a timely manner before they have a chance to be tenured, and hence require a major garbage collection to reclaim their memory.

All of this background prepares us to identify memory leaks. Memory is leaked in Java when an object maintains an unwanted reference to another object, hence stopping the garbage collector from reclaiming its memory. In light of the architecture of the Sun JVM, objects that are not dereferenced will make their way through Eden and the survivor spaces, into the old generation. Furthermore, in a multiuser Web-based environment, if multiple requests are being made to leaky code, we will see a pattern of growth in the old generation.

Figure 14-5 highlights potential candidates for leaked objects: objects that survive multiple major collections in the tenured space. Not all objects in the tenured space represent memory leaks, but all leaked objects will eventually end up in the tenured space. If a true memory leak exists, the tenured space will begin filling up with leaked objects until it runs out of memory.

Therefore, we want to track the effectiveness of garbage collection in the old generation: each time that a major garbage collection runs, how much memory is it able to reclaim? Is the memory use in the old generation growing according to any discernable pattern?

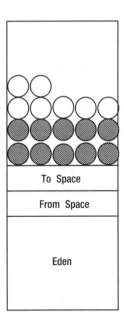

Figure 14-5. *The shaded objects are those that have survived multiple major collections and are potential memory leaks.*

Some of this information is available through monitoring APIs, and detailed information is available through verbose garbage collection logs. The level of logging affects the performance of the JVM, and as with almost any monitoring technology, the more detailed (and useful) information you want, the more expensive it is to obtain. For the purposes of determining whether a memory leak exists, I use relatively standard settings that show the overall change in generational memory between garbage collections and draw conclusions from that. Sun reports the overhead for this level of logging at approximately 5 percent, and many of my clients run with these settings enabled all the time to ensure that they can manage and tune garbage collection. The following settings usually give you enough information to analyze:

```
-verbose:gc -Xloggc:gc.log -XX:+PrintGCDetails -XX:+PrintGCTimeStamps
```

Observable trends in the heap overall can point to a potential memory leak, but looking specifically at the growth rate of the old generation can be more definitive. But remember that none of this investigation is conclusive: in order to conclusively determine that you have a memory leak, you need to run your application off-line in a memory profiler.

IBM JVM Memory Management

The IBM JVM works a little differently. Rather than starting with a large generational heap, it maintains all objects in a single space and frees memory as the heap grows. It runs different levels of garbage collections, and you can read in Chapter 9 about the various tuning options to optimize those collections. The main behavior of this heap is that it starts relatively small, fills up, and at some point executes a mark-sweep-compact garbage collection to clean up dead objects as well as to compact live objects at the bottom of the heap. As the heap grows, long-lived objects get pushed to the bottom of the heap. So your best bet for identifying potential memory leaks is to observe the behavior of the heap in its entirety: is the heap trending upward?

Resolving Memory Leaks

Memory leaks are elusive, but if you can identify the request causing the memory leak, then your work is much easier. Take your application to a development environment, and run it inside a memory profiler, as described in Chapter 5, performing the following steps:

1. Start your application inside the memory profiler.

2. Execute your use case (make the request) once to allow the application to load all of the objects that it needs in memory to satisfy the request; this reduces the amount of noise that you have to sift through later.

3. Take a snapshot of the heap to capture all objects in the heap before the use case has been executed.

4. Execute your use case again.

5. Take another snapshot of the heap to capture all objects in the heap after the use case has been executed.

6. Compare the two snapshots, and look for objects that should not remain in the heap after executing the use case.

At this point, you will need access to developers involved in coding the request you are testing, so that they can make a determination about whether an object is, in fact, being leaked or if it is supposed to remain in memory for some purpose.

If nothing screams out as a leaked object after performing this exercise, one trick I sometimes use is to perform step 4 a distinct number of times. For example, I might configure my load tester to execute the request 17 times, in hopes that my leak analysis might show 17 instances of something (or some multiple of 17). This technique is not always effective, but it has greatly helped me out when each execution of a request leaks objects.

If you cannot isolate the memory leak to a specific request, then you have two options:

- Profile each suspected request until you find the memory leak.

- Configure a monitoring tool with memory capabilities.

The first option is feasible in a small application or if you were lucky enough to partially isolate the problem, but not very feasible for large applications. The second option is more effective if you can gain access to the monitoring tools. These tools track object creation and destruction counts through bytecode instrumentation and typically report the number of objects held in predefined or user-defined classes, such as the Collections classes, as a result of individual requests. For example, a monitoring tool might report that the /action/login.do request left 100 objects in a HashMap after it completed. This report does not tell you where the memory leak is in the code or the specific object that it leaks, but it tells you, with very low overhead, what requests you need to look at inside a memory profiler. Finding memory leaks in a production environment without crashing your application server is tricky, but tools with these monitoring capabilities make your job much easier!

Artificial Memory Leaks

A few issues can appear to be memory leaks that in actuality are not. I refer to these as *artificial memory leaks*, and they may appear in the following situations:

- Premature analysis

- Leaky sessions

- Permanent space anomalies

This section examines each artificial memory leak, describing how to detect it and how to work around it.

Premature Analysis

To avoid a false positive when searching for memory leaks, you need to ensure that you are observing and analyzing the heap at the appropriate time. The danger is that, because a certain number of long-lived objects need to be in the heap, a trend may look deceiving until the heap reaches a steady state and contains its core objects. Wait until your application reaches this steady state prior to performing any trend analysis on the heap.

To detect whether or not you are analyzing the heap prematurely, continue monitoring it after your analysis snapshot for a couple hours to see if the upward heap trend levels off or if it continues upward indefinitely. If the trend levels off, then capture a new memory recording at this point. If the trend continues upward, then analyze the memory session you have.

Leaky Sessions

Memory leaks tend to occur during Web requests, but during a Web request objects can be stored only in a finite number of places. Those places include the following:

- Page scope

- Request scope

- Session scope

- Application scope

- Static variables

- Long-lived class variables, such as inside a servlet itself

When implementing JSPs, any variable created inside the JSP itself will be eligible for garbage collection as soon as the page completes; these variables exist for the lifetime of a single page.

Attributes and parameters that are passed from the Web server to the application server, as well as attributes that are passed between servlets and JSPs, live inside an `HttpServletRequest` object. The `HttpServletRequest` object serves as a communication mechanism for various components in your dynamic Web tier, but as soon as the request is complete and the socket connected to the user is closed, the servlet container frees all variables stored in the `HttpServletRequest`. These variables exist for the lifetime of a single request.

HTTP is a stateless protocol, meaning that a client makes a request of the server, the server responds to the request, the communication is terminated, and the conversation is complete. Because we appreciate being able to log on to a Web page, add items to a shopping cart, and then check out, Web servers have devised a mechanism to define an extended conversation that spans multiple requests—the session. Attributes and parameters can be stored on a per user basis inside an `HttpSession` object, and then accessed by any servlet or JSP in the application when that user accesses them. In this way, the login page can locate your information and add it to the `HttpSession`, so that the shopping cart can add items to it and the check out page can access your credit card number to bill you. For a stateless protocol, the client always initiates the communication with the server, requiring the server to know how long the maximum break in communications can be before it considers the conversation over and discards the user's data. This length of time is referred to as the session time-out, and it is configurable inside the application server. Unless objects are explicitly removed from the session or the session is programmatically invalidated, objects will stay in the session for at least the duration of the time-out, measured from the last time the user accessed the Web server.

While the session manages objects on a per-user basis, the `ServletContext` object manages objects on an application basis. The `ServletContext` is sometimes referred to as *application scope*, because through a servlet's `ServletContext` or a JSP's application object, you are able to maintain and share objects with all other servlets and JSPs for all users in the same application. The `ServletContext` is a prime location to place application configuration information and to cache application-wide data, such as database JNDI lookup results.

If data is not stored in one of these four predefined areas: page scope, request scope, session scope, or application scope, objects may be stored in the following objects:

- Static variables

- Long-lived class variables

Static variables are maintained in the JVM on a per-class basis and do not require a class instance to be alive in the heap for the static variable to exist. All class instances share the same static variable values, so changing a static variable in one class instance affects all other instances of the same class type. Therefore, if the application places an object into a static variable for a class and nullifies that variable, the static object is not reclaimed by the JVM. These static objects are prime locations for leaking memory!

Finally, objects can be added to internal data structures or member variables inside long-lived classes such as servlets. When a servlet is created and loaded into memory, it has only one instance in memory, and multiple threads are configured to access that servlet instance. If it loads configuration information in its `init()` method, stores it in class variables, and reads that information while servicing requests, then all instances are assured of seeing the same information. One common problem that I have seen is the use of servlet class variables to store data such as page caches. These caches, in and of themselves, are good to have, but probably the worst place to manage them is from inside a servlet. If you are considering using a cache, then you are best served by integrating a third-party cache, like Tangosol's Coherence, into your application framework for that specific purpose.

When page- or request-scoped variables maintain references to objects, they are automatically cleaned up before the request completes. Likewise, if session-scoped variables maintain references to objects, they are automatically cleaned up when your application explicitly invalidates the session or when the session time-out is exceeded.

Probably the greatest number of false positives in memory leak detection that I see are *leaky sessions*. A leaky session does not leak anything at all; it consumes memory, resembling a memory leak, but its memory is eventually reclaimed. If the application server is about to run out of memory, the best strategy to determine whether you have a memory leak or a poorly managed session is to stop all input to this application server instance, wait for the sessions to time out, and then see if memory is reclaimed. Obviously, this procedure is not possible in production, but it offers a surefire way to test in production staging, with your load tester, if you suspect that you may have large sessions rather than a memory leak.

In general, if you have excessively large sessions, the true resolution is to refactor your application to reduce session memory overhead. The following two workaround solutions can minimize the impact of excessively large sessions:

- Increase the heap size to support your sessions.

- Decrease the session time-out to invalidate sessions more quickly.

A larger heap will spend more time in garbage collection, which is not an ideal situation, but a better one than an OutOfMemoryError. Increase the size of your heap to be able to support your sessions for the duration of your time-out value; this means that you need enough memory to hold all active user sessions as well as all sessions for users who abandon your Web site within the session time-out interval. If the business rules permit, decreasing the session time-out will cause session data to time out earlier and lessen the impact on the heap memory it is occupying.

In summary, here are the steps to perform, prioritized from most desirable to least desirable:

- Refactor your application to store the minimum about of information that is necessary in session-scoped variables.

- Encourage your users to log out of your application and explicitly invalidate sessions when users log out.

- Decrease your session time-out to force memory to be reclaimed sooner.

- Increase your heap size.

However, unwanted object references maintained from application-scoped variables, static variables, and long-lived classes are, in fact, memory leaks that need to be analyzed in a memory profiler.

Permanent Space Anomalies

The purpose of the permanent space in the JVM process memory is typically misunderstood. The heap itself only contains class instances, but before the JVM can create an instance of a class on the heap, it must load the class bytecode (.class file) into the process memory. It can then use that class bytecode to create an instance of the object in the heap. The space in the process memory that the JVM uses to store the bytecode versions of classes is the permanent space.

Figure 14-6 illustrates the relationship between the permanent space and the heap: it exists inside the JVM process memory but is not part of the heap itself.

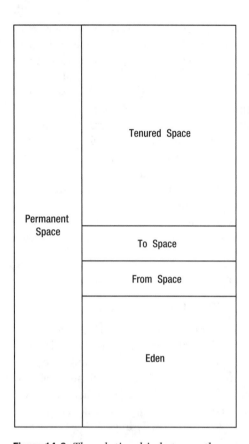

Figure 14-6. *The relationship between the permanent space and the heap*

In general you want the permanent space to be large enough to hold all classes in your application, because reading classes from the file system is obviously more expensive than reading them from memory. To help you ensure that classes are not unloaded from the permanent space, the JVM has a tuning option:

```
-noclassgc
```

This option tells the JVM not to perform garbage collection on (and unload) the class files in the permanent space. This tuning option is very intelligent, but it raises a question: what does the JVM do if the permanent space is full when it needs to load a new class? In my observation, the JVM examines the permanent space and sees that it needs memory, so it triggers a major garbage collection. The garbage collection cleans up the heap, but cannot touch the permanent space, so its efforts are fruitless. The JVM then looks at the permanent space again, sees that it is full, and repeats the process again, and again, and again.

When I first encountered this problem, the customer was complaining of very poor performance and an eventual OutOfMemoryError after a certain amount of time. After examining verbose garbage collection logs in conjunction with heap utilization and process memory utilization charts, I soon discovered that the heap was running well, but the process was running out of memory. This customer maintained literally thousands of JSPs, and as such each one was translated to Java code, compiled to bytecode, and loaded in the permanent space before creating an instance in the heap. Their environment was running out of permanent space, but because of the -noclassgc tuning option on the heap, the JVM was unable to unload classes to make room for new ones. To correct this out-of-memory error, I configured their heap with a huge permanent space (512MB) and disabled the -noclassgc JVM option.

As Figure 14-7 illustrates, when the permanent space becomes full, it triggers a full garbage collection that cleans up Eden and the survivor spaces, but does not reclaim any memory from the permanent space.

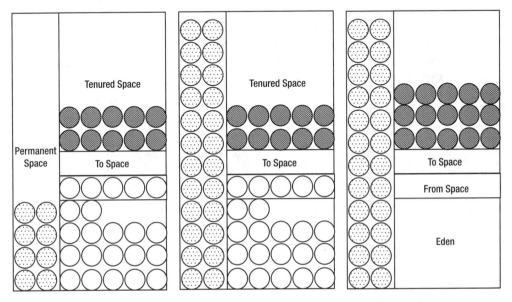

Figure 14-7. *Garbage collection behavior when the permanent space becomes full*

■**Note** When sizing the permanent space, consider using 128MB, unless your applications have a large number of classes, in which case you can consider using 256MB. If you have to configure the permanent space to use anything more, then you are only masking the symptoms of a significant architectural issue. Configuring the permanent space to 512MB is OK while you address your architectural issues, but just realize that it is only a temporary solution to buy you time while you address the real problems. Creating a 512MB permanent space is analogous to getting painkillers from your doctor for a broken foot. True, the painkillers make you feel better, but eventually they will wear off, and your foot will still be broken. The real solution is to have the doctor set your foot and put a cast on it to let it heal. The painkillers can help while the doctor sets your foot, but they are used to mask the symptoms of the problem while the core problem is resolved.

As a general recommendation, when configuring the permanent space, make it large enough to hold all of your classes, but allow the JVM to unload classes when it needs to. Size it large enough so that hopefully it will not unload classes, but a minor slowdown to load classes from the file system is far more preferable than a JVM OutOfMemoryError crash!

Thread Pools

The main entry point into any Web or application server is a process that receives a request and places it into a request queue for an execution thread to process. After tuning memory, the tuning option with the biggest impact in an application server is the size of the execution thread pool. The size of the thread pool controls the number of simultaneous requests that can be processed at one time. If the pool is sized too small, then requests will wait in the queue for processing, and if the pool is sized too large, then the CPU will spend too much time switching contexts between the various threads.

Each server has a socket it listens on. A process that receives an incoming request places the request into an execution queue, and the request is subsequently removed from the queue by an execution thread and processed. Figure 14-8 illustrates the components that make up the request processing infrastructure inside a server.

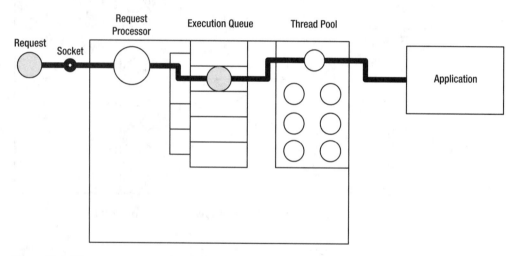

Figure 14-8. *The request processing infrastructure inside a server*

Thread Pools That Are Too Small

When my clients complain of degraded performance at relatively low load that worsens measurably as the load increases, I first check the thread pools. Specifically, I am looking for the following information:

- Thread pool utilization

- Number of pending requests (queue depth)

When the thread pool is 100 percent in use and requests are pending, the response time degrades substantially, because requests that otherwise would be serviced quickly spend additional time inside a queue waiting for an execution thread. During this time CPU utilization is usually low, because the application server is not doing enough work to keep the CPU busy. At this point, I increase the size of the thread pool in steps, monitoring the throughput of the application until it begins to decrease. You need consistent load or, even better, an accurate load tester to ensure your measurements' accuracy. Once you observe a dip in the throughput, lower the thread pool size down one step, to the size where throughput was maximized.

Figure 14-9 illustrates the behavior of a thread pool that is sized too small.

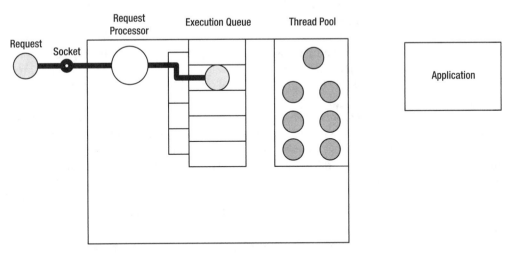

Figure 14-9. *When all threads are in use, requests back up in the execution queue. In this scenario, the thread pool utilization is at 100 percent and the queue length (number of requests in the execution queue) is growing.*

Every time I read performance tuning documents, one thing that bothers me is that they never recommend specific values for the size of your thread pools. Because these values depend so much on what your application is doing, the documents are completely accurate to generalize their recommendations; but it would greatly benefit the reader if they presented best practice starting values or ranges of values. For example, consider the following two applications:

- One application retrieves a string from memory and forwards it to a JSP for presentation.

- Another application queries 1,000 metric values from a database and computes the average, variance, and standard deviation against those metrics.

The first application responds to requests very rapidly, maybe returning in less than 0.25 seconds, and does not make much use of the CPU. The second application may take 3 seconds to respond and is CPU intensive. Therefore, configuring a thread pool with 100 threads for the first application may be too low, because the application can support 200 simultaneous requests; but 100 threads may be too high for the second application, because it saturates the CPU at 50 threads.

However, most applications do not exhibit this extreme dynamic in functionality. Most do similar things, but do them for different domains. Therefore, my recommendation is for you to configure between 50 and 75 threads per CPU. For some applications this number may be too low, and for others it may be too high, but as a best practice I start with 50 to 75 threads per CPU, monitor the CPU performance along with application throughput, and make adjustments.

Thread Pools That Are Too Large

In addition to having thread pools that are sized too small, environments can be configured with too many threads. When load increases in these environments, the CPU is consistently high, and response time is poor, because the CPU spends too much time switching contexts between threads and little time allowing the threads to perform their work.

The main indication that a thread pool is too large is a consistently high CPU utilization rate. Many times high CPU utilization is associated with garbage collection, but high CPU utilization during garbage collection differs in one main way from that of thread pool saturation: garbage collection causes CPU spikes, while saturated thread pools cause consistently high CPU utilization.

When this occurs, requests may be pending in the queue, but not always, because pending requests do not affect the CPU as processing requests do. Decreasing the thread pool size may cause requests to wait, but having requests waiting is better than processing them if processing the requests saturates the CPU utilization. A saturated CPU results in abysmal performance across the board, and performance is better if a request arrives, waits in a queue, and then is processed optimally. Consider the following analogy: many highways have metering lights that control the rate that traffic that can enter a crowded highway. In my opinion, the lights are ineffective, but the theory is sound. You arrive, wait in line behind the light for your turn, and then enter the highway. If all of the traffic entered the highway at the same time, we would be in complete gridlock, with no one able to move, but by slowing down the rate that new cars are added to the highway, the traffic is able to move. In practice, most metropolitan areas have so much traffic that the metering lights do not help, and what they really need is a few more lanes (CPUs), but if the lights could actually slow down the rate enough, then the highway traffic would flow better.

To fix a saturated thread pool, reduce the thread pool size in steps until the CPU is running between 75 and 85 percent during normal user load. If the size of the queue becomes too unmanageable, then you need to do one of the following two things:

- Run your application in a code profiler, and tune the application code.

- Add additional hardware.

If your user load has exceeded the capacity of your environment, you need to either change what you are doing (refactor and tune code) to lessen the CPU impact or add CPUs.

JDBC Connection Pools

Most Java EE applications connect to a back-end data source, and often these applications communicate with that back-end data source through a JDBC connection. Because database connections can be expensive to create, application servers opt to pool a specific number of connections and share them among processes running in the same application server instance. If a request needs a database connection when one is unavailable in the connection pool, and the connection pool is unable to create a new connection, then the request must wait for a connection to become available before it can complete its operation. Conversely, if the database connection pool is too large, then the application server wastes resources, and the application has the potential to force too much load on the database. As with all of our tuning efforts, the goal is to find the most appropriate place for a request to wait to minimize its impact on saturated resources; having a request waiting outside the database is best if the database is under duress.

An application server with an inadequately sized connection is characterized by the following:

- Slow-running application

- Low CPU utilization

- High database connection pool utilization

- Threads waiting for a database connection

- High execution thread utilization

- Pending requests in the request queue (potentially)

- Database CPU utilization that is medium to low (because enough requests cannot be sent to it to make it work hard)

If you observe these characteristics, increase the size of the connection pool until database connection pool utilization is running at 70 to 80 percent utilization during average load and threads are rarely observed waiting for a connection. Be cognizant of the load on the database, however, because you do not want to force enough load to the database to saturate its resources.

JDBC Prepared Statements

Another important tuning aspect related to JDBC is the correct sizing of JDBC connection prepared statement caches. When your application executes an SQL statement against the database, it does so by passing through three phases:

- Preparation

- Execution

- Retrieval

During the preparation phase, the database driver may ask the database to compute an execute plan for the query. During the execution phase, the database executes the query and returns a reference to a result set. During the retrieval phase, the application iterates over the result set and obtains the requested information.

The database driver optimizes this process: the first time you prepare a statement, it asks the database to prepare an execution plan and caches the result. On subsequent preparations, it loads the already prepared statement from the cache without having to go back to the database.

When the prepared statement cache is sized too small, the database driver is forced to prepare noncached statements again, which incurs additional processing time as well as network time if the database connection goes back to the database. The primary symptom of an inadequately sized prepared statement cache is a significant amount of JDBC processing time spent repeatedly preparing the same statement. The breakdown of time that you would expect is for the preparation time to be high initially and then begin to diminish on subsequent calls.

To complicate things ever so slightly, prepared statements are cached on a per-connection basis, meaning that a cached statement can be prepared for each connection. The impact of this complication is that if you have 100 statements that you want to cache, but you have 50 database connections in your connection pool, then you need enough memory to hold 5,000 prepared statements.

Through performance monitoring, determine how many unique SQL statements your application is running, and from those unique statements, consider how many of them are executed very frequently.

Entity Bean and Stateful Session Bean Caches

While stateless objects can be pooled, stateful objects like entity beans and stateful session beans need to be cached, because each bean instance is unique. When you need a stateful object, you need a specific instance of that object, and a generic instance will not suffice. As an analogy, consider that when you check out of a supermarket which cashier you use doesn't matter; any cashier will do. In this example, cashiers can be pooled, because your only requirement is a cashier, not Steve the cashier. But when you leave the supermarket, you want to bring your children with you; other peoples' children will not suffice: you need your own. In this example, children need to be cached.

The benefit to using a cache is that you can serve requests from memory rather than going across the network to load an object from a database. Figure 14-10 illustrates this benefit. Because caches hold stateful information, they need to be configured at a finite size. If they were able to grow without bound, then your entire database would eventually be in memory! The size of the cache and the number of unique, frequently accessed objects dictate the performance of the cache.

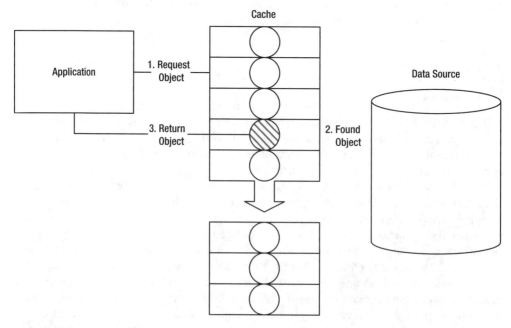

Figure 14-10. *The application requests an object from the cache that is in the cache, so a reference to that object is returned without making a network trip to the database.*

When a cache is sized too small, the cache management overhead can dramatically impact the performance of the cache. Specifically, when a request queries for an object that is not present in a full cache, then the following steps, illustrated in Figure 14-11, must be performed:

1. The application requests an object.

2. The cache is examined to see if the object is already in the cache.

3. An object is chosen to remove from the cache (typically using a least-recently-used algorithm).

4. The object is removed from the cache (passivated).

5. The new object is loaded from the database into the cache (activated).

6. A reference to the object is returned to the application.

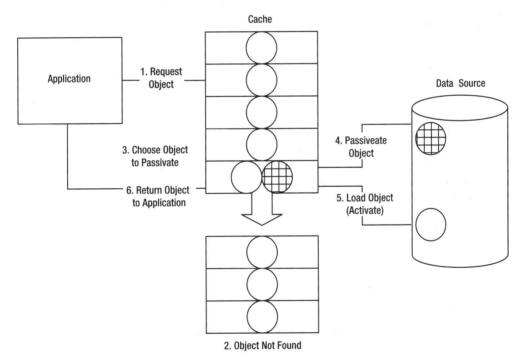

Figure 14-11. *Because the requested object is not in the cache, an object must be selected for removal from the cache and removed from it, so the new object loaded from the database can be added to the cache before returning a reference back to the application.*

If these steps must be performed for the majority of requested objects, then using a cache would not be the best idea in the first place! When this process occurs frequently, the cache is said to thrash. Recall that removing an object from the cache is called passivation, and loading an object loaded from persistent storage into the cache is called activation. The percentage of requests that are served by the cache is the hit ratio, and the percentage that are not served is the miss ratio.

While the cache is being initialized, its hit ratio will be zero, and its activation count will be high, so you need to observe the cache performance after it is initialized. To work around the initialization phase, you can monitor the passivation count as compared to the total requests for objects in the cache, because passivations will only occur after the cache has been initialized. But in general, we are mostly concerned with the cache miss ratio. If the miss ratio is greater than 25 percent, then the cache is probably too small. Furthermore, if the miss count is above 75 percent, then either the cache is too small or the object probably should not be cached.

Once you determine that your cache is too small, try increasing its size and measure the improvement. If the miss ratio comes down to less than 20 percent, then your cache is well sized, but if increasing the size of the cache does not have much of an effect, then you need to work with the application technical owner to determine whether the object should be cached or whether the application needs to be refactored with respect to that object.

Stateless Session Bean and Message-Driven Bean Pools

Stateless session beans and message-driven beans implement business processes, and as such do not maintain their states between invocations. When your application needs access to these beans' business functionality, it obtains a bean instance from a pool, calls one or more of its methods, and then returns the bean instance to the pool. If your application needs the same bean type later, it obtains another one from the pool, but receiving the same instance is not guaranteed.

Pools allow an application to share resources, but they present another potential wait point for your application. If there is not an available bean in the pool, then requests will wait for a bean to be returned to the pool before continuing. These pools are tuned pretty well by default in most applications servers, but I have seen environments where customers have introduced problems by sizing them too small. Stateless bean pools should generally be sized the same as your execution thread pool, because a thread can use only one instance at a time; anything more would be wasteful. Furthermore, some application servers optimize pool sizes to match the thread count, but as a safety precaution, you should configure them this way yourself.

Transactions

One of the benefits to using enterprise Java is its inherent support for transactions. By adding an annotation to methods in a Java EE 5 EJB, you can control how the method participates in transactions. A transaction can complete in one of the following two ways:

- It can be committed.

- It can be rolled back.

When a transaction is committed, it has completed successfully, but when it rolls back, something went wrong. Rollbacks come in the following two flavors:

- Application rollbacks

- Nonapplication rollbacks

An application rollback is usually the result of a business rule. Consider a Web application that asks users to take a survey to enter a drawing for a prize. The application may ask the user to enter an age, and a business rule might state that users need to be 18 years of age or older to enter the drawing. If a 16-year-old submits information, the application may throw an exception that redirects the user to a Web page informing that user that he or she is not eligible to enter the drawing. Because the application threw an exception, the transaction in which the application was running rolled back. This rollback is a normal programming practice and should be alarming only if the number of application rollbacks becomes a measurable percentage of the total number of transactions.

A nonapplication rollback, on the other hand, is a very bad thing. The three types of nonapplication rollbacks follow:

- System rollback

- Time-out rollback

- Resource rollback

A system rollback means that something went very wrong in the application server itself, and the chances of recovery are slim. A time-out rollback indicates that some process within the application server timed out while processing a request; unless your time-outs are set very low, this constitutes a serious problem. A resource rollback means that when the application server was managing its resources internally, it had a problem with one of them. For example, if you configure your application server to test database connections by executing a simple SQL statement, and the database becomes unavailable to the application server, then anything interacting with that resource will receive a resource rollback.

Nonapplication rollbacks are always serious issues that require immediate attention, but you do need to be cognizant of the frequency of application rollbacks. Many times people overreact to the wrong types of exceptions, so knowing what each type means to your application is important.

Summary

While each application and each environment is different, a common set of issues tends to plague most environments. This chapter focused not on application code issues, but on the following environmental issues that can manifest poor performance:

- Out-of-memory errors

- Thread pool sizes

- JDBC connection pool sizes

- JDBC prepared statement cache sizes

- Cache sizes

- Pool sizes

- Excessive transaction rollbacks

In order to effectively diagnose performance problems, you need to understand how problem symptoms map the root cause of the underlying problem. If you can triage the problem to application code, then you need to forward the problem to the application support delegate, but if the problem is in the environment, then resolving it is within your control.

The root of a problem depends on many factors, but some indicators can increase your confidence when diagnosing problems and completely eliminate others. I hope this chapter can serve as a beginning troubleshooting guide for your Java EE environment that you can customize to your environment as issues arise.

CHAPTER 15

■■■

Next Steps

I appreciate you embarking on this journey into the world of performance management with me, and I trust that your efforts will be fruitful. Rather than leave this book as a collection of performance management topics, in this chapter I conclude it with a call to action and help you identify your next steps in taking control of the performance of your applications. To start, I will discuss some of the tools and online resources that can help make your job that much easier.

Tools of the Trade

Administrators (especially those with a development background) are sometimes reluctant to use third-party tools, as they would rather build what they need on their own. But tools only help you do your job better—it is your talent in using them and your domain expertise that makes them effective. If you compare tools to weapons, you might be the finest sharpshooter in the world, but if you have only a slingshot at your disposal, you will not be very effective. On the other hand, if you couldn't shoot the side of a barn from 20 feet, then the best rifle will not help you either. But when you have the skills and the proper tools, you can be hugely effective.

This book described quite a few tools that can help you effectively perform your job function. In this section, my aim is to provide you with the criteria that I use when evaluating tools as well as list some vendor links for you to evaluate on your own.

Load Tester

In this book, we used load testers in two capacities:

- To simulate end-user behavior

- To perform capacity assessments

To simulate end-user behavior, consider the nature of your requests as well as the robustness of your environment. For example, if your application is strictly Web-based, then you have more options than if you also have thick clients or advanced Web components (such as applets or Flash applications) accessing your server. In the Web scenario, you only need to simulate HTTP GETs and POSTs, something that can be accomplished with many open source tools. But if you have a thick client that makes RMI calls or submits an XML payload to a servlet, you need that type of capability in your load tester. In this case, your choices are to either write a custom load tester or purchase an advanced commercial offering.

When performing a capacity assessment, you need strict control over the ramp-up behavior as well as the ability to graduate load at a specific pace. For example, if the expected load is 500 users and you have validated that you can support that load, then during your capacity assessment you want to ramp up to 500 users in your normal fashion, but then start increasing load at your predefined graduated step size and rate, such as increasing the load by 20 users every ten minutes. In addition, you need to be able to gather performance analysis information during the load test, so either that capability has to be built into the load tester or you need to have a strong integration between your load tester and performance analysis tool. Even though load testing tools are valuable, they offer little in terms of Java diagnostic detail.

Mercury LoadRunner is the most popular commercial tool in the load testing market, and quite a few open source offerings are available as well. You can find a sampling of these products at the following Web sites:

- Mercury LoadRunner (commercial): `www.mercury.com/us/products/performance-center/loadrunner`

- OpenSTA (free and open source): `www.opensta.org`

- Apache JMeter (free and open source): `http://jakarta.apache.org/jmeter`

- The Grinder (free and open source): `http://sourceforge.net/projects/grinder`

- PushToTest TestMaker (free and open source): `www.pushtotest.com`

This list is by no means exhaustive; it represents the load testers that I have first- or secondhand experience with. I will keep this book's companion Web site up to date, so if I missed your favorite load tester, go to `www.javasrc.com` and submit it.

Performance Profilers

When you use a performance profiler in the development phase of your application, the profiler requires three specific components:

- Code profiler

- Memory profiler

- Coverage profiler

The code profiler needs to provide line-of-code–level profiling, identifying where in your code you are spending all the majority of execution time, in terms of both CPU cycles and elapsed time. Furthermore, it needs to report the number of times each line of code is being executed. As a secondary requirement, it should allow you to track where you are allocating objects and the number of objects being allocated. This information will help you identify and eliminate code-level bottlenecks.

The memory profiler needs to provide the following capabilities:

- Capture heap snapshots

- Compare heap snapshots

- Trace heap objects to the line of code that allocated them

With these capabilities, you can follow the performance unit testing methodologies presented in Chapter 5 to perform use cases, determine exactly what objects your use cases left in memory, and then trace those objects back to the lines of code that allocated them. This procedure enables you to track down Java memory leaks.

The other memory problem associated with Java applications is *object cycling*, or the rapid creation and destruction of temporary objects, which creates an unnecessary burden on the garbage collector and hence reduces application performance. To detect object cycling, you need a memory profiler that monitors garbage collection behavior and can identify and summarize the objects that were garbage collected. It should also provide you with the capability to trace garbage collected items to the line of code that allocated them.

The final optional feature is the concept of triggers, which can promote a finer grain of memory debugging. A *trigger* is an event inside your code that the profiler watches for that causes an action to occur. For example, a trigger might be configured to take a heap snapshot when a particular EJB method is invoked and then take another snapshot when the method completes. You have no way of manually obtaining this level of granularity without writing a test case that invokes only that single method (which may not be possible without establishing the context in which your application invokes it), so triggers can provide fine-grained control over your performance debugging efforts.

As you learned in Chapter 5, you should perform performance unit tests against the same unit tests as your functional unit tests, so it is also very important that you have a coverage profiler to tell you exactly what lines of code are and are not being executed by your unit tests. Your coverage profiler establishes your confidence level in your functional and performance unit tests. For example, if you do not detect any cycling objects, memory leaks, or performance bottlenecks, but you are testing only 10 percent of your code, what is your confidence in your analysis? The answer is near zero! But if you verify that you are testing 95 percent of your code and all conditions (for example, both `if` conditions and `else` conditions), then your confidence in your analysis is very high.

All of these profilers can be run manually, but if you want to embrace a formal testing process, then these tools also need to have an automation interface. In other words, the tools need to provide the following capabilities: execute unit tests during profiling offline (maybe during a weekend build), capture snapshots, and generate reports for you. These automation features not only reduce your testing efforts, but also provide free regression testing, because the tests are running in an automated fashion on a consistent basis, even six months after the code is complete.

The commercial offering that basically owns the profiling market is Quest's JProbe Suite. Other products are available and are listed here, but JProbe was the first profiler in the market and has continued to be the leader.

- JProbe Suite: www.quest.com/jprobe

- ej-technologies' JProfiler: www.ej-technologies.com

- Borland Optimizeit: www.borland.com/us/products/optimizeit

> ■**Note** In the interest of full disclosure, at the time of this writing I work for Quest Software. Therefore, I have the greatest exposure to Quest tools, and I use them on a daily basis to solve my customers' problems. But because I work in the IT industry, I am aware of the other major vendors in these spaces, and I want to present to you as many options as possible.

Performance Analysis Tools

Performance analysis tools need to be able to analyze QA, production staging, and production environments and provide the following information:

- Describe application performance down to the method level

- Trace requests across JVMs and clustered servers

- Identify the Java EE perspective of the performance of external dependencies

- Correlate application server information with application performance information (for example, compare thread pools, connection pools, and JVM heap information with request response information)

- Integrate with Web servers to trace requests between Web servers and application servers

- Run under high-load scenarios with low overhead

In summary, the performance analysis tool needs to combine bytecode instrumentation with the ability to identify and trace a request across JVMs to reconstruct complete user requests as well as gather application server information through a management interface like JMX. Chapter 4 discussed the underlying nature of these technologies and introduced some of the inherent complexity associated with them.

Products in this space include the following:

- Quest's Application Assurance Suite: www.quest.com/application_assurance

- Wily Introscope: www.wilytech.com/solutions/products/Introscope.html

- Mercury Diagnostics for J2EE: www.mercury.com/us/products/diagnostics

24×7 Unattended Monitoring

In order to support a production environment, you need a 24×7 unattended monitoring solution that provides a deep level of monitoring across a breadth of technologies and that includes intelligent alerting. Monitoring only your Java EE environment is not sufficient, because problems can occur anywhere within the distributed layered execution model upon which your application runs. For example, if you are running a BEA WebLogic Server that is connecting to an Oracle database, and there is latch contention inside Oracle, then the monitoring solution needs to direct the help desk to triage the problem to the appropriate DBA.

Furthermore, the monitoring solution needs to provide alerting rules that go well beyond simple threshold alerting and provide an understanding of the business process. This is referred to as *intelligent alerting*, or combining performance metrics from disparate sources to derive a business value and determine a business impact. A simple alert informing you that a particular thread pool is above 80 percent utilized is not nearly as useful as a rule that tells you that the standard deviation of response times is growing at an alarming rate because garbage collection is running frequently, CPU utilization is above 90 percent, throughput is down, and requests are awaiting a thread from the thread pool. In the former scenario, you might resize your thread pool, but with the additional analysis provided by the intelligent rule, you know that users are being affected by poorly performing garbage collection behavior, so you might change your heap configuration. Intelligent alerting provides you with an assessment of user impact as well as a clearer diagnostic pathway to discovering the root cause of a problem.

The ideal solution provides cross-IT coverage by monitoring all aspects of the application environment and presents this coverage through a unified, customizable dashboard. The dashboard tools should provide proactive discovery of problems before end users experience problems and should be able to kick-start an investigation triage process to identify the root cause.

This space has quite a few product offerings, including the following:

- Quest's Performance Management Suite for Java and Portals: `www.quest.com/performance_management`

- Mercury Diagnostics: `www.mercury.com/us/products/diagnostics`

- Symantec I^3 for J2EE: `www.veritas.com/Products/www?c=product&refId=315`

- IBM Tivoli: `www.ibm.com/tivoli`

- BMC Performance Manager: `www.bmc.com/products/products_services_detail/0,,0_0_0_302,00.html`

End-User Experience Monitors

Several times in this book I mentioned the importance of understanding your users' behavior, because your tuning efforts are valid only for the load that the environment is subjected to. If you properly mimic end-user behavior, then your tuning efforts will be good; if you do not, then you cannot have confidence that your environment will meet your users' needs. As such, you need a mechanism to discover what your users are doing, and how often your users are doing those things and in what relative balance. This is referred to as *identifying the balanced and representative service requests*.

There are two approaches to gathering this information:

- Performing access log analysis

- Using an end-user experience monitor

Access log analysis can show you a breakdown of what requests were executed and in what balance, but access logs do not have any inherent understanding of your business. They work well for a certain subset of Java EE applications, mostly for Web-based applications with explicit URLs. Access logs typically do not capture request parameters or the body of POSTs; therefore, front controller servlets that differentiate requests based off of request parameters as well as applications that submit XML payloads to a single servlet are not good candidates. But if you are using a framework like the Apache Struts Action Framework and differentiating requests by explicit actions (`.do` extensions), then performing access log analysis can be a good strategy.

You have many log file analyzers to choose from (more than 100 are available at the time of this writing)—here's just a sampling:

- WebTrends: www.webtrends.com

- Quest's Funnel Web Analyzer: www.quest.com/funnel_web_analyzer

- SPSS's Predictive Web Analytics: www.spss.com/pwa

- The Webalizer: www.mrunix.net/webalizer

- WebSTAT: www.webstat.com

For more advanced cases where business functionality cannot be determined by looking at the URL itself, an end-user experience monitor can provide the insight that you need. You can configure the monitor to understand your business processes, so that rather than presenting a set of disparate requests, it can assign business values to those requests.

The only tools in this market are Quest's Foglight Experience Monitor (www.quest.com/foglight_experience_monitor) and Quest's Foglight Experience Viewer (www.quest.com/foglight_experience_viewer). These tools boast the ability to gather deep information and present it in the context of your business processes with 0 percent overhead because they simply sniff network traffic as it occurs and redirect information to a central analysis engine while the request is processed by the Web server.

Online Communities

To support this book, as well as to continue my efforts to promote formal performance management and effect positive change in Java EE performance, I have launched a Web community at www.javasrc.com. On JavaSRC, you will find active discussions around performance tuning and performance management, links to the latest vendor products, sample code and tools, articles and white papers, and online education. At the time of this writing the community is under development, but my aim is that by the time you get this book home (or it arrives from your favorite online e-tailer), the site will be moving full-steam ahead. In addition to running JavaSRC, I publish weekly articles, many of which are performance related, on www.informit.com in the Java Reference Guide.

Finally, here are links to sites that I visit on a regular basis to find performance-related discussions:

- TheServerSide.com: www.theserverside.com

- Java Performance Tuning: www.javaperformancetuning.com

- Sun Developer Network (SDN): http://developers.sun.com

- Java.net: www.java.net

- dev2dev (BEA's developer site): http://dev2dev.bea.com

- IBM developerWorks: http://www-128.ibm.com/developerworks

- JBoss Forums (especially the Performance Tuning forum): www.jboss.org

Developing a Performance Management Plan

Now that you have learned the performance management processes and methodologies, the next step is to start developing a performance management plan for your area within your organization and then put it into motion.

- If you are an architect, it is time to start communicating with application business owners and defining performance criteria inside use cases.

- If you are a developer, it is time to start writing unit tests, running them through performance profilers, and configuring an automated and repeatable process. Once you understand the tools you have chosen and the process you have embraced, document it and encourage other developers to follow it.

- If you are on the QA team, it is time to push application business owners and application technical owners to define performance criteria in use cases and then evaluate the application performance against those performance criteria.

- If you are on the performance testing team, it is time to start performing production staging tests and capacity assessments. You need to perform trend analysis against production metrics, build forecasts against those trends, and construct a capacity plan that responds to forecasts and ensures the integrity of your business.

- If you are on the production support team, it is time to build a production support workflow document calling out specific people in your triage process. You need to maintain historical information and track your effectiveness at resolving production issues.

Summary

This chapter began by covering a variety of tools that can help make your job easier and online resources where you can find performance-related discussions. The chapter concluded by outlining the next steps each job role within an organization should take in developing a performance management plan.

Whatever your role in your organization, you can effect a positive change in the performance of your applications. The key is to take the first step from conceptual knowledge to practical application. Good luck!

Index

Sources

The following source references are presented by chapter.

Chapter 1

Documentation

BEA. "WebLogic Server Performance and Tuning." BEA WebLogic Server and WebLogic Express 8.1 Documentation, http://edocs.bea.com/wls/docs81/perform/index.html.

EJB 3.0 Expert Group. "JSR 220: Enterprise JavaBeans, Version 3.0." Sun Microsystems, Inc., May 11, 2006.

Haines, Steven and John Newsom. "Formal Production Support Workflow." Quest Software, Inc., 2005 (unreleased).

Quest Software, Inc. *Foglight 4.2 User's Manual.* 2006.

Quest Software, Inc. *Installing JProbe Products Installation Guide Version 6.0.* July 2005.

Quest Software, Inc. *JProbe Coverage User's Guide 6.0.* July 2005.

Quest Software, Inc. *JProbe Memory Debugger Developer's Guide 6.0.* July 2005.

Quest Software, Inc. *JProbe Profiler Developer's Guide 6.0.* July 2005.

Roehm, Birgit et al. *IBM WebSphere V5.1 Performance, Scalability, and High Availability WebSphere Handbook Series.* International Business Machines Corporation, http://www.redbooks.ibm.com/redbooks/SG246198/wwhelp/wwhimpl/java/html/wwhelp.htm.

Other

Quest Software, Inc., marketing department. Various slide presentations, 2000–2006.

Chapter 2

Documentation

Haines, Steven. "WebLogic 7 Expert Analysis." Quest Software, Inc., 2003.

Haines, Steven. "WebSphere 5 Expert Analysis." Quest Software, Inc., 2003.

Quest Software, Inc. *Foglight 4.2 User's Manual.* 2006.

Quest Software, Inc. *Installing JProbe Products Installation Guide Version 6.0.* July 2005.

Quest Software, Inc. *JProbe Coverage User's Guide 6.0.* July 2005.

Quest Software, Inc. *JProbe Memory Debugger Developer's Guide 6.0.* July 2005.

Quest Software, Inc. *JProbe Profiler Developer's Guide 6.0.* July 2005.

Quest Software, Inc. *PerformaSure User's Guide Version 4.2.* 2005.

Sun Microsystems, Inc. "Tuning Garbage Collection with the 5.0 Java™ Virtual Machine." `http://java.sun.com/docs/hotspot/gc5.0/gc_tuning_5.html`.

Other

Quest Software, Inc., marketing department. Various slide presentations, 2000–2006.

Chapter 3

Documentation

Hrasna, Hans (specification lead). Java™ 2 Platform, Enterprise Edition Management Specification (JSR-77). Sun Microsystems, Inc., 2002.

Quest Software, Inc. *Installing JProbe Products Installation Guide Version 6.0.* July 2005.

Quest Software, Inc. *JProbe Coverage User's Guide 6.0.* July 2005.

Quest Software, Inc. *JProbe Memory Debugger Developer's Guide 6.0.* July 2005.

Quest Software, Inc. *JProbe Profiler Developer's Guide 6.0.* July 2005.

Quest Software, Inc. *PerformaSure User's Guide Version 4.2.* 2005.

Sun Microsystems, Inc. Java™ Management Extensions Instrumentation and Agent Specification, v1.2. October 2002.

Other

Quest Software, Inc., marketing department. Various slide presentations, 2000–2006.

Chapter 4

Documentation

Haines, Steven. JMX Statistics servlet source code. Quest Software, Inc., 2001.

Quest Software, Inc. *Installing JProbe Products Installation Guide Version 6.0.* July 2005.

Quest Software, Inc. *JProbe Coverage User's Guide 6.0.* July 2005.

Quest Software, Inc. *JProbe Memory Debugger Developer's Guide 6.0.* July 2005.

Quest Software, Inc. *JProbe Profiler Developer's Guide 6.0.* July 2005.

Quest Software, Inc. *PerformaSure User's Guide Version 4.2.* 2005.

Chapter 5

Documentation

Quest Software, Inc. *Installing JProbe Products Installation Guide Version 6.0.* July 2005.

Quest Software, Inc. *JProbe Coverage User's Guide 6.0.* July 2005.

Quest Software, Inc. *JProbe Memory Debugger Developer's Guide 6.0.* July 2005.

Quest Software, Inc. *JProbe Profiler Developer's Guide 6.0.* July 2005.

Other

Quest Software, Inc., marketing department. Various slide presentations, 2000–2006.

Web Sites

- JUnit.org: `http://junit.org`

Chapter 6

Documentation

Quest Software, Inc. *Funnel Web Analyzer User Guide.* 2002.

Quest Software, Inc. *PerformaSure User's Guide Version 4.2.* 2005.

Quest Software, Inc. *Quest User Experience Monitor User Guide.* 2005.

Roehm, Birgit et al. *IBM WebSphere V5.1 Performance, Scalability, and High Availability*

WebSphere Handbook Series. International Business Machines Corporation, `http://www.redbooks.ibm.com/redbooks/SG246198/wwhelp/wwhimpl/java/html/wwhelp.htm`.

Other

Quest Software, Inc., marketing department. Various slide presentations, 2000–2006.

Chapter 7

Articles

Fleury, Marc. "Why I Love EJBs." Red Hat Inc., 2002.

Documentation

BEA. "WebLogic Server Performance and Tuning." BEA WebLogic Server and WebLogic Express 8.1 Documentation, `http://edocs.bea.com/wls/docs81/perform/index.html`.

Haines, Steven. "WebLogic 7 Expert Analysis." Quest Software, Inc., 2003.

Haines, Steven. "WebSphere 5 Expert Analysis." Quest Software, Inc., 2003.

International Business Machines Corporation. "IBM Developer Kit and Runtime Environment, Java™ 2 Technology Edition, Version 1.4.2, Diagnostics Guide." April 2006.

International Business Machines Corporation. "IBM JVM Garbage Collection and Storage Allocation Techniques." November 2003.

Roehm, Birgit et al. *IBM WebSphere V5.1 Performance, Scalability, and High Availability WebSphere Handbook Series.* International Business Machines Corporation, `http://www.redbooks.ibm.com/redbooks/SG246198/wwhelp/wwhimpl/java/html/wwhelp.htm`.

Shannon, Bill. Java™ 2 Platform Enterprise Edition Specification, v1.4. Sun Microsystems, Inc., 2003.

Sun Microsystems, Inc. "Tuning Garbage Collection with the 5.0 Java™ Virtual Machine." `http://java.sun.com/docs/hotspot/gc5.0/gc_tuning_5.html`.

Other

Quest Software, Inc., marketing department. Various slide presentations, 2000–2006.

Software

- Apache Ant: `http://ant.apache.org`

- visualgc (Visual Garbage Collection Monitoring Tool): `http://java.sun.com/performance/jvmstat/visualgc.html`

Chapter 8

Documentation

BEA. "WebLogic Server Performance and Tuning." BEA WebLogic Server and WebLogic Express 8.1 Documentation, `http://edocs.bea.com/wls/docs81/perform/index.html`.

Haines, Steven. "WebLogic 7 Expert Analysis." Quest Software, Inc., 2003.

Haines, Steven. "WebSphere 5 Expert Analysis." Quest Software, Inc., 2003.

Quest Software, Inc. *Funnel Web Analyzer User Guide*. 2002.

Quest Software, Inc. *Quest User Experience Monitor User Guide*. 2005.

Roehm, Birgit et al. *IBM WebSphere V5.1 Performance, Scalability, and High Availability WebSphere Handbook Series*. International Business Machines Corporation, `http://www.redbooks.ibm.com/redbooks/SG246198/wwhelp/wwhimpl/java/html/wwhelp.htm`.

Other

Ellison, Larry. CES Keynote 2003. Oracle Inc., 2003.

Quest Software, Inc., marketing department. Various slide presentations, 2000–2006.

Chapter 9

Software

- Mercury Load Runner: `http://www.mercury.com`

Chapter 10

Documentation

BEA. "WebLogic Server Performance and Tuning." BEA WebLogic Server and WebLogic Express 8.1 Documentation, `http://edocs.bea.com/wls/docs81/perform/index.html`.

Quest Software, Inc. *Foglight 4.2 User's Manual*. 2006.

Quest Software, Inc. *PerformaSure User's Guide Version 4.2*. 2005.

Roehm, Birgit et al. *IBM WebSphere V5.1 Performance, Scalability, and High Availability WebSphere Handbook Series*. International Business Machines Corporation, `http://www.redbooks.ibm.com/redbooks/SG246198/wwhelp/wwhimpl/java/html/wwhelp.htm`.

Sun Microsystems, Inc. "Tuning Garbage Collection with the 5.0 Java™ Virtual Machine." `http://java.sun.com/docs/hotspot/gc5.0/gc_tuning_5.html`.

Chapter 11

Documentation

Haines, Steven and John Newsom. "Formal Production Support Workflow," Quest Software, Inc., 2005 (unreleased).

Other

Quest Software, Inc., marketing department. Various slide presentations, 2000–2006.

Chapter 12

Haines, Steven. "Performance Tuning Professional Services Offering." Quest Software, Inc., 2003–2005.

Quest Software, Inc. *Funnel Web Analyzer User Guide*. 2002.

Quest Software, Inc. *PerformaSure User's Guide Version 4.2*. 2005.

Quest Software, Inc. *Quest User Experience Monitor User Guide*. 2005.

Chapter 13

Documentation

Haines, Steven. "Performance Tuning Professional Services Offering." Quest Software, Inc., 2003–2005.

Chapter 14

Documentation

BEA. "WebLogic Server Performance and Tuning." BEA WebLogic Server and WebLogic Express 8.1 Documentation, `http://edocs.bea.com/wls/docs81/perform/index.html`.

Haines, Steven. "Performance Tuning Professional Services Offering." Quest Software, Inc., 2003–2005.

Haines, Steven. "WebLogic 7 Expert Analysis." Quest Software, Inc., 2003.

Haines, Steven. "WebSphere 5 Expert Analysis." Quest Software, Inc., 2003.

Roehm, Birgit et al. *IBM WebSphere V5.1 Performance, Scalability, and High Availability WebSphere Handbook Series.* International Business Machines Corporation, `http://www.redbooks.ibm.com/redbooks/SG246198/wwhelp/wwhimpl/java/html/wwhelp.htm`.

Sun Microsystems, Inc. "Tuning Garbage Collection with the 5.0 Java™ Virtual Machine." `http://java.sun.com/docs/hotspot/gc5.0/gc_tuning_5.html`.

Chapter 15

Software

- Apache JMeter: `http://jakarta.apache.org/jmeter`

- Application Assurance Suite for Java and Portals: `http://www.quest.com/application%5Fassurance`

- BMC Application Management: `http://www.bmc.com/products/products_services_detail/0,,0_0_0_302,00.html`

- Borland Optimizeit Enterprise Suite: `http://www.borland.com/us/products/optimizeit`

- Foglight Experience Monitor: `http://www.quest.com/foglight%5Fexperience%5Fmonitor`

- Foglight Experience Viewer: `http://www.quest.com/foglight%5Fexperience%5Fviewer`

- Funnel Web Analyzer: `http://www.quest.com/funnel%5Fweb%5Fanalyzer`

- JProbe Suite: `http://www.quest.com/jprobe`

- JProfiler: `http://www.ej-technologies.com/products/jprofiler/overview.html`

- Mercury Diagnostics: `http://www.mercury.com/us/products/diagnostics`

- Mercury LoadRunner: `http://www.mercury.com/us/products/performance-center/loadrunner`

- OpenSTA (Open System Testing Architecture): `http://www.opensta.org`

- Performance Management Suite for Java and Portals: `http://www.quest.com/performance%5Fmanagement`

- Predictive Web Analytics: http://www.spss.com/pwa

- PushToTest Test Maker: http://www.pushtotest.com

- Symantec i[3] for J2EE: http://www.symantec.com/enterprise/products/overview.jsp?pcid=1021&pvid=315_1

- The Grinder: http://sourceforge.net/projects/grinder

- The Webalizer: http://www.mrunix.net/webalizer

- Tivoli: http://www-306.ibm.com/software/tivoli

- WebSTAT: http://www.webstat.com

- WebTrends Analytics: http://www.webtrends.com

- Wily's Interscope: http://www.wilytech.com/solutions/products/Introscope.html

Web Sites/Online Communities

- Dev2Dev: http://dev2dev.bea.com

- developerWorks: http://www-128.ibm.com/developerworks

- Java.net: http://www.java.net

- Java Performance Tuning: http://www.javaperformancetuning.com

- JBoss Forums: http://www.jboss.org

- Sun Developer Network (SDN): http://developers.sun.com

- TheServerSide.com: http://theserverside.com

You Need the Companion eBook

Your purchase of this book entitles you to buy the companion PDF-version eBook for only $10. Take the weightless companion with you anywhere.

We believe this Apress title will prove so indispensable that you'll want to carry it with you everywhere, which is why we are offering the companion eBook (in PDF format) for $10 to customers who purchase this book now. Convenient and fully searchable, the PDF version of any content-rich, page-heavy Apress book makes a valuable addition to your programming library. You can easily find and copy code—or perform examples by quickly toggling between instructions and the application. Even simultaneously tackling a donut, diet soda, and complex code becomes simplified with hands-free eBooks!

Once you purchase your book, getting the $10 companion eBook is simple:

❶ Visit **www.apress.com/promo/tendollars/**.

❷ Complete a basic registration form to receive a randomly generated question about this title.

❸ Answer the question correctly in 60 seconds, and you will receive a promotional code to redeem for the $10.00 eBook.

2560 Ninth Street • Suite 219 • Berkeley, CA 94710

eBookshop

ASP **Today**

Apress®
THE EXPERT'S VOICE™

Offer valid through 05/07.